OFFICIAL
Netscape Navigator 2.0
BOOK

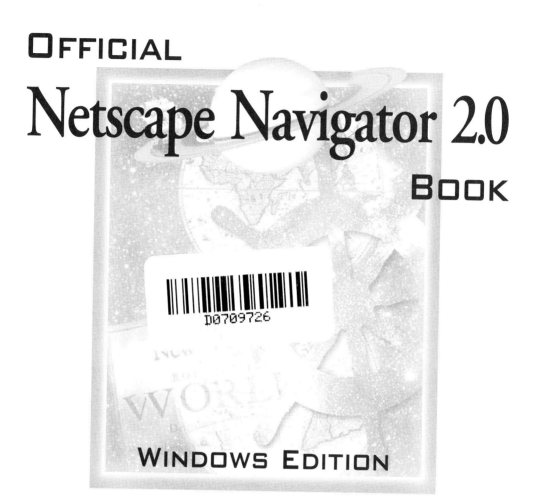

WINDOWS EDITION

**The definitive guide
to the world's most
popular Internet navigator**

Phil James

Contributing writers:
Walt Bruce
Mark L. Chambers
Clay Shirky
Rob Tidrow

NETSCAPE
PRESS

An imprint of
Ventana Communications Group

Official Netscape Navigator 2.0 Book, Windows Edition: The Definitive Guide to the World's Most Popular Internet Navigator

Library of Congress Cataloging-in-Publication Data

James, Phil.

    Official Netscape Navigator 2.0 book / Phil James. — Windows ed., 1st ed.

        p. cm.

        Includes index.

        ISBN 1-56604-347-6

        1. Netscape. 2. World Wide Web (Information retrieval system)

3. Internet (Computer network) I. Title.

      TK5105.882.J35 1995

      025.04—dc20   95-47901

                       CIP

First Edition 9 8 7 6 5 4

Printed in the United States of America

Published and distributed to the trade by Ventana Communications Group, Inc., P.O. Box 13964, Research Triangle Park, NC 27709-3964   919/544-9404   (FAX 919/544-9472)

President/CEO
Josef Woodman

**Vice President of
Content Development**
Karen A. Bluestein

Managing Editor
Pam Richardson

Editorial Staff
Kristin Miller, Amy Moyers,
Melanie Stepp

Production Manager
John Cotterman

Technology Operations Manager
Kerry Foster

Print Department
Dan Koehler

Marketing Product Manager
Diane Lennox

Art Director
Marcia Webb

Design Staff
Jennifer Rowe, Laura Stalzer

Acquisitions Editor
Cheri Robinson

Developmental Editor
Tim Mattson

Project Editor
Lynn Jaluvka

Copy Editor
Ellen Strader

Assistant Editor
Bradley King

Technical Director
Cheryl Friedman

Technical Reviewer
Brian Little, The Imagination
Workshop

Desktop Publishers
Patrick Berry, Lance Kozlowski,
Jaimie Livingston

Proofreader
Angela Anderson

Indexer
Richard T. Evans, Infodex

Book Design
Marcia Webb

Cover Illustration
Charles Overbeck

About the Author

Phil James has been wandering around cyberspace, often aimlessly, for more than a decade. He is a software design consultant, performance artist, part-time musician, author of several other Ventana books including *The Internet Guide for Windows 95*, and a literary writer whose stories have appeared in a variety of print and electronic zines. Lately you can often find his fiction in *Word* magazine, at http://www.word.com.

ACKNOWLEDGMENTS

Gone are the days when a book like this was principally the work of the author. Now there's a whole team of people struggling to meet impossible deadlines. I owe a big thank you to all the people at Ventana Communications Group who made this project happen, especially Cheri Robinson, Lynn Jaluvka, Tim Mattson, John Cotterman, Patrick Berry, Jaimie Livingston, Marcia Webb, and Cheryl Friedman.

I also want to thank my contributing writers Walt Bruce, Mark Chambers, Clay Shirky, and Rob Tidrow, as well as the technical editor, Brian Little. Oh yes, and Dick Cravens, too, for some very last-minute screen shots.

—Phil James

Contents

chapter five Newsgroups.................... 201

Foreword

We've come a long way in two years. Businesses large and small have adopted TCP/IP, the underlying protocol of the Internet, as their means of communicating both within the company and with the outside world. Individuals now cruise the Net from home, using it for everything from personal finance to entertainment. And the simple graphical interface pioneered in Mosaic and extended in Netscape Navigator has become *the* standard method for accessing electronic information.

Where is all of this going? Well, the possibilities are endless. As you'll discover, Netscape Navigator 2.0 is not just an isolated piece of software. You can think of it as an integrated communications suite, since it includes not only Web capabilities but e-mail, threaded newsgroups, and FTP. But it's a platform as well. What I mean by this is that other developers can extend its capabilities in a variety of directions for creating what we call "live online applications" and "live objects." Since there was no way for us to foresee all the things people might want to do on the Net, we designed Netscape Navigator 2.0 to provide the framework for new ways of interacting. You might click on a link and moments later be navigating through a three-dimensional virtual-reality world, or buying and selling stocks in real-time, or participating in a video conference complete with sound and full-motion images. Because of its support for live online applications and live objects, the technology is already there to do all of this from within Netscape Navigator 2.0. Gone are the days of having to buy and learn dozens of programs.

We live in tremendously exciting times. The Internet is opening up new possibilities in commerce, education, research, government, and entertainment. At Netscape we're proud that we can provide you with the tools for accessing these resources.

—*Marc Andreessen*
Vice President of Technology
Netscape Communications Corporation

Introduction

I'm sure you've noticed that almost every night some computer-related story makes it onto the evening news. Since network executives are selling a product, and since nice, happy information doesn't sell as well as calamities and horrors, the computer-related news items are overwhelmingly negative. Hackers, stolen information, and child porn: these are the mainstays of computer journalism on TV and in glossy general-interest magazines.

But this past year was exceptional in that there were several very encouraging stories, stories that even the most jaded commentators couldn't force into a negative slant. First of all, Windows 95 came out. Some of us in the computer industry had been looking over beta versions of the software for what seemed like 50 years, and when Windows 95 was finally released, we couldn't quite believe it. In spite of some minor glitches, it was, all in all, a successful and, some would say, miraculous birth.

Another positive story was the acceptance of "Internet" as a household word. 1995 was the year your aunt and uncle in Montana learned to say "e-mail" and my in-laws started calling me with questions about IP addresses. History caught up with us info-geeks, and we suddenly found ourselves respectable citizens. (Well, almost.)

For many of us, however, the most interesting story was the meteoric rise of a previously unknown software company named Netscape. There are not many companies that have grown so quickly, and there are even fewer that have earned so much respect from the industry. If you wanted to start exploring the Internet a year ago, your head would have been buzzing with arcane terminology. (I even wrote a book or two full of arcane terminology!) But now a new Internet user needs to add only a few words to his or her vocabulary, and certainly the most prominent of these is *Netscape*.

Netscape's success is not simply an artifact of our celebrity culture, in which people and businesses step up to the plate for their 15 minutes of fame. No, in this case, there are more substantial factors. First of all, there's the "right time, right place" factor. The founders of Netscape knew that a graphical World Wide Web browser was the single most important piece of software you could produce right now. Secondly, they knew that to succeed, they must integrate a full range of Internet services. Netscape Navigator 2.0 is aimed at a public that no longer wants—and will no longer tolerate—the dozens of little applications that used to be necessary to perform even the most routine Internet tasks. Finally, Netscape recognized the importance of open platforms. With its support for plug-ins and other extensions, Netscape Navigator 2.0 is positioned to follow the curving path into the future for many years to come.

OK, I've tooted Netscape's horn enough, I guess. (We don't want to drive their stock prices *too* high, do we?) Let's take a moment to look at what Netscape's latest release, Netscape Navigator 2.0, means to you:

- You can browse through the enormous range of multimedia information available on the World Wide Web. You can do advanced research without flying off to some university library, you can read the latest stock quotes, you can listen to clips of songs before you go out and plunk down $15 for a CD, you can probably even learn to dance the lambada with animated step-by-step lessons. Remember the lambada?

- You can access all the older, less flashy repositories of information: specialized Gopher and Telnet sites, vast file archives, and databases full of bizarre and arcane data.

- You can exchange electronic mail quickly and reliably with Internet users around the world. You can even exchange messages with users of private online services connected to the Net. Fire up Netscape Navigator 2.0, and you are almost by default a "global citizen."

- You can join the ranks of thousands of electronic consumers and actually make purchases online. And with Netscape Navigator 2.0's built-in security features, transferring sensitive financial data is safer than it ever has been.

WHO CAN USE THIS BOOK

This book is aimed at anyone who knows how to use some version of Windows and wants to get busy on the Net. It's also aimed at anyone who's been on the Net for a while but wants to upgrade to Netscape Navigator 2.0. Here's what you need:

- A PC with at least 8MB of RAM and Windows 95, Windows 3.1, or Windows NT installed.

- If you haven't already installed Netscape Navigator 2.0, about 5MB of space on your hard drive.

- For the version of this book that comes with a CD-ROM, a CD-ROM drive.

- A TCP/IP local area network (LAN) or a way to get on the Internet.

- For home access via an Internet access provider, a modem, preferably one that can run at 28.8 kbps.

The last two requirements need some explanation. First of all, you can gather from what I said that Internet access is not really necessary in all cases. Thousands of people are using Netscape Navigator 2.0 to share multimedia information within their own companies. This use relies not on the Internet but on *intranets*, enterprise-wide networks that a local system administrator sets up. All that's needed is a LAN or wide area network (WAN) that can run the TCP/IP protocols (if you don't know what that means, don't worry: your system administrator will).

But let's say you're a home user who wants to get out into the big Internet ocean. Chances are that unless you're a very ambitious and wealthy computer nerd (no longer an oxymoron in the Age of Gates), you don't have a direct connection to the Net. That means you need a modem and an account with an Internet service provider. Neither is hard to get or very expensive any more. Of course, you should get the fastest modem you can afford, preferably one that can run at 28.8 kbps, but a 14.4 kbps modem will still do the job.

For those of you who bought the version of this book that has a CD-ROM inside the back cover, here's something you *don't* need: Netscape Navigator 2.0 itself. That's right, the CD includes the official software right from Netscape!

How This Book Is Organized

Chapter 1, "The Web & the Net," provides an overview of the Internet: where it came from, some of its features, and where it's going. You'll learn what the difference really is between the Internet and the World Wide Web, and you'll learn enough about the technical underpinnings of the Net to understand any other technical discussions in the book. We'll even throw in some hints on using the Net so that the natives don't spot you as a "newbie."

In **Chapter 2, "Getting Started,"** you will actually install and configure the Netscape Navigator 2.0 software. This chapter includes hints on selecting an Internet access provider, and it goes pretty deeply into configuring Windows 95 for Internet access. Once you work through the instructions here, you'll be ready to start exploring.

Chapter 3, "A Quick Look Around," introduces you to the Netscape Navigator 2.0 interface and the basics of navigating the Web. In a few short minutes, you'll be cruising, surfing, or whatever the term is this year.

Electronic mail is one of the most important "meat and potatoes" Internet applications, and **Chapter 4, "Netscape Mail,"** covers it fully. Step-by-step tutorials guide you through the excellent e-mail facilities that are built right into Netscape Navigator 2.0, and in no time you'll be zipping off messages as if you'd been doing it for years.

Chapter 5, "Newsgroups," introduces you to one of the most fascinating services available on the Net. Usenet newsgroups are forums where Internet users with particular interests trade information, insights, and even files. There are groups devoted to everything from astrophysics to zydeco, and with the excellent newsgroup functionality built right into the Netscape software, you'll be able to join in quickly.

In **Chapter 6, "Getting Files via FTP,"** you'll learn how to explore file archives and download files via FTP, the standard file transfer protocol on the Net. There are archives of informational files, technical files, shareware and freeware programs, games, graphics, video clips. . . . *Warning:* Get a bigger hard drive. You're not going to believe what's available.

Chapter 7, "Gopher & Telnet," introduces you to two old Internet friends: Gopher and Telnet. These Internet services have been around for quite a while, but are still useful tools in certain situations. Netscape Navigator 2.0 includes support for both.

Of course the real *fun* of the World Wide Web is its multimedia capabilities. **Chapter 8, "Sound & Graphics in Netscape Navigator 2.0,"** explains how Netscape Navigator 2.0 uses graphics and sound. We show you some of what's available out there, and we walk you through configuring Netscape Navigator 2.0 so that it uses your system optimally in dealing with these new types of information.

In **Chapter 9, "Advanced Netscape Navigator 2.0,"** we go beyond the basics and show you some of the more forward-looking features of a forward-looking piece of software. Don't be scared off by the word "advanced": none of these features are difficult to use.

Want to do your banking on the Net? Before you do, you might want to read **Chapter 10, "Commerce & Security on the Net."** This chapter gives you the lowdown on Netscape Navigator 2.0's impressive security features. We'll never get rid of greed and crime, but Netscape's technology helps a lot.

In **Chapter 11, "Our Favorite Sites,"** we tell you about some of our own favorite Internet resources. This list is not exhaustive, since that would require volumes. Instead, these are a few road-side attractions that we've found exciting, informative, fun, or just plain weird. You can also think of them as jumping off places for your own explorations. If you have purchased the version of this book that has a companion CD-ROM in the back cover, you also have an electronic version of Chapter 11. You can browse the listings electronically, simply clicking the links to visit sites you're interested in.

THE ONLINE COMPANION: NETSCAPEPRESS.COM

To further enhance this book, we're providing an online companion for this and other Netscape Press titles. The online companion at netscapepress.com includes an area where you can download files we've mentioned; a Web version of Chapter 11, so that you don't have to type in all the Internet addresses we provide; and even a facility for sending us your comments on this book. Please feel free to log on as often as you want; there are no additional charges.

To get to netscapepress.com, simply point your Netscape Navigator 2.0 to http://www.netscapepress.com/. (If you don't know what I'm talking about, you will by the end of Chapter 2.)

OK, enough introduction. Let's go take a look at this Internet thing that everyone's talking about!

chapter one

The Net & the Web

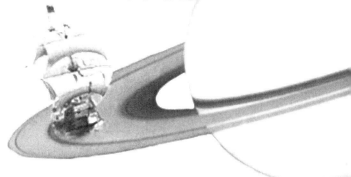

Internet. World Wide Web. Just about everywhere you go these days you overhear somebody using these words. And not just the words themselves, but dozens of phrases derived from them. If you pay attention to the mass media hype, you'd think that most people spend a significant portion of their time "cruising the Net," or "checking out Web sites," or even "surfing cyberspace" (now *there's* a mixed metaphor to make your old English professor cringe).

As with most new technologies, jargon precedes popular understanding. New terminology makes it possible to explore new ideas, but it also exacerbates the epidemic of Geek Answer Syndrome. There is no shortage of people who will blab on authoritatively but incorrectly about anything to do with information technology, flashing their vocabulary like bright plumage. Well now you can tell them to take a walk, because in the next few minutes we'll make sure that you *really* understand what the Net is, what the Web is, and how you can use these exciting new resources. By the time you've finished this chapter you won't be a cybergeek, but you'll be able to answer these questions and probably more:

- Just what *is* the Internet? How did it start? How did it evolve?
- What kinds of services and information are available on the Net?
- How does Internet addressing work?
- What is the World Wide Web? How is it related to the Net?
- What is hypertext? How about hypermedia?
- How does Netscape Navigator give you access to the Web and the rest of the Net?
- Are there any general guidelines for using the Internet?

ENTERPRISE NETSCAPING

This book concentrates on using Netscape Navigator 2.0 to cruise around the Internet, but there are other ways you can harness its power. For instance, if your office is on a LAN you can use Netscape Navigator 2.0 to share multimedia information among employees. You might want to create a colorful tutorial for coworkers, or your personnel department might want to enliven the company expense regulations with songs and animation. Everybody connected to the network could then view these multimedia files using Netscape Navigator 2.0. In addition, you could use Netscape Navigator 2.0 as a front-end for accessing *any* kind of files, not just multimedia ones. You can even use Netscape Navigator 2.0 for your company e-mail. Throughout this book I'll include occasional sidebars that point out interesting uses for Netscape Navigator 2.0 on enterprise-wide "intranets."

WHAT IS THE INTERNET?

It's really a lot simpler than you'd guess. A network is a collection of computers that are connected together so they can share information, and the Internet is a network of networks. It lets individuals on one network share information with users on another network that may be thousands of miles away. The shared information can take many forms. For instance, you can use the Internet to send e-mail messages, or to download files, or to view video clips, or listen to music. You can even use the Net for banking and shopping. It's a lot like the phone system, except that instead of just talking you can exchange all different kinds of information.

The physical Internet looks like a vast net of wires. A few high-speed "backbone" cables branch out into other cables, which in turn radiate outward into finer strands. Most of the developed areas of the world have already been wired, so by routing your information or requests through this vast system you can reach other Internet users all over the world. Fortunately the routing happens automatically, just as it does with telephone calls, so you don't need to know *how* data gets from your computer to a computer in Timbuktu.

And the system is democratic. Anyone can use it. You don't even have to have your own network in order to connect—you can communicate using the current infrastructure by plugging into somebody else's network. Maybe you're already doing this. If you have a Serial Line Internet Protocol (SLIP) or Point-to-Point Protocol (PPP) account (see Chapter 2), you simply connect via modem and phone line to your access provider's network site (known as a "point of presence"). The actual transmission of data is free, but you'll probably need to pay the access provider for the time you spend accessing its equipment.

There are hundreds of thousands of users sitting at their PCs right now, gathering information from far-flung reaches of the globe. Pretty soon the Internet will be accepted as a simple fact of modern life, and people will forget how it got there to begin with.

ORIGINS OF THE INTERNET

I'm not going to get into this very deeply. There are other books, even a couple of mine, that cover the topic in more detail. But it may be useful for you to have a little background. If you really don't care about the history, just skip this section. On the other hand, if you want to be the hit of the next propeller-head party you attend, memorize the following four paragraphs:

As with many technological advances, the Internet began as a military research project. It was the early 1970s, a time full of menace to civilization as we knew it: leisure suits, wide ties, platform shoes, and the threat of nuclear war. The U.S. Defense Department implemented a network, called ARPAnet, that was designed so that even if part of its physical structure were destroyed, information could still be sent to any remaining destination.

In the early 1980s, local area networks at a variety of research institutions started hooking into ARPAnet. They were able to do this by using the same underlying technology that ARPAnet used to transfer data and make sure it got to the right place.

Then in the late 1980s, the National Science Foundation (NSF) established five supercomputer centers and connected them via their own network, NSFnet. Based on the same technology as ARPAnet, the sites were physically linked by special phone lines. Since the phone companies charged by the mile for these lines, it was very expensive to gather information from one of these centers. The NSF decided to create several regional networks with dozens of connected sites; any data could be passed along the line from one node to another, saving on the costly line charges.

The rest of the Internet's history is one of expansion. As new educational institutions and government agencies developed their own networks and joined NSFnet, the original wiring quickly became overloaded. Much faster lines were put in, faster computers were installed, and what is now known as the Internet opened its virtual doors to most of the academic and government community. Universities from other nations, not to mention foreign governments, started joining the Net. In the early 1990s, commercial organizations began to jump on board, and it is now common for companies to promote, and even sell, all sorts of products and services over the Net.

The latest trend on the Internet is the rapid growth of personal information, with individuals making available all sorts of things they'd like to share with the world. I can almost guarantee you that somebody you know has a poem out on the Net, and that another friend has provided humanity with a picture of a favorite pet cat. And of course you can access all of this stuff with Netscape Navigator 2.0. Andy Warhol predicted a time when everyone in the world would enjoy 15 minutes of fame. Well, notwithstanding Kato Kaelin, that hasn't quite happened, but we are fast approaching a time when everybody can enjoy 15 *kilobytes* of fame.

WHAT'S OUT THERE

What services does the Internet actually provide the average user right now? Let's take a slightly deeper look at a few that can have a real impact on your life:

ELECTRONIC MAIL

Thanks to the Internet, you can send messages to just about anybody who has a computer and a network connection or a modem. If the individual you want to contact is not directly on the Net, you can use Netscape Navigator 2.0 to send a message to him or her on one of the popular online services such as CompuServe or America Online.

There are a number of advantages to sending messages via e-mail instead of the U.S. Postal Service (known affectionately as "snail mail" by e-mail advocates). First of all, there's the speed. It may take only seconds for your message to reach somebody on the other side of the world. The recipient can read your text immediately on the screen, respond to it right away, save it for later, print it out, or quickly forward it to somebody else. You can create electronic mailing lists for sending notices to hundreds or even thousands of people at once. Messages you receive can be organized into convenient electronic folders and saved for as long as you want without taking up any office space. And with e-mail, it's possible to verify very quickly that your message has indeed arrived at its destination. Because of these advantages, and several others that you'll learn about in Chapter 4, e-mail has become my principal means of communicating with the world. I receive several dozen e-mail messages a day and send about as many. In several months I generate more messages than all the old-fashioned paper letters I've written in my life!

Netscape Navigator 2.0 includes full-featured e-mail support, and Figure 1-1 shows what its main Mail window looks like.

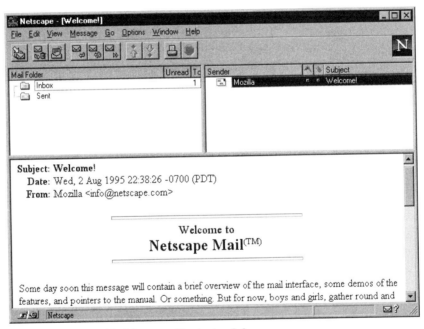

Figure 1-1: *E-mail in Netscape Navigator 2.0.*

RESEARCH

Locating specific information used to be a tedious and time-consuming process. Remember digging through library card catalogs and then wandering through dusty stacks of books, only to discover that what you needed wasn't even at this library? Now finding references to topics can be as simple as typing in a keyword and clicking a button—from the privacy of your own home! The Internet includes entire libraries of specialized information, and thousands of these are accessible, free of charge, to the general public.

The Internet also supports a variety of research techniques and styles. Suppose you're trying to come up with a topic for a speech you have to deliver. At first you might want to browse a variety of materials to refine your subject area. This process is much like going to an area in a library and starting to pull books off the shelf, except that on the Internet you can leap from library to library, following associative links or trains of thought. Once you've determined the exact subject of your speech, you may need to track down some very specific information, such as statistics to back up a particular point (statistics always make it sound like you know what you're talking about, don't they?). Once again there are Internet services that will help you, powerful search tools that will scurry around the Net and quickly find your needle in the information haystack. Netscape Navigator 2.0 gives you access to these tools through the Net Search feature on the Netscape home page, shown in Figure 1-2.

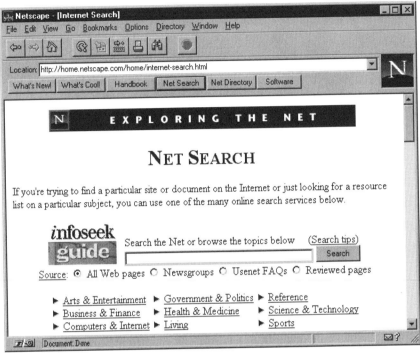

Figure 1-2: *Net Search gives you access to a variety of search tools from the Netscape home page.*

UNDER THE HOOD: TCP/IP

You can probably get through life just fine without understanding the technical underpinnings of the Net. But if you like the nuts and bolts stuff, boy have I got a sidebar for you!

TCP/IP really means "the TCP/IP protocol suite." It is a group of protocols that allow data to be transmitted correctly from one machine to another over the Net. And what exactly is a protocol? It's simply a set of standardized conventions for communication. In the human world a typical protocol is saying "Your Honor" when you talk to a judge. In the world of data communications a protocol might require that a sending machine include a special string of characters before and after every chunk of data so that the receiving machine can determine where that data begins and ends.

The TCP part of TCP/IP stands for Transmission Control Protocol. It divides any information you send into manageable blocks; conversely, it reconstructs received blocks into a stream of information. TCP does not require that all the blocks be received in the right sequence, since it attaches sequence numbers for reassembly. TCP also includes error checking; if blocks are missing or garbled, it requests that they be resent. When you run Internet applications you remain blissfully unaware of all of this activity, since the TCP software layer "sits below" the application software. Information is passed from the application software to TCP without any human intervention; at the other end, reassembled information is passed *from* TCP to the appropriate software program.

The IP part of TCP/IP stands for Internet Protocol. The Internet Protocol is the real workhorse of the Internet. When you send something over the Internet, TCP passes its packets on to IP. This is roughly like dropping a letter at the post office, because IP repackages the data and makes sure that all of it gets delivered from point to point on the Internet on its way to the final destination: the specified IP or domain name address. Conversely, when IP receives packets, it "delivers" them up to TCP. There are other low-level Internet protocols, but these are the two most important ones, the basis of most Internet communication.

NEWS & INFORMATION

This is the age of information, and success in many fields depends on getting the latest news as quickly as possible. The Internet provides numerous sources for specialized, up-to-date information. You may want to subscribe to an electronic mailing list, for instance, that keeps you posted on the latest developments in nanotechnology; you may want to get stock prices more current than those you can read in your local newspaper; or you may want to participate in a Usenet newsgroup where specialists in some arcane area of knowledge keep you abreast of what you need to know. Because of its scope and speed, the Internet is by far the most efficient way to make sure you maintain expert status in your little corner of the information universe. Netscape Navigator 2.0 gets you the information you need!

Figure 1-3 shows you what a list of Usenet newsgroups look like from Netscape Navigator 2.0.

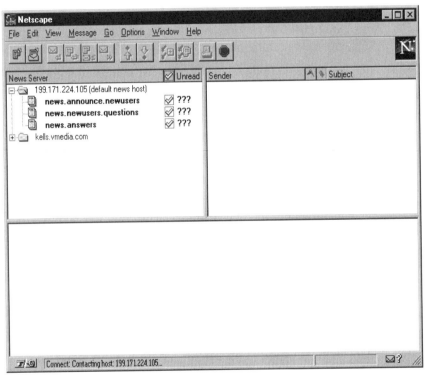

Figure 1-3: *A few Usenet newsgroups.*

SOFTWARE

One of the most astounding features of the Internet is the availability of thousands and thousands of software programs that you can download at no charge. In fact, until recently you couldn't even buy commercial Internet client programs for PCs that were anywhere near as good as the freeware and shareware available on the Net. (For more information about freeware and shareware, see Chapter 6.) That situation is starting to change, but there still are times when you need a program dedicated to a very specific task, such as playing a new kind of sound or video file.

Many of the sites that allow you to download programs are large, and most do not include descriptions of the files. Fortunately Netscape Navigator 2.0 helps you locate and download exactly what you need.

Figure 1-4 shows you some of the direcories of files available at Netscape's own FTP site.

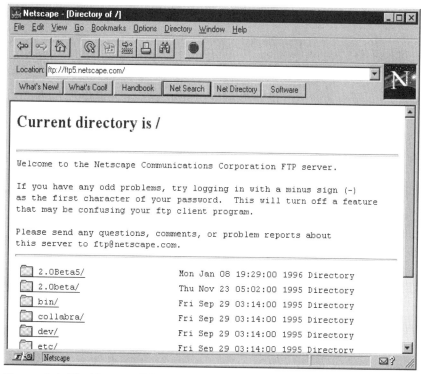

Figure 1-4: *The Netscape FTP site.*

PROMOTION, SHOPPING & ONLINE TRANSACTIONS

For years the Internet was a commerce-free zone. It was funded and monitored by dedicated bureaucrats and academicians who instituted strict usage policies restricting anything that smelled vaguely of money. Well, all that's changed. Now there are vast areas of cyberspace that look less like research libraries than like your local mall, and most major corporations maintain Web sites where they promote their products and services.

Figure 1-5 shows Open Market's Index to hundreds of commercial sites (http://www.directory.net).

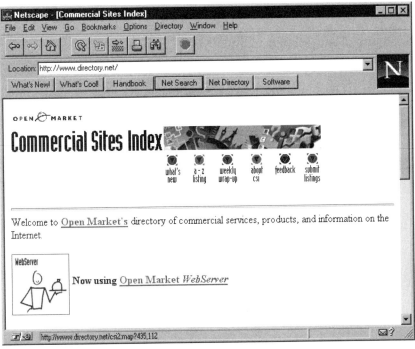

Figure 1-5: *Open Market's Commercial Sites Index.*

RECREATION

Planning a vacation? The Internet can provide current travel information on just about any area of the globe. Considering taking up a new sport? Want to find out about the latest foreign movies? The Internet can point you to the resources you need.

But the Internet not only supplies information *about* recreational activities, it also provides its own diversions and amusements. If you like interactive online games, for instance, you might be in danger of staying glued to your keyboard and monitor well into the wee hours. Figure 1-6 shows one of the many games sites available to you via the Web.

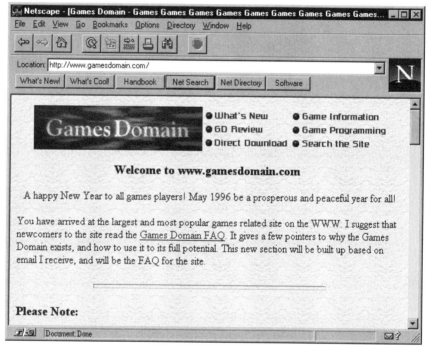

Figure 1-6: *The Games Domain site on the World Wide Web.*

And if you're a more cyber-gregarious person than I am, the Internet offers plenty of opportunities for meeting friends and chatting online. Then of course the World Wide Web, which we'll talk about later in this chapter, is full of unclassifiable forms of fun and nonsense, and Netscape Navigator 2.0 brings it all right into your own home.

But before discussing the Web, we need to take a quick look at how information actually gets from one place to another on the Web. A basic understanding of Internet addressing will make it easier for you to find the sites with information you're interested in.

INTERNET ADDRESSING

The whole basis of the Internet is that machines are constantly sending messages to other machines. Some of these messages are software commands, some are requests for data, and some include the human-readable data itself. Obviously there has to be a way for information to get to the proper recipient, and so the underlying suite of Internet protocols includes an addressing scheme. At the heart of the addressing scheme is the concept of domains.

DOMAINS & DOMAIN NAMES

By _domain_, we simply mean where a computer resides. For instance, a specific computer at the University of Missouri is in the _missouri_ domain, which in turn is within the top-level _edu_ domain, the domain that includes all Internet-connected colleges and universities in the United States. The complete domain name of a machine called _bigcat_ at the University of Missouri, for instance, would be _bigcat.missouri.edu_. No other machine anywhere on the Internet has the same domain name. Every name is registered with a special Internet organization to ensure that it is unique.

I have an e-mail account on echonyc.com. To reach my account, all you need to do is add my username to the domain name. My username is pjames, so my full e-mail address is _pjames@echonyc. com_. If you wanted to visit the Web pages at echonyc.com, however, you'd simply tell Netscape Navigator 2.0 to get a document from the Web server machine at that site, www.echonyc.com.

At first these addresses might look impossible to pronounce, but pronunciation conventions have developed. Pjames@echonyc. com is pronounced "p-james at echo-n-y-c dot com," and ftp.vmedia.com is pronounced "f-t-p dot v-media dot com." Of course usernames don't have to be as simple as mine. If your LAN administrator or access provider lets you choose your own name, you might want to be zzzx_12_qwerty@serviceprovider.com. Then again you might not. Keep in mind that people who send you e-mail need to remember your address.

Fortunately, the Internet doesn't care about case-sensitivity in addresses. You can send a message to pJaMeS@EcHoNyC.cOm, and I will still get it. But most experienced Internet users stick with lowercase when typing addresses—it's just easier. If you use both uppercase and lowercase letters in your addresses, some of the old-timers will chuckle at the newcomer, more often called a "clueless newbie."

As I mentioned earlier, the last part of a domain name address is called the top-level domain. There are six standardized domain names corresponding to types of organizations, as shown in Table 1-1.

Domain	Type of Organization
com	Commercial entity
edu	Educational institution
gov	Government agency or department
mil	Military organization
net	Network resource
org	Other type of organization, usually a not-for-profit

Table 1-1: *Top-level domains.*

In addition, Internet sites outside the United States are identified by a special two-letter, top-level domain name. For instance, a computer in Finland would have a top-level domain name of *fi*, and a computer in Germany would have a top-level domain name of *de* (for Deutschland). As you start cruising around the Net, you will run into these foreign domain names on a daily basis. There is even a two-letter designation for the United States (you guessed it, *us*), but it is rarely used since the six "organization type" names are more descriptive.

IP ADDRESSES

Pretty simple, isn't it? Well, luckily for those of us who make a living explaining such things, it's not *quite* that simple. Domain name addresses are really easy-to-remember translations of the kind of addresses the Internet really uses, numeric *IP addresses*. IP stands for "Internet Protocol." You may have read about IP in the sidebar above, "Under the Hood: TCP/IP." For now, it's only important to understand the difference between the two kinds of addresses.

If you're my age, you probably remember when phone numbers always began with the name of the exchange, as in "Murray Hill Seven, Five Five Five Five." You can think of Murray Hill Seven, the exchange, as a top-level domain name. But in fact your telephone didn't really care about the words Murray Hill Seven, it simply transmitted down the line the fact that you had dialed the numbers 647. You can think of 647 as the top-level portion of the IP address. When you use a domain name address to attach to a Web server, for instance, a special Internet service known as a Domain Name Service (DNS) looks up the name and replaces it with an IP number. And as long as you're connected to the Net, you have your own IP address so that remote machines know how to send you the information you request.

IP addresses are structured very much like domain name addresses, but backwards. They consist of four numbers, each less than 256, separated by periods. The rightmost number specifies the actual machine, while those to the left identify the network and subnetwork. When I link to the Net via my PPP account with the access provider ThoughtPort, for instance, my IP address is 199.171.225.100. The "100" part of that address is my actual computer on the ThoughtPort network.

OK, that's enough technical talk for now. Let's move ahead to one of the most fascinating Internet resources available, the World Wide Web.

WHAT IS THE WORLD WIDE WEB?

There is a lot of confusion among the general public about what the Web really is, and especially about how it relates to the Internet as a whole. Let's clarify these issues right now.

The World Wide Web is, quite simply, a global hypermedia document that resides on and stretches across most of the Internet. Whoa! What the !@#$ am I talking about? To understand the Web you really need to know what we mean by hypertext and hypermedia.

HYPERTEXT AND HYPERMEDIA

Imagine you are reading this book on your computer screen instead of on the page. As you read along, you notice that some of the words are underlined and may appear in a different color or **font**, just like that. In this example, you try clicking your mouse on the word font. Magically, a new document appears on your screen, explaining what fonts are. This new document also contains words and phrases that you can click on, taking you to yet other documents or to other places in the same document. That's what *hypertext* is all about: the nonlinear presentation of text, letting you jump from idea to idea following your own associative pathways. The clickable words and phrases are known as links, and the activity of moving around through these linked documents is known as *browsing*.

Now imagine that when you click on the **font** link you don't just get a text explaining fonts. Instead, a fancy picture pops up, a colorful depiction of fonts through the ages from Guttenberg to Adobe. Perhaps you're even presented with a video clip complete with Charlton Heston narration and a corny John Williams score. Congratulations! You've just learned what hypermedia is: the nonlinear presentation not just of text, but of a variety of other media including graphics and sound.

HYPERMEDIA ON THE NET

So what's this got to do with the Internet? Well, this is where it gets interesting. When you click on a link, the document that you get—whether it's text, graphics, sound, or full-motion video—does not have to be on the same machine as the original document. Thanks to a special protocol known as HyperText Transfer Protocol (HTTP), the primary protocol for the World Wide Web, you can access documents *on any public World Wide Web server on the Internet!* The original document might be on your own computer, or on the Netscape site; the video clip about fonts might reside on a machine in Hollywood or Timbuktu. Now here's the conceptual leap that makes this new technology so exciting: you can think of the collection of all the documents linked together as one big hypermedia document.

Let's go back to our original definition of the Web: a global hypermedia document that resides on and stretches across most of the Internet. Make sense now?

WHAT'S SO GREAT ABOUT HYPERMEDIA?

Suppose you're reading one of those wonderful but frustrating Russian novels in which 36 major characters are introduced during the first two chapters. If you're anything like me, you'll continually find yourself flipping back and forth trying to keep track of who's who. Was Natasha Galanskaya the one who ran away with the Count against her father's wishes, or was that Natalia Balanchina? Wouldn't it be great if you could just push a button on a character's name and instantaneously be transported to a full description of that character's relevant history? Well, you can't do that in a book or a magazine or even a regular computer document, but the magic of hypermedia makes it possible. ➡

Let's look at another example of how hypermedia can improve the communication process, and even make learning more fun and interesting. Suppose you're a high school student studying astrophysics. One option is to open your textbooks and review the mathematics of planetary motion in the abstract. Even if you enjoy solving a few motion problems, it's still a fairly boring exercise. But what if your physics lab computer is linked to the Web and takes you to a virtual textbook with animations that show the orbits of the bodies, in full color and motion? Or plays back short lectures on the day's exercises, by the foremost authority in the field? Educators and trainers know the power of multimedia to speed learning and increase students' retention levels. This type of presentation has become popular in education and corporate training environments, as it presents information in an interesting and entertaining format.

When we click on the graphics, video, and sound objects embedded in a compound-document Web page, we are fulfilling prophesies made years ago for a global information system. When you're up and running with Netscape Navigator 2.0, you'll see exactly what all the excitement's about.

SERVERS & BROWSERS

The Web utilizes what is sometimes called a client-server model. Special machines or software known as World Wide Web servers make the linked hypermedia documents available to the public. Individuals then move around through these documents using software known as Web clients or, more commonly, Web *browsers*. Obviously a Web browser has to be able to display or "play" a wide variety of hypermedia formats.

Because the World Wide Web uses a standardized protocol (HTTP) for transferring the information across the Internet, and because all Web software adheres to this protocol, any kind of Web browser will work with any kind of Web server. For instance, a site may decide to use one of the server packages developed by Netscape, but any World Wide Web browser will be able to access the information available at that site. Conversely, the browser we are discussing in this book, Netscape Navigator 2.0, can access hypermedia documents on any Web server anywhere in the world.

WHAT'S A HOME PAGE?

Once you start exploring the World Wide Web, you'll encounter the term *home page* or *homepage* over and over again, and it won't always be used the same way. Here are some of the things it can mean:

- A home page is the document that's displayed by a Web browser such as Netscape Navigator 2.0 when you first load the program. This document may be located on your local machine or at a remote site. In the case of Netscape Navigator, the default home page is a document located at Netscape's own Web site, but as with most other browsers, you can change this.

- A home page is the top-level document at a particular Web site. For instance, a typical small business's home page would contain a title, a logo, some introductory information, and a bunch of links to more detailed marketing information.

- A home page is a personal Web document created by an individual and made available to the public (Joe Blow's 15 kilobytes of fame). Many access providers now let users copy Web documents to their public Web servers, and the Net sprouts hundreds of new personal home pages every day. You'd be surprised who's out there!

- In some contexts, a home page is simply any hypertext Web document, though I have to admit it bugs me when I hear people use the term this way.

A QUICK DIP IN ACRONYM SOUP

OK, let's get all of our technical-sounding acronyms out of the way in OSF (one swell foop). There are only two you really need to worry about: HTML and URL. Not only will they give you a better handle on navigating around the Web, but if you pepper your conversation with them, many people will think you are really cool in a geeky sort of way.

HTML

All Web pages that contain text are written in a language called HTML, which stands for HyperText Markup Language. HTML is a subset of SGML (Standard Generalized Markup Language), a very generalized system originally designed for typesetting and document page description. HTML is simply ordinary ASCII text with embedded codes (usually referred to as *tags*) that represent instructions for displaying the text or for linking to other Web documents. For example, <I>italic</I> or <B>bold</B> in a Web document tells the browser to display the phrase "italic or bold" with the word "italic" in italics and the word "bold" in boldface. It is important to understand that HTML does *not* indicate exactly what the resulting text should look like—that is up to the browser software. On a system that can't display true italic or bold fonts, for instance, the browser might just display the words in a differ-ent color. When you author your own Web document, you simply label various text elements rather than specifying exactly what the text will look like. This makes HTML a universal language, ensur-ing that Web pages are displayable in one way or another on any conceivable machine or operating platform.

Figure 1-7 shows a typical Web page, and Figure 1-8 shows what some of the HTML source for it looks like.

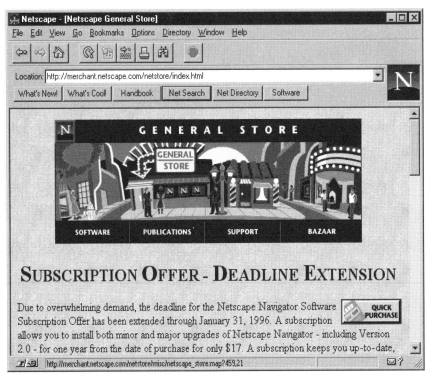

Figure 1-7: *A typical HTML document.*

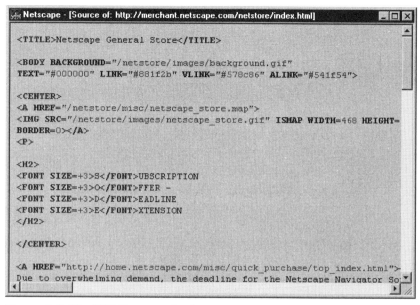

Figure 1-8: *The HTML source for the same page.*

TIP

Yes, Netscape Navigator 2.0 not only displays Web documents properly, it lets you see the source for any document it displays! This is especially useful if you're learning how to create your own Web page. Simply select Document Source from the View menu.

HTML is an evolving language. Tim Berners-Lee of the European Particle Physical Laboratory (CERN) in Switzerland, started it all in 1990 by releasing an initial specification to the public. It was pretty basic, supporting only the basic text handling tags. Berners-Lee started an Internet mailing list to solicit suggestions for refining and adding to the language, and in 1992 Dan Connolly released a "level 1" HTML specification. As soon as it was released, work began on a level 2 specification that would contain more advanced text handling capabilities. HTML 2.0, now completed and approved by a standards body known as the Internet Engineering Task Force (IETF), also includes support for interactive forms and imagemaps. Interactive forms let you enter data on the screen that is then sent to the host site, and imagemaps let you link to other documents by clicking on "hot spots" within an image. Most good browsers now support the HTML 2.0 features.

HTML Filenames

Files that contain HTML tags are known as HTML files, and they always have an extension of either .HTM or .HTML. On UNIX and other systems that support long filenames, the extension is .HTML; on DOS-based systems, it's .HTM. This extension tells the browser it is dealing with a hypertext document rather than some other type of hypermedia document, such as an image or audio file.

What's next? HTML 3.0, of course! Netscape has been at the forefront of the collaborative design process in proposing *and implementing* new features for HTML 3.0. Many of these exciting new extensions are covered later in this book, particularly in Chapter 9, "Advanced Netscape Navigator 2.0."

MORE HISTORY

If you're the kind of person who likes to know all about the origins and evolution of new information technologies, here are some sites to try once you've learned how to use Netscape Navigator 2.0:

- **About the World Wide Web (http://www.nmsi.ac.uk/ usage/).**

- **World Wide Web and CERN (http://www1.cern.ch/CERN/ WorldWideWeb/WWWandCERN.html).**

- **The World Wide Web: Origins and Beyond (http:// homepage.seas.upenn.edu/~lzeltser/WWW/).**

I mentioned before that HTML also includes the format for specifying links to other documents or to other areas of the same document. Here's what one of these links looks like:

```
<a href="http://www.faraway.com/explain-directory/
explain.html">Click here for an explanation</a>
```

Looks a little strange, doesn't it? That's OK. All you really need to know is that when you click the phrase "Click here for an explanation" a new HTML document (the file explain.html, which is located at a remote site) pops up. This will all make more sense when you learn about URLs, and so without further ado. . . .

URL

URL stands for Uniform Resource Locator. Back when $10 was worth something, that's what we used to call a bunch of $10 words, but it's really pretty simple. URLs are like signs pointing to hypermedia documents on the Web. They provide the protocol and addressing information that Netscape Navigator 2.0 or another browser uses to connect to the target document. The first part of a URL specifies the type of data or the protocol necessary to retrieve the data, the second part specifies the server where the information is located, and the optional third part specifies the exact path to that data. For instance, the URL http://www.vmedia. com/vvc/index.html tells Netscape Navigator 2.0 to retrieve the file index.html from the vvc directory at www.vmedia.com (Ventana Online's Web server) using the HTTP protocol, the basic support protocol on the Web. (See Chapters 6 and 7 for information about accessing resources available via other major Internet protocols, including FTP and Gopher.)

URLs are used in several different ways. First of all, they are part of the HTML tags that tell your browser to jump to a remote document. In the middle of an HTML file, for instance, the above URL might be used like this:

```
<a href="http://www.vmedia.com/vvc/index.html">Click
here to go to the Ventana Online home page!</a>
```

You can also type URLs directly into Netscape Navigator 2.0 to jump immediately to a remote document. And finally, you can add URLs to Netscape Navigator 2.0 as "bookmarks" for easy access at some later time.

NETSCAPE NAVIGATOR 2.0 & THE FUTURE OF THE WEB

Remember how I said that any Web browser can access hypermedia documents from anywhere on the Web? If that's true, why would you choose one browser over another, especially since there are a number of shareware and even freeware browsers available?

Well, here's the catch: while any browser can *access* available documents, different software packages vary greatly in their ability to *present* hypermedia information to you. For instance, some browsers are exclusively text-based. If you click on a link to a graphics document, all you'll get is a message saying something like "There is a picture here." But even among browsers that support a wide variety of hypermedia formats, there are still differences. For instance, different browsers support different versions or different features of HTML. Some browsers, for instance, will not let you enter information into interactive forms that may be essential for online shopping, or may not be able to display text in table format. As I mentioned earlier, Netscape Navigator 2.0 not only supports the full range of standard HTML features, it also supports a huge number of *proposed* HTML features, formatting options that are very likely to become standards in the next couple of years. (You'll learn more about some of these leading-edge features in Chapter 9.) With Netscape Navigator 2.0, you can view the future of the Web today.

SOME POINTERS ON USING THE NET

OK, we talked about the Internet a little, then about the World Wide Web. We're going to end this chapter by focusing once more on the Internet as a whole. The Web, after all, is really only one feature—albeit a dazzling one—of the new information landscape. And remember, Netscape Navigator 2.0 is more than a Web browser, it is more like a luxury cruise-mobile for exploring *all* the resources of the Net. And so in this section, I'd like to give you some very general pointers on using the Net effectively and efficiently.

Some people view the Internet as an experiment in grassroots self-governance. There aren't many laws, and there aren't many cops, and the best way to keep it that way is with generosity and common sense. If the Internet is to stay the wide-open magical place it is today, users will have to keep concentrating on the welfare of the community as a whole instead of exploiting it for individual gain. The Net can be seen as an *information environment* in which everything is interconnected, and we should all practice our "Internet ecology."

The online culture has developed its own guidelines, and before actually exploring the Net, it's a good idea to get familiar with some of these mostly unwritten rules of the road. Here are just a few that will make your Internet travels more efficient, more pleasant, and more "ecological." I think these guidelines are so important that I try to include the following subsections in every book I write. (Sure took that Harlequin Romance editor by surprise!)

AVOID TRAFFIC JAMS

They call it a superhighway, but sometimes it's more like driving through Bombay. Every day several thousand clueless newbies start exploring the Net. (Don't worry, you're not one of them: you bought this book!) Servers can support only a certain number of clients, and routers start to seem "sludgy" when they're called upon to transfer packets of data for thousands of users. Certain sites are practically impossible to reach, especially those distributing the latest free software or pictures of naked people.

To avoid traffic jams, and to avoid creating them, follow these simple rules of thumb:

- Connect during nonbusiness hours whenever possible. (Since this is a world-wide system, remember to compensate for different time zones!)

- If you're unable to connect with a particular server—for instance, if you get an "unable to connect with host" message when you try to access a Web page—wait a while before trying again. Bombarding the Net with unsuccessful connection attempts only adds to the problem.

- Use what are known as "mirror sites" for downloading files via FTP. Since some of the large anonymous FTP servers are so busy, a number of hosts sprinkled around the Net have been kind enough to "mirror" the exact contents, keeping their file lists completely up-to-date. The original site usually informs you about these mirror sites in its sign-on message. FTPing to a mirror is just like FTPing to the original host, except that you'll be out of the heaviest traffic.

- Find the closest source for what you need. Don't Telnet to Timbuktu if you can get the same information by FTPing to Peoria. When you access far-flung reaches of the globe, your packets of information must travel point-to-point through dozens of locations.

- Don't create unnecessary message traffic. This is especially important in Usenet newsgroups (see Chapter 5). If you have something to say, by all means say it, but the Net provides a useful venue for practicing eloquent restraint. Don't send the text of your Great American Novel to the whole world, simply tell users where they can find it. And remember that even a short message like "Ha ha ha!" expands to several hundred bytes of control and addressing information and may require the services of dozens of routers. Sending a message like this may look free to you, but it definitely costs the community as a whole.

■ Log off properly. If you don't follow the proper procedure for logging off from a particular Telnet site, for instance, a connection may be left open, perhaps making it difficult for others to log in.

UNDERSTAND ACCEPTABLE USE

Certain networks on the Internet, including the large backbones, have published standards for information that may be transmitted via their equipment and cabling. When you sign up with an access provider, you are mailed or e-mailed a document that outlines the acceptable use policies in effect for the networks used by that provider. You must adhere to these strictly! Besides the obvious prohibitions against using the network for trafficking in drugs and bombs, these policies usually make clear what kinds of commercial activities are permitted.

Here's a typical list of prohibitions from an acceptable use policy statement:

■ Users may not transmit any data or programs that cause disruption of service for others.

■ Users may not transmit any form of computer worm or virus.

■ Users must not use the network to violate intellectual property laws by distributing copyrighted or otherwise protected information, documents or software programs.

■ Users may not distribute unsolicited advertising.

But the written policies are really only the beginning of acceptable use. Common sense and respect for others should be your guiding principles when communicating over the Net. The Internet is not a good place for personal attacks and threats, as they frequently escalate into full-blown "flame wars" that waste resources. It's not necessarily a good place for challenging local community ethical standards, either, since various factions are looking for excuses to impose more stringent regulation. Make sure that you post your materials at the appropriate sites.

RESPECT & PROTECT PRIVACY

Privacy is the big hot topic on the Internet today. To what extent should government agencies have access to private Internet communications? Should the content of public sites be regulated? Should there be safeguards against commercial entities adding you to electronic mailing lists? It remains to be seen how these issues will be decided, but it is very clear that the Internet community expects its citizens to respect the privacy of other individuals. Nothing will get you in more trouble than trying to "hack" somebody else's account, trying to take advantage of technological loopholes to access private data, or publishing confidential information.

At the same time, you should realize that in a culture as large as the Internet there are going to be occasional problems with privacy, and you should do what you can to protect yourself and others by keeping your accounts secure:

- Always use good, specific passwords; your spouse's name or the name of a *Star Trek* character just won't do it.

- Change your passwords often.

- Always inform the appropriate network administrators when you think there may have been a security breach.

- If you're worried about particularly sensitive information, use some form of encryption such as Pretty Good Privacy (PGP), which is available on most large anonymous FTP sites.

■ And just in case, don't make any information available on the Net if you wouldn't want it to appear on the front page of *USA Today* or your hometown newspaper.

BE WILLING TO ASK FOR HELP

In my experience, the most annoying Internet users are those who "know just enough to be dangerous." They go crashing around the Internet, leaving a mess for others to clean up. Look, the Internet is full of *real* experts; if you don't know how to do something, just ask. You'll be amazed at how helpful and friendly the seasoned Net veterans can be. I've asked some pretty stupid questions on the Internet, but only rarely have I received a snooty response.

Of course, before asking questions of other users, you should look for available resources such as help files or appropriate technical documents. The Netscape site, which appears as soon as you load Netscape Navigator 2.0, is full of useful information. Many Usenet newsgroups even maintain files of frequently asked questions, called FAQs. But if you've exhausted other resources, there's nothing wrong with a plea for help.

DON'T BE AFRAID TO EXPLORE

On the other hand, one of the most valuable ways to learn how to use the Net is simply to explore. As long as you're not trying to do something too tricky or arcane, common sense will usually get you where you want to go. Half the fun of the Internet is wandering around guided as much by your instincts as by a conscious plan. Certainly you can do no harm by getting out there and seeing the world!

MOVING ON

What makes Netscape Navigator 2.0 the premier product for accessing the Internet is not its slick interface, or its availability on a variety of platforms, or its solid reliability, or even its early support of forward-looking Web features. What really sets this product apart is that it lets you do *everything you need to do on the Net*. In addition to browsing the Web, you can use Netscape Navigator 2.0 to send and receive e-mail; to read and post Usenet newsgroup messages; to gather files; and to explore a wide range of specialized Internet services. In the following chapters, we'll be exploring all aspects of this versatility using a hands-on approach, and you'll see for yourself that becoming a seasoned Internaut is easy and fun.

But first let's make sure your system is ready for the trip. The next chapter guides you through the process of getting connected to the Net if you're not already "wired," as well as installing and configuring Netscape Navigator 2.0. If you've already done all of this, you may just want to skim Chapter 2 and then move ahead to Chapter 3, where the *real* fun begins!

chapter two

Getting Started

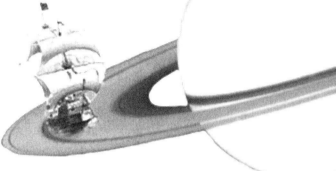

After learning about some of the resources available on the Net, you're probably eager to get busy exploring this vast new electronic world. Thanks to Netscape Navigator 2.0, it's easy. But as with any journey, there are a few preparations to deal with first. In this chapter, we'll show you:

- How to make sure you have the necessary hardware and software.

- How to connect to the Internet (with extensive coverage of Windows 95's built-in connectivity features).

- How to install Netscape Navigator 2.0 if you have the version of this book with CD-ROM.

- How to configure Netscape Navigator 2.0 so that it works the way you want it to.

OK, first things first. What exactly do you need to run Netscape Navigator 2.0?

HARDWARE & SOFTWARE REQUIREMENTS

To run the Windows or Windows 95 version of Netscape Navigator 2.0, you need:

- A 386 or better computer running Windows 3.1, Windows for Workgroups, Windows 95, or Windows NT.

- At least 8MB of RAM, preferably much more (especially with Windows 95).

- A live connection to the Internet, either via your LAN or via a SLIP or PPP connection with an Internet access provider. If you're using SLIP or PPP, you also need:

  - A modem properly connected to your computer. The modem should be at least 14.4 baud.

  - An account with an Internet access provider. If you don't already have one, see the section later in this chapter called "Finding an Internet Access Provider."

  - Software for establishing your connection with your Internet access provider and for providing TCP/IP communications on your machine. (More about this below in the section "Connecting to the Internet.")

TRAP

If you are a Windows 3.1 user and have an older version of Win32s on your system (version 1.15 or below), you may need to remove it before installing Netscape Navigator 2.0. Navigator installs a newer version of Win32s. For more information, please see the Readme file.

CONNECTING TO THE INTERNET

Before you can use Netscape Navigator 2.0, you have to be connected to the Internet. There are several different types of Internet connections. The simplest, from the point of view of the end user of Netscape Navigator 2.0, is a *permanent LAN connection*.

PERMANENT LAN CONNECTIONS

These days businesses large and small use LANs, or local area networks, to share files as well as devices such as printers. LANs are a cost-effective way to coordinate tasks, and they eliminate the need for multiple copies of business documents. And as a bonus, many office LANs are wired directly into the Internet via a special leased line, often a high-speed T1.

Hardwired connections like this really only make economic sense when several individuals on a LAN need to access the Internet simultaneously, or when an organization wants to make a Telnet, FTP, or Web server available for access by remote Internet users. At this point leased lines are still too expensive for you to hardwire your home. Besides, the Internet is so addicting that round-the-clock access might be dangerous!

If your workplace already has Internet connectivity, you may be able to fire up Netscape Navigator 2.0 and visit some great inter-active game sites right away—on your break, of course. But if you haven't accessed the Internet from work already, there may be a few preliminary steps before you can go online. Your network administrator may need to configure the TCP/IP software on your local machine, or change some aspects of your network account. The good news is that there's very little you have to do yourself. Once you can connect to the Internet from your desk, you're ready to travel anywhere in cyberspace with Netscape Navigator 2.0. And if you plan to use Netscape Navigator 2.0 with a permanent LAN connection, you can probably skip the next few sections of this chapter and move ahead to "Internet Connectivity Software."

TIP

If you're on a LAN that supports TCP/IP, you don't necessarily *need a connection to the Internet. Netscape Navigator 2.0 can be used within your organization for accessing documents and sharing multimedia resources on your local file servers without ever connecting to the outside world. While this book emphasizes the Internet, most of the information also applies to this more specialized use of the product. Please see your network administrator for more information.*

But what about Internet access for the home, or for businesses that don't require a round-the-clock hardwired connection? That's where we get into SLIP and PPP.

SLIP & PPP CONNECTIONS TO THE NET

If you don't have to be linked to the Internet all the time, you can get what is known as a Serial Line Internet Protocol (SLIP) or Point-to-Point Protocol (PPP) account with an Internet access provider. These are dial-up accounts that give you the same full access to the Net as hardwired connections, but you are online only during the time your computer is actually linked by phone with your access provider.

Here's how it works: Whenever you want to be "live on the Net," you click an icon and your computer places a modem call to the access provider. After the remote computer determines that you are in fact a valid customer, it connects you to the Internet, and you communicate using Netscape Navigator 2.0 or any other Internet software just as if you were wired in directly via a LAN. The information you send and receive is in the correct format for communicating over the Net. In addition, each packet of data is "wrapped" with extra information that allows it to be transmitted or received by modem instead of coaxial network cable. This extra envelope is the SLIP or PPP protocol. You need to use only one of them, whichever one your access provider supports.

Most access providers charge by the hour for SLIP or PPP connectivity, but your bill will be much, *much* lower than with a leased line connection, sometimes as low as $20 a month.

WHAT ABOUT ISDN?

Normal telephone lines are low-bandwidth analog lines; compared to digital lines, they can't handle large amounts of information very quickly. An ISDN line is a special kind of all-digital line that your phone company may be able to run to your house or office. There are some hefty installation fees, and then you're usually charged by how much you use the line. This fee is in addition to whatever hourly rates you pay your Internet access provider.

In order to use your ISDN line for Internet access, you need a few pieces of specialized equipment and an account with an access provider that supports ISDN connectivity. Unfortunately, you still need to understand some complex terminology before even ordering a line from your phone company. It is beyond the scope of this book to address these issues, and for most individual users ISDN is not yet a cost-effective option. If you want to investigate this connectivity method further, there's lots of information available on the Net itself.

FINDING AN INTERNET ACCESS PROVIDER

You might already have a SLIP or PPP account with an Internet access provider. For instance, if you have already installed the Personal Edition of Netscape Navigator 2.0, you may have already signed up with an access provider. But if you don't currently have a way to get on the Net, this section's for you!

These days there are hundreds of providers to choose from, and there's a good chance you can find one with a local access number. But you might not find the access provider of your dreams in the Yellow Pages, since it's not worth it for companies to list every local point-of-presence. But who needs the Yellow Pages anyway in this electronic age? Just find a friend who is already connected to the Internet and get him or her to point Netscape Navigator 2.0 or some other less cool Web browser to http://thelist.com. (Don't worry, this will all make sense after Chapter 3, "A Quick Look Around.") This document claims to include the most complete list of Internet access providers, conveniently arranged by geographic area. And if there isn't an access number in your area, you can always sign up with one of the larger providers that offer 800 number service for a small extra fee.

Figure 2-1 shows a small portion of the access provider list, displayed in Netscape Navigator 2.0, of course.

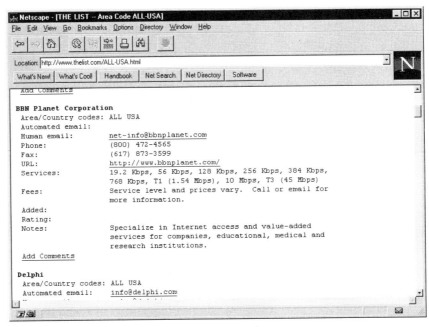

Figure 2-1: *THE LIST of Internet access providers.*

But with all these access providers out there, how do you choose one? Of course, you should call several and compare their charges. Just a year or two ago, pricing was all over the map. Luckily, increased competition has both lowered and leveled the pricing, but there can still be a lot of variation. For instance, many access providers offer a number of hours per month for a set fee, and after that charge on an hourly basis. You should ask how many hours are included in the base monthly charge as well as what the rates are for additional online time.

Besides cost, there are a number of other questions you should ask as you shop around for an Internet access provider:

- Do I get an Internet e-mail account at no extra charge? (The answer should be yes.)

- Do you support 28.8 kbps modems? (Even if you don't have a 28.8 kbps modem now, who knows when you might? The answer to this should be yes.)

- Do you have a network news server that includes a full range of Usenet newsgroups? (The answer should be yes, and there should be no extra charge for newsgroup access.)

- Do you have a Web server where I can put up my own Web pages? (This is a service you may not need. If you do, shop around carefully; extra charges for this vary from zero to hundreds of dollars!)

- Which do you provide, SLIP service or PPP service? PPP is preferable, though this is not all that important.

TRAP

Windows 95 gives you Internet support and PPP connectivity right out of the box, but SLIP will not work with Windows 95 unless you install the Internet components from Microsoft Plus! or the special SLIP client software that's available only on the CD-ROM version of Windows 95.

- Can you assign me a fixed IP address rather than dynamically assigning one each time I call in? (This is not essential unless you want to set your machine up as a server that can be accessed by the general public.)

- How do you provide technical support? (The answer should be that real-time support is available via a toll-free voice line, and same-day support is available via e-mail and fax.)

And of course if you're considering a small, local access provider, ask around to make sure that they can adequately handle the current traffic, that they can grow to handle the traffic for years to come, and that they can generate enough revenue to stay in business. Once you've given everyone your e-mail address, it can be a real pain to switch providers.

TIP

Many of the large online information services such as America Online, CompuServe, and the Microsoft Network now provide Internet access via dial-up SLIP and PPP. You might want to check out their rates and the availability of access numbers in your area.

INTERNET CONNECTIVITY SOFTWARE

So far everything's been pretty simple and straightforward, right? Well, here's where it gets a bit complicated. Don't worry, the information in this section is the hairiest stuff in the book. If you get through it without scratching your head a time or two you may be geekier than I am.

If the designers of PC operating systems had foreseen back in the dark ages (the eighties) that "Internet" would become a household word, they would have built a TCP/IP layer right into DOS. What is a TCP/IP layer? When you type a message into an e-mail program, for instance, it has to be formatted for transmission over the Net; in addition, it has to have an address attached so that it gets to the right destination. Conversely, incoming messages have to have the addressing information stripped off and have to be reconstituted into something you can read. This process of packaging and unpackaging Internet information is the task of the *Transmission Control Protocol/Internet Protocol* (TCP/IP) layer.

Since the designers of PC systems software *couldn't* see into the future, you need an additional piece of software to provide this functionality—at least if you're running a pre-Windows 95 version of Windows. If you're directly connected to the Internet via a LAN, that's all you'll need. But to establish an active account with a SLIP or PPP service provider, you also need software that dials an access number and packages TCP/IP packets so that they can be sent out via modem. Fortunately, most TCP/IP software for Windows also includes a dialer and SLIP or PPP features.

And what if you have Windows 95? Well, you're lucky! Windows 95 has TCP/IP built right in, as well as PPP and a dialer. That's the good news. The not-so-good news is that you still have to configure the software, and Windows 95's Internet configuration is one of those tasks that gives writers like me a nice warm feeling of job security.

Whether you install separate Internet connectivity software on a Windows 3.1 system or configure Windows 95 for Internet access, there are a bunch of account-specific Internet addresses and other numbers you will need to enter. When you sign up with an Internet access provider, you are usually sent a data sheet that includes this configuration information. Now's the time to drag that piece of paper out and transfer the information into the handy little chart in Table 2-1.

Name of access provider:	*Spirit One*
PPP, SLIP, or CSLIP:	*PPP*
Local access number: *70 #*	*220 5080*
My user ID:	*mmcKay*
My account password:	*aKs 8 bat*
My IP address, if any:	*Dy 020.0. or Dynam*
Subnet mask, if any:	*255.255.255.0*
Primary DNS address, if any:	*205. 139. 108. 2*
Secondary DNS address, if any:	*204 . 70. 128 .1*
Address of mail server:	
My e-mail account name:	*mmcKay @ spiritone .com*
My e-mail password:	*aKs 8 bat*

Table 2-1: *Personal Internet access information.*

SAME
E-Add

INcomeing Mail. Spirtowe. Com

By the way, if you pass this book on to somebody else, or if you keep it where it is accessible to people who are just dying for some free time on the Net, make sure *not* to include your passwords in the above table!

Out   smTP

WHERE TO GET INTERNET CONNECTIVITY SOFTWARE FOR WINDOWS 3.1

As I already mentioned, Windows 95 has Internet functionality built right in. In a few minutes, I'll show you how to configure Windows 95 for getting on the Net, but what about you Windows 3.1 users? Where do *you* get software for Internet access?

The answer is, it's all over the place! Here are a few of your options:

- Netscape sells a special version of Netscape Navigator 2.0 called the Personal Edition. This software operates exactly like the program included on the CD-ROM that comes with this book, but also includes TCP/IP software as well as a dialer and SLIP or PPP options. It even includes a special introductory offer from an access provider.

- Ventana Communications Group, Inc., has released several excellent products, such as the Windows Internet Membership Kit and the World Wide Web Kit, that include connectivity software and special offers from access providers.

- There are several shareware Internet connectivity products available from most large electronic bulletin board systems and online services. The best known of these is Trumpet 2.0, which has almost become a standard for Windows 3.1 SLIP and PPP users.

- Microsoft offers a TCP/IP add-on for Windows for Workgroups. Contact Microsoft for further information on this product.

Obviously it's impossible to cover installing and configuring all these different pieces of software! If you're a Windows 3.1 user, you're on your own until we get into installing Netscape Navigator 2.0 itself. But don't worry: all of the products just mentioned come with pretty good documentation, and armed with the chart you filled out above, you should do just fine. You can also call your access provider for technical support. Most access providers are familiar with a broad range of connectivity software.

If you're a Windows 95 user, though, or if you're thinking about installing Windows 95, I can help you out a bit more. Read on!

SETTING UP WINDOWS 95

If you plan on spending a lot of time on the Internet, Windows 95 provides some advantages over previous versions of Windows:

- As I mentioned before, TCP/IP and SLIP or PPP connectivity are built right into the operating system, so you don't need extra software just to get on the Net.

- Windows 95 lets you use 32-bit Windows applications such as the Windows 95 version of Netscape Navigator 2.0. Thirty-two-bit programs generally run faster, and they may include more features than their 16-bit counterparts. In addition, many vendors of Internet applications are now concentrating almost exclusively on Windows 95 versions.

- The Windows 95 user interface is easier for most users, so you can move around the Net faster.

- With Windows 95, you are less likely to experience crashes or other annoying software problems while connected to the Net.

If you're going to spend a lot of time on the Net *and* if you're considering installing Windows 95 anyway, I'd recommend you go ahead and do it now.

OK, let's assume you took my advice and just got through installing a brand new copy of Windows 95. (Or maybe you already had it installed and didn't even need my advice.) Now let's get your system set up for Internet connectivity. If you plan to connect to the Internet via your company's LAN, go on to the next section. If you plan to use a SLIP or PPP connection, skip ahead to "Setting Up Windows 95 for a SLIP or PPP Connection."

SETTING UP WINDOWS 95 FOR A PERMANENT LAN CONNECTION TO THE NET

First of all, a warning: *Do not proceed with this section until you've told your network administrator what you're doing!* If you proceed on your own without involving the proper technical personnel in your company, I hereby explicitly waive any responsibility for the chewing out you're about to get.

OK, your LAN administrator has said you can go ahead on your own, and has given you a bunch of information such as your IP address, subnet mask, and DNS address. To set up the connection:

1. Select Settings from the Windows 95 Start menu, and then select Control Panel from the cascading submenu. The Control Panel folder appears, as shown in Figure 2-2.

Figure 2-2: *The Windows 95 Control Panel.*

2. Double-click the Network icon. The Configuration tab pops up, as shown in Figure 2-3.

   ■ Don't worry if the network components you have listed are different from mine.

3. If both TCP/IP and your network adapter (the name of your network card) appear on your list, skip ahead to the section "Configuring Your Network Components."

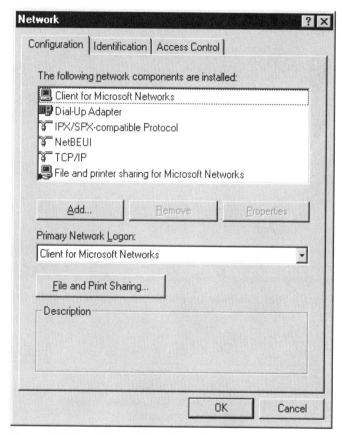

Figure 2-3: *The Network Configuration tab.*

ADDING TCP/IP & YOUR ADAPTER

1. While sill in the Network Configuration tab, click the Add button. The Select Network Component Type dialog box appears, as shown in Figure 2-4.

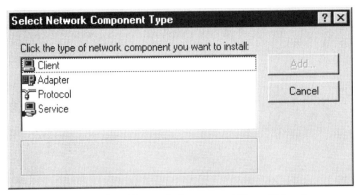

Figure 2-4: *The Select Network Component Type dialog box.*

2. Select Protocol and click Add. The Select Network Protocol dialog box appears.

3. Select Microsoft in the left panel, then TCP/IP in the right panel, as shown in Figure 2-5.

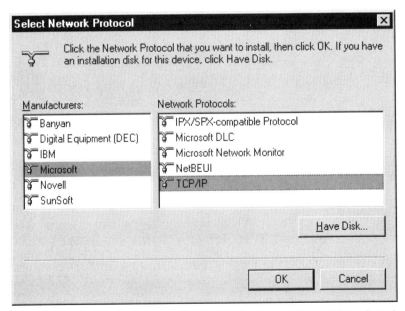

Figure 2-5: *The Select Network Protocol dialog box, with TCP/IP selected.*

4. Click OK. You are returned to the Configuration tab, which should now contain TCP/IP, as shown in Figure 2-6.

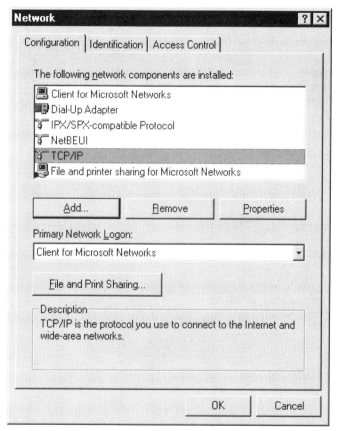

Figure 2-6: *The Configuration tab with new TCP/IP component selected.*

5. If your network adapter appears in the list of network components, you can skip ahead to the section "Configuring Your Network Components." Otherwise, click the Add button again.

6. When the Select Network Component Type dialog box appears, as shown earlier in Figure 2-4, select Adapter and click Add. The Select Network Adapters dialog box appears, as shown in Figure 2-7.

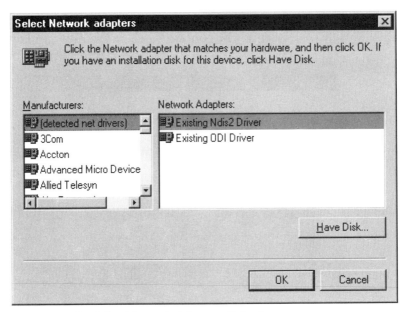

Figure 2-7: *The Select Network Adapters dialog box.*

7. Select the manufacturer of your network card from the left panel, then the exact model of the card from the right panel. Click OK. You are returned to the Configuration tab, which now contains both TCP/IP and your network adapter.

Now you can go ahead and configure your network components.

CONFIGURING YOUR NETWORK COMPONENTS

With the Configuration tab still displayed:

1. Select your network adapter, then click Properties. A Properties dialog box pops up, similar to the one in Figure 2-8.

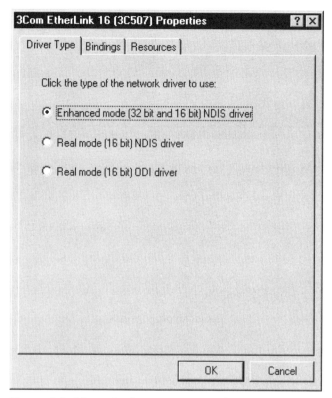

Figure 2-8: *Network adapter Properties dialog box.*

■ The title bar of this dialog box will reflect the name of your actual network card, and the tabs might differ from mine.

2. Select the Bindings tab, as shown in Figure 2-9.

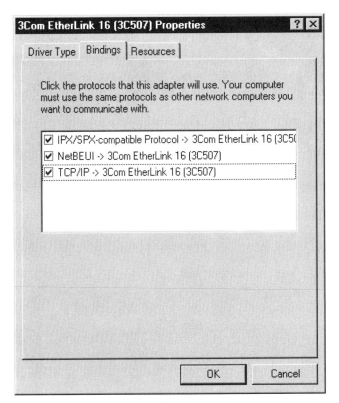

Figure 2-9: *The Bindings tab.*

3. If they are not already checked, check the TCP/IP and NetBEUI check boxes. You should also check the boxes for any other protocols that are necessary on your LAN. (Here's where a call to your network administrator might be helpful!) When you're done checking boxes in the Bindings tab, click OK to return to the Configuration tab.

4. Select TCP/IP and click the Properties button. The TCP/IP Properties appear, with the IP Address tab selected, as shown in Figure 2-10.

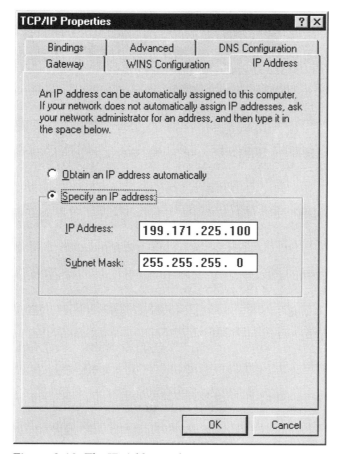

Figure 2-10: *The IP Address tab.*

5. Select the Specify an IP Address radio button, then in the appropriate fields, enter the IP address and subnet mask you were given by your LAN administrator. Typically the subnet mask is 255.255.255.0 or 255.255.0.0.

If you're on a Novell network, you may be able to find your IP address in the file NET.CFG. Usually this file is located in the root directory of your hard drive.

6. Select the WINS configuration tab and click the Disable WINS Resolution radio button, unless you've been given different instructions.

7. Select the Gateway tab and enter the IP address of the default gateway on your LAN. Again, this is a number you should get from your network administrator or, in the case of Novell networks, from your NET.CFG file.

8. Select the Bindings tab. By default the Client for Microsoft Networks check box is checked. Do not change this, but make sure that any other necessary clients are checked.

9. Select the Advanced tab and make sure the Set This Protocol To Be the Default Protocol check box is checked.

10. Select the DNS Configuration tab:

   ■ Click the Enable DNS radio button. Enter your username in the Host box and the domain name of your company's DNS server in the Domain box.

   ■ In the DNS Server Search Order box, enter the IP address for your company's main DNS server and click Add. If your network administrator has given you an alternate DNS address, enter that now and click Add again.

   ■ In the Domain Suffix Search Order box, type in the domain suffix for your company's DNS and click Add. You can add several domain suffixes the same way you added entries in the DNS Server Search Order box.

   Your completed DNS Configuration tab should look something like Figure 2-11.

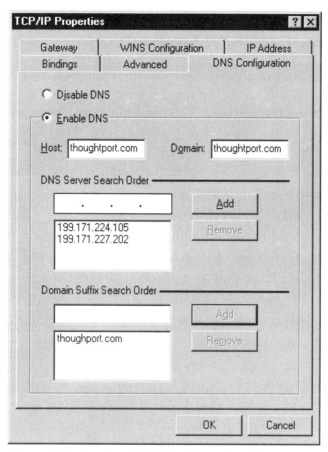

Figure 2-11: *Completed DNS Configuration tab.*

11. Click OK to return to the Configuration tab, then OK again to exit the Network Properties dialog box. Windows 95 will ask you if you want to reboot your system. Click Yes.

Once Windows 95 comes back up, you're ready to install and run Netscape Navigator 2.0 or virtually any Internet software for Windows. You're just a few small steps away from getting out on the Net. And since you're not using a SLIP or PPP dial-up connection, you get to skip ahead a few pages to the section "Installing Netscape Navigator 2.0."

SETTING UP WINDOWS 95 FOR A SLIP OR PPP CONNECTION

There are a few more steps to setting up a SLIP or PPP connection using Windows 95, but it's still pretty easy. I'll take you through it from beginning to end. The main things you need are patience, the ability to follow directions carefully, and about 20 minutes. There are a few other requirements:

- Windows 95 successfully installed on your machine.

- A modem installed in or attached to your computer, preferably 28.8 kbps, though 14.4 kbps is OK.

- Your original Windows 95 CD-ROM or disks (CD-ROM required for SLIP support, though not for PPP).

- A PPP or SLIP account with an Internet access provider.

- The following information, all of which you should have received from your PPP service provider:

  - Your user ID.

  - Your account password.

  - The IP address assigned to you by your access provider. (*Note:* Some access providers do not give you your own IP address, but dynamically assign you a new one each time your computer logs on. If you were not assigned an IP address, this is probably the way it works for you.)

  - The DNS address(es) for your access provider.

  - What kind of account this is (PPP, SLIP, or CSLIP).

INSTALLING YOUR MODEM

OK, got all your supplies? The first step is telling Windows 95 about your modem. (If you already configured your modem when you installed Windows 95, you can skip this section. I'll meet you around the bend, in the "Adding Dial-Up Networking" section.) I'll assume you've completed the physical part of the installation, attaching your modem to your computer and to a wall jack following the manufacturer's instructions. Now it's time to go to Windows 95's Modems facility. To install your modem:

1. Select Settings from the Windows 95 Start menu, and then select Control Panel from the cascading submenu. The Control Panel folder appears, as shown earlier in Figure 2-2.

2. Double-click the Modems icon. The Modems Properties dialog box appears, with the General tab selected as shown in Figure 2-12.

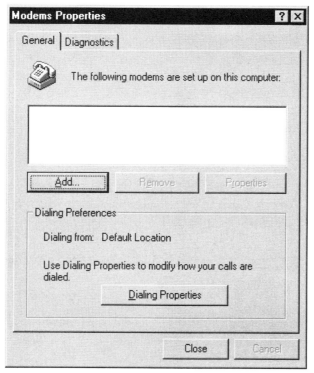

Figure 2-12: *The General tab.*

■ If your modem already appears in the list, Windows 95 has already installed it for you automatically. You can skip ahead to the section "Dialing Properties."

3. Click Add. The Install New Modem Wizard appears, as shown in Figure 2-13.

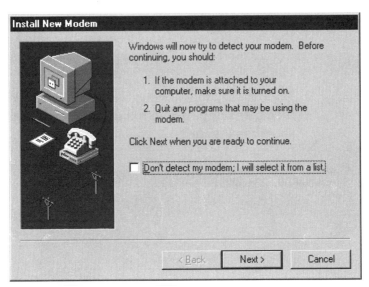

Figure 2-13: *The Install New Modem Wizard.*

4. Click Next. Windows 95 spends a few moments trying to detect your modem and then pops up the Verify Modem dialog box, as shown in Figure 2-14.

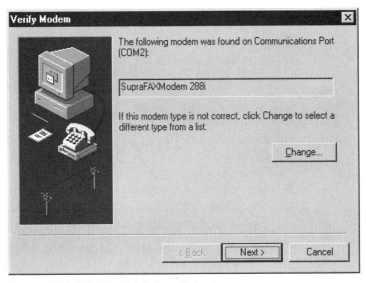

Figure 2-14: *The Verify Modem dialog box.*

5. If Windows 95 has not correctly identified your modem, you can click the Change button to select it manually. Otherwise, click Next and then Finish to exit the Install New Modem Wizard.

Now we'll configure your Dialing Properties. This configuration option is also accessed from the General tab of the Modems Properties dialog box, so stay right where you are!

DIALING PROPERTIES

The Windows 95 Dialing Properties tell your modem how to dial calls from your location. For instance, you may have to dial 9 to get an outside line, and you probably need to dial 1 for long-distance calls. Perhaps you even want to use a credit card for all your data calls. You may have already dealt with the Dialing Properties when you first installed Windows 95, but in case you didn't, or in case you want to change them, here's what you do:

1. In the General tab of the Modems Properties dialog box, as shown earlier in Figure 2-12, click the Dialing Properties button. The My Locations tab appears, as shown in Figure 2-15.

2. In the Where I Am section of the tab, type in your area code and select your country from the drop-down list. Do *not* change the field that contains the words "Default Location."

3. In the How I Dial From This Location section, fill in all the fields appropriately for your phone system. For home phones, several of the fields can be left blank. If you check the Dial Using Calling Card check box, you are prompted for further information.

4. If you will always log on to the Internet from this location, you're done. Simply click OK to return to the General tab and then click OK again to save your changes and exit the Properties sheet. But let's say you're using a laptop that you transport between home and work, and you'll be accessing the Internet from both places. In that case you'll probably need to create a new location with its own dialing properties.

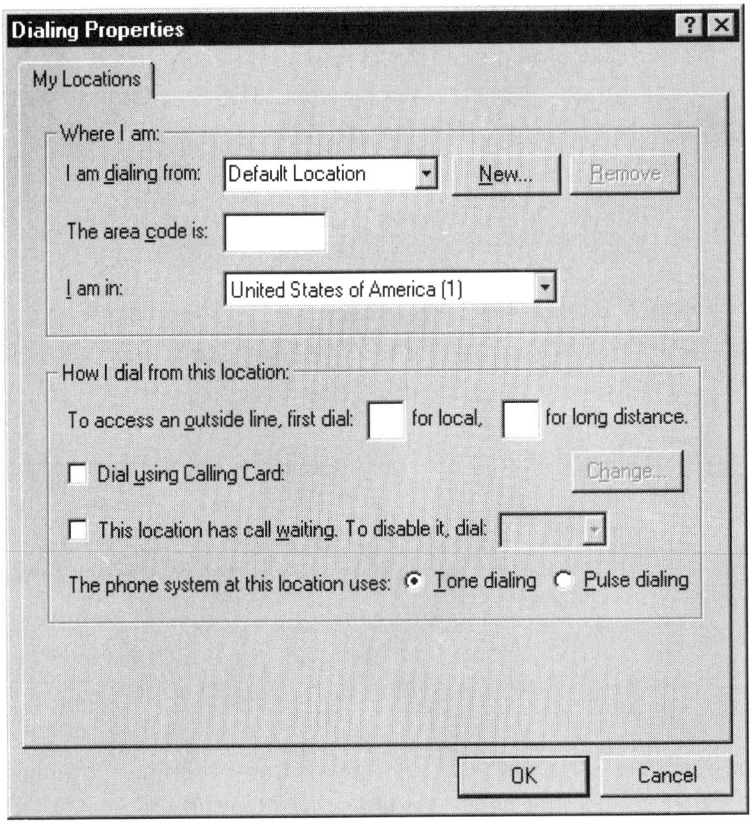

Figure 2-15: *The My Locations tab.*

TIP

If you're using a laptop that you transport between home and work, or if you'll be accessing the Internet from more than one office, you can create a new location with its own dialing properties. Click the New button in the My Locations tab, enter the name of the new location, and type in any changes to the dialing properties. Dial-Up Networking will let you choose from among any new locations you add here.

ADDING DIAL-UP NETWORKING

Dial-Up Networking is the Windows 95 component that lets you attach to your Internet access provider via SLIP or PPP. You may have installed it when you first installed Windows 95, but in case you didn't:

1. Select Settings from the Windows 95 Start menu, and then select Control Panel from the cascading submenu. The Control Panel folder appears.

2. Double-click the Add/Remove Programs icon. The Add/Remove Programs Properties sheet pops up.

3. Select the Windows Setup tab, shown in Figure 2-16.

TIP

As you can see by skimming ahead, setting up your Windows 95 system for SLIP or PPP Internet connectivity is not difficult, but it does take some time. If you'd rather travel in the fast lane, pick up a copy of Microsoft Plus!, an excellent add-on to Windows 95. It includes an Internet Setup Wizard that will make this whole process much simpler.

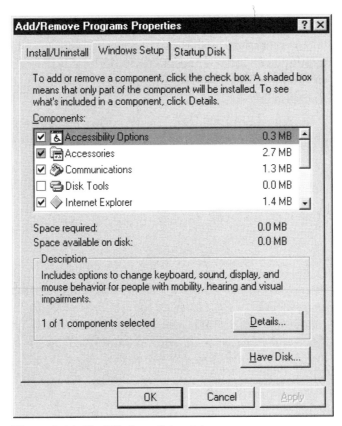

Figure 2-16: *The Windows Setup tab.*

4. In the list of components, highlight the Communications entry and click the Details button. The Communications dialog box appears, as shown in Figure 2-17.

Figure 2-17: *The Communications dialog box.*

- Follow any instructions for inserting or removing your Windows 95 CD-ROM or disk.

5. If Dial-Up Networking is already checked, skip ahead to the next section, "Adding TCP/IP." Otherwise, check Dial-Up Networking and then click OK. You are returned to the Windows Setup tab, with Communications now checked.

- If you want, you can add other components as well at this time.

6. Click OK. The Copying Files message box appears, and after a few moments Windows 95 informs you that you must restart your computer in order for the changes to take effect. Go ahead and do that now.

ADDING TCP/IP

When you hook up your computer to the Internet, whether by cables or a dial-up connection, it must use the same TCP/IP protocols for sending and receiving data as every other entity on the Net. TCP/IP functionality is included on your Windows 95 CD or disks, but it is not installed automatically.

To add TCP/IP to Windows 95:

1. Select Settings from the Windows 95 Start menu, and then select Control Panel from the cascading submenu. The Control Panel folder appears.

2. Double-click the Network icon. The Configuration tab pops up, as shown in Figure 2-18.

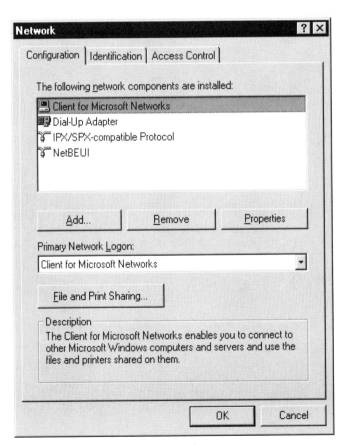

Figure 2-18: *The Configuration tab.*

■ Don't worry if you have other network components in the list. When you added Dial-Up Networking to Windows 95, the system added some components necessary for remote access to Novell or Microsoft LANs. If you are not currently on a LAN and are not planning to connect your machine to other computers, and if you only want to use Dial-Up Networking to connect to the Internet, you can remove these extra components. But whatever you do, *do not remove the Dial-Up Adapter!*

3. If TCP/IP already appears in your list, skip ahead to the section "Dial-Up Adapter Properties." Otherwise, click the Add button. The Select Network Component Type dialog box appears, as shown in Figure 2-19.

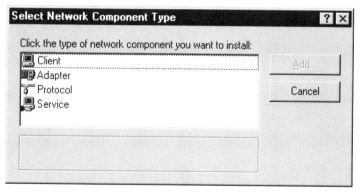

Figure 2-19: *The Select Network Component Type dialog box.*

4. Select Protocol and click Add. The Select Network Protocol dialog box appears.

5. Select Microsoft in the left panel, then TCP/IP in the right panel, as shown in Figure 2-20.

6. Click OK. You are returned to the Configuration tab, which should now contain TCP/IP, as shown in Figure 2-21.

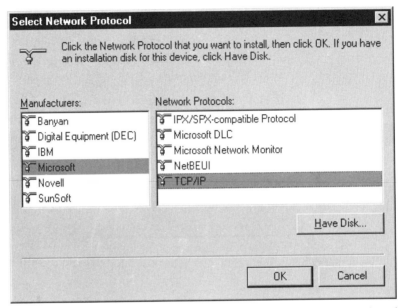

Figure 2-20: *The Select Network Protocol dialog box with TCP/IP selected.*

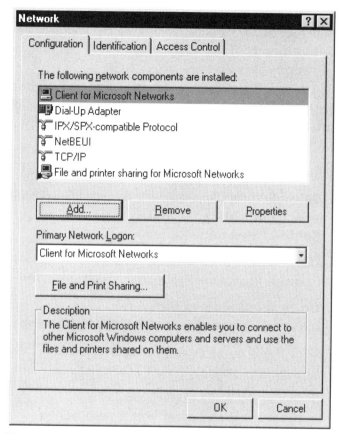

Figure 2-21: *The Configuration tab with new TCP/IP component added.*

Now we just need to make sure that the two network components we care about, the Dial-Up Adapter and TCP/IP, are configured properly. This part is easy.

ADDING SLIP SUPPORT

As I mentioned before, some Internet access providers use PPP for dial-up access and some use SLIP.

The base Windows 95 product supports PPP, but it does not support SLIP (or CSLIP) connections right out of the box. Fortunately, if you have the CD-ROM version of Windows 95, you can add this capability very simply. Here's how:

1. Insert the original Windows 95 CD in your CD-ROM drive.

2. Select Settings from the Windows 95 Start menu, and then select Control Panel from the cascading submenu. The Control Panel folder appears.

3. Double-click the Add/Remove Programs icon. The Add/Remove Programs Properties sheet pops up.

4. Go to the Windows Setup tab, then click the Have Disk button. The Install From Disk dialog box pops up.

5. Click the Browse button, then in the Open dialog box navigate to the file ADMIN\APPTOOLS\DSCRIPT\RNAPLUS.INF on your CD-ROM drive. Click OK.

6. In the Have Disk dialog box, select SLIP and Scripting for Dial-Up Networking and then click Install. SLIP and CSLIP support are added to your system.

DIAL-UP ADAPTER PROPERTIES

Let's quickly check the Dial-Up Adapter properties. You probably won't have to change anything, but since you're somebody who likes getting under the hood, you should know where to find these settings in case you need to adjust them later. To access the Dial-Up Adapter settings:

1. In the Configuration tab, select Dial-Up Adapter and then click the Properties button. The Dial-Up Adapter Properties sheet appears, with the Driver Type tab selected. Don't change anything in this tab.

2. Select the Bindings tab. This is where you associate the Dial-Up Adapter with a particular set of networking protocols. In this case, it should be associated with TCP/IP. Make sure that TCP/IP is checked, as shown in Figure 2-22. If it is not, check it.

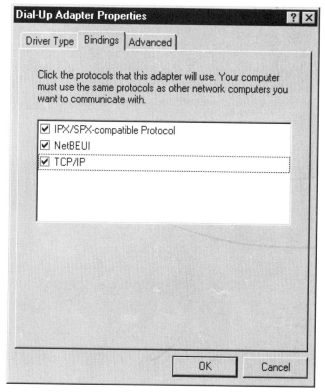

Figure 2-22: *The Bindings tab with TCP/IP selected.*

3. Now select the Advanced tab. The only setting that applies here is whether or not you want a troubleshooting log file recorded when the Dial-Up Adapter attempts to connect with your Internet access provider. The default is No, but if at some point you experience difficulties with your link, you might want to temporarily change this to Yes.

4. Click OK. You are returned to the Configuration tab.

TCP/IP PROPERTIES

Now let's take a look at the TCP/IP properties:

1. Back in the Configuration tab, select TCP/IP and click the Properties button. The TCP/IP Properties sheet appears, with the IP Address tab selected, as shown in Figure 2-23.

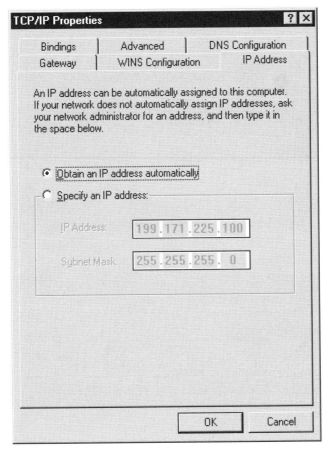

Figure 2-23: *The IP Address tab.*

2. If your Internet access provider assigns IP addresses dynamically, make sure the Obtain an IP Address Automatically radio button is selected. You can skip ahead to step 4.

FIXED & DYNAMIC IP ADDRESSES

Some Internet access providers assign you a fixed IP address, and others let you obtain a different one automatically each time you log on. The second method, known as *dynamic address assignment*, is becoming more common for home and small business accounts. Which is better? It doesn't really matter a lot. The only reason you might need a fixed IP address is if you plan to set up any sort of server software on your computer—in other words, if you want to let Internet users log in to your machine to get files or view Web documents. Obviously in this scenario, they'd need to know your Internet address, so your address couldn't be constantly changing! But for most uses of the Net, a dynamic address is just fine.

3. If your Internet access provider has assigned you a fixed IP address, click the Specify an IP Address radio button and enter your assigned IP address. In addition, enter the subnet mask for this address.

TIP

Chances are good that the subnet mask is 255.255.255.0.

4. Now select the DNS Configuration tab, as shown in Figure 2-24.

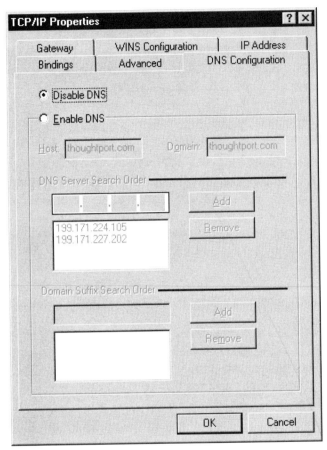

Figure 2-24: *The DNS Configuration tab.*

5. Unless you've received different instructions from your Internet access provider, enter the DNS address or addresses you've been given:

■ Click the Enable DNS radio button. Enter your user name in the Host box and the domain name of your company's DNS server in the Domain box.

■ In the DNS Server Search Order box, enter the IP address for your company's main DNS server and click Add. If your network administrator has given you an alternate DNS address, enter that now and click Add again.

■ In the Domain Suffix Search Order box, type in the domain suffix for your company's DNS and click Add. You can add several domain suffixes the same way you added entries in the DNS Server Search Order box.

Your completed DNS Configuration tab should look something like Figure 2-11 earlier in the chapter.

6. Unless you're a serious propeller-head, leave the rest of the tabs in these Properties alone! Click OK to return to the Configuration tab, then click OK again to exit the Network properties sheet.

Windows 95 may copy some files from your CD-ROM or disks and then tell you that you need to restart your computer for these changes to take effect. If so, press the Restart button, and I'll meet you in an hour or two when your system is back up. (Just kidding.)

ADDING A DIAL-UP CONNECTION

OK, now that you've got the Dial-Up Adapter and some network components installed, your computer is ready to behave itself on the Net, sending and receiving properly formatted information just like the zillions of other computers online right now. But first you have to tell Windows 95 how to actually connect to your Internet access provider. It's really pretty straightforward:

1. Double-click the My Computer icon on your Windows 95 desktop. The My Computer folder opens, revealing several icons.

2. Double-click the Dial-Up Networking icon. The Dial-Up Networking folder opens.

3. Now double-click the Make New Connection icon. The Make New Connection Wizard appears, as shown in Figure 2-25.

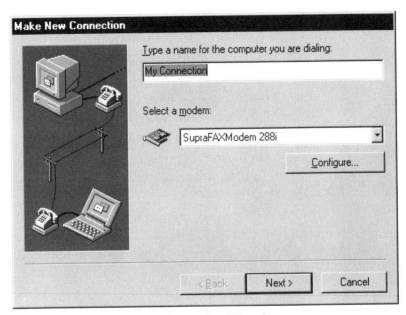

Figure 2-25: *The Make New Connection Wizard.*

4. Enter the name of your access provider in the box labeled Type a Name for the Computer You Are Dialing. Since I use ThoughtPort as my access provider, for instance, I'd type **ThoughtPort**.

5. Make sure your modem appears in the Select a Modem box. If not, drop down the list to select it.

6. Click the Configure button. The properties for your modem appear, with the General tab selected.

7. You can adjust your modem's properties in the General and Connection tabs. I won't go through all this stuff now, but if your modem was on the Windows 95 list when you installed it, the default settings should be fine. If it wasn't on the list, please consult your modem manual and set it for the best throughput for your access provider's baud rate. For now, move on to the Options tab, as shown in Figure 2-26.

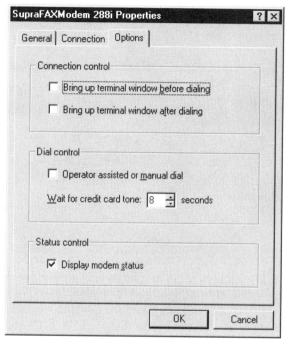

Figure 2-26: *The Options tab.*

8. Assuming that you'll be using your modem to dial the call to your access provider rather than dialing manually, leave everything in this tab unchecked, with two exceptions: you *should* check Bring Up Terminal Window After Dialing and Display Modem Status.

   ■ You need to bring up the terminal window after dialing in order to complete the process of logging on to your Internet access provider.

   ■ Displaying modem status will make it much easier to troubleshoot connection problems.

9. Click OK to return to the Make New Connection Wizard, then click Next. The phone number page appears, as shown in Figure 2-27.

10. Type in the correct information, then click Next.

11. Follow any further instructions that appear, and complete the configuration by clicking the Finish button.

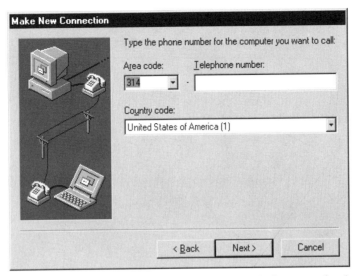

Figure 2-27: *The Make New Connection Wizard phone number information.*

CONFIGURING YOUR NEW DIAL-UP CONNECTION

OK, now for a few finishing touches. You have to configure your new connection to work properly with the Internet settings given to you by your access provider.

In the Dial-Up Networking folder, which is still open on your desktop, there is now an icon for your particular access provider. For instance, in my case the icon is labeled ThoughtPort, as shown in Figure 2-28.

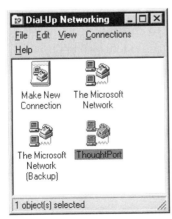

Figure 2-28: *The Dial-Up Networking folder with a new connection.*

To configure the properties for this new connection:

1. Click the icon with the secondary (usually the right) mouse button, then choose Properties from the pop-up menu. The connection's properties pop up, with the General tab selected as shown in Figure 2-29.

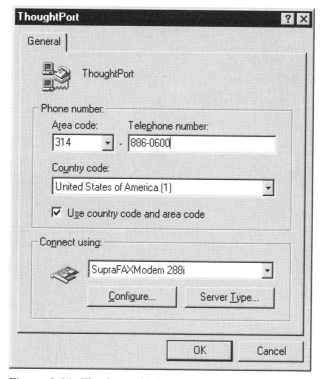

Figure 2-29: *The General tab.*

2. Click the Server Type button. The Server Types dialog box appears. You should complete it so that it looks something like Figure 2-30.

   ■ Select your server type from the Dial-Up Server drop-down list:

      ■ For PPP, choose PPP: Windows 95, Windows NT 3.5, Internet.

      ■ For SLIP, choose SLIP: UNIX Connection.

- For CSLIP (or SLIP that supports IP header compression) choose CSLIP: UNIX Connection with IP Header Compression.

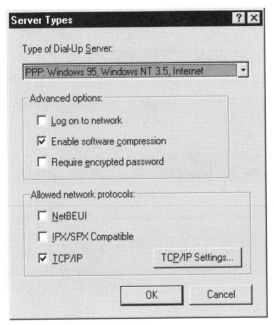

Figure 2-30: *The Server Types dialog box.*

- In the Advanced Options section, only Enable Software Compression should be checked. If you have problems with communications later, ask your access provider if this option should be turned off.

- In the Allowed Network Protocols section, only TCP/IP should be checked.

3. Click the TCP/IP Settings button. The TCP/IP Settings dialog box for this connection appears.

4. If your access provider dynamically assigns you an IP address each time you dial in, click the Server Assigned IP Address radio button. Otherwise, click the Specify an IP

Address radio button and type in the IP address assigned to you by your access provider.

5. Unless you've been given different instructions, click the Specify Name Server Addresses radio button and type in the DNS address or addresses assigned to you by your access provider.

   ■ You can ignore the two WINS fields.

6. Unless you've received specific instructions to the contrary from your access provider, you should check the bottom two check boxes, Use IP Header Compression and Use Default Gateway on Remote Network.

   ■ If your access provider has assigned you specific IP and DNS addresses, your completed page should look something like Figure 2-31.

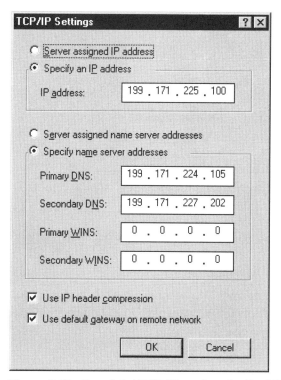

Figure 2-31: *Completed TCP/IP settings for fixed IP and DNS addresses.*

■ If your access provider assigns you an IP address dynamically each time you call in, your completed page should look something like Figure 2-32.

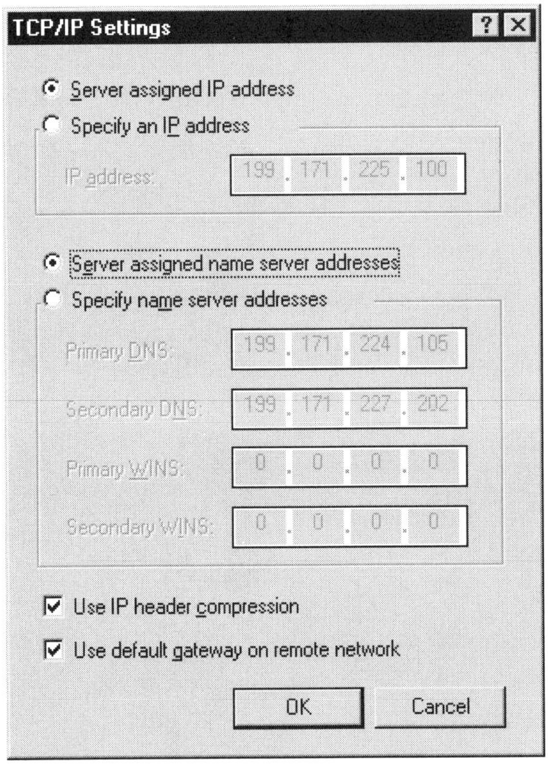

Figure 2-32: *Completed TCP/IP settings for dynamically assigned IP addresses.*

7. Click OK to return to the Server Types page, then OK again to return to the General tab, and finally OK again to save your new connection properties.

Congratulations! You've created and configured a new PPP or SLIP connection to the Internet. To get connected, just follow the instructions in the following section, "Getting On & Off the Net."

TIP

To get on and off the Net, you'll be accessing your new connection icon on a regular basis. You can simplify this process by creating a shortcut on your desktop. Simply press the Ctrl key and use your mouse to drag a copy of the icon from the Dial-Up Networking folder out to the desktop.

GETTING ON & OFF THE NET

This is the fun part. Now that you've gone through this admittedly tedious setup process, the Internet is only a few clicks away.

To log on to the Internet using your access provider:

1. Double-click the icon for your access provider in the Dial-Up Networking folder or on your desktop. The Connect To dialog box appears, as shown in Figure 2-33.

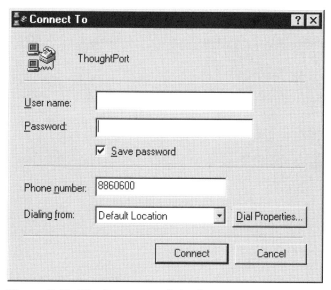

Figure 2-33: *The Connect To dialog box.*

- Don't bother filling in the User Name and Password fields, since you need to type these in when the terminal window pops up after you establish a modem connection with the host. In the case of most service providers, filling in your user ID and password in these fields won't do you any good.

- If you're calling from a different location than usual, you may want to reconfigure the Dial Properties by clicking the Dial Properties button.

2. Click Connect. The Connecting message box appears, and once your modem connection is established, the Post-Dial Terminal Screen pops up, as shown in Figure 2-34.

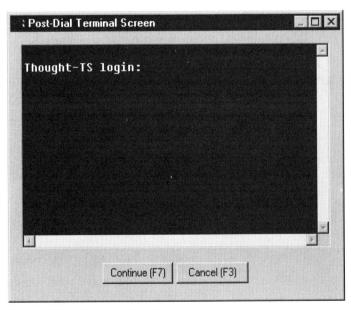

Figure 2-34: *The Post-Dial Terminal Screen.*

3. When prompted by the host system, type in your user ID, password, and any other information that is required. You may need detailed information from your access provider to get this right. If the host system assigns you an IP address at this point or presents you with other important information, be sure to jot it down! When you've completed the process, click the Continue button or press F7.

LOGGING ON—THE HARD WAY & THE EASY WAY
Each time you call your Internet access provider, you need to enter a user ID and password before you're actually connected to the Net. There may be other prompts as well. In order to complete this login process, Windows 95 can be configured to bring up a terminal window that lets you interact with the host computer. If you do not do this, you probably won't be able to establish your link.

Wouldn't it be nice if the software took care of this for you, sending your user ID and password to the host computer as well as responding to other prompts at the appropriate times? Well, Windows 95 *can* do this—but not right out of the box. You have to add the *scripting tool* that's only on the CD version of Windows 95 (it installs along with the SLIP software). This is the way it works: you write a short text file (the script) telling the scripting facility what to do. Your script includes commands that tell the software what prompts to wait for, how to respond to the prompts, how long to pause at certain points, and so forth. When you call your access provider, the script starts running, and *presto!*—you're online without ever typing a thing.

Unfortunately it's beyond the scope of this book to show you how to use the Windows 95 scripting facility, but if you want more information—OK, here comes a blatant authorial plug—take a look at my book *Internet Guide for Windows 95*, which covers this topic in detail.

■ If you are connecting to a system that dynamically assigns you a different IP address every time you log in, another dialog box may pop up asking you to verify or enter your IP address. Enter the IP address that you just jotted down and click OK to continue with the connection process.

After a few seconds, the Connected message box appears, as shown in Figure 2-35. You're on the Net, and you can now use Netscape Navigator 2.0 or just about *any* Windows Internet client programs for e-mail, Web-browsing, Telnet, or FTP.

Figure 2-35: *The Connected message box.*

As you might guess, breaking your Internet connection is even easier than establishing it. Look at the Connected message box in Figure 2-35. Let's see if you can figure out how to disconnect. Yep, you got it!

TIP

If you've installed Microsoft's Internet Explorer or the Internet Jumpstart Kit on Microsoft Plus!, then by default, Dial-Up Networking runs automatically whenever you attempt to use Netscape Navigator 2.0 and are not already connected to the Net. This feature is called AutoDial, and it means you don't ever really need to double-click the dial-up icon for your access provider in order to connect. In addition, your link to the Internet is broken automatically after 20 minutes of idle time. If you leave your machine in the middle of a long FTP file transfer, for instance, the transfer will be completed and then you will automatically be disconnected from the Net after 20 minutes.

If you don't like AutoDial or want to change some of its settings, double-click the Internet icon in Control Panel and make your changes in the AutoDial tab.

And now that you're able to establish a connection with the Internet, let's install Netscape Navigator 2.0 so that you have something to do out there.

INSTALLING NETSCAPE NAVIGATOR 2.0

This section is for those of you who have the version of the book with the CD-ROM. If you have already installed Netscape Navigator 2.0, you can skip this section. Or if you want to install Netscape Navigator 2.0 Personal Edition, or a copy of the software you have downloaded from the Internet, make sure to carefully follow the instructions included with the program. Remember, Readme files are our friends.

After all that Windows 95 configuration, this is going to be a breeze. Let's get right down to business:

1. Insert the CD at the back of this book into your CD-ROM drive.

2. Select Run from the Windows 95 Start menu or the Windows 3.1x File menu. In the Run dialog box that appears, type **D:\VIEWER**, where **D:** is the drive name of your CD-ROM. For instance, if your CD-ROM drive is E, type **E:\VIEWER**.

   ■ If you are using Windows 95 and have Auto Start enabled, the main window may appear automatically when you put the CD in; in that case you do not need to follow step 2 above.

3. Click CD Contents in the window. A new window appears, showing the actual contents of the CD.

In case the CD has changed slightly since this book went to print, you should follow any instructions that appear for installing Netscape Navigator 2.0. You can also click Help for further information. The next few steps, however, describe the general process:

1. If you are using Windows 95 or Windows NT, use your mouse to select the folder that contains the Windows 95 version of the program. If you are using Windows 3.1, make sure to select the folder that contains the Windows 3.1 version.

If you are using Windows 95 or Windows NT but want to continue accessing the Internet with a 16-bit TCP/IP stack such as Trumpet or the access software that's part of Netscape Navigator 1.2 Personal Edition, you must *install the Windows 3.1 version of Netscape Navigator 2.0. The Windows 95 version will only work with a 32-bit TCP/IP stack.*

2. Once you have selected the proper folder, be sure to read any README files it contains. Again, follow instructions for installing the program. Move your mouse cursor over the correct setup or installation file in either the Windows 95 or Windows 3.1 folder, depending on your system. A separate window displays information about the file.

3. Once you have chosen the proper installation file, simply click the Install button to begin the process. After a few moments an Install Wizard appears.

4. Read the Welcome message and then click Next. The Choose Destination Location dialog box appears, as shown in Figure 2-36.

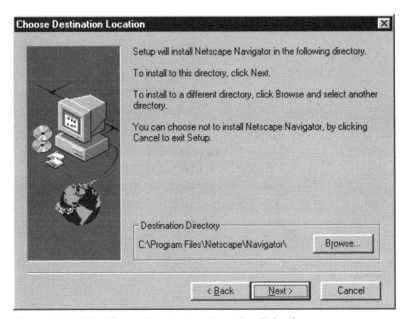

Figure 2-36: *The Choose Destination Location dialog box.*

5. If you want to change the drive or directory where Netscape Navigator 2.0 is stored, click the Browse button and choose a new destination directory. In most cases, you should leave this dialog box as it is and simply click Next.

6. Once you click Next, a new setup window appears, as shown in Figure 2-37.

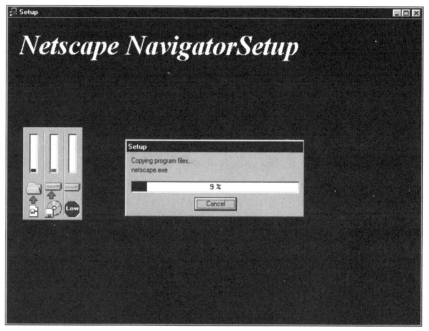

Figure 2-37: *The Netscape Navigator Setup window.*

This window could use a little explaining. First of all, the Setup progress bar right in the middle indicates the install program's progress as it copies files to the destination directory. On the left side of the window, another control gives you more detailed information about when the program is extracting files, when it is copying them from the CD-ROM, and how much space you have on your drive. Once the program files have been installed, a dialog box pops up, asking if you want to connect to the Netscape Setup site to continue, as shown in Figure 2-38. But before you answer this question, read on!

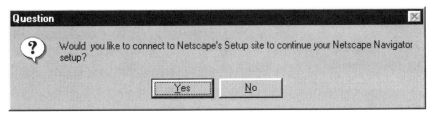

Figure 2-38: *The dialog box asking if you want to connect to the Netscape Setup site.*

To register your copy of Navigator click Yes. After filling out a short questionnaire, you'll receive your registration number.

ANSWERING THE QUESTION

OK, why am I making such a big deal about one simple click of the mouse? It seems like a fairly easy question to answer, doesn't it?

If you're the adventurous sort who likes to explore new ways of doing things, you should definitely click Yes. Clicking Yes takes you out onto the Net right away to complete your configuration using instructions provided at Netscape's own site. But in order for this method to work, a few things have to be in order:

- You must currently be connected to the Internet via a direct connection or a SLIP or PPP connection to your access provider.

- Or, your Internet access software must be configured so that it dials your access provider automatically when you launch an Internet program. (Remember the discussion of AutoDial back in the section on Windows 95 setup?)

If you are not currently connected to the Internet and you do not have an automatic dialing feature installed, then you must click No in this dialog box.

Let's assume for a moment that you are already connected to the Internet and you click Yes. What happens next is that Netscape Navigator 2.0 is launched, and within a few seconds the main window appears, as shown in Figure 2-39.

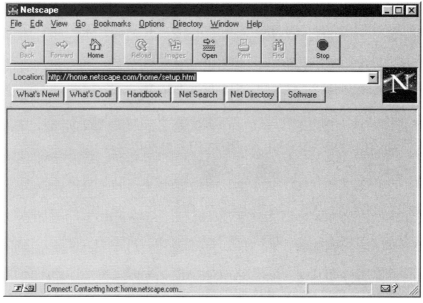

Figure 2-39: *The main Netscape Navigator 2.0 window, about to access the Netscape Setup site.*

At this point, you're on your own: all you have to do is follow the instructions that appear. If you can't figure out how to move around at all in the program, you might skim the first few pages of Chapter 3, "A Quick Look Around." And if you get completely disoriented, don't worry: just click the Home button and join the rest of the class down below in the section called "Configuring Netscape Navigator 2.0."

And what if you decide to answer No to the question? Will you be missing anything? Not to worry: I'll be covering all the same stuff the Netscape people tell you online anyway! If you click No, the installation program exits, and the next thing you see on your desktop is the new Navigator folder or program group, containing Netscape Navigator 2.0 itself and a Readme file, as shown below in Figure 2-40.

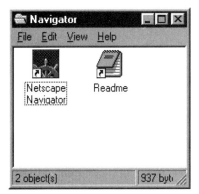

Figure 2-40: *The Navigator folder.*

You can create a convenient shortcut to Netscape Navigator 2.0 by dragging its icon from the Netscape folder right out to the Windows 95 desktop.

Since only intelligent people buy my books, I'm not going to remind you how important it is to read the Readme file right away. I won't even bother telling you that Readme files often contain crucial, last-minute information, information that can mean the difference between pleasant, trouble-free navigating and late-night wrestling matches with the software.

OK, on to configuring Netscape Navigator 2.0. Even if you worked through Netscape's own online setup instructions, you should still read the next section to check your configuration and gain a better understanding of some of the options.

CONFIGURING NETSCAPE NAVIGATOR 2.0

Once it's installed, Netscape Navigator 2.0 needs very little configuration. Most of the default options will work just fine for you, and there are only a few dialog boxes where you have to enter specific information in order to activate a particular feature. For instance, you have to enter your e-mail address in order for e-mail to work.

Most of the configuration options are covered in detail in the appropriate chapters of this book, but for now let's take a quick look around in case you want to start customizing the program on your own. To look at the configuration options:

1. Make sure you are connected to the Internet, either directly or through a SLIP or PPP connection with your access provider. If you are using SLIP or PPP and are not currently connected, double-click the Dial-Up Connection icon for your access provider.

   ■ If you have AutoDial turned on, you can skip this step. Windows 95 will attempt to connect to your access provider after you launch the program.

   ■ If you are using Windows 3.1 rather than Windows 95, or if you are using Windows 95's built-in networking, follow the instructions that came with your TCP/IP software for accessing the Internet.

2. Double-click the Netscape Navigator 2.0 icon to launch the program. The main window appears, and the Netscape home page starts loading, as shown in Figure 2-41.

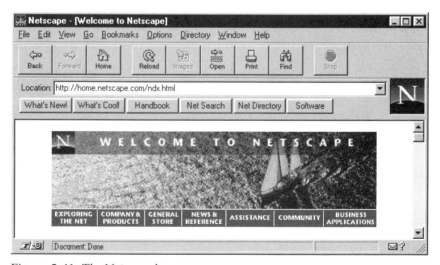

Figure 2-41: *The Netscape home page.*

That colorful Netscape page probably makes you eager to start exploring right away, but hold on—that's coming up in Chapter 3, "A Quick Look Around."

3. Click the Options menu. The menu drops down, as shown in Figure 2-42.

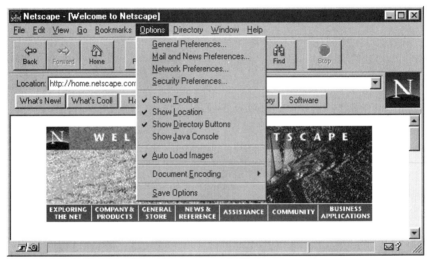

Figure 2-42: *The Options menu.*

ADJUSTING NAVIGATOR'S LOOK & FEEL
In the second section of the Options menu are several "checkmark" items, or toggles. When these items are checked, they are active; when unchecked, they are inactive. Most of them have to do with user interface objects that are displayed in the main Netscape Navigator 2.0 window. Later on, when you get more familiar with the program, you may not need all of the "window dressing." You can play around with these items to see what works best for the way you use the program. But for now leave them alone, or set them back to the default settings after trying them out. That way your screen will look pretty much like the illustrations in this book.

In the top section of the Options menu there are four items representing different areas of Netscape Navigator 2.0 that can be customized: General Preferences, Mail and News Preferences, Network Preferences, and Security Preferences. The Mail and News settings are covered in Chapters 4 and 5, respectively; the Network settings are covered in Chapter 9; and the Security settings are covered in Chapter 10. We won't bother looking at those options right now, but let's glance at the General Preferences options so you get a sense of what kind of customization is possible in Netscape Navigator 2.0.

GENERAL PREFERENCES

To access the General Preferences, select General Preferences from the Options menu, shown earlier in Figure 2-42. The Preferences dialog box appears, with the Appearance tab selected as shown in Figure 2-43. If that tab isn't selected, click it now.

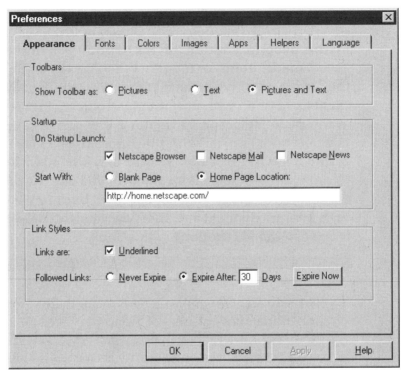

Figure 2-43: *The Appearance tab.*

Now we'll go very quickly through each of the tabs, pointing out where you can get more information on each one.

APPEARANCE

In the Appearance tab you can make several choices that determine how Netscape Navigator 2.0 will look on your screen:

■ You can choose whether the toolbar buttons will be displayed as Pictures, Text, or Pictures and Text. The default is Pictures and Text, but you can change this to one of the other options if you find the text annoying, or the pictures too busy.

■ You can choose which Web document, if any, Netscape Navigator 2.0 displays when you launch the program. The default is the Netscape home page, located at the Netscape site. In Chapter 3, "A Quick Look Around," we'll talk about why you might want to change this.

■ As you learned in Chapter 1, "The Net & the Web," Web documents contain links to other documents. You have to be able to recognize these links, and Netscape Navigator 2.0 lets you choose whether or not they should be underlined so that you recognize them more easily.

■ Once you've clicked on a link to access a new document, or a new section of the current document, the link changes color to indicate that you've used it. The Appearance tab lets you choose how long the link will stay this new color. More about this in Chapter 3.

FONTS

The Fonts tab lets you associate incoming data with particular display fonts. In the United States, just about all the Web information you receive will be in the ISO-Latin-1 character set, and this character set will be displayed using the default Times New Roman and Courier New fonts. Chapter 9, "Advanced Netscape Navigator 2.0," includes more information on changing these settings.

COLORS

The Colors tab lets you change the default colors for text and links that are displayed in Netscape Navigator 2.0. In addition, it lets you specify a new background color, or even a .GIF file for the display background. You can also decide here whether or not you want Netscape Navigator 2.0 always to use these colors rather than responding to the special color requests in Web documents.

IMAGES

The Images tab, shown in Figure 2-44, lets you specify how images are displayed. In most cases you should leave these settings alone, but on fast network connections you might want to click the While Loading radio button to display images a little quicker. More about these settings in Chapter 8, "Sound & Graphics in Netscape Navigator 2.0."

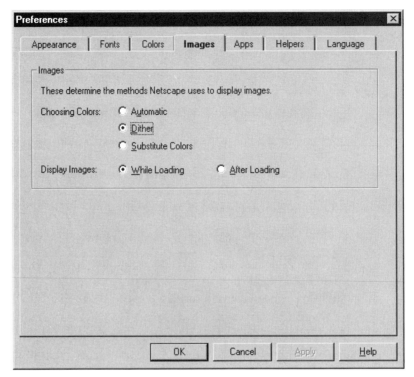

Figure 2-44: *The Images tab.*

APPS

To access Telnet resources, Netscape Navigator 2.0 can launch a separate application anywhere on your hard drive. This allows you the maximum flexibility in connecting to sites via Telnet or TN3270 (please see Chapter 7 if you don't know what I'm talking about). The Apps tab lets you choose what applications to use. In addition, it lets you specify an external text viewer or editor to look at the source HTML code of Web documents you view, and you can even choose the work directory Netscape Navigator 2.0 uses to store temporary files.

HELPERS

Helper applications are separate programs on your system that handle particular tasks for Netscape Navigator 2.0. For instance, a helper application might play a sound that's included in a Web document, or display a video clip. When Netscape Navigator 2.0 encounters particular kinds of files that are part of Web documents, it launches the appropriate helper applications. You will read lots more about helper applications and this tab in chapters 7, 8, and 9.

LANGUAGE

The Language tab is self-explanatory: this is where you choose the language used by Netscape Navigator 2.0. Some of us are eagerly awaiting a Klingon radio button in this tab.

When you're done looking through the General Preferences tabs, simply click the Cancel button to return to the main Netscape Navigator 2.0 window. Now you can either exit the program or get busy exploring the Net. I know which I'd do!

MOVING ON

By now you know how to get on and off the Internet, and you have Netscape Navigator 2.0 installed on your computer. Netscape Navigator 2.0 is so easy to use that I'd be surprised if you have any trouble at all cruising around and discovering exciting new resources on the Net.

In the next chapter, you'll learn all the basics of using Netscape Navigator 2.0 effectively, and subsequent chapters will show you how to take advantage of some of the program's most powerful features. Before you know it, you'll be a seasoned Net explorer, cruising from newsgroups to file archives to hypermedia Web sites with a few easy clicks of the mouse.

chapter three

A Quick Look Around

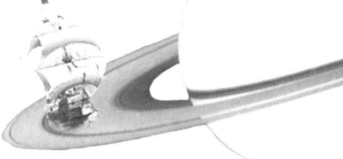

Now that you've installed Netscape Navigator 2.0 and configured it so that it works properly on your system, it's time to take a look around the Net. In this chapter, you'll learn some of the basics of the program and of Internet navigation. You'll learn:

- How to use the various controls in the program.

- How to move around a Web document, and how to get from one document to another.

- How to take advantage of exciting Web resources like Yahoo, where you can easily search for specific topics and keywords on pages all around the world.

- How to use navigation aids such as the history list, bookmarks, and desktop shortcuts.

Netscape Navigator 2.0 is so simple to use that you can really master the program by trial and error. I taught my daughter how to use it by saying, "When you see some words that are underlined and in another color, click on them. That takes you to other places." After an hour she was whizzing around the Web like a seasoned veteran. Of course, she is 13 years old and learns this kind of stuff a lot faster than those of us who were born before PCs and Nintendo. By the end of this chapter, you may not quite be an adolescent Web-geek, but you'll know how to use the main features of Netscape Navigator 2.0 and how to find what you're looking for quickly and easily. Now let's get going!

THE NETSCAPE NAVIGATOR 2.0 WINDOW

We'll start by taking a closer look at the Netscape Navigator 2.0 main window:

1. Make sure you are connected to the Internet, either directly or through a SLIP or PPP connection with your access provider. If you are using a SLIP or PPP connection and are not currently connected, double-click the Dial-Up Connection icon for your access provider.

   ■ If you are using Windows 3.1 rather than Windows 95, or if you are using Windows 95 and are not using its built-in networking functionality, follow the instructions that came with your TCP/IP software for accessing the Internet.

2. Double-click the Netscape Navigator 2.0 icon to launch the program. The main window appears, and the Netscape home page starts loading as shown in Figure 3-1.

   ■ By default, Netscape Navigator 2.0 uses the Netscape home page as your personal home page (your *home page* is the document that loads automatically when you launch the program). Depending on the speed of your Internet connection and how busy the Netscape site is, this might take a few moments. Later in the chapter, you'll learn how you can select a different Web document as your home page in the sidebar "Changing Your Home Page."

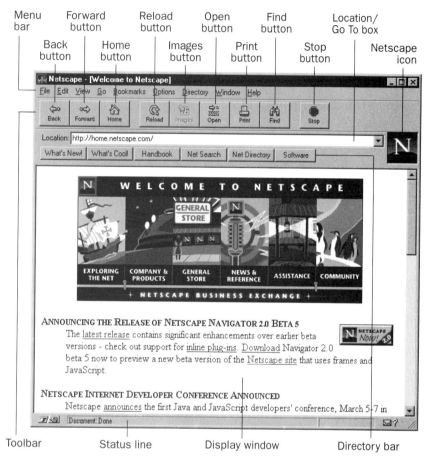

Figure 3-1: *The Netscape Navigator 2.0 window with the Netscape home page.*

Let's identify each of the major components of the Netscape
Navigator 2.0 window:

■ **The menu bar**. Like any other Windows program, Netscape
Navigator 2.0 arranges all of its user-accessible features in a
menu bar across the top of the window. Some menu families like File and Edit are familiar and practically self-
explanatory, while others are unique to an Internet application. We'll discuss the Bookmarks and Directory menu
families in detail later in this chapter, in the "Bookmarks"
section and in the "Directory Menu" sidebar.

■ **The toolbar**. Again, a toolbar is a familiar feature in most Windows programs. You click each individual button to control a different program function. The toolbar is such an easy way to use the program that you may never resort to the menus.

   You won't be tested on this since we're going to cover each button more thoroughly later on, but from left to right, the Netscape Navigator 2.0 buttons are:

   ■ **The Back and Forward buttons**. Pressing these cycles through the documents you have already viewed. You can revisit these documents in reverse order (relative to the order in which you originally viewed them) by pressing the Back button, and then you can retrace your path using the Forward button.

   ■ **The Home button**. Pressing this button returns you to your home page.

   ■ **The Reload button**. Pressing this button reloads the currently displayed document into the Netscape Navigator 2.0 window.

   ■ **The Images button**. This button is operational only if you've turned off the Auto Load Images option on the Options menu. With Auto Load Images off, Web pages are displayed without graphics. Instead, icons appear where the graphics normally would be loaded. When you press this button, Netscape Navigator 2.0 loads the images for the current page.

TIP

If you have a slow Internet connection, surf the Web in text-only mode (which is much, much faster than graphics mode) and load graphics only for those pages with images you'd like to see.

■ **The Open button**. Pressing this button pops up a dialog box that lets you type in a URL to open a new document, as shown in Figure 3-2. (If you don't know what I mean by a URL, please refer to Chapter 1, "The Net & the Web.")

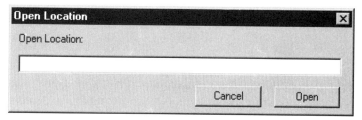

Figure 3-2: *The Open Location dialog box.*

■ **The Print button**. Pressing this button prints the currently displayed document.

■ **The Find button**. Pressing this button lets you search for a word or phrase in the currently displayed document.

■ **The Stop button**. When this button is red, Netscape Navigator 2.0 is loading a document into the window. Pressing this button stops the document from loading.

That's it for the menu bar and the toolbar. Now let's move on down to some of the other components of the main Netscape Navigator 2.0 window:

■ **The Location or Go To box**. This text box has a morphing (changing) label. When Netscape Navigator 2.0 is displaying a home page, the box is labeled Location. If you want to enter a URL manually, you can either type it or paste it directly into this field (the label changes to Go To while you're typing the new URL). Press Enter when you've finished entering the URL, and Netscape Navigator 2.0 jumps to that page.

TIP

*You'll notice an arrow button directly to the right of the Location box. You can click this button to display a drop-down list of the sites you've recently visited. Click any site in the list to return to it. (**Note:** This list only shows pages whose URLs you have entered in the Location or Open boxes.)*

■ **The directory bar**. The directory bar is made up of buttons, much like the toolbar. But the directory buttons display only commands from the Directory menu. For example, clicking the What's New button on the directory bar is the same as selecting the What's New entry from the Directory menu—just a little more convenient. Both actions result in Netscape Navigator 2.0 displaying Netscape's own What's New page, as shown in Figure 3-3.

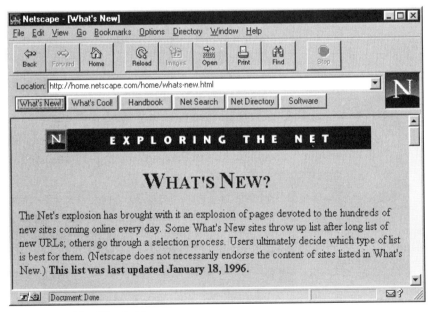

Figure 3-3: *The What's New page.*

We'll be looking at each of the Directory Bar buttons more closely later, under "The Directory Buttons," but for now let's continue our overview of the Netscape Navigator 2.0 main window.

- **The Netscape icon**. Although it's not really a control, the Netscape logo at the top right of the Netscape Navigator 2.0 window is very useful nonetheless. When this icon is animated with shooting stars, it indicates that the program is busy retrieving data from a Web site. When the icon is motionless, Navigator has received the entire document and is ready for your next action. ***Bonus:*** Clicking on the Netscape icon while you're connected to the Net will take you directly to Netscape's home page.

- **The display window**. The display window is the most important area within Netscape Navigator 2.0. This is where Netscape Navigator 2.0 displays the formatted text, links, hotspots, form fields, graphics, and other items that make up a Web page. Some of these fields and controls are "static," like a standard paragraph of text, while others are "active" and actually perform a function. Some controls may be immediately obvious, like a button, while others may be hidden. For example, the Netscape page in Figure 3-4 includes a Welcome to Netscape graphic with hotspots. When you click on these hotspots, you are magically teleported to other Web pages, just as if you'd clicked a text link. You'll learn more about these components of a Web page later in this chapter. For now, though, just remember that if your mouse cursor turns into a hand with a pointing finger, you can click there to do something or go somewhere!

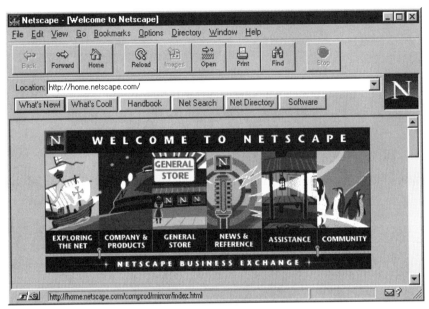

Figure 3-4: *A graphic menu with hotspots.*

TIP

Netscape Navigator 2.0 includes standard scroll bars along the right and bottom edges of the display window. If you resize the window (or if a Web page is longer than one screen length, which is usually the case), these controls let you scroll the display so that you can view the entire page.

- **The status line.** Navigator uses the last line of the window to display current status information. For example, if you're currently receiving a picture from a Web site, Netscape Navigator 2.0 fills in the status line with the name of the image file and a status bar that indicates the progress of the transfer. Or if you move your mouse pointer over a link, the status line shows its URL, as you can see in Figure 3-5.

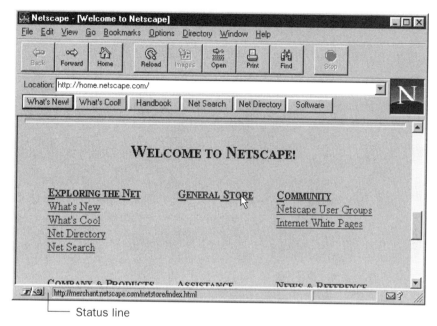

Status line

Figure 3-5: *The Netscape Navigator 2.0 status line showing the URL of a link.*

Note the small icon that looks like a broken key on the left side of the status line. This icon indicates whether or not your current session is using a special secure protocol for financial and business transactions. As you might guess, when the icon is "broken," the session is not secure. (Don't worry—you don't really need heavy-duty security for most of what you'll be doing on the Web.) You'll learn more about Netscape Navigator 2.0's security features in Chapter 10.

In addition, a small envelope icon at the far right of the status line links you to the Netscape Navigator 2.0 mail window. You simply click it to access your e-mail. If the icon has an exclamation point next to it, you have new mail. If it has a question mark next to it, Netscape Navigator 2.0 is configured so that it cannot automatically check your mail server for new messages. You'll learn more about e-mail in Chapter 4.

LOCAL AREA URLS

As I mentioned in Chapter 1, "The Net & the Web," you don't even need the Internet to use Netscape Navigator 2.0 effectively. If you're on a local area network (LAN), you can use the program to access documents within your own organization. For instance, employees could call up the latest sales data, or view a fancy multimedia demonstration of a new product or service.

To access a document that is stored locally rather than at a remote site, press Ctrl+O or select Open File from Netscape Navigator 2.0's File menu. A File Open dialog box pops up. Now you can simply choose the document you want. HTML documents appear with the Netscape logo, but you could also choose to view text or graphic files.

You can also access a locally stored document by clicking a link to it within another document. For instance, you may want to construct a home page that contains links to a variety of important files on your LAN. The URL for a locally stored file looks a little different from other URLs, and you should know how to construct one in case you ever need to enter one directly in the Location box. A local file URL starts with file:. After that there are *three* forward slashes rather than the usual two, the letter name of the local or network drive, a vertical bar (the pipe symbol...Shift+\), and the path to the file. Got all that? Here's an example, an HTML file called PRODUCT.HTM that's located in the Public directory on the Q drive of your LAN: file:///Ql/Public/PRODUCT.HTM.

Of course Netscape Navigator 2.0 supports all the same media on a LAN as it does on the Net. You can use the program to play sound files, run video clips, and even gather information from other employees using HTML forms (see "Forms on the Web" later in this chapter). And of course a document can contain a mix of links to Internet sites and to local files. This power and flexibility make Netscape Navigator 2.0 an excellent tool for disseminating enterprise-wide information.

LINKS & HOTSPOTS

Let's continue our discussion of Web navigation with the most common active control found within Web pages: the *link*. A link is a special text string embedded within a document. It tells Netscape Navigator 2.0 to jump to another document or to a different place in the current document. Linked documents may be physically stored at the same site or another site halfway across the world. As I explained in Chapter 1, "The Net & the Web," this is the essence of hypertext.

Links are considered "followed" once you click on them to display the new information. Netscape Navigator 2.0 changes the color of a followed link to indicate that you've used it before. This color coding can help you retrace your steps.

To use a link, simply move your mouse pointer over the link text and click. But how can you be sure you're on a link? It's really simple.

HOW CAN I TELL I'M ON A LINK?

Netscape Navigator 2.0 provides a number of visual cues to indicate the presence of a link:

- By default, links are underlined and appear in blue, while regular inactive text is not underlined and appears black. If you return to a page after using one of its links, the link now appears in purple to indicate that you've been there. You can always click the same link again; it does not become inactive once you've clicked it. The change in color is only a helpful reminder.

- As I mentioned earlier, if you rest your mouse cursor on a link, the status line changes to indicate the link's URL. No URL in the status line, no link!

- As I also mentioned earlier, your mouse cursor changes to a pointing hand when it rests on a link.

Figure 3-6 shows a section of Netscape's own online handbook that contains a number of links.

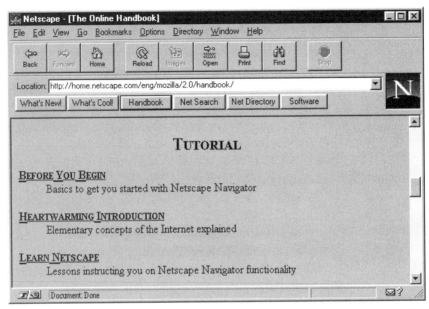

Figure 3-6: *Netscape's Online Handbook, showing typical links to more detailed information.*

TIP

Often the context of the text containing the link indicates what the link will do. For instance, "download PROGRAM.ZIP now" and "jump to the index" are self-explanatory.

CHANGING WHAT LINKS LOOK LIKE
You can change the properties of link text from the Options menu. Click the General item to display the Preferences dialog box. In the Colors tab, you can change the default colors for links you've used and those you haven't tried yet. In the Appearance tab you can specify whether links should be underlined or not. Here you can also set how many days it takes for a followed link to "expire" (expired links are returned to the default color, just as if you had never followed them).

USING HOTSPOTS

Hotspots are just like links, except they are embedded within graphical information rather than text. Like links, hotspots perform an action when you click them. You might click one to jump to another page, or to view an image or even play a piece of music. Sometimes hotspots are smaller "thumbnail" versions of full-size images that you can download, or they may be beautifully designed arrows pointing to the next in a series of linked documents. Many sites also use hotspots as "menu items" within larger images that serve as menu systems. In the Netscape home page, for instance, you can click on various areas within the same graphic to jump to different documents. Let's give this a try:

1. Make sure you are connected to the Internet, either directly or through a SLIP or PPP connection with your access provider. If you are using SLIP or PPP connection and are not currently connected, double-click the Dial-Up Connection icon for your access provider.

   ■ If you are using Windows 3.1 rather than Windows 95, or if you are not using Windows 95's built-in networking, follow the instructions that came with your TCP/IP software for accessing the Internet.

2. Double-click the Netscape Navigator 2.0 icon to launch the program. The main window appears, and the Netscape home page starts loading, as shown earlier in Figure 3-1.

3. In the large graphic near the top of the page, click the General Store section. The General Store appears, as shown in Figure 3-7.

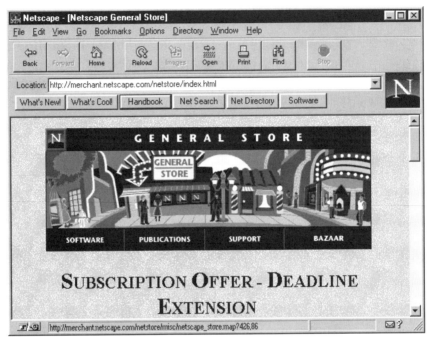

Figure 3-7: *The General Store.*

Congratulations! You just used a hotspot to get from the Netscape home page to the General Store. Traveling sure is simple in cyberspace.

In this example, it was easy to find the hotspots in the graphic because they included text. But there are other ways to indicate hotspots as well. Sometimes they are displayed with a colored border, or the author of a Web page might refer to a hotspot in a line of text such as "Click the right arrow to move to the next page."

TIP

If you click a link or hotspot with the right mouse button, a context menu appears that lets you manipulate that link or hotspot in a number of ways. For instance, you can (1) open another display window for the target, so that you have both the original document and the new one on your screen at the same time; (2) copy the link to an HTML file; or (3) save the link as a bookmark (see "Bookmarks" later in the chapter). You can even use the context menu to navigate back or forward from the current document instead of using the Back and Forward buttons.

USING THE NETSCAPE NAVIGATOR 2.0 TOOLBAR

As I mentioned earlier, the Netscape Navigator 2.0 toolbar is the program's control center. You can use these buttons like the forward and reverse gears of a car, moving back and forth through Web documents. You can also use them to print the contents of any page or to locate a specific word or phrase within the text of a page.

Of course, all these functions are also available from the menu bar, but most Internet surfers find that the graphical nature of the Web lends itself to mouse control, making the toolbar the easiest and most convenient method for harnessing the power of Netscape Navigator 2.0.

In this section, we'll discuss the buttons you'll use the most as we navigate through the Netscape's own Web site.

TRAP

Note that pages on the Netscape Web site may change from time to time, so the screens and links we use may not agree exactly with what you see on your screen. However, you should still be able to follow the steps in a general fashion.

THE FORWARD & BACK BUTTONS

You've already seen how easy it is to get to a new document by clicking on a link or hotspot. But what if you need to return to a previously viewed page? Perhaps you forgot to download a file, or you suddenly decide to back up and follow a different information trail. This is where the first two buttons on the toolbar come into play. Back and Forward allow you to retrace your steps to a previous page or, if you've already backtracked, to jump forward to the last page you accessed.

To see how this works, follow these steps:

1. Make sure you are connected to the Internet either directly or via your SLIP or PPP access provider. If Netscape Navigator 2.0 is not currently running, launch it by double-clicking its icon.

2. In the Netscape home page, click the hotspot for the General Store.

   ■ If you're already at the General Store because you're a good student who followed the last set of directions, just stay there!

3. Now click the Back button. We're back where we started, at the Netscape home page. Guess what the Forward button does? Go ahead and click it now. As you probably guessed, the General Store page pops up once more.

4. Now click a new link or hotspot. It doesn't really matter which one. Once the new document appears, click the Back button twice. Yes, as you probably expected the Back button can lead sequentially back through all the pages you have visited. And of course Forward works the same way, in reverse.

THE HOME BUTTON

You can click new links and dance around with the Forward and Back buttons as long as you want, but eventually you might get dizzy and long for home. To return to the Netscape home page:

1. Click the Home button.

That's it. (I love throwing in these one-step procedures.)

WHY DO I NEED A HOME PAGE, ANYWAY?

You may be asking, "Why do I need a home page, anyway?" There are several reasons:

■ A home page helps you stay oriented with a familiar starting point. Imagine what surfing would be like if you started without a home base—or, even worse, jumped to a random page every time you started the program!

■ Many seasoned Web surfers set their home pages to their favorite site, especially if the contents of the page change often. This way, you can check your favorite page each time you begin a Netscape Navigator 2.0 session. If you have your own personal Web page, for example, you might set it as your home page.

■ Some pages are especially designed to offer as much as possible for new Web surfers, making them ideal launching pads for Web exploration. For example, the Netscape home page offers links to the newest and most popular pages, Web search tools, and a wealth of exciting Internet resources—all from one screen.

As you can see, the Home button returns you directly to whatever home page you've selected with a single click of your mouse. And by the way, changing your home page is easy. To find out how, see the "Changing Your Home Page" sidebar.

CHANGING YOUR HOME PAGE

Why change your home page? First, a purely practical reason: if your current home page is particularly busy or it's operated on a slower connection, it may take 30 seconds or so to load the page! Delays like that can get quite tiring after a few sessions, so you'd probably want to select a faster site (or perhaps even use a page you've created on your local hard disk). If you're really interested in saving time, you can even set your home page as "blank," so there's no load time at all.

Additionally, your interests are likely to change. You can save valuable Internet time by constructing a customized home page and including in it the sites you access the most. (To learn how to do this, see Chapter 9, "Advanced Netscape Navigator 2.0.")

To change your home page, follow these steps:

1. Select General Preferences from the Options menu.

2. Select the Appearance tab.

3. Click the Home Page Location radio button and type in the URL of your new home page. Make sure you spell the address correctly! If you've saved or created a page on your local hard drive, you can enter the URL for the file instead of a remote site.

4. Click OK, then make sure to select Save Options from the Options menu.

THE PRINT BUTTON

OK, so you've found the Secret to Life's Eternal Mystery on a particular Web page, and you'd like to save it for future reference. You could highlight the text with your mouse and copy the text to the Windows Clipboard, but why not print out the whole thing? That way you can keep a hard copy of all of the contents of the page, including the images.

To print the contents of a page, click the Print button. Like most Windows applications, Navigator provides standard options that you can access from within the Print dialog box, and you can change the appearance of printed documents by selecting Page Setup from the File menu.

You can also display a preview image of the output before you print it by selecting the Print Preview option from the File menu. Figure 3-8 shows a print preview of the Netscape home page.

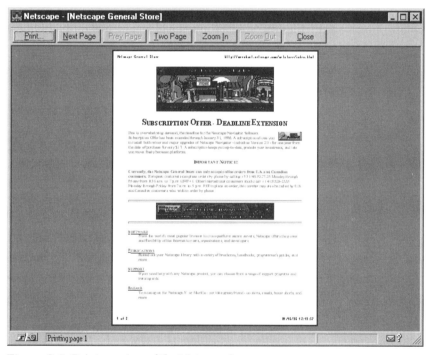

Figure 3-8: *Print preview of the Netscape home page.*

THE FIND BUTTON

From time to time you'll encounter huge documents that are crowded with text and links. Scrolling slowly through a mountain of text line by line is one method of locating that link you remember, but Netscape Navigator 2.0 makes it much easier with the Find command.

Let's look for a specific string of text in Netscape's own Internet Directory:

1. Make sure you are connected to the Internet either directly or via your SLIP or PPP access provider. If Netscape Navigator 2.0 is not currently running, launch it by double-clicking its icon.

2. Click the Net Directory button. Netscape's Internet Directory page appears, as shown in Figure 3-9.

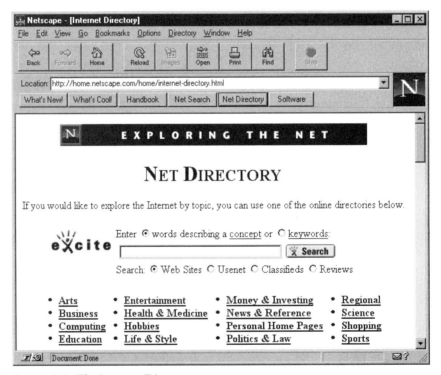

Figure 3-9: *The Internet Directory page.*

3. Click the Find button. Netscape Navigator 2.0 displays the Find dialog box, as shown in Figure 3-10.

Figure 3-10: *The Find dialog box.*

4. For the purposes of this tutorial, type the words **New York** in the Find What field and click the Find Next button. In a flash, Netscape Navigator 2.0 finds a mention of my old home town, highlights it, and displays the surrounding section of the document, as shown in Figure 3-11.

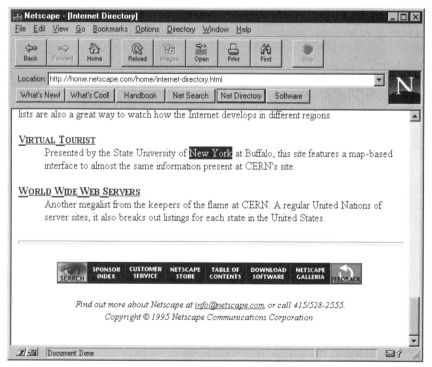

Figure 3-11: *The results of a successful Find command.*

- If you need a case-sensitive search, enable the Match Case option; Netscape Navigator 2.0 will display only those instances in which the capitalization matches your entry. You can also specify in which direction the program should search—click the Up radio button to search upward through the document or the Down radio button to move downward. The search begins at the current cursor position.

5. To search for more occurrences of the same string, click the Find Next button again. In this case, there are no more occurrences of New York, so Netscape Navigator 2.0 displays the message shown in Figure 3-12.

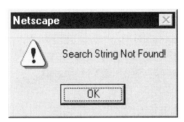

Figure 3-12: *The results of an unsuccessful Find command.*

THE STOP BUTTON

Our final stop on the Netscape Navigator 2.0 toolbar is the Stop button. If you need to abort the transfer of any data to or from Navigator, click this button. You might not need the Stop button often, but when you do it'll make the difference between continuing your session or waiting for what seems like a lifetime for the transfer attempt to finally time out.

Why do some pages seem to take forever to load? Possible reasons for a long wait can include:

- **Heavy usage on the Web site you're calling**. Try calling during low-traffic hours—late at night or early in the morning.

■ **Heavy usage on the system that provides your Internet connection**. Check with your access provider to see when the system is being used the least. Remember that the server where a particular page is located may be in another part of the world, so you may have to make allowances for time differences.

■ **Extra-large graphics or files you're receiving**. (Remember, you can always keep track of where you are in the transfer process by watching the progress bar that appears in the Navigator status line).

■ **A slow data pipeline**. In plain English, this means that some sites are connected to the Web by leased modem lines or older networks, and these slower connections can be bottlenecks.

TIP

If Navigator is attempting to receive a Web page or a file and the transfer seems "stuck," you can often retrieve the data successfully by aborting the current transfer with the Stop button and immediately trying the same link again.

Here's a good rule of thumb: the best time to surf the Net is when you really should be sleeping.

So far we've looked at Web pages that simply present information. But Netscape Navigator 2.0 supports more interactive uses of the Internet as well. In the next section, we'll look at a different kind of Web page, the fill-out form.

MULTIPLE CONNECTIONS

You can display several Web documents at once with Netscape Navigator 2.0. Select New Web Browser from the File menu, or simply press Ctrl+N. Another window appears, and you can use it, like the first window, to navigate to any site.

And why would you want to connect to more than one site at a time?

- **If you're researching a specific topic and you've found more than one page with pertinent information or links, it's a good idea to load each page in a separate window if you need to compare them.**

- **Certain sites may be particularly slow, and opening an additional window allows you to continue exploring while you wait for the display of the first page to finish.**

- **Extra-large files like .MOV or .AVI animations may take several minutes to download. With a second window, you can continue surfing while you wait.**

It's important to remember that each window you load will use the original connection you've made to the Internet; opening too many windows will slow down the overall speed of *all* of them!

FORMS ON THE WEB

"Please fill in your name, address, and phone number." You've been doing it your whole life on paper, and now you can do it electronically too.

Forms are scattered all over the Web. Some let you fill in a search word and then find it for you in a collection of documents; some let you buy a CD or new software product; some even engage you in a real-time conversation. Whatever their purpose,

World Wide Web forms share a common look and feel when displayed in Netscape Navigator 2.0. Here's an example:

1. Make sure you are connected to the Internet either directly or via your SLIP or PPP access provider. If Netscape Navigator 2.0 is not currently running, launch it by double-clicking its icon.

2. Click the Open button. The Open Location dialog box appears.

   ■ Yes, you could simply type the new URL in the Netsite box. It's a good idea, though, to try the various ways to accomplish a particular task in Netscape Navigator 2.0 so you can see which feels easiest to you.

3. In the Open Location field, type **http://hoohoo.ncsa.uiuc.edu/archie.html** and click Open. The Archie request form appears, as shown in Figure 3-13.

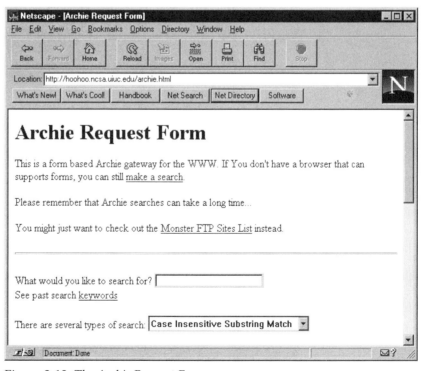

Figure 3-13: *The Archie Request Form.*

Archie is an Internet service that's been around much longer than the Web. It is a tool for finding files at FTP sites (see Chapter 6). But until the Web came along and provided convenient fill-out forms like this one, Archie was much more difficult to use.

Take a few minutes to scroll through this page and examine its various forms elements. There are boxes you can type text into, drop-down lists, and radio buttons. There is also a Submit button that lets you send your request once you have completed filling in the information. If you want, type something in the What Would You Like to Search for? box and then click the Submit button. Let's say you typed the word **Netscape** and left all the other fields alone. In a few seconds you'd be presented with something like Figure 3-14.

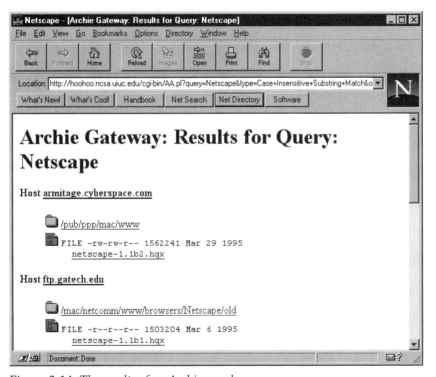

Figure 3-14: *The results of an Archie search.*

As the commercial uses of the Internet become more prominent, we'll see more and more forms for actual transactions. Already you can buy all kinds of products directly over the Net, and the Web's forms interface makes it easy. By the way, Netscape has been a leader in Internet security, and Netscape Navigator 2.0 indicates when a form is not secure by displaying the following text:

```
Any information you submit is insecure and could be
observed by a third party while in transit. If you are
submitting passwords, credit card numbers, or other
information you would like to keep private, it would be
safer for you to cancel the submission.
```

This may sound a bit frightening, but security is typically not a problem with the vast majority of forms you'll fill out online. As a rule, simply take the same precautions as you would if someone were asking similar questions over the telephone. If you feel uncomfortable providing a particular piece of private information, you'll probably want to follow Navigator's recommendation and cancel the form without submitting it. Chapter 10, "Commerce & Security on the Net," discusses security issues in more detail.

As more and more companies start collecting data and even selling products via the Internet, online forms may become the bread-and-butter interface on the Web. But fortunately the Web is not all bread and butter, it's champagne and Jell-O too. Let's take a look at something a bit more fun than forms: *frames*.

UNDERSTANDING FRAMES

One of the coolest new features of Netscape Navigator 2.0 is its support for frames. Frames are distinct areas within the Netscape Navigator 2.0 display area. Special HTML commands in a Web document tell the program to partition the display. Each frame is a stand-alone environment that recognizes mouse clicks, has its own scroll bars, and can include all the features of any Web page. Each frame has its own distinct URL. In short, each frame is actually a window displaying its own Web page. Netscape Navigator 2.0 can actually "freeze" one of the frames so that it stays onscreen all the time while you interact with the links and hotspots in another frame. You might see logos, advertisements, or tables of contents handled in this fashion.

Let's take a look at an example of frames, as shown in Figure 3-15. Figure 3-15 is the Netscape Web site at http://home.netscape.com/comprod/products/navigator/version_2.0/index.html.

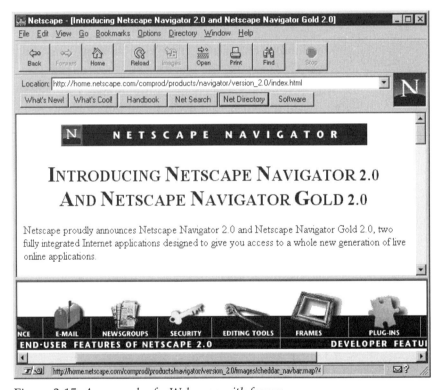

Figure 3-15: *An example of a Web page with frames.*

Because each frame is its own entity, make sure you select the appropriate frame (by clicking) when you decide to print something. Only the contents of the selected frame, and not the entire display window, print. In addition, you can reload the contents of individual frames by selecting Reload Frame from the View menu, and you can even e-mail the contents of a frame by selecting Mail Frame from the File menu.

The way developers use frames makes Web sites very flexible and dynamic for the user. At the Netscape Communications Web site, notice how each frame is used differently. The top frame displays product descriptions and features. The bottom frame is used to navigate among different features, such as Performance, E-Mail, Editing Tools, and so on. Also, notice how the scroll bars let you scroll up and down in the top pane and horizontally in the bottom frame.

Other sites use frames to display different types of elements. One frame, for instance, may contain text, while another contains graphics. As you click and read through the text, the graphics can change or rotate based on the text displayed. Frames are also used with multimedia or 3D objects. One pane may contain instructions or a story about how to navigate a VRML world with WebFX, while the other contains the actual VRML objects. (What, you don't know what VRML and WebFX are? Please turn to Chapter 9, "Advanced Netscape Navigator 2.0.")

TIP

The Back and Forward buttons won't work to go back to the previous contents of an individual frame. Instead, click the right mouse button and select either Back in Frame or Forward in Frame from the context menu that pops up.

By now you're well on your way to gathering a wide variety of information from the Web. In the next few sections, we'll look at some ways of organizing all this information.

THE HISTORY LIST & BOOKMARKS

As you travel around the World Wide Web, you'll often find yourself jumping back to the same pages over and over again. From time to time you may also need a specific URL that you visited two or three sessions ago. And you're certain to find a number of Web pages that become your favorites, so you'll want to visit them often.

Netscape Navigator 2.0 provides several methods for keeping track of where you are on the Web—and where you've been. In this section, we'll discuss the two important features that help you maintain your own Web road map: the history list, which keeps track of where you've been in the current session, and bookmarks, which are permanent pointers to your favorite Web pages.

USING THE HISTORY LIST

The history list is actually a collection of entries automatically maintained by Netscape Navigator 2.0. Each entry represents a single site you have visited in the current session. Each time you load a new Web page, the URL for that site is saved in your history list. This makes the history list an excellent tool for jumping among pages while you check references.

There are three ways to access your history list. First, the simplest:

1. After you have viewed several documents using Netscape Navigator 2.0, click the down arrow just to the right of the Location box. The history list appears right there, as shown in Figure 3-16. Note that the list is scrollable, with only the most recent five pages showing.

2. Click any entry in the list to return to that document.

TRAP

The Location box history list includes only URLs you've entered in the box itself or using the Open button; it does not include any sites you've visited by clicking on a link. The other methods of accessing your online history, described later in this chapter, show all the sites you've visited.

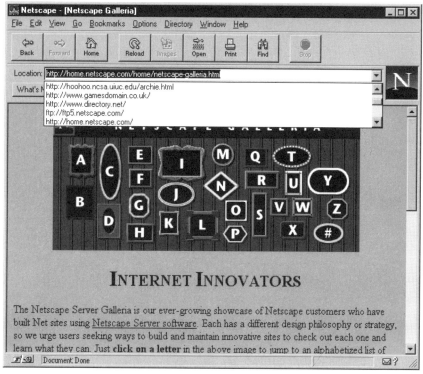

Figure 3-16: *The drop-down history list.*

You can also return to a previously viewed page right from Netscape Navigator 2.0's Go menu. Simply click Go. You will see the history list at the bottom of the menu, as shown in Figure 3-17. Once again, you can simply select one of the entries to jump to it immediately.

Lastly, you can display the history list within a dialog box, which allows for a neater and more complete presentation of each entry:

1. Select History from the Window menu, or simply press Ctrl+H. Netscape Navigator 2.0 displays the History dialog box, as shown in Figure 3-18.

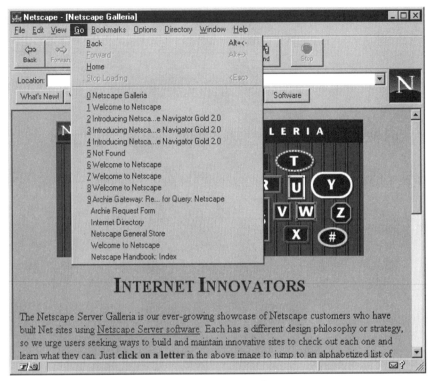

Figure 3-17: *The Go menu, showing the history list.*

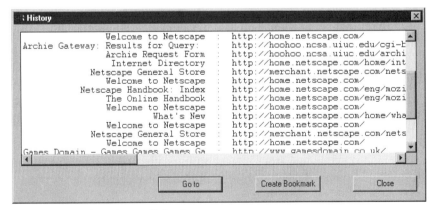

Figure 3-18: *The History dialog box.*

- Notice that each entry appears as a single line, complete with both the page title and its URL address.

2. To jump to a particular page, simply double-click directly on the entry or select it and click the Go To button.

3. To add a history entry to your bookmarks, click the Create Bookmark button. (We'll cover bookmarks in the next section.)

TRAP

Remember, your history list is erased when you finish your session. The Location box list is maintained, but again, it contains only URLs you've entered yourself. That's why bookmarks are important.

BOOKMARKS

Now that you're familiar with the history list, you may be saying to yourself, "Well, that's great for a single session, but what about documents that I want to return to at some later date?" Luckily you don't have to resort to paper and pencil or try to maintain a text file of your favorite sites—Netscape Navigator 2.0 provides you with bookmarks, which are saved permanently in your own "Web page directory." You can also create a simple Web page of your own that includes your favorite sites; we'll discuss this in Chapter 9, "Advanced Netscape Navigator 2.0."

ADDING & USING BOOKMARKS

The two actions you'll perform most often with bookmarks are (1) adding them and (2) using them to jump to a stored URL. To add a bookmark for the document that's currently displayed in Netscape Navigator 2.0:

- Select Add Bookmark from the Bookmarks menu, or simply press Ctrl+D.

Using bookmarks to jump to a document is just as easy:

■ Click the Bookmarks menu, then select one of the bookmarks that appears at the bottom (see Figure 3-19). You are
immediately teleported to the selected URL.

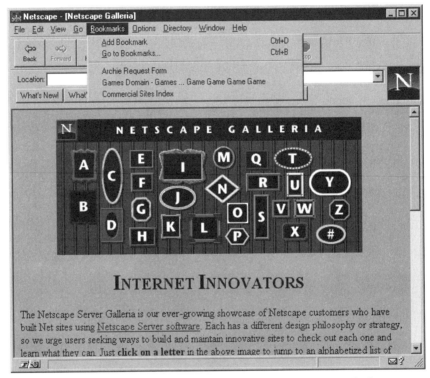

Figure 3-19: *The Bookmarks menu, showing list of bookmarks at the bottom.*

As with the history list, Netscape Navigator 2.0 provides a
fuller, alternative interface to your bookmarks: the Bookmarks
window.

THE BOOKMARKS WINDOW

Now that you know how to use bookmarks at the simplest level,
let's advance a bit. Just as history entries can be displayed in the
History dialog box, you can also display a bookmark list that
offers a lot more functionality than the Bookmarks menu. To open
the Bookmarks window, select Go to Bookmarks from the Book-

marks menu, or simply press Ctrl+B. The Bookmarks window appears, as shown in Figure 3-20.

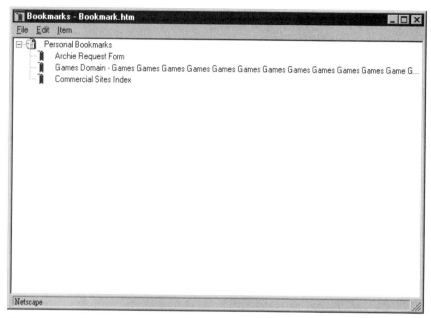

Figure 3-20: *The Bookmarks window.*

■ Depending on what sites you've already added to your bookmarks list, your window may look different from mine.

■ The top-level bookmark folder may include your own name instead of simply reading "Main Bookmarks" or "Personal Bookmarks."

As you can see, Netscape Navigator 2.0 displays the contents of the current bookmark file in a tree format, with entries appearing under the folder icon. You'll notice that the default bookmark file, Main Bookmarks, contains a single entry, Welcome to Netscape. The Bookmarks window has its own menu bar, which we'll refer to as we explain the other Bookmark functions. But to jump to the document represented by a bookmark entry you don't even need the menu. Simply double-click the entry itself.

> **TIP**
>
> *Netscape Navigator 2.0 lets you use more than one bookmark file and also makes it easy to switch between files. From the File menu in the Bookmarks window, you can choose Open to select a new file, or Save As to save the current file under a new name.*

ADDING FEATURES TO NETSCAPE NAVIGATOR 2.0

Netscape offers a collection of add-on modules called the Netscape Power Pack that enhances the functionality of several existing Navigator features, as well as adding completely new capabilities to Navigator.

SmartMarks, one of the modules included in the Power Pack, allows you to keep track of changes in your favorite Web pages. It also includes improved Web search features and bookmark organization tools. Other modules provide support for QuickTime digital movies and RealAudio audio files, Internet chat, and Adobe Acrobat PDF documents.

ORGANIZING YOUR BOOKMARKS

If you're familiar with the Windows drag-and-drop function and the tree structure common in Windows 95 applications like Explorer, you'll have no problem organizing your bookmarks any way you like.

For example, let's say you'd like to categorize your bookmarks by subject matter, with each subject represented by its own folder. For the purposes of this exercise, we'll add a new folder called Computers under the existing Main Bookmarks folder.

First, to create a new bookmarks folder:

1. Highlight the existing folder under which the new folder should be created. In this case, the existing folder is Main Bookmarks.

2. Choose Insert Folder from the Item menu. Netscape Navigator 2.0 displays the Bookmark Properties dialog box shown in Figure 3-21.

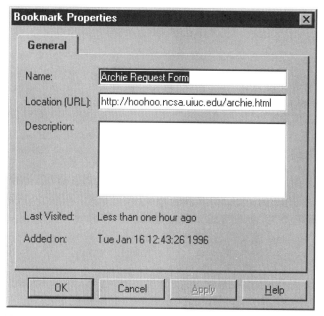

Figure 3-21: *The Bookmark Properties dialog box.*

3. Type **Computers** in the Name field. If you like, you can add a simple text description that will display when you right-click on the folder and select Properties.

4. Click OK to save the folder.

Now that you've added the Computers folder, you can either create new bookmark entries within it, or move existing entries into it.

To create a new bookmark:

1. Highlight the folder under which the new entry should be created. In this case, we'll click Computers.

2. Select Insert Bookmark from the Item menu. Netscape Navigator 2.0 displays the Bookmark Properties dialog box, shown above in Figure 3-21.

3. Type the name for your new bookmark in the Name field. As an example, let's use **A nifty Computer URL**. If you like, you can add a simple text description that will display when you right-click on the entry and select Properties.

4. Type the URL into the Location field. Make sure you type the complete address correctly!

5. Click OK to save the entry. Your Bookmarks window should now look something like Figure 3-22.

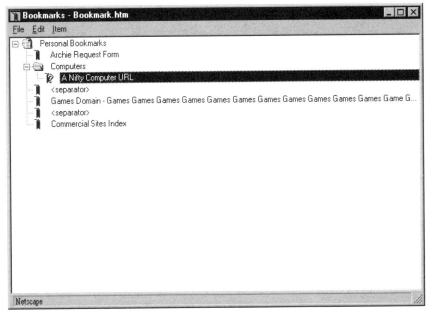

Figure 3-22: *The Bookmarks window with new entry.*

It's even easier to move an existing bookmark into a folder. Click and drag the entry icon (which looks like a sheet of paper with the edge folded down) and drop it on top of the desired folder. Notice that your cursor changes appearance to indicate you're dragging the entry to a new spot. The entry will now appear as a sub-branch under the folder.

When you add entries under a folder, Netscape Navigator 2.0 also displays the entries and folder hierarchy as part of the Bookmarks menu. Folders with entries in them appear with arrows on the right side of the menu; when you select the folder, the folder name expands to show the bookmark entries within.

If you'd like to separate your entries or folders on the Bookmarks menu, highlight the name in the Bookmarks window and select Insert Separator from the Bookmarks dialog box Item menu. When you return to the Bookmarks menu, you'll see a line separating that entry or folder from the others on the menu.

TIP

Once you've expanded your entries within several folders, it may be harder to find a particular entry. Of course, you can use the Find command in the Bookmarks window, but it also helps to close folders you're not using. Closing a folder hides all the Bookmark entries under it. To close a folder, double-click its icon; to expand it and display the entries it contains, double-click its icon again.

CHECKING FOR WHAT'S NEW

Let's suppose it's been a week or two since you last surfed the Web (after all, there is more to life than the Internet), and you'd like to catch up on any changes to your favorite bookmarked Web sites. Unfortunately, you have dozens of sites, and not enough time to check all of them for updated information.

Fortunately, Netscape Navigator 2.0's advanced What's New feature takes all the hassle out of keeping up-to-date with some or all of the sites you've added to your Bookmark files. To check for updated Web pages in a Bookmark file, follow these steps:

1. If you want to scan a selected group of sites, highlight them with your mouse.

2. Choose What's New from the File menu. Netscape Navigator 2.0 displays the What's New dialog box shown in Figure 3-23.

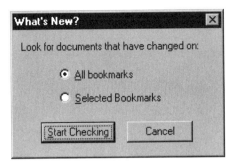

Figure 3-23: *The What's New dialog box.*

3. To check all documents for updated information, choose All Bookmarks. To check only the sites currently selected in the Bookmarks window, click on Selected Bookmarks.

4. Click Start Checking to begin the scanning process.

Netscape Navigator 2.0 will report the sites where any information has been updated or changed.

IMPORTING & EXPORTING BOOKMARKS

As you build your collection of bookmarks, you may want to share your favorite Web sites with others. In fact, many Web surfers keep a "favorite sites" file or "hotlist" in HTML format that they can share with others through Internet mail. Netscape Navigator 2.0 makes it simple to import a bookmark file (bring new entries from some other HTML file into your bookmark file) or export your entries (create an HTML hotlist that others can use).

Remember, an HTML file is simply a text document that contains links to other Web documents. HTML documents are standardized so that all Web browsers can interpret them correctly. That's why importing and exporting allow you to trade files with any Web user, whether or not they have Netscape Navigator 2.0.

From the Netscape Navigator 2.0 window, follow these steps to *import* a bookmark file:

1. Select Go to Bookmarks from the Bookmarks menu. The Bookmarks window appears, as shown earlier in Figure 3-20.

2. From the Bookmarks window File menu, select Import. Netscape Navigator 2.0 displays a standard Windows or Windows 95 file open dialog, as shown in Figure 3-24.

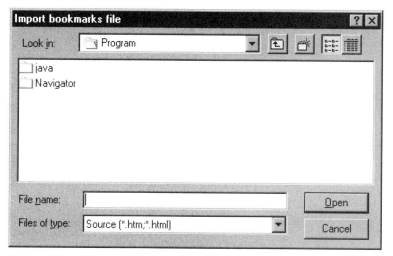

Figure 3-24: *The File Open dialog box.*

3. Navigate to the directory where the HTML file is stored and then double-click it.

From the Navigator display window, follow these steps to *export* a bookmark file:

1. Select Go to Bookmarks from the Bookmarks menu. The Bookmarks window appears, as shown earlier in Figure 3-20.

2. Select the bookmark file you want to export.

3. From the Bookmarks window's File menu, select the Save As command. Netscape Navigator 2.0 displays the standard Windows or Windows 95 file save dialog, as shown in Figure 3-25.

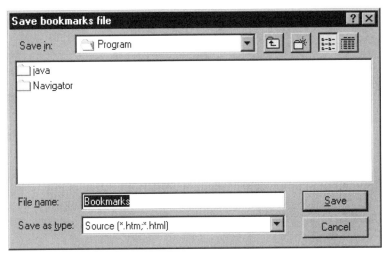

Figure 3-25: *The File Save dialog box.*

4. Save the file in any location and under any name you want. Make sure the file type is set to Source (*.htm, *.html).

NETSCAPE NAVIGATOR 2.0 SHORTCUTS FOR WINDOWS 95

If you're running Netscape Navigator 2.0 under Windows 95, you can create iconized desktop shortcuts that will make connecting to your favorite Web page as easy as a click of your mouse!

There are two ways to create shortcuts:

■ If you click and drag a link, the pointer will change to indicate that the link can now be dropped onto your desktop. A highlighted link is shown in Figure 3-26, while the new desktop shortcut should look something like Figure 3-27.

■ You can click your right mouse button on a link and then select Internet Shortcut from the context menu that pops up.

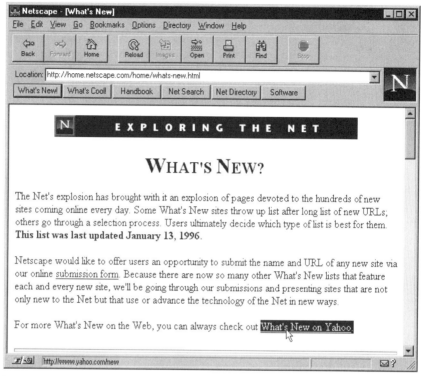

Figure 3-26: *A highlighted link, soon to become a desktop shortcut.*

Figure 3-27: *A Netscape shortcut icon on the desktop.*

Now that you're familiar with some of the program's main features, let's take a quick look at the information Netscape makes available to you with a single mouse click.

THE DIRECTORY BUTTONS

Already you know how to use many of Netscape Navigator 2.0's main features, and you're probably pretty used to leaping from link to link across the vast stretches of the Internet. One of the great things about Netscape Navigator 2.0 is that it not only provides the tools for getting places, it actually has some of the best Web links built right in. The Directory buttons serve as quick and easy shortcuts to some of the most important Internet resources. We'll also pop in on one of the most popular and well-known sites on the Web: the Yahoo Web page search site.

THE WHAT'S NEW BUTTON

Let's face it: the World Wide Web is an immense world within cyberspace, and it's getting bigger every day. Even the mass-market magazines are listing Web sites these days, and your Net-surfing friends will certainly send you their share of cool URLs.

But where do you go for the very latest sites? Wouldn't it be nice to check a single page for the "best of the newest" sites that have recently opened?

That's the idea behind the first button on the Directory bar, What's New. This button brings up a page that acts as a doorway to the latest sites on the Web, and it's one of the most popular starting points for owners of Netscape Navigator 2.0. In this section, let's check the What's New page and jump to a new site. Follow these steps:

1. Make sure you are connected to the Internet either directly or via your SLIP or PPP access provider. If Netscape Navigator 2.0 is not currently running, launch it by double-clicking its icon.

2. Click the What's New button on the Directory bar. Netscape's What's New page appears, as shown in Figure 3-28.

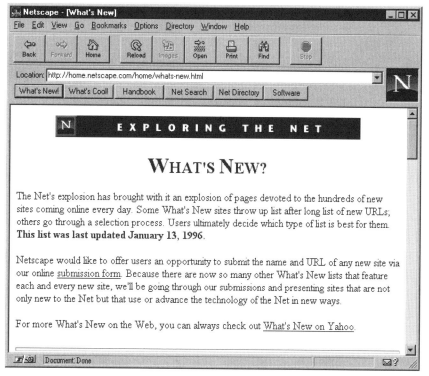

Figure 3-28: *The What's New page.*

TIP

You can click the Directory buttons no matter where you are on the Net. You don't have to be displaying documents from the Netscape site for these buttons to work.

3. Scroll down until you see the links to new sites, along with their descriptions. To jump to one of these new pages, simply click its link.

4. To return to the What's New page, simply click the What's New button again.

THE WHAT'S COOL BUTTON

The What's Cool button has a similar function to the What's New button. It brings up a page full of links to documents that may not be brand new, but which:

■ Are especially well designed or colorful.

■ Have unique resources, like extensive image libraries or databases.

■ Offer animation or unusual Web applications.

■ Have proven particularly popular with Web surfers.

Figure 3-29 shows what was on the What's Cool page when this book went to press.

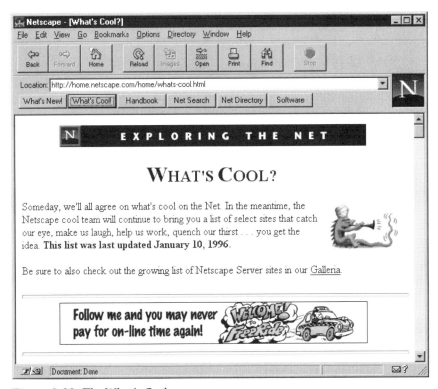

Figure 3-29: *The What's Cool page.*

THE ONLINE HANDBOOK BUTTON

Unlike most other Windows applications, some of the more advanced online help for Netscape Navigator 2.0 does not use the Windows Help program. Instead, it loads a hypermedia online handbook that's really a large collection of linked Web documents. Handbook screens feature cross-referencing and an extensive index, and it's a great resource if you have technical questions that we haven't answered in this book.

Let's open the Handbook to the first page of online help. Make sure you're connected to the Net, then click the Handbook button. After a few seconds, Netscape Navigator 2.0 loads the help document, as shown in Figure 3-30.

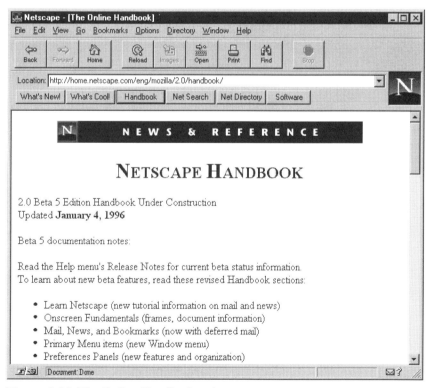

Figure 3-30: *The Online Handbook main page.*

Note the first set of topics listed in the Handbook. Four of these topics are of special interest:

- **Before You Begin.** This Handbook section offers a "quick start" tutorial for new users of Netscape Navigator 2.0, including some of the basics we've covered so far in this chapter. If you feel you'd benefit from additional introductory material after you finish this chapter, Before You Begin is a good next step.

- **Primary Menu Items.** In this section, you'll find details about each item on the Netscape Navigator 2.0 menu bar and each dialog box displayed by the program. If you need help with a particular menu command or a field in a dialog box, check here.

- **Application Features.** This is the advanced section of the Handbook, and it covers many of the topics we'll discuss in more depth later in this book. Once you've become more experienced with browsing and the Netscape Navigator 2.0 user interface, take a few minutes to review the contents of this section.

- **The Index.** Finally, this section makes it easy to search for help on a particular topic. Once you're familiar with Netscape Navigator 2.0, the Index is likely to be the section of the Handbook you use the most.

In fact, let's go ahead and use the Index to locate a specific topic. In this example, let's suppose you want to find out how to save an image you've found on a Web page to your hard drive. Follow these steps:

1. From the Directory bar, click the Handbook button. Netscape Navigator 2.0 displays the first screen of the Handbook, as shown earlier in Figure 3-30.

2. Scroll down until you see the Index at the bottom of the page. Each letter of the alphabet appears, and each is actually a separate link that takes you to a new Web document. Since we're interested in images, click *I*.

The *I* section in the index appears, as shown in Figure 3-31.

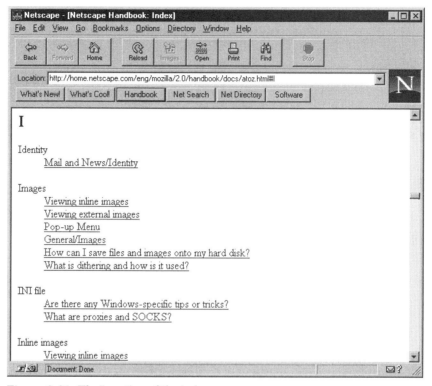

Figure 3-31: *The* I *section of the index.*

Voilà! There's our topic: "How can I save files and images onto my hard disk?" You'll notice that it is also a link. Click the entry to jump to that discussion elsewhere in the Handbook pages.

THE NET SEARCH BUTTON

As we mentioned earlier, the sheer size of the World Wide Web makes it extremely difficult to locate a particular piece of information or a specific Web page by simply fishing for the right URL. For this reason, topical search engines have been around for as long as the Web itself.

Search engines usually look through an index of documents for a query string that you specify. Some search tools also allow you to add logical operators like "either," "and," and "or" so that you can perform more sophisticated searches.

Netscape Navigator 2.0 provides you with links to all the search engines you're likely to need. Clicking the Net Search button brings up the Net Search page, shown in Figure 3-32.

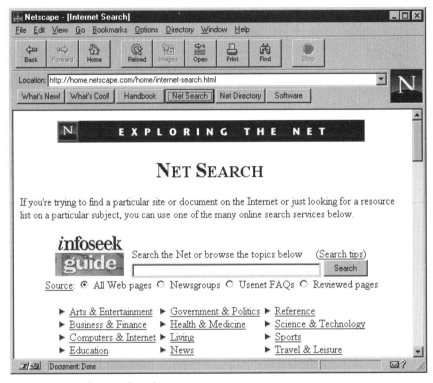

Figure 3-32: *The Net Search page.*

You can access the InfoSeek engine directly from this page, while the other search engines are called using links to their own pages.
    Let's search for a specific topic:

1. Click one of the radio buttons beneath the search field. For instance, if you just want to search Web pages, click the All Web Pages radio button.

2. Enter the string **batman** in the search field and then click the Search button. InfoSeek returns the search results shown in Figure 3-33.

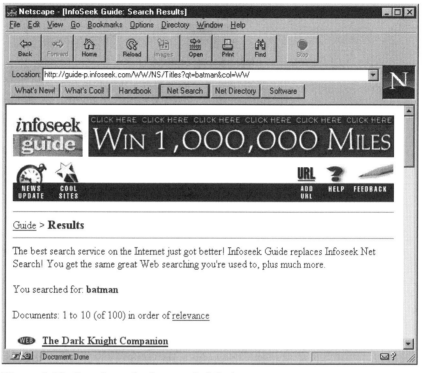

Figure 3-33: *Search results from an InfoSeek query.*

3. To jump directly to one of the pages, simply click on the corresponding link.

A Net search is not guaranteed to locate every site on a particular topic, but if you're hunting for reference material or just surfing because you're interested in the subject, you'll find more than enough sites to keep you busy.

THE NET DIRECTORY BUTTON

Next, we arrive at the Net Directory button. In Web-speak, a *directory* provides a similar function to a search engine: it helps you find documents you're interested in. Unlike a search engine, however, a directory arranges Web pages by topic. For example, sites are grouped into sections like "Art," "Science," "Computers,"

"Business," and so on. In this way, a Net directory is more akin to a tourist's guidebook, and it appeals more to those who like a broad range of sites rather than the focus provided by a search engine.

Of course, not all directories are quite so generic. For example, throughout the Web you'll find many pages featuring specialized directories covering only music, for example, or only films. As you become more experienced in surfing the Web, you'll encounter directory sites that literally provide hours of exploration before you've exhausted their resources.

The Netscape Net Directory page includes several links to other directories, but undoubtedly the best (and most famous) directory is the Yahoo Web Guide.

THE SOFTWARE BUTTON

Finally, let's take a look at the last Directory button. Click the Software button to display the Netscape Navigator Upgrade page, which contains all the details on purchasing and upgrading Netscape software. The Upgrade page provides information on the Netscape Navigator Subscription Program and the latest-released versions of Navigator for different computers. Of course, you'll also find a number of convenient links for downloading demonstration software.

Just think of the Software Button as your Netscape software catalog, complete with the option to purchase products online.

EXPLORING YAHOO

For a taste of the limitless expanse of information available on the Web today, there's no better site to begin with than Yahoo. This Web guide started as a hobby project by Stanford University students David Filo and Jerry Yang in April 1994. Since then, Yahoo has mushroomed into a profitable business that's become a career, but Filo and Yang still offer their original service free of charge to everyone, and the site has become the home page for uncounted Web surfers.

What are we waiting for? Let's start exploring! To access Yahoo:

1. Make sure you are connected to the Internet either directly or via your SLIP or PPP access provider. If Netscape Navigator 2.0 is not currently running, launch it by double-clicking its icon.

2. Click the Net Directory button to load the Netscape Net Directory page.

   ■ Netscape has provided convenient links to each of the major subjects on the Yahoo page, so you don't even really need to load the Yahoo top-level page itself. But just so you can see what Yahoo looks like, let's do this the slightly slower way.

3. Click the link Yahoo Directory. Netscape Navigator 2.0 displays the Yahoo top page, as shown in Figure 3-34.

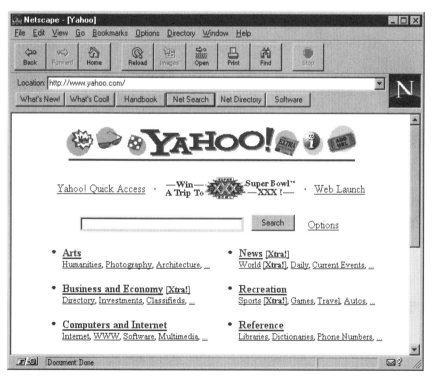

Figure 3-34: *The Yahoo Web site.*

You can see that each section in the guide is actually a link. In fact, each section is further broken down into subsections, and these subsections are links as well. If you don't see the subsection you're looking for, click on the ellipsis (...) link to display more.

Like the Net Search page, Yahoo also provides its own search engine, which operates in a similar fashion as the InfoSeek engine we tried out in the previous section. You can specify keywords, URLs, or simple text strings as search targets. Click the Options link to learn more about the Boolean search operators available.

Yahoo also offers these other features through the hotspots that surround the title graphic:

- **What's New.** A listing of the latest sites added to the guide.

- **Cool Sites.** Those sites that are especially unusual or inventive.

- **Reuters News Headlines.** Headlines and news summaries in text format from the Yahoo newswire.

- **What's Popular.** The sites on the Web that receive the most user traffic. Of course, these sites are often the slowest as well, but that's the penalty you pay for Internet success!

- **Write Us.** Like most Web pages, the Yahoo site provides an Internet e-mail link so that you can leave electronic mail to the administrators.

- **Add URL.** How can you inform the staff at Yahoo about the new Web site you just put online? Click here! This function allows you to submit the URL of your favorite site. Yahoo displays a form that you can fill out with all the information.

- **Random Link.** If you're looking for something new and unexpected, or if you just like to waste time, click the Random hotspot to display a site selected totally at random from the Yahoo guide.

- **Info.** This hotspot displays helpful information about Yahoo, including more information about the different features available at the site that change from time to time.

It's a good idea to check the Yahoo site at least once per session, since it's constantly changing and new pages are added every day. This site is probably the best indication of the enormous popularity and constant expansion of the World Wide Web, so make sure you add it to your bookmark file the first time you visit.

THE DIRECTORY MENU

The Netscape Navigator 2.0 Directory menu contains all of the same commands available using the Directory buttons, but it also offers other resources of interest to new users:

- **Netscape Galleria.** The Netscape Galleria is a collection of links to Web servers running Netscape's server software, including the Commerce Server package for secure online financial transactions. Some of these sites are commercial; others focus on educational and scientific content. If you're interested in running a Web server, this page offers a great chance to sample what other individuals and companies have done.

- **The Internet White Pages.** Looking for an individual's Internet mail address? You'll find it's very similar to searching for a needle in a haystack, but the Internet White Pages can help.

- **About the Internet.** This menu item is provided for those who would like additional information about the Internet itself. The links on this page jump to other pages that provide both basic concepts and technical details on every aspect of the Internet and the World Wide Web, including the history of the Internet and current demographic statistics.

MOVING ON

In this chapter, you learned the basics of surfing the World Wide Web, as well as how to operate the major features of Netscape Navigator 2.0. You now know how to search for a particular site, as well as where you can find the newest and coolest pages on the Web.

In the next chapter, we get serious about Netscape Mail. You'll learn how to compose electronic mail to others, read mail they've sent to you, and reply to mail messages. We'll discuss features that Netscape Navigator 2.0 provides for electronic mail power users as well, including mailing lists and message forwarding.

chapter four

Netscape Mail

Netscape isn't content with just making the world's best Web browser. In Netscape Navigator 2.0, Netscape has created a multi-purpose software product that can do much more than just display Web documents.

The most basic of all Internet tools is electronic mail, or e-mail. E-mail is the most widely used software tool of any kind, and Netscape Navigator 2.0 provides a separate interface just to handle this messaging service. In this chapter, we'll show you how to use the Netscape Navigator 2.0 e-mail window to send, receive, read, and store e-mail. This window, shown in Figure 4-1, is accessed by selecting Netscape Mail from Navigator's Window menu.

TIP

If you're already using Microsoft Exchange for e-mail in Windows 95, you can integrate it with Netscape Navigator 2.0. See the sidebar "Using Netscape Navigator 2.0 with Microsoft Exchange" on page 199.

Figure 4-1: *The Netscape Mail window.*

Before we get into that, however, let's begin with a few words about e-mail itself.

WHAT IS E-MAIL & HOW DOES IT WORK?

E-mail, as you probably know, is the electronic messaging service of the Net. When you send a message to a friend via e-mail, that message travels from your machine over the Internet until it arrives at your friend's machine, or to a special electronic post office on a machine he or she can access. The message is then kept there until your friend retrieves it and reads it. How does the Internet know how to get a piece of e-mail from your machine to your friend's post office account? It works just about like snail mail: all the necessary delivery information is contained in your friend's e-mail address.

When you write a piece of e-mail, the most important thing you should do is get the address right. The first rule of e-mail addressing is to remember that every character counts. If there is a mistake in the address you enter—even one wrong letter—the mail will simply be returned to you as undeliverable.

The standard form for an Internet address is *user@domain*. This address is in two parts, separated by an @ sign (press Shift+2 on your keyboard). The part before the @ is the username, and the part after the @ is the domain name—the name of the machine where that user has an e-mail account. It is important that e-mail addresses not have any spaces in them.

Usernames are how users are identified by their Internet access providers. For instance, the username part of Count Dracula's e-mail address, dracula@transylvania.com, is *dracula*. Domain names are the names of the machines themselves. The domain name in the address, *transylvania.com*, identifies the name of a machine, transylvania. The *.com* at the end of the domain name means that this is a commercial service. There are also *.gov* services, which are governmental institutions; *.edu* services, which are at educational institutions; and so on. We touched on some of this in Chapter 1, "The Net & the Web." Sometimes addresses will end with information about a country or network instead of a type of service. For example, addresses ending in .ca are in Canada, and addresses ending in .uk are in the United Kingdom.

WHAT'S MY E-MAIL ADDRESS?

Your e-mail address is your identity in the online world; you will have been given your e-mail address by the people who provide you with Internet access. If you are on an office LAN, your Internet e-mail address may be your network login name followed by an @ sign and the domain name of your company. Then again, it may not—you really need to check with your LAN administrator.

If you get on the Net using a SLIP or PPP account, you can usually figure out your e-mail address. If your login name is *frank* and your Internet access provider is *graveyard.com*, then your e-mail address is probably frank@graveyard.com. If this isn't correct, then you will have to call your access provider to figure out what your address is.

TIP

If your Internet access provider doesn't provide you with an e-mail account, you should seriously consider switching access providers!

EXCHANGING MESSAGES WITH ONLINE SERVICES

What if you have friends who are not connected directly to the Internet via a LAN or a SLIP or PPP account, but are users of some online service such as America Online (AOL) or CompuServe? Can you exchange e-mail messages with them?

Sure! Users of CompuServe, MCI Mail, AT&T Mail, Prodigy, or AOL can send you e-mail using your regular Internet address. Typically, the procedure is no more complex than sending a message to another user of the service. You can also send e-mail to a user on any of these services, using Netscape Navigator 2.0 in the same way you would when communicating with another individual on the Net. The only difference is the addressing. If an online service user gives you his or her ID, you have to know how to turn it into a valid Internet address so that any message you send can be delivered. The method for translating addresses varies from service to service.

COMPUSERVE

User IDs on CompuServe take the form of two numbers separated by a comma, as in 71234,5678. To send e-mail to a CompuServe subscriber, you address it to that ID number at (@) the domain compuserve.com. The only trick is that the comma must be replaced by a period. Thus the Internet e-mail address for the user whose ID is 71234,5678 would be:

71234.5678@compuserve.com

That's all there is to it; you send the message just like any other e-mail.

MCI MAIL

MCI Mail users really have three IDs: a number; a "handle," or abbreviated name; and a normal full name. For instance, the user Jake Barns might have the following set of IDs:

123-4567
jbarns
Jake Barns

To send e-mail to Jake, you could use any of the following Internet e-mail addresses:

1234567@mcimail.com
jbarns@mcimail.com
jake_barns@mcimail.com

Please note that in the user number, you drop the hyphen, and in the full name you have to add an underscore (_) character between the first and last names.

AMERICA ONLINE

All you need to know is the AOL user's "screen name"; you then just add the at sign (@) and the domain aol.com. A valid Internet e-mail address for an AOL user might be, for instance:

aoluser@aol.com

Note that even if the AOL user has a space in his or her AOL name—John Doe, for instance—you can ignore that space and simply address your e-mail to johndoe@aol.com.

PRODIGY

This is just like America Online. You send e-mail to a particular user ID at prodigy.com. Here's an example:

abc123@prodigy.com

AT&T MAIL

As with AOL and Prodigy, each AT&T Mail user has a unique username. To address a message, you simply append @attmail.com to the username. A valid address might be as follows:

msmuffet@attmail.com

CONFIGURING NETSCAPE NAVIGATOR 2.0 MAIL

Now that you know about e-mail addresses, you are ready to configure the Netscape Navigator 2.0 Mail window for your personal use. To begin with, Netscape Navigator 2.0 needs to know a few basic things about you.:

1. With Netscape Navigator 2.0 loaded, select Mail and News Preferences from the Options menu. The Preferences dialog box appears, with the Servers tab selected as shown in Figure 4-2.

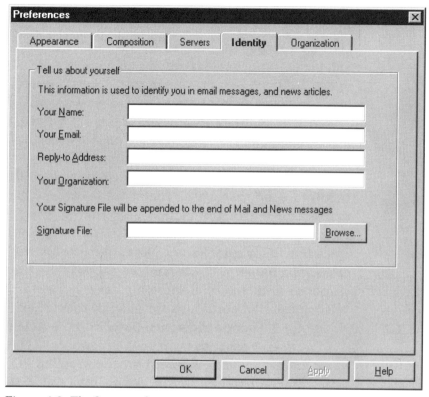

Figure 4-2: *The Servers tab.*

- If the Servers tab isn't automatically selected when you choose Mail and News Preferences from the Options menu, select it now.

- In the Servers tab, there are two pieces of information Netscape Navigator 2.0 needs: your SMTP (Simple Mail Transport Protocol—aren't you glad you asked?) address, and your POP3 (Post Office Protocol) address. These are the network addresses the program uses to send and receive your e-mail. If you don't know what these addresses are for your Internet access provider, you still can probably figure them out.

SMTP & POP3

Like all Internet programs, Netscape Navigator 2.0 relies on established protocols to send and receive data. As explained earlier in this book, protocols are simply conventions that allow one piece of software to exchange data with another. For instance, a client program might expect a particular kind of acknowledgment after it sends a packet of data. Both sender and receiver need to play by the same rules.

Internet mail programs use SMTP (Simple Mail Transport Protocol) to *send* messages. The client, Netscape Navigator 2.0, first establishes a connection with the remote SMTP server, the machine that acts as host for the recipient's e-mail account. Once the link is established, Netscape Navigator 2.0 sends the recipient's name. If the server can accept mail for that user, it responds with an OK. If there are several intended recipients, this negotiation continues for each of them. Finally Netscape Navigator 2.0 sends the actual body of the e-mail message.

To *retrieve* messages from your e-mail server, Netscape Navigator 2.0 uses a very different protocol, called POP3 (Post Office Protocol, version 3). I won't go into the details of POP3 because they're somewhat complex, but it's important to make sure that your e-mail account is on a server that supports this protocol (most do).

2. Enter the domain name for your Internet access provider in the SMTP field. Count Dracula would enter **transylvania.com**.

3. Now enter the domain name for your Internet access provider in the POP field. Once again, Count Dracula would enter **transylvania.com**, as shown in Figure 4-3.

4. Enter your username in the Pop User Name field. Count Dracula would enter **dracula**, as shown in Figure 4-3.

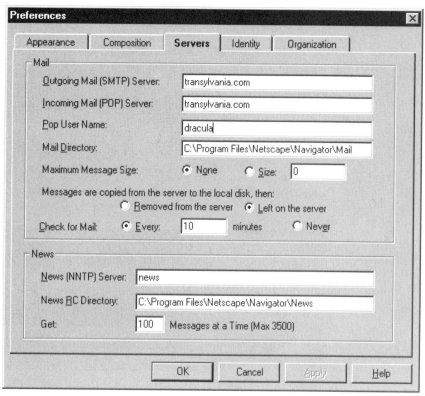

Figure 4-3: *Configuring the Directories options.*

5. Unless you have very strong feelings about how your hard drive should be organized, leave the Mail Directory field alone. The default location should be fine for storing mail files.

6. Unless you want to limit the size of messages you receive, leave the None radio button selected in the Maximum Message Size area. If you decide to limit the size, the value you enter is the maximum number of lines.

7. Select the Removed From the Server radio button if you want all messages deleted from your post office account when you retrieve your mail. If you want your messages to remain on the server so that you can download them again later, select the Left on the Server radio button.

■ If you decide to leave retrieved messages on your post office server, you may receive the same messages over and over when Netscape Navigator 2.0 gets new mail.

8. In the Check for Mail area, tell Netscape Navigator 2.0 how often you want the program to log on to your post office server to collect any new messages.

■ If you click the Never radio button, you will have to click the Get Mail button in the Netscape Mail window every time you want to check for messages.

Next, select the Identity tab, shown in Figure 4-4.

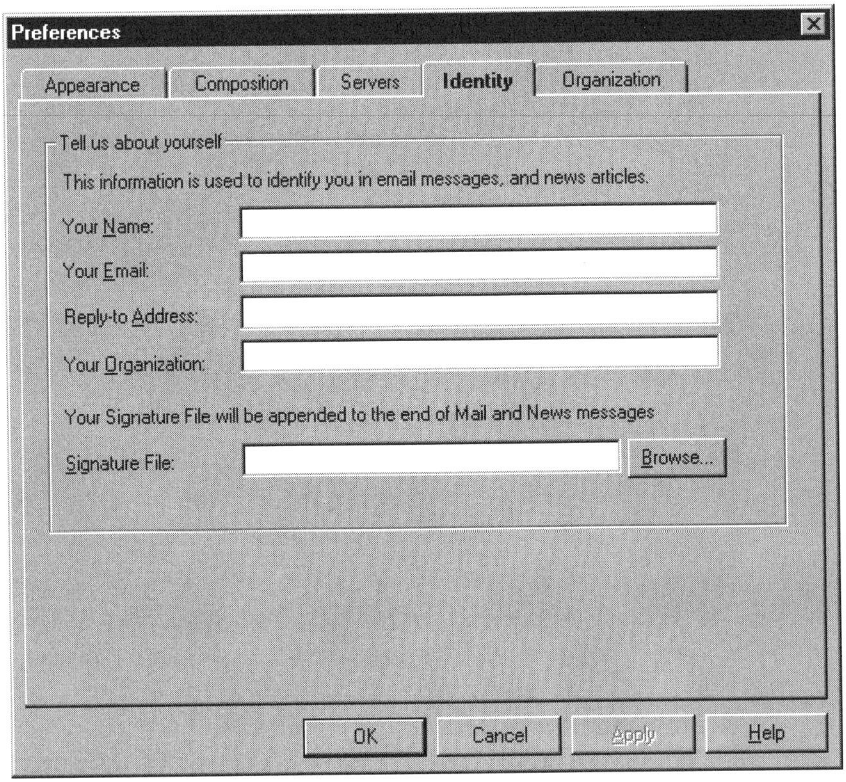

Figure 4-4: *The Identity tab.*

Here's where you enter the information that will appear on all your outgoing mail. To configure your identity preferences:

1. Type your name into the Your Name field. Dracula would enter **Count Dracula**.

2. Type your e-mail address into the Your E-mail field. Dracula would enter **dracula@transylvania.com**.

3. Optionally, enter an alternate e-mail address in the Reply-to Address field. This is the address others will use when replying to your messages. It isn't likely you'll need to do this. You would only use Reply-to Address if, for instance, you wanted to send mail out from Netscape Navigator 2.0 using a commercial access provider, but you wanted to get replies on another account, such as an account you have through school.

4. Optionally, enter the name of an organization or affiliation in the Your Organization field. This simply adds an identifying tag to your mail. Think of it as a kind of electronic letterhead, there if you want it but not really necessary.

5. Optionally, create a signature file for yourself and specify where to find it in the Signature File field.

WHAT'S A SIGNATURE FILE?

A signature file is simply a file that gets tacked on to the end of every piece of mail, so if Dracula always wants to add a closing line like

Count Dracula, Moderator, Bloodsuckers Anonymous Mailing List

he would simply create a text file called something like SIG.TXT with a text editor such as Notepad, save it on his hard drive and use the Browse button to tell Netscape Navigator 2.0 where to find it. Like Your Organization, a signature file (often called a ".sig" on the Net) can be used to include more information in your mail, but isn't necessary. If you do include a signature file, make sure it is short (no more than four lines long) and pertinent (long and/or pointless .sig files tend to attract flames for wasting bandwidth).

Your completed Identity tab will look something like Figure 4-5.

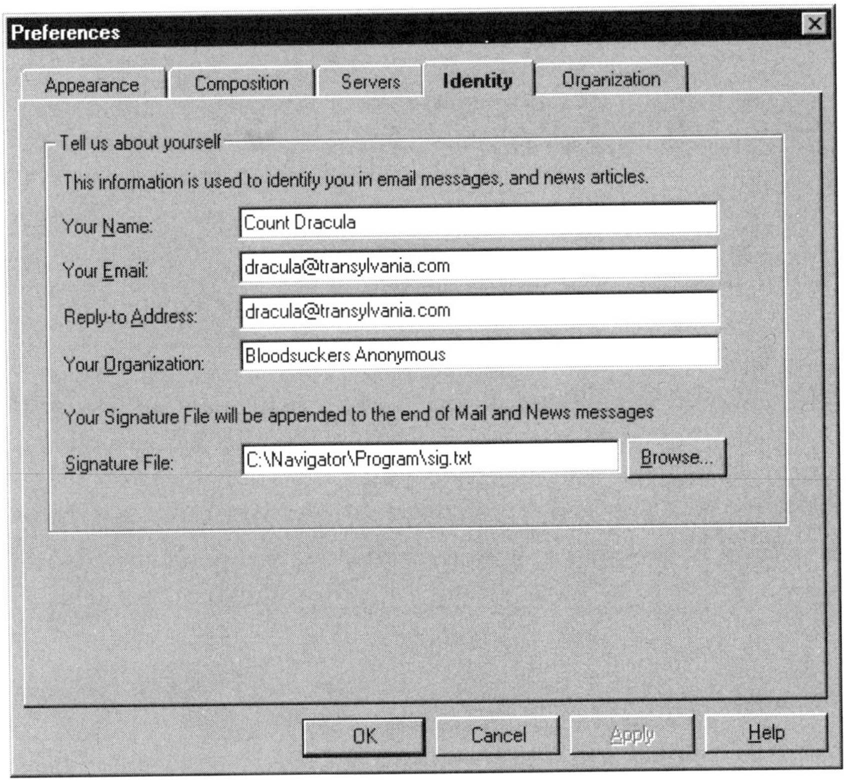

Figure 4-5: *A configured Identity tab.*

Click OK to leave the Preferences dialog box and save your changes. Now it's time to try out the basic mail operations: sending and receiving a message.

TIP

You can change the fonts Netscape Navigator 2.0 uses to display messages by selecting the Appearance tab from the Preferences dialog box. If you don't like the default fonts, you might want to experiment a bit.

SENDING & RECEIVING E-MAIL

Once you have configured your preferences, you are ready to send yourself a message. That might seem at first like an odd thing to do, but it's the best way to try out both sending and receiving e-mail. Let's get started.

SENDING AN E-MAIL MESSAGE

While you are still in Netscape Navigator 2.0 and connected to the Internet, select New Mail Message from the File menu or simply press Ctrl+M. If you are already in the Netscape Mail window, click the To:Mail button. Whichever method you use, the Message Composition window appears, as shown in Figure 4-6.

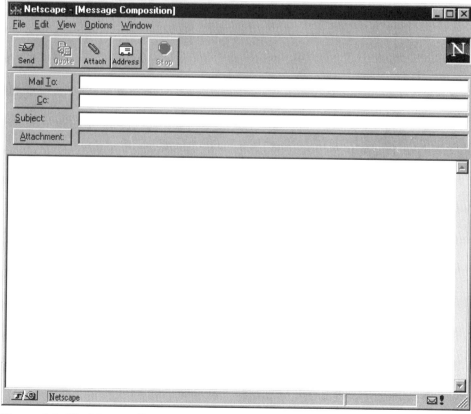

Figure 4-6: *The Message Composition window.*

As you can see, this window is divided into two parts. The top part contains the header information about the message, the text that will appear at the very beginning of the message when it is received. The bottom part is the pane where you type in your actual message.

Each of the headers in the top pane has a particular specific function:

- **Mail To.** The Mail To field is where you enter the e-mail address of your recipient. If you want to send the same piece of mail to more than one person, just enter all their addresses in the Mail To field, separating each address with a comma.

- **Cc.** The Cc field works like carbon copies in the old-fashioned world of paper and typewriter—a copy of your message is sent to everyone listed on the Cc: line. Typically, the message is sent to these recipients for their information, and they don't need to reply. Note that the designated recipient or recipients of the mail will see who has been Cc'ed.

TIP

Click the Mail To, Cc, or Address button to select addresses from your Address Book. You can read about setting up your Address Book later, in the section called, unsurprisingly, "The Address Book."

- **Subject.** The Subject header is whatever you want it to be—it tells the recipient what your letter is about. Try to keep your Subject lines short and informative.

- **Attachment.** Netscape Navigator 2.0 allows you to attach other files stored on your computer to your mail, so that when you send the mail, a copy of that file travels along with the mail. You can also send URLs, links to files that aren't even on your machine but that will appear in your recipient's Mail window! We'll talk more about this in the section "Attaching Files to Messages."

There are other header lines you can add to your e-mail—Reply To, Newgroups, Followups To, From and Bcc lines—which you add by selecting them under View in the menu (or, if you want to see everything, just select Show All).

- **Reply To.** The Reply To line is where you can put the e-mail address of another account where you want responses sent.

- **Bcc.** Bcc, for *Blind Cc,* is used when you want to send a copy of a letter to someone but do not want that person's name to appear in the Cc line. The recipient or recipients of the mail who are listed on the Mail To and Cc lines will not know who has been Bcc'ed.

- **Newsgroups.** In this field, you can list the names of any Usenet newsgroups you'd like your epistle posted to. Select Newsgroups from the View menu. You will learn more about Usenet newsgroups in Chapter 5.

- **Followups To.** This field is also for use with Usenet news-groups. For more information, please see "Replying to an Article" in Chapter 5, "Newsgroups."

Some of the addressing fields, like Mail To, Cc, and Bcc, have buttons next to them. Clicking these buttons will open your Address Book and allow you to select your recipients by mouse clicks. We'll talk more about the Address Book in just a bit.

To write a test letter to yourself, you really only need to fill in a couple of these fields:

1. Fill in the Mail To field with your own e-mail address.

2. Fill in the Subject field with a subject like **Letter from me**.

3. Write yourself a message in the pane below the headers, just as you would type new text into a word processor document. In the end, you should have a message that looks something like the one in Figure 4-7.

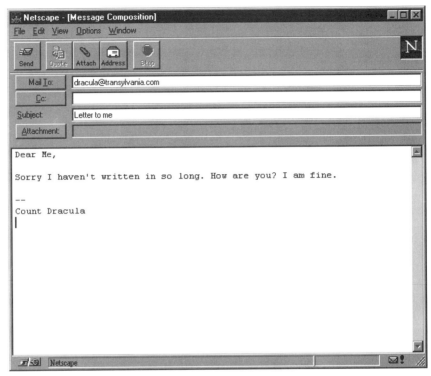

Figure 4-7: *A test letter to yourself.*

MAILTO: TAGS
Besides calling up the Message Composition window, Netscape Navigator 2.0 offers another way to send mail. Web pages can include special HTML tags called MAILTO: tags. They look just like ordinary links, although often they appear in italics. When you click one of these, Netscape Navigator 2.0 pops up the Message Composition window, allowing you to send a message to the recipient indicated in the Mail To tag.

MAILTO: tags provide a convenient way to solicit feedback or comments in a Web document.

Once you have the Mail To and Subject fields filled out and you've entered some text in the text pane, you are ready to actually send your message.

1. Make sure you are connected to the Internet, either directly or through a SLIP or PPP connection with your access provider. If you are using SLIP or PPP and are not currently connected, double-click the Dial-Up Connection icon for your access provider.

2. While you are still in the Message Composition window, click the Send button in the toolbar.

If everything is set correctly, Netscape Navigator 2.0 will contact your Internet access provider and send the message. If it can't send the message properly, make sure that your Internet connection is really open, and check the name of the SMTP and POP servers in the Servers tab, shown earlier in Figure 4-2. If all of this is correct and you still can't send a message, you may need to contact your Internet access provider to make sure you have the right names for the machines handling the mail on your system.

Netscape Navigator 2.0 is also configured to save a copy of your outgoing messages in a folder called "Send." If you don't want a copy of these messages, you can delete them, which you will learn how to do later in this chapter under "Organizing Your Mail Folders."

RETRIEVING E-MAIL

Now that you have sent yourself a message, you can go ahead and retrieve it from your post office server:

1. You should still be connected to the Internet. Back in the Netscape Navigator 2.0 main window, click the small envelope icon at the bottom right corner. You will immediately be asked for a password.

2. In the Password Entry dialog box, enter your e-mail password. If you're connecting to the Internet via SLIP or PPP, this is probably the same password you use to connect to your Internet access provider.

TIP

Netscape Navigator 2.0 asks for this password the first time you retrieve e-mail after launching the program, but once you connect to your e-mail post office, it will not ask you for a password again during your current session.

Once you enter your password, Netscape Navigator 2.0 logs you in to your post office account to retrieve your mail.

■ If you have configured Netscape Navigator 2.0 so that it does not retrieve mail automatically, you need to click the Get Mail button in order to get your waiting message.

If this is the first mail message you have sent, your test message is the only one that will be retrieved (if you don't see your test message in the mail window, press the Get Mail button to check once more). But if you are already using the e-mail address you filled in earlier in Preferences, Netscape Navigator 2.0 will get the rest of your e-mail stored at that address as well.

TIP

Once Netscape Navigator 2.0 retrieves any e-mail from your post office server it puts an exclamation point next to the envelope icon in the main browser window. That way you know immediately when new mail has arrived, even if you are not in the Netscape Mail window.

Let's assume that the test message was the first piece of e-mail you have ever received. Once Netscape Navigator 2.0 retrieves it, your mail window will look like the one in Figure 4-8.

As you can see, this window is divided into three panes— Folders in the upper left, Messages in the upper right, and the main reading window below. Each of these panes has information sorted in columns. In the Folders pane, you will see an Inbox, where incoming mail is stored, with a list of Unread and Total messages. (If the test message is the only mail you have, both Unread and Total will read "1.")

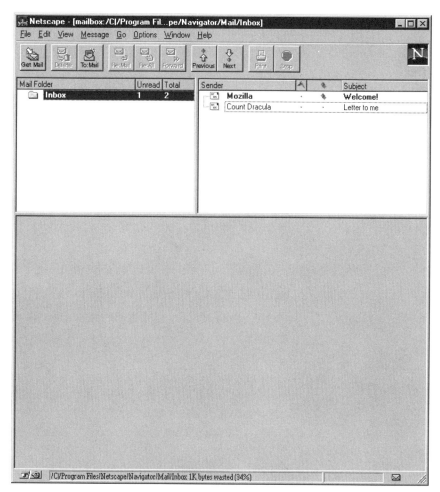

Figure 4-8: *Mail window after retrieving new e-mail message.*

If you select the Inbox folder by clicking it, you will see the headers of the message or messages contained in it displayed in the right-hand Messages pane, as shown in Figure 4-9.

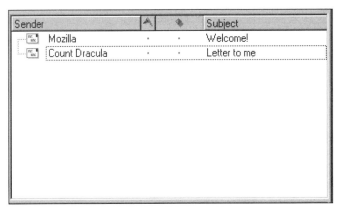

Figure 4-9: *Information about received mail in the Messages pane.*

The Messages pane shows you several things:

■ The Subject line of the incoming mail.

■ Whether you have marked the messages (a method of flagging important mail). Marked messages are indicated with a red flag.

■ Whether you have read the message yet. Unread messages are flagged with a green diamond that may look like a dot if your eyes are like mine.

■ The Sender line.

■ The date of the message.

The width of each of these columns is adjustable. To change the size of the columns:

1. Position your mouse over the border of the column until it displays a pair of arrows pointing left and right.

2. Now click and drag the border of the column to the left or right, depending on which column you want to widen.

The borders between the panes operate exactly the same way, and you will probably want to shrink the size of the Folders pane to the left so that you can have more room to expand the From and Subject headers of your e-mail in the Messages pane, as shown in Figure 4-10.

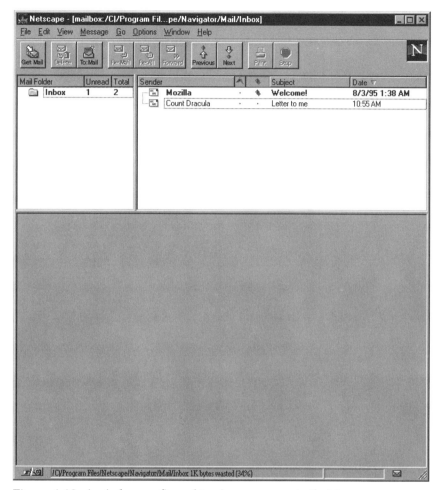

Figure 4-10: *A window configured to give more room to the Messages pane, where information about the mail (like Sender and Subject) is displayed.*

TIP

> *To flag a message you've received, simply select it and click the dot in the flag column. You might want to flag messages that really need to be answered, thus differentiating them from those that are merely informational. Once you have replied to a message, you can unflag it by clicking in the flag column again.*

Now let's actually read the test message:

1. If your Inbox folder is not currently open, open it by clicking it in the Folder pane. The headers of your messages appear in the Messages pane.

2. Click the Subject line of the mail you want to read. The message itself is now displayed in the lower window for reading, as in Figure 4-11.

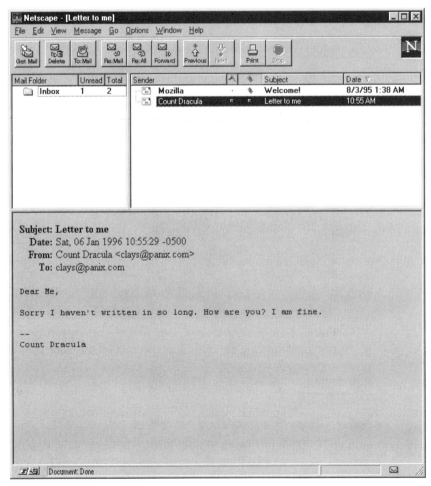

Figure 4-11: *New mail opened in the mail window.*

Since you've been nice enough to send yourself a message, maybe you should be polite and send yourself a reply. Replying to e-mail is the last of the basic messaging functions.

REPLYING TO E-MAIL

Replying to a piece of e-mail differs from sending new mail in several important ways. First of all, when you reply, Netscape Navigator 2.0 fills in the Mail To field automatically, since the intended recipient is simply the sender of the original message. The program also fills in the Subject field with "Re:" and the subject of the mail you are replying to.

There is another important difference: the program lets you use a special quote feature to include the text of the e-mail you are responding to right in the body of your reply.

Let's try it:

1. In the Mail window, select a received message and click the Re:Mail button.

2. When the Message Composition window opens, the text of the letter to which you are replying appears in the bottom pane. You will notice that every line begins with a ">"— this is the Internet standard for indicating quoted material.

At this point, you can add whatever text you like below the quoted text. You can also add other people to the Mail To or Cc fields if you like. If the message you have quoted is long, or if you want to respond to only one or two sentences of a letter, it is considered polite to delete the portions not relevant to your reply, although it is bad etiquette to delete or alter quoted text without indicating removals by inserting [...] or (**snip**) or some other indication that you edited the quoted material.

Following these steps for replying to your test message, you should end up with a New Message Composition window like the one shown in Figure 4-12.

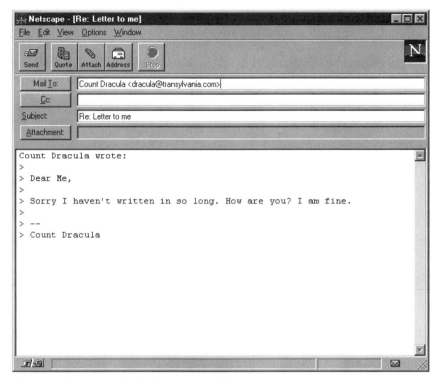

Figure 4-12: _A reply including quote of the original message._

Once you've completed your reply, sending it is just like sending a new message: simply click the Send button.

REPLY TO ALL & FORWARD

There are two other ways to reply to a letter—Re:All and Forward. The ordinary Re:Mail function just grabs the e-mail addresses of everyone on the From field, but it ignores everyone in the Cc field. Re:All will send your reply out to everyone in both the From and Cc fields. This is a good way to have a kind of group conversation via e-mail, since Re:All allows you to address the same group of people the sender of the letter addressed originally.

To select the Re:All option when you are reading a message, simply click the Re:All button on the toolbar.

E-MAIL ETIQUETTE

■ Keep in mind that e-mail can be saved, and you can find that what you write in haste can come back to haunt you. Every piece of e-mail is potentially permanent, so before you say something in e-mail, make sure you really mean it because you may see it again later.

■ Don't assume that the person getting your mail can always understand what you meant when you wrote it. E-mail can be very impersonal. We instinctively understand the difference between a bill, a business letter, and a post card when they arrive in our mail box, but all e-mail looks the same. Without this context, it is easy to misinterpret and to be misinterpreted, so write carefully. If someone has written a message that upsets you, don't rule out the possibility that he or she didn't mean it the way you took it.

■ Don't send abusive mail. This advice seems obvious, but the line can sometimes be hard to draw. What seems like a straightforward comment to you may be read as an insult by someone else. There is one Golden Rule: if someone complains about mail you are sending them, stop.

■ Reread your message before you send it. It is so easy to dash off a thoughtless message; the only defense is to reread everything you write before sending it. That goes double if you are angry when writing, in which case it is best to save the message and reread it later before deciding whether or not to send it. Once you send a message, there is no way to retract it.

You use Forward when you want to send a letter along to someone other than the people listed in the From or Cc fields. Forward is similar to Re:Mail, with a couple of differences. The Subject line is filled in with the subject line of the letter labeled

Fwd instead of Re (with the entire field enclosed in square brackets), and the Mail To field is not filled in. To select the Forward button when you are reading a message, simply click the Forward button in the toolbar.

The message being forwarded is automatically included as an attachment to the mail rather than as text in your actual message. Clicking the Quote button will include the text of the forwarded letter, bracketed by >'s, but if you use this feature to annotate the forwarded letter, remember to delete the attachment so that you don't send two copies of the same letter.

THE ADDRESS BOOK

Now that you know how to send and retrieve e-mail messages, you're ready to start communicating with anybody who has an Internet e-mail address. Chances are that you already know dozens or even hundreds of individuals and businesses with e-mail accounts, but how do you remember all these addresses? E-mail addresses are a little easier than phone numbers because they often include part of a name or some other meaningful information, but as the Net grows and names get used up, e-mail add-resses will become more and more devoid of any real-world significance. I suspect that some day they'll be like license plates, and you'll have to pay extra for a meaningful one!

Of course, you can jot e-mail addresses in a paper address book, but that's pretty old-fashioned for a Net geek like you. Fortunately, Netscape Navigator 2.0 provides an electronic address book for storing frequently used e-mail addresses.

The Address Book has two options—it allows you to enter single addresses and groups of addresses. To use the Address Book:

1. Select Address book from the Netscape Navigator 2.0's Window menu. A window like the one in Figure 4-13 pops up.

Figure 4-13: *The Address Book.*

■ As in other hierarchical tree displays, clicking the plus sign to the left of an item expands it to show all the entries it contains. Clicking the minus sign closes, or collapses, the item. In the Address Book window, an open book icon indicates an expanded mail folder, while a closed book indicates a collapsed folder.

2. To add a new user, select Add User from the Item menu. A dialog box like the one in Figure 4-14 appears.

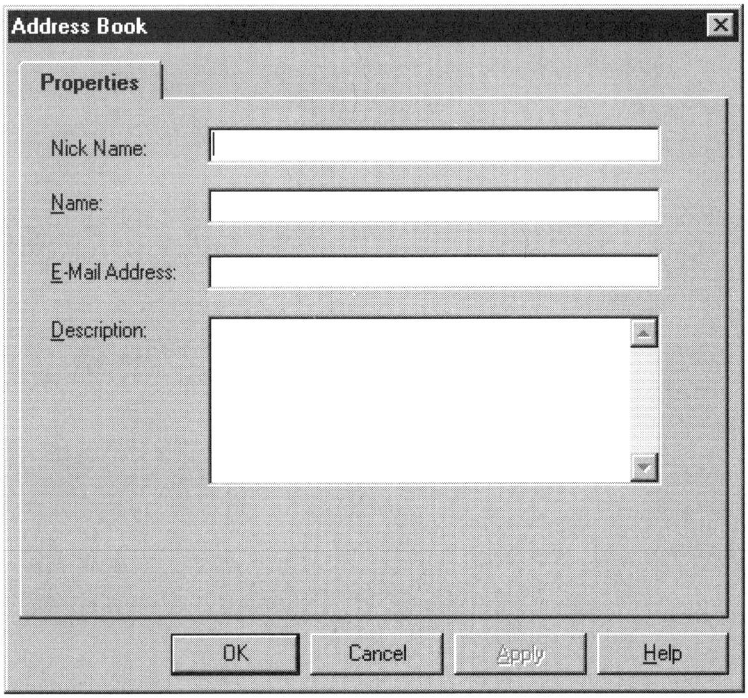

Figure 4-14: *Add User dialog box.*

3. Fill in the Nick Name field. It doesn't matter what you enter as long as it's easy for you to remember and to associate with this entry. The nick name is your way of remembering who the recipient is.

4. Fill in the Name field with an actual name.

5. Fill in the E-Mail Address field with a complete e-mail address for the new entry.

6. Optionally, fill in the Description field. This field is just for your reference.

7. Click OK. You are returned to the Address Book window, and the new entry appears under your top-level folder, with a little "person" icon next to it.

Let's say you entered your own address in the Address Book with the nickname **me**. Now, when you go to write a new piece of mail, you only need to write **me** in the Mail To field; Netscape Navigator 2.0 will fill in the real information automatically. This means that you can reduce e-mail addresses to a few easy-to-remember keystrokes. Why type in **president@whitehouse.gov** when you can simply enter **bill**? (Or **bob**, or **ross**, or whatever.)

You can also add lists of recipients to the Address Book. That way, a single nickname can represent as many addresses as you want. For instance, you could create an Address Book entry called Candidates that let you automatically send the same message to Bill, Bob, and Ross. To create a list:

1. In the Address Book window, select Add List from the Item menu. A dialog box like the one in Figure 4-15 appears.

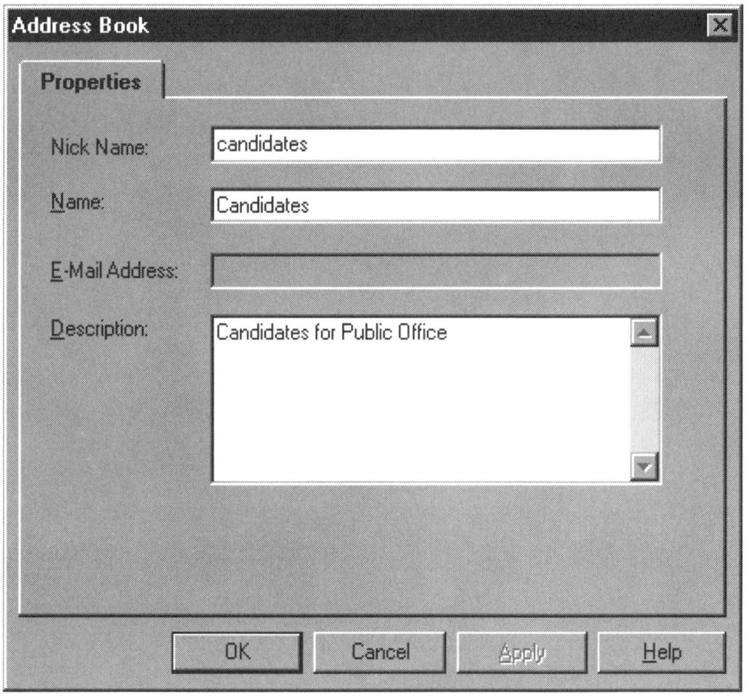

Figure 4-15: *Add List dialog box.*

2. Fill in the Nick Name field with an easy-to-type nickname.

3. Fill in the Name field with the name of your list, for instance, Candidates.

4. Optionally, fill in the Description field. This field is just for your reference.

5. Click OK.

6. Back in the Address Book window, drag the names of people you want included into the new list from the main address book. You will get a new folder in your address book with all these names in it, like the one shown in Figure 4-16.

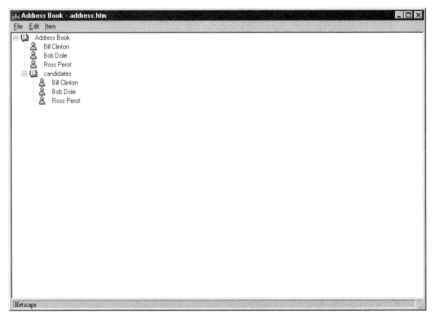

Figure 4-16: *A new folder (address list) in the Address Book window.*

TIP

You can also add entries to a list by selecting the folder and then clicking Add User in the Item menu.

MULTIMEDIA MAIL

Netscape Navigator 2.0 is really a multimedia program, and as you might guess, it can handle more than just plain text in e-mail. It can also display HTML formatting and GIF or JPEG images in the e-mail window, just as it can in the main Web browser window. You can see this in the piece of welcome mail included by Netscape in every browser, part of which is shown in Figure 4-17.

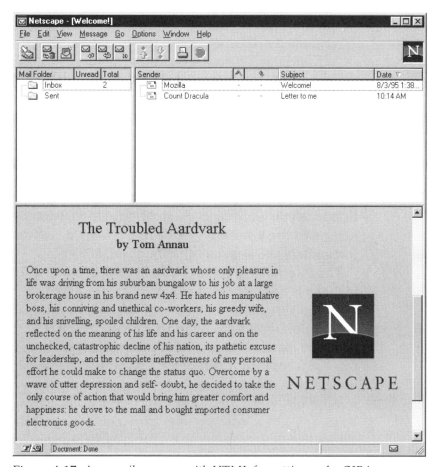

Figure 4-17: *An e-mail message with HTML formatting and a GIF image.*

When you send someone a piece of mail with HTML tags in it, Netscape Navigator 2.0 interprets these tags just as it would if they were in a Web page. This is how the mesage in Figure 4-17 is able to have text in bold face and italics. Although a course in HTML is beyond the scope of this chapter, if you know HTML and you are sending mail to someone else who uses Netscape, you can format the text, include inline images, and even add links to your mail. In fact, Netscape Navigator 2.0 is so good at handling HTML that if someone mentions a URL in a piece of mail, the program will recognize it as a URL and turn it into a link automatically! Just click on it, and you are transported to the site mentioned in the message.

In addition, when you send someone a GIF or JPEG image via e-mail, Netscape Navigator 2.0 opens it directly in the mail window, displaying the image for the recipient. This means you can now mail images directly to other Netscape Navigator 2.0 users. All of this allows you to create truly multimedia mail.

FINDING PEOPLE ON THE NET

Suppose you want to find somebody's e-mail address. You can just go to the Internet "phone book" and look it up, right? Unfortunately the answer is, "No, not yet."

The Internet's greatest advantage as a communications tool is that it is decentralized, which allows small organizations and even individuals to take care of setting up their own Internet connection with little need to consult a central authority. The greatest disadvantage of this method is that it is, well, a little too decentralized to allow for anything like a net-wide "phone book." Instead there are several partial systems for looking people up, many of them good, but none of them perfect. Netscape in its wisdom has provided a page called Internet White Pages, accessible as a Web page from Netscape Navigator 2.0's Directory menu. Figure 4-18 shows what it looks like:

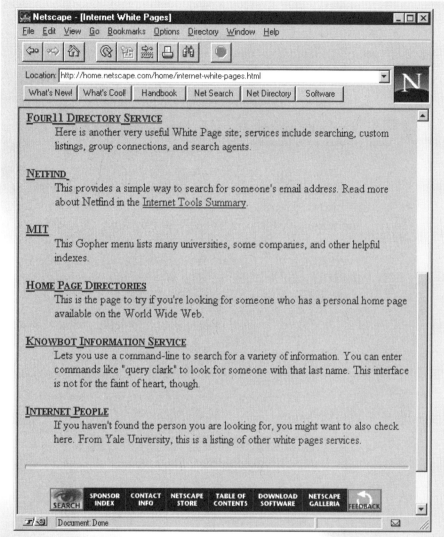

Figure 4-18: *Netscape's "Internet White Pages" page.*

This page gives you access to a variety of different search services. Be warned that many of the systems like the Knowbot have arcane interfaces, but with a little practice you can extract useful information from them.

TIP

To learn a little bit about how to use HTML tags, see the section "Creating Your Own Home Page" in Chapter 9, "Advanced Netscape Navigator 2.0."

ATTACHING FILES TO MESSAGES

Besides including HTML tags and inline images in messages, you can also include entire HTML files or attach any kind of file, text or binary. There are no restrictions on the type of material you can include with your message. You can send spreadsheets, graphics, sounds, word processor files, programs, you name it. You can even attach files that are not on your own computer by sending the URLs for the files as attachments to your message!

To attach a file to an e-mail message:

1. Follow all the steps outlined earlier for creating a new e-mail message.

2. Before sending the message, click the Attachment button in the Message Composition window. The Attachments dialog box appears, as shown in Figure 4-19.

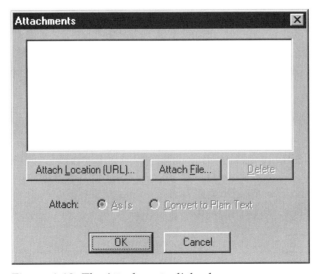

Figure 4-19: *The Attachments dialog box.*

3. Click either the Attach File button or the Attach Location (URL) button to send a file with your message or to include a link to a file that is on a remote computer.

   ■ Any kind of file can be attached to your mail. But if you are sending an HTML file, you can choose to send it as is (with its HTML formatting) or as plain text, without any special formatting. Select either the As Is or the Convert to Plain Text radio button.

4. Once you have selected a file or typed in a URL, click OK to return to the Attachment dialog box.

TIP

You can add as many files as you want to the attachment list before you close it.

5. Click OK to attach the file(s) and return to the Message Composition window.

6. Send the message, including any attachment, by clicking the Send button.

MAKING SURE YOUR ATTACHED FILES ARRIVE SAFELY
Internet e-mail is a system designed primarily for exchanging text messages, and attached files require special handling by Internet software. Netscape Navigator 2.0's default settings will work fine in most cases, but if somebody complains that a binary file you attached to a message was corrupt or wouldn't run, here's what to do:

1. Select Mail and News Preferences from the Options menu in the main window.

2. Select the Composition tab.

3. Click the MIME Compliant (Quoted Printable) radio button.

This makes Netscape Navigator 2.0 use an alternate method of encoding when it sends attached binary files.

DEALING WITH ATTACHED
FILES YOU RECEIVE

Not only does Netscape Navigator 2.0 let you attach all kinds of files to e-mail messages, it also includes special options for dealing with attached files that you receive. For instance, as I mentioned before, when you receive an image file, it is automatically displayed as an image.

But Netscape Navigator 2.0 cannot automatically handle every type of file you might receive. Obviously there are thousands of different file formats, and new ones come along every day. Although Netscape Navigator 2.0 can't possibly know about all these different file types, it includes a facility for using special *helper applications* to handle them. For example, if you receive a Microsoft Word document attached to an e-mail message, Netscape Navigator 2.0 will automatically launch Word, if it's available on your system.

If you're an advanced user, you can customize the way Netscape Navigator 2.0 associates particular types of files with different helper applications, but that topic is beyond the scope of this chapter. For a full discussion of helper applications, turn to the section "Helper Applications" in Chapter 6, "Getting Files via FTP." All of the information there applies to e-mail as well as FTP.

ORGANIZING YOUR MAIL FOLDERS

Once you start receiving lots of e-mail, your Inbox folder can get pretty crowded. Luckily, Netscape Navigator 2.0 lets you create new folders besides the Inbox. It also lets you move messages around from folder to folder. Maybe you want to distinguish between personal mail and business correspondence. You can create new folders called "Friends" and "Business" to help you keep them separate.

To create a new folder:

1. In the Netscape Mail window, select the New Folder option from the File menu. The New Folder dialog box appears, as shown in Figure 4-20.

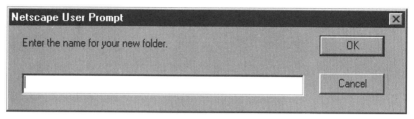

Figure 4-20: *New Folder dialog box.*

2. Enter a name such as **Friends** in the dialog box and press Enter.

The folder you just created will appear in the Folders pane alongside the Inbox folder, as shown in Figure 4-21.

Once you have created a new folder, you can move mail into it to organize your e-mail in the same way you organize files on your desktop into folders. There are several ways to move e-mail around:

■ You can move a piece of mail into a folder by dragging and dropping the letter icon from the Messages pane into the folder icon in the Folders pane.

■ You can use Move under Messages to move a selected letter or letters to another folder.

■ You can use Copy to copy selected mail while leaving a copy where it is as well.

What about removing e-mail you don't want to keep around any more? That's even easier!

1. Select one or more pieces of mail by clicking them.

2. Click the Delete button on the toolbar.

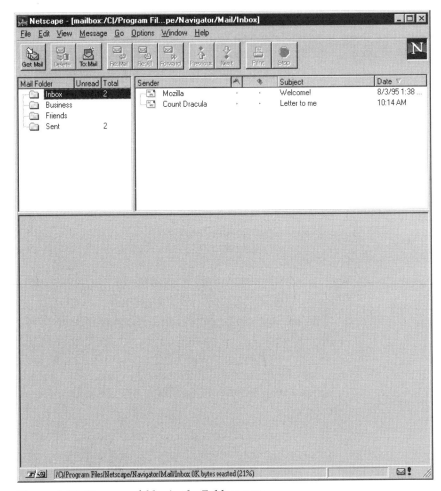

Figure 4-21: *Two new folder in the Folders pane.*

When you do this, a folder called Trash is created in the Folders pane. The Trash folder allows you to remove messages without making them unrecoverable. There are two ways to empty the Trash folder so that the e-mail in it is truly deleted.

1. Click the Trash folder in the folders pane. You should now see a list of messages to be trashed.

2. Select all the messages you want to delete.

3. Click Delete on the toolbar.

> **TIP**
>
> *If you don't need to look at the mail in the Trash folder before deleting it, selecting Empty Trash Folder from the File menu deletes all the mail in the Trash folder.*

SORTING E-MAIL MESSAGES WITHIN FOLDERS

Folders provide a convenient way to sort mail into broad categories, but you still need ways to sort different pieces of mail within a folder. The Messages pane provides several ways to do this:

- By default, mail in a folder is sorted in chronological order, with the earliest mail at the top of the folder and the latest mail at the bottom. To sort alphabetically by subject, click on the Subject bar at the top of the message pane, as shown in Figure 4-22. Note that the program ignores any "Re:"s when sorting by subject.

Sender			Subject ▽	Date
Ewan Kirk	·	◆		11/22/95 2:51...
Rayman, Graham	·	◆		12/18/95 14:4...
Joergen Knudsen	·	◆		12/22/95 13:5...
Kim Scheinberg	·	◆		Wed 14:07 PM
TOM@ecw.org	·	◆	Re: "turtles all the...	12/14/95 16:1...
Phil James	·	◆	(Fwd) screen shots...	Wed 13:16 PM
MANHEIMER K...	·	◆	:revision	12/14/95 14:4...
Jason Chervokas	·	◆	@NY Vol. 1, No. 10	Fri 20:34 PM
Hendra Agusnar	·	◆	<FTP EMAIL> resp...	9:29 AM
cardmaster@big...	·	◆	500White	12/14/95 14:1...
Danny Burstein	·	◆	a bunch of consult...	Fri 15:00 PM
Cameron Laird	·	◆	Re: A journalist wo...	Mon 17:26 PM
Wordsmith	·	◆	A.Word.A.Day--de...	Fri 0:28 AM
Wordsmith	·	◆	A.Word.A.Day--jan...	12/17/95 0:28...
geordie pace	·	◆	Re: ads;lfjghakdsf...	Fri 15:02 PM
Nick Routledge	·	◆	Alchemy and Addi...	10/20/95 14:2...
outlawyer@cris....	·	◆	alt.hate	12/17/95 19:4...
Imagesmith	·	◆	Alt.hate feedback	12/16/95 22:2...

Figure 4-22: *Mail sorted by subject.*

■ You can also sort by sender name, as shown in Figure 4-23. To do this, simply click the Sender bar.

Sender ▽	▲	◆	Subject	Date
Alan Sondheim	·	◆	Voices from the Net	5/28/95 22:19...
Andrea Kimmich...	·	◆	greetings	12/8/95 12:39...
Andrea Kimmich...	·	◆	internship opportu...	Thu 16:15 PM
andrew (a.m.) w...	·	◆	Re: Forbidden wor...	Fri 11:35 AM
Andrew Funk	·	◆	Re: Your book...	12/8/95 12:06...
Arnold Dreyblatt	·	◆	Re: Arnold Dreyblatt	11/16/95 15:5...
autoreply	·	◆	Solaris 2.5 x86 Ha...	Fri 8:44 AM
Barbara Hamel	·	◆	Re: An odd request	12/30/95 23:4...
Bo Bradham	·	◆	Re: An interesting ...	Tue 14:07 PM
Bowe, Marisa	·	◆	Re: Last Invoice	12/14/95 13:1...
Bowe, Marisa	·	◆	Re: net.hate	12/18/95 13:1...
Bowe, Marisa	·	◆	Re[2]: bye (fwd)	12/19/95 17:2...
Bruce Tindall	·	◆	Re: Forbidden wor...	Fri 11:12 AM
Cameron Laird	·	◆	Re: A journalist wo...	Mon 17:26 PM
cardmaster@big...	·	◆	the subject?	12/13/95 16:5...
cardmaster@big...	·	◆	500White	12/14/95 14:1...
cati laporte	·	◆	check out the smo...	10/17/95 20:5...
Christoph Rodatz	·	◆	Internet and Theat...	5/12/95 9:40 ...

Figure 4-23: *Mail sorted by sender.*

TRAP

Clicking Sender sorts your messages in alphabetical order by the first character in the From line, whether it is a first name or a last name. This can make your message list confusing.

■ You can reverse any of these sorting tools by selecting Ascending in the Sort menu under View. This makes date sorting run from most recent to earliest, and alphabetical sorting run from Z to A, as shown in Figure 4-24.

Messages can also be sorted by Subject, Date, Sender, or by thread (shared subject field).

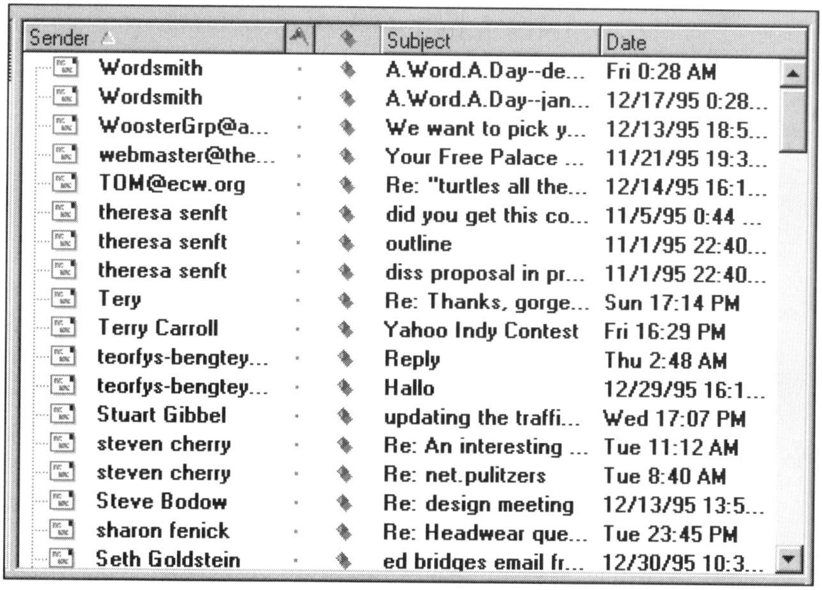

Sender ▲		◆	Subject	Date
Wordsmith	·	◆	A.Word.A.Day--de...	Fri 0:28 AM
Wordsmith	·	◆	A.Word.A.Day--jan...	12/17/95 0:28...
WoosterGrp@a...	·	◆	We want to pick y...	12/13/95 18:5...
webmaster@the...	·	◆	Your Free Palace ...	11/21/95 19:3...
TOM@ecw.org	·	◆	Re: "turtles all the...	12/14/95 16:1...
theresa senft	·	◆	did you get this co...	11/5/95 0:44 ...
theresa senft	·	◆	outline	11/1/95 22:40...
theresa senft	·	◆	diss proposal in pr...	11/1/95 22:40...
Tery	·	◆	Re: Thanks, gorge...	Sun 17:14 PM
Terry Carroll	·	◆	Yahoo Indy Contest	Fri 16:29 PM
teorfys-bengtey...	·	◆	Reply	Thu 2:48 AM
teorfys-bengtey...	·	◆	Hallo	12/29/95 16:1...
Stuart Gibbel	·	◆	updating the traffi...	Wed 17:07 PM
steven cherry	·	◆	Re: An interesting ...	Tue 11:12 AM
steven cherry	·	◆	Re: net.pulitzers	Tue 8:40 AM
Steve Bodow	·	◆	Re: design meeting	12/13/95 13:5...
sharon fenick	·	◆	Re: Headwear que...	Tue 23:45 PM
Seth Goldstein		◆	ed bridges email fr...	12/30/95 10:3...

Figure 4-24: *Mail sorted by name in reverse order.*

■ Selecting Thread Messages from the Sort menu (under the View menu) selects all messages in the same folder that are grouped together by a shared Subject line, such as an original letter and a number of replies to it.

CHANGING THE DEFAULT SORTING OPTIONS

There are two mail sorting options that you can access by selecting Mail and News Preferences from the Options menu and then choosing the Organization tab. You can sort your mail by *threading*, which means that all messages with a shared subject line will be grouped together automatically. You can also change the default sorting Netscape Navigator 2.0 provides when you open the Mail window. As you've seen, sorting by date is the default, but you can change the default to sorting by subject or by name.

MAILING LISTS

Internet e-mail is not just for exchanging private messages. It can also be used for gigantic group conversations among Internet users via an Internet service known as *mailing lists.*

A mailing list is simply a list of the e-mail addresses of everyone who wants to send and receive mail about a certain topic. There are mailing lists for discussing bonsai trees, rap music, adoption, cars, computer software, folk dancing, and on and on. There are thousands of lists, with new ones being created every week.

Adding your e-mail address to a mailing list is a way of joining these conversations. This is called *subscribing*, and removing your e-mail address from such a list is called *unsubscribing.* Once you've subscribed to a list, any mail you send to the list address gets sent back out to all the other e-mail addresses included on the list, and any mail from any of the other subscribers also gets sent to you.

When you subscribe to a mailing list, you immediately begin receiving mail from the other subscribers. If, after reading what other people on the list are talking about for a few days, you have something to add, you send mail back to the list address, and everyone else on the list sees your message.

So how do you find out what mailing lists are out there, and how to subscribe to them? The closest thing the Net has to an official list is Stephanie da Silva's list of Publicly Accessible Mailing Lists, originally created by Chuq Von Rospach. This list is an impressive compendium of mailing lists with a name, a short description, and information on how to subscribe for each one. The list itself is currently in 17 parts, arranged alphabetically and stored on a machine at MIT.

How do you retrieve this list of lists? Simple, you use Netscape Mail:

1. From the main Netscape Navigator 2.0 window, select New Mail Message from the File menu (or simply press Ctrl+N). The New Message Composition window appears.

2. Enter **mail-server@rtfm.mit.edu** in the Mail To field.

3. Enter **Mailing Lists** in the Subject field. (Do this for your own information. The MIT mail-server doesn't care what's in the Subject field.)

4. Type only one line in the body of the message:

`send pub/usenet/news.answers/mail/mailing-lists/part01`

Your completed message should look like the one in Figure 4-25.

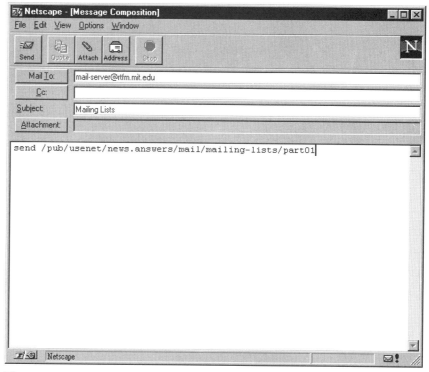

Figure 4-25: *Mail ready to go to the MIT mail server.*

This message instructs the MIT mail server, a kind of electronic file clerk, to send you Part 1 of the list. The list is large, and Part 1 shows you the names of all the mailing lists described in the other 16 parts, so take a look and make sure it's something you're interested in.

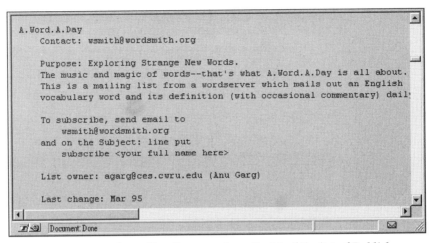

```
A.Word.A.Day
    Contact: wsmith@wordsmith.org

    Purpose: Exploring Strange New Words.
    The music and magic of words--that's what A.Word.A.Day is all about.
    This is a mailing list from a wordserver which mails out an English
    vocabulary word and its definition (with occasional commentary) daily

    To subscribe, send email to
        wsmith@wordsmith.org
    and on the Subject: line put
        subscribe <your full name here>

    List owner: agarg@ces.cwru.edu (Anu Garg)

    Last change: Mar 95
```

Figure 4-26: *A sample mailing list entry from Part 1 of the list of Publicly Accessible Mailing Lists.*

If there are mailing lists you'd like to subscribe to, send another piece of mail to mail-server@rtfm.mit.edu with just this line:

```
send pub/usenet/news.answers/mail/mailing-lists/part*
```

The asterisk there instead of an actual number means "Send me all the files." You should then receive 17 pieces of mail, containing the whole file cut into parts, with all the information you need to subscribe to mailing lists.

USING MAILING LISTS

There are a few differences between sending and receiving mail from a mailing list and sending and receiving personal mail, because mailing lists are a public forum. When you send a message to a mailing list, you don't even know how many people are reading it, much less who all of them are. This changes the way people read and write e-mail. Mailing lists are famous for long-running, voluminous, and often quite heated exchanges of e-mail, and because they are public forums, there are different rules of conduct there.

MAILING LIST ETIQUETTE

- **Read before you write.**   This is Rule #1. Before you send e-mail to a mailing list, remember that you are writing for a particular audience, and make sure that what you have to say is relevant. The rule of thumb when dealing with mailing lists is to read what other people are saying for a about a week before sending any mail yourself, to make sure that any questions or comments you might have are pertinent. (Reading a list without posting is called *lurking*.)

- **Don't waste people's time.**   This advice seems self-evident, but you will often see people posting mail that adds nothing to the discussion. Don't jump into a conversation just to tell everyone you agree with what someone else has said. If you are quoting another person's message, only quote what is relevant to your point. Nothing wastes people's time more than scrolling through screen after screen of a message they have already read once, only to read "I think you are completely correct" at the end.

- **Use private e-mail when appropriate.**   When you read something posted to a mailing list, you have a choice between replying to the writer in private or sending your reply to the entire list. If you merely want to say you agree, or ask where you can get a copy of something mentioned in the post, send e-mail to the writer instead of to the list.

- **Use the Subject line carefully.**   As with private e-mail, the Subject line is the first thing anyone sees in mail from you, and it tells people whether they are interested in what you have to say. Use the Subject line to describe, as succinctly as possible, the contents of your mail.

One of the main differences between mailing list mail and personal mail is that when you want to reply to a message, you have a choice between replying only to the author of the article or sending the reply out to the whole list. If you have something to add to the debate, you should send your mail to the list, but if you just want to say that you agree with what someone has said, send it to the author only. The best way to tell what's appropriate is to read what other people are posting to the list to see what kinds of things are being discussed in public.

When replying to something you have read on a mailing list, make sure to examine the Mail To field of your outgoing mail. Different mailing lists handle the return address differently. On some lists, when you use the Reply function, the Mail To field is set up assuming that you want to send mail out to the whole mailing list, while on others it is set up assuming that you want to reply only to the author of the original post. If you want to reply to the whole group, you would select Reply to All.

TIP

Checking the Mail To line of your mail before you reply will prevent you from sending mail you meant to be private to everyone on the list or from sending mail you meant to be public only to one other person.

One concept that you will sometimes hear discussed on mailing lists is the *signal-to-noise ratio*. This is an engineering term that has been pressed into service to describe the percentage of messages sent to any given mailing list that are useful or interesting. Lists where there is generally an engaged and articulate discussion going on are said to have a high signal-to-noise ratio, while lists where the subscribers are posting messages needlessly are said to have a low signal-to-noise ratio. Good mailing list etiquette helps create a high signal-to-noise ratio. As with regular e-mail, there are a few general guidelines for etiquette on mailing lists.

USING NETSCAPE NAVIGATOR 2.0 WITH MICROSOFT EXCHANGE

This chapter has shown you how to use Netscape Navigator 2.0's excellent e-mail features to send messages to anyone on the Net. But what if you're already using Microsoft Exchange, the e-mail client that comes with Windows 95? You might already have spent hours configuring it to behave just the way you want, and why should you go through that process all over again?

No problem! Simply select Mail and News Preferences from the Options menu and then go to the Appearance tab. At the bottom of the tab, you can select the Use Exchange Client for Mail and News radio button. You'll never see the Netscape Mail window again.

But how does this work? Well, suppose you are viewing a Web document that has a Mail To link in it. When you click the link, you will now see Exchange instead of Netscape Navigator 2.0's Message Composition window. And even if you select New Mail Message from Netscape Navigator 2.0's File menu, you'll find yourself in Exchange.

MOVING ON

In this chapter, you've learned about using Netscape Navigator 2.0 to exchange e-mail with other Internet users, and you've worked with some of the program's powerful messaging features. In the next chapter, you'll learn another way to communicate with others on the Net: Usenet News. Like e-mail, News is a way of sending and receiving messages, but where mail is usually private, News provides a public forum. Netscape Navigator 2.0 also includes a separate interface, similar to the Netscape Mail window, just for handling News.

chapter five

Newsgroups

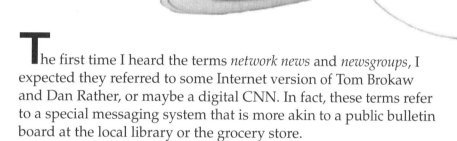

The first time I heard the terms *network news* and *newsgroups*, I expected they referred to some Internet version of Tom Brokaw and Dan Rather, or maybe a digital CNN. In fact, these terms refer to a special messaging system that is more akin to a public bulletin board at the local library or the grocery store.

It turns out that Netscape Navigator 2.0 is not only the best World Wide Web browser around but is also a top-notch *news reader*—a program that enables you to access and participate in newsgroups. After reading this chapter, you'll be able to read and respond to newsgroup articles and begin your own discussions. This chapter introduces you to *Usenet* (the "official" name for network news and newsgroups) and explains how to use Netscape Navigator 2.0 to get all the "news" that is fit to "print"—as well as some that might make Tom and Dan and maybe even Ted Turner blush!

INTRODUCTION TO USENET

Before we look at how to use Netscape as a news reader, let's take a quick look at Usenet itself.

WHAT IS IT & HOW DOES IT WORK?

Usenet (also known as Netnews) was originally developed for UNIX systems in 1979. It has become a worldwide network of thousands of Usenet sites, known as *news hosts* or *news servers*, running many operating systems (such as UNIX, MS-DOS, and Windows NT) on various types of computers. Millions of people share messages electronically over these Usenet sites. The messages are sent from news server to news server using UNIX-to-UNIX Copy Protocol (UUCP).

People post their Usenet messages or articles to categories known as newsgroups instead of to individuals (as would be the case with e-mail). A newsgroup is a great place to exchange ideas, ask questions, or discuss opinions and experiences. It's the place to learn what both your neighbor next door and someone in Moscow you've never met think about almost any subject imaginable. Everyone who subscribes to a newsgroup can read and respond to the articles posted there. Popular newsgroup categories include computers (of course), business, biology, recreation, science, social issues, miscellaneous, and alternative discussions.

Individual discussions posted to a particular newsgroup are known as *threads*. I post a message. You post a response. Someone else responds to your response. And so it goes. Generally speaking, all threads posted to a particular newsgroup share a common theme: music, cars, sports, electronics, and so on.

Most newsgroups are unmoderated, which means subscribers may post directly to the newsgroup. In moderated newsgroups, a moderator screens the messages and posts only messages deemed of interest to other subscribers.

Usenet servers don't have to be connected to the Internet; many are not. But because thousands of Usenet sites do have access to the Internet, the Internet has become the most commonly used electronic postal route for network news. The total number of distinct newsgroups on the Internet is in the thousands and growing daily. Consequently, millions of people who may have started using the Internet to gain access to the World Wide Web or to the Internet's electronic mail find that they can participate in Usenet newsgroups as well, provided they have the right client software. News servers on the Internet use Network News Transfer Protocol (NNTP) to communicate with client software. Luckily for you, Netscape Navigator 2.0 knows NNTP.

Before you can use Netscape Navigator 2.0 to access newsgroups, you must do two things:

1. **Obtain access to a news server**. Generally speaking, most Internet service providers (ISPs) run news servers. If you haven't already done so, ask your ISP for the name of the news server to which you have access (the name will be something like *news.myisp.com*). Later in this chapter (in the "Configuring Network News" section), you'll learn how to configure Netscape Navigator 2.0 to access this news server.

2. **Subscribe to one or more newsgroups**. Subscribing to a newsgroup is nothing more than adding it to the list of newsgroups you want your news reader software (Netscape Navigator 2.0 in this case) to check each time you go online. Follow the procedures described in this chapter (in the "Subscribing & Unsubscribing to Newsgroups" section) to subscribe to newsgroups.

HOW MANY NEWSGROUPS CAN I GET?

How many angels can dance on the head of a pin? Nobody knows, and the same is true regarding the total number of newsgroups available at any time via the Internet. To impose some order on the basically anarchic structure of Usenet, newsgroups have a fairly strict hierarchical naming convention. Newsgroup names look similar to Internet addresses, and are a series of words or abbreviations separated by dots:

```
rec.arts.movies.reviews
```

The first word in the name denotes the major category to which the newsgroup belongs. A few of the major, hierarchical categories of Usenet newsgroups are:

- **alt.** *Alternative* newsgroups contain articles that are often very interesting, but can be on the controversial side, if not downright disgusting. Reader beware! This major category alone accounts for thousands of Usenet newsgroups.

- **comp.** *Computer* newsgroups discuss computer-related issues.

- **misc.** The *miscellaneous* newsgroups category (as you no doubt have guessed) is a catch-all category for discussions that don't fit into one of the other categories.

- **news.** The *news* category is for newsgroups discussing Usenet network news itself. These newsgroups are a great source of information about Usenet.

- **rec.** *Recreation* newsgroups discuss recreation, sports, and the arts.

- **sci.** *Science* newsgroups cover scientific topics.

- **soc.** *Social* newsgroups focus on issues of perceived social importance.

- **talk.** If you like good arguments, *talk* newsgroups are the place for you.

Newsgroups in these categories are usually distributed world-wide. Originally, Usenet consisted only of the newsgroups comp, news, rec, sci, soc, talk, and misc. All other newsgroups were referred to as *alternative* newsgroups. The term Usenet is now more commonly used to refer to the collection of all newsgroups

Other major categories that may be distributed throughout the world include bionet (biology newsgroups), biz (business newsgroups), and vmsnet (discussions about the VMS computer operating system). Many other topical major categories are usually distributed around the world as well. Geographical, organizational, and commercial newsgroups are usually distributed only within their area of interest.

Newsgroups in the *bit* major category are actually an alternative distribution method for Bitnet LISTSERV mailing lists. Conversely, many newsgroups also distribute articles via mailing lists to users who don't have access to a news server. In effect, the pertinent messages are mailed to the user's electronic mail box, enabling the user to get network news via a simple dial-up Internet e-mail account.

Because of the sheer volume of Usenet traffic, and due to the timely nature of much of newsgroup content, most newsgroups put a limit on the number of days an article will be available for reading. Past the time limit, an article is said to have expired and is removed from the newsgroup. The time limit varies from newsgroup to newsgroup, but many longstanding newsgroups keep archives of expired articles.

Do you have access to all the newsgroups on the Internet? Maybe, maybe not, depending on your news server. Later in this chapter, we'll see how to get a list of all the newsgroups available through your server.

The best way to gain an understanding of Usenet news is to browse through several newsgroups, reading the messages but not responding. This practice is affectionately known as *lurking.* In this case, lurking for a while makes a lot of sense. Before you know it, you'll feel compelled to jump in there and participate in the conversation.

CONFIGURING NETSCAPE NEWS

Even though you're probably anxious to try your hand at network news, there's still a little bit of housekeeping we need to take care of. Before Netscape Navigator 2.0 can access news, you have to give it the name of your news server. While you're at it, you may also want to configure the way news is displayed.

SPECIFYING YOUR NETWORK NEWS SERVER

Because Usenet is a network of news servers, you need access to one or more of these servers in order to participate in network news. The server uses the NNTP protocol to communicate with Netscape Navigator 2.0's news reader. The server keeps track of which articles have been posted to which newsgroups. Netscape Navigator 2.0 keeps track of the newsgroups in which you are interested as well as the articles you have read.

To specify a news server:

1. Double-click the Netscape Navigator 2.0 icon to launch the program. The main window appears. If you are connected to the Internet, the Netscape home page starts loading as shown in Figure 5-1.

   ■   You need not be online to configure Netscape News. If you're not connected to the Internet, simply click the Stop button in the main Netscape window so that the program will stop trying to load the Netscape home page.

Figure 5-1: *The main Netscape Browser window displaying the Netscape home page.*

TIP

By default, Netscape Navigator 2.0 starts in the Browser window and attempts to load the Netscape home page. This behavior can be changed to (1) start in either Netscape Mail or Netscape News and (2) load a blank page rather than the home page. To display the screen where you can make these changes, select General Preferences from the Options menu and click the Appearance tab.

2. In the Netscape Navigator 2.0 main window, choose Mail and News Preferences from the Options menu. Netscape displays the Preferences dialog box, as shown in Figure 5-2. The tab last accessed will be displayed.

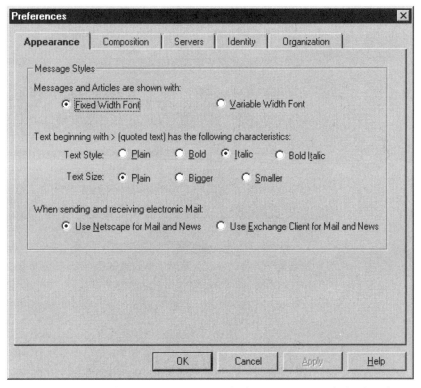

Figure 5-2: *The Preferences dialog box with the Appearance tab displayed.*

3. Click the Servers tab, as shown in Figure 5-3.

4. In the text box labeled News (NNTP) Server, type the name of the news server you will be using. If you don't know this address, obtain it from your ISP or from your system administrator (if you are configuring Netscape News on your computer at work).

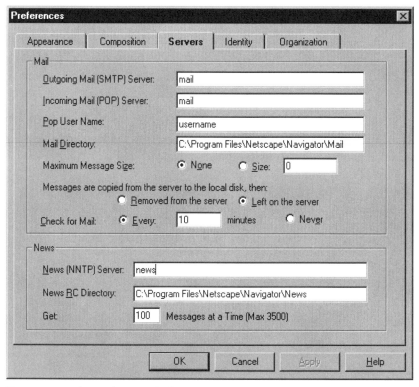

Figure 5-3: *The Preferences dialog box with the Servers tab displayed.*

5. As we mentioned earlier, your news reader software keeps track of your favorite newsgroups as well as the articles you've already read. Most news reader programs store this information using a standard format in a file known as a NEWS.RC file.

If you are an experienced Internet user, you may already have been using another news reader to get your network news. To avoid the hassle of resubscribing to your favorite newsgroups, just point Netscape Navigator 2.0 to the NEWS.RC file generated by your previous news reader. Type the full path of the directory containing NEWS.RC in the News RC Directory text box. If you've never used a news reader, just accept the default setting. Netscape Navigator 2.0 will create a new *newsrc* file and automatically subscribe you to three newsgroups that contain articles of particular interest to new Usenet users. As you subscribe to newsgroups, Netscape Navigator 2.0 stores this information in NEWS.RC.

6. If you are interested in configuring other Netscape News characteristics, such as font width, proceed to the next section in this chapter. Otherwise, you are finished specifying a news server. Click the OK button in the Preferences dialog box to confirm any changes you made and return to the main Netscape Navigator 2.0 window.

TIP

Although most people have access to only one news server, you may have access to multiple news servers. To open a news server other than the one listed in the Servers tab of the Preferences dialog box, choose Open News Host from the News window's File menu and specify the server's name.

You are now ready to take a look at network news. You might want to skim through the sections that describe how to configure Netscape News, but you probably don't need to change the default settings. Then proceed to the "Subscribing to & Unsubscribing From Newsgroups" section to try out your first newsgroup.

CONFIGURING THE WAY
YOUR NEWS IS DISPLAYED

One of the most obvious improvements in personal computers over the past 10 years has been the advent of *graphical user interfaces* (GUIs) such as Windows. A hallmark of GUIs is the capability to display text in multiple typefaces (fonts). Later versions of Windows and all versions of the Mac operating system are capable of displaying fonts in which each character has a unique width (*variable width,* also known as *proportional spacing*), rather than all characters having the same width (*fixed width,* also known as *monospacing*). You are used to seeing proportional spacing in most printed material, such as books, magazines, and newspapers.

Netscape Navigator 2.0 gives you the option of displaying newsgroup messages in either variable-width or fixed-width spacing. Usenet was developed several years before the IBM PC was introduced and almost 10 years before proportional spacing was introduced to PC users in Windows. If you are a purist and would prefer to view newsgroup articles in their "natural" state—fixed-width spacing—you have that option with Navigator.

Since news articles are often a continuation of an ongoing discussion (that is, another article in the same thread), articles often include quoted portions of earlier articles in the same discussion. News reader programs typically denote quoted sections of text by placing an angle bracket (>)at the left margin. Netscape Navigator 2.0 enables you to control the font style and size of these quoted sections as well.

Since electronic mail messages and network news messages are closely related in purpose, Netscape's Mail window and News window are very similar. When you configure the appearance of your network news, you are also configuring the appearance of your e-mail.

To set how Netscape Navigator 2.0 displays news and e-mail:

1. Select Mail and News Preferences from the Options menu. Click the Appearance tab.

2. If you want text displayed in a fixed-width font (the default option), click the Fixed Width Font option button. If you prefer variable-width spacing, click the Variable Width Font option button. (*Note:* You can select the font itself using the Display properties dialog in the Windows Control Panel.)

3. Choose from among the following options to determine how Netscape News will display quoted text in e-mail messages and news articles:

   ■ Plain

   ■ **Bold**

   ■ *Italic*

   ■ ***Bold Italic***

4. Select one of the following options to determine the size of quoted text:

   ■ Plain

   ■ Bigger

   ■ Smaller

5. Click the OK button to save the selections you have made.

USING THE MICROSOFT EXCHANGE MAIL & NEWS CLIENTS

Windows 95 includes an Internet mail client called Exchange that can be set up to provide a universal inbox for all your electronic correspondence. If you would prefer to use Microsoft Exchange, rather than Netscape Navigator 2.0, as your mail client and news reader, choose the Use Exchange Client for Mail and News option on the Appearance tab of the Preferences dialog box. Refer to your Windows 95 documentation for instructions on setting up and configuring Exchange as your Internet mail and news client.

STORING NEWS

As you have learned, e-mail messages and network news articles are closely related. Navigator's facilities for the two types of messages are nearly identical. However, one significant difference between e-mail and news is in where incoming messages are stored. While you have the option to store e-mail messages on the server or on your local hard disk, incoming news articles always reside on the server. The news reader displays them to your screen during an online session, but doesn't keep a copy on your hard disk. If you like, you can save an article using the Save As option from the File menu, but Navigator does not do so automatically.

Even though Netscape Navigator 2.0 doesn't automatically keep a copy of news articles that you have read, you may want to have Netscape Navigator 2.0 automatically save a copy of all articles that you post to a newsgroup. You can choose to e-mail a copy to yourself, to add the article to a running text file, or both.

To change how Navigator handles copies of outgoing news articles:

1. Choose Mail and News Preferences from the Options menu. Netscape Navigator 2.0 displays the Preferences dialog box.

2. Click the Composition tab to display the dialog shown in Figure 5-4.

3. To have a copy of each outgoing news article sent to a particular e-mail address, type the address in the News Messages text box.

4. To have the contents of each outgoing article copied to a specific text file stored on your computer, type the full path and name of the file in the News File text box. Each news article you send will be added to the end of the file.

5. Click the OK button to save your changes and return to the Netscape window.

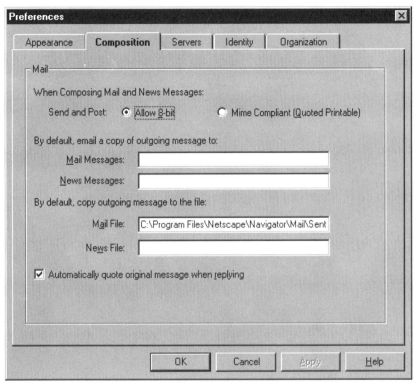

Figure 5-4: *The Preferences dialog box with the Composition tab displayed.*

CONFIGURING THREADING & SORTING

As you may recall, a series of news articles on the same topic is called a thread. Usually the articles in a thread make sense only if they are read together in chronological order. Netscape Navigator 2.0 makes it very easy to see the relationship between related articles and to follow the thread of the discussion. But this threading feature is an option, and in order to use it, you must first turn it on.

Netscape Navigator 2.0 also enables you to choose how you want messages sorted: by date, by subject, or by sender. You can configure the threading feature and the sort order from the same configuration window.

To activate the newsgroup threading feature and select a sorting order:

1. Choose Mail and News Preferences from the Options menu. Netscape displays the Preferences dialog box.

2. Click the Organization tab to display the dialog shown in Figure 5-5.

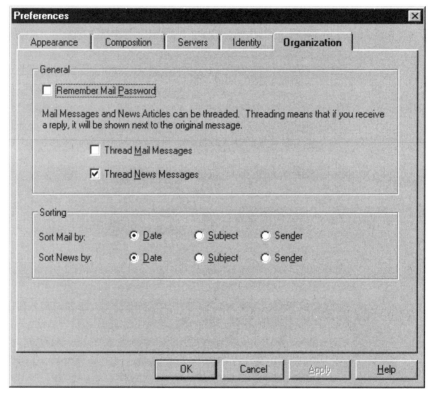

Figure 5-5: *The Preferences dialog box with the Organization tab displayed.*

3. Click the Thread News Messages check box to have articles in the same thread listed together, in chronological order. If you don't activate this option, Netscape Navigator 2.0's news reader will list newsgroup articles in the order received.

- As an alternative way to toggle the threading feature, select the Sort option from the View menu and then choose Thread Messages.

4. You can also specify how articles will be sorted by choosing the Date, Subject, or Sender option button. If you have chosen the Thread News Messages check box, you probably should sort messages by subject, at least for starters. You can change the sort order later if you like. If you choose to sort articles by date, by sender, or by message number you will still see the articles in each thread grouped together on the screen, but the order in which the threads appear (as well as the order of the articles within each thread) will be by date, sender, or message number, as you specified.

5. Click the OK button to save the changes you have made and return to the Netscape window.

ARRANGING THE NEWSGROUP LIST, MESSAGE HEADING & MESSAGE PANES

You can also configure the arrangement of Netscape Navigator 2.0's News window. Before we do that, however, let's go online so that we'll have something to look at as we arrange the parts of the window:

1. Make sure you are connected to the Internet, either directly or through a SLIP or PPP connection with your access provider. If you are using a SLIP or PPP connection and are not currently connected, click the Dial-Up Connection icon for your access provider (or if you are not using the Windows 95 Internet software, click the icon you use to connect to your ISP).

   - If you are using Windows 3.1 rather than Windows 95, or if you are not using Windows 95's built-in networking, follow the instructions that came with your TCP/IP software for accessing the Internet.

2. If Netscape Navigator 2.0 isn't already running, click the Netscape Navigator 2.0 icon to launch the program. The main Netscape (browser) window appears, and the Netscape home page starts loading.

3. Select Netscape News from the Window menu to display the main News window, shown in Figure 5-6.

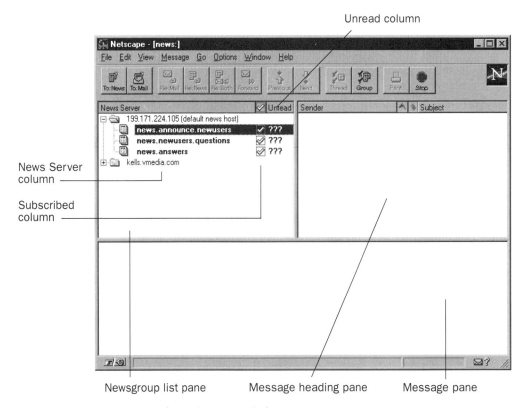

Figure 5-6: *The main News window.*

The main News window is divided into three panels: the *newsgroup list pane* in the upper left portion of the window; the *message heading pane* at upper right; and the *message pane* across the bottom. This screen is almost identical to the Mail window that you learned about in Chapter 4, "Netscape Mail." You can control the size of each pane by placing the mouse pointer on a panel border and dragging the pointer in the appropriate direction.

ARRANGING THE NEWSGROUP LIST PANE

Obviously, the *newsgroup list pane* lists newsgroups. The first time you use Netscape News, the program lists your news server in the News Server column of the newsgroup list pane and lists three newsgroups intended to provide helpful information to new users of Usenet network news: *news.announce.newusers*, *news.newusers*, and *news.answers*. (If, during configuration, you specified the location of your NEWS.RC file, Netscape News also lists the newsgroups to which you're subscribed.)

The newsgroup list pane has four columns:

■ **News Server**. This column lists one or more news servers. By default, it lists the news server you specified when you configured Netscape News. If you know of other news servers to which you have access, you can add them to this list in the Newsgroup window by selecting Open News Host from the File menu and typing the news server's name in the dialog that opens. Each available news server is denoted by a folder icon at the left margin of the Newsgroup list pane.

■ **Subscribed**. The Subscribed column (the one with the checkmark at the top) contains an icon that resembles a checkmark if you are subscribed to a newsgroup.

■ **Unread**. This column contains a number in each row that indicates the number of articles in the respective newsgroup that you have yet to read.

■ **Total**. This column indicates the total number of articles in the newsgroup.

You can control the width of each column by placing the mouse pointer on the right or left border of the column heading and dragging it in the appropriate direction.

ARRANGING THE MESSAGE HEADING PANE

So that we can examine the message headings and message panes of the window, let's display a message from the *news.announce. newusers* newsgroup:

1. In the Newsgroup list pane, click the *news.announce.newusers* newsgroup icon. In the message heading pane, Netscape News displays a message heading for each article currently found in this newsgroup. Figure 5-7 shows 11 message headings.

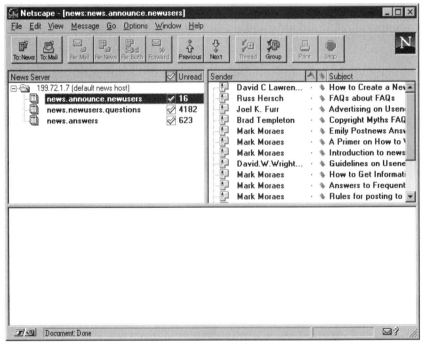

Figure 5-7: *The News window with the news.announce.newusers newsgroup selected.*

2. In the message heading pane, click one of the messages. Netscape News displays the selected article in the message pane.

The message heading pane provides information about each article that may be helpful when you're trying to determine which article to read. This information is displayed in five columns:

- **Sender**. This column lists the name of the individual who posted the article to the newsgroup.

- **Flagged**. The flagged column contains a flag icon if you have *flagged* the article using the Flag Message option in the message pane. This feature is discussed in "Flagging Articles To Be Read Later" later in this chapter.

- **Read**. The Read column contains a green diamond if you haven't yet read the article.

- **Subject**. This column lists the subject of the article. The subject of each article was assigned by the article's author.

- **Date**. This column lists the date and time the article was posted to the newsgroup.

You can control the width of each column by placing the mouse pointer on the right or left border of the column heading and dragging the border in the appropriate direction.

You have learned already that you can establish a default sort order for articles in the message heading pane. You can also instantly sort the list again using either of two methods:

- Choose Sort from the View menu and click by Date, by Subject, by Sender, or by Message Number; or

- In the message heading pane, click the Sender, Subject, or Date column heading.

Navigator puts a downward pointer in the column heading of the column by which articles are currently sorted.

By default, the message headings are sorted in descending order. To sort in ascending order, choose Sort from the View menu and click the Ascending option. To toggle off this option, returning to descending order, repeat the same step.

ARRANGING THE MESSAGE PANE

The message pane displays *header* information at the top of each article. By default, the message pane lists the article's Subject, Date, From, Organization, Newsgroups, and References header information (see Figure 5-8).

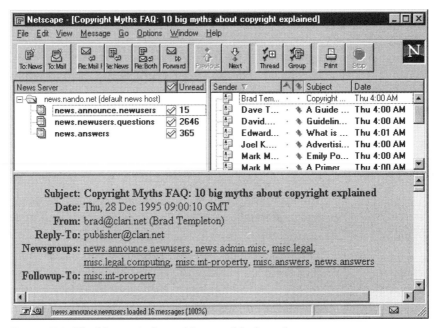

Figure 5-8: *The News window with an article from the news.announce.newusers newsgroup selected.*

To display additional header information, select the Show All Headers option on the Options menu (see Figure 5-9).

You can control the size of the message pane by placing the mouse pointer on one of its borders and dragging the border in the appropriate direction.

DETERMINING WHICH NEWSGROUPS & ARTICLES WILL DISPLAY

Since there are literally thousands of newsgroups and hundreds of thousands of news articles, there obviously must be ways for you to filter newsgroups and news articles and list a select few for your consideration. We have already discussed briefly the concept of subscribing to newsgroups, and we'll cover the procedure of subscribing to newsgroups in one of the next sections in this chapter. Netscape Navigator 2.0's Options menu also provides several other ways to help you keep the volume of news articles listed on your screen to a manageable level.

Use the following options on the News window's Options menu (shown in Figure 5-9) to control which newsgroups and articles (messages) are listed on your screen (note that tick marks indicate menu options that are currently active).

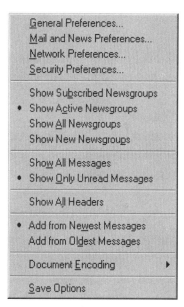

Figure 5-9: *The News window's Options menu.*

- **Show Subscribed Newsgroups**. This option causes Netscape News to list only newsgroups to which you have subscribed. With this option checked, Netscape News lists all subscribed newsgroups, even if they contain no unread articles.

- **Show Active Newsgroups**. This option lists only subscribed newsgroups that contain articles you have yet to read. This option is active by default.

- **Show All Newsgroups**. This option lists all the newsgroups currently available through your news server. We'll try this option out later in the chapter so that you can subscribe to a few more newsgroups. Be aware, however, that choosing this option causes Netscape Navigator 2.0 to download to your disk a file that may take a few minutes to retrieve.

- **Show New Newsgroups**. Choose this option when you want to list all newsgroups available through your news server that have been added since you last connected to the server.

- **Show All Messages**. This option causes Netscape News to list the message headings of all messages found in the selected newsgroup.

- **Show Only Unread Messages**. This option, active by default, lists in the message heading pane only unread messages from the selected newsgroup.

- **Add From Newest Messages.** This option, active by default, tells Netscape News to display the newest message headings from the current newsgroup first.

- **Add From Oldest Messages.** This option causes the oldest message headings to be listed first.

If you make any changes to these options and would like to establish your changes as the preferred configuration, select Save Options from the Options menu.

SUBSCRIBING TO & UNSUBSCRIBING FROM NEWSGROUPS

The concept of subscribing to network newsgroups is a bit of a misnomer. You don't really subscribe to newsgroups as you might subscribe to a magazine. If your news server has access to a particular newsgroup, then so do you. In the Usenet context, subscribing to a newsgroup simply involves instructing your news reader—Netscape News, in this case—to list articles from that newsgroup in the News window.

DEFAULT NEWSGROUPS

The first time you use Netscape News, the program lists your news server in the News Server column of the newsgroup list pane and lists three newsgroups: *news.announce.newusers*, *news.newusers.questions*, and *news.answers* (see Figure 5-10), assuming of course that these newsgroups are available through your news server. These newsgroups are specifically intended to provide helpful information to new users of Usenet network news. (*Note:* If, during configuration, you specified the location of your NEWS.RC file, Netscape News lists the newsgroups to which you're subscribed.)

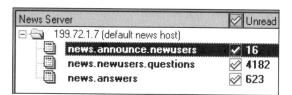

Figure 5-10: *The default newsgroups in the newsgroup list pane of the News window.*

Notice that a checkmark in a newsgroup's Subscribed column indicates that you're subscribed to that newsgroup.

GETTING A LIST OF ALL NEWSGROUPS

Before you can subscribe to a newsgroup, you have to instruct Netscape News to display a list of all newsgroups available through your news server. To do so:

1. Make sure you are connected to the Internet, either directly or through a SLIP or PPP connection with your access provider. If you are using SLIP or PPP connection and are not currently connected, click the Dial-Up Connection icon for your access provider (or if you are not using the Windows 95 Internet software, click the icon you use to connect to your ISP).

   ■ If you are using Windows 3.1 rather than Windows 95, follow the instructions that came with your TCP/IP software for accessing the Internet.

2. If Netscape Navigator 2.0 isn't already running, click the Netscape Navigator 2.0 icon to launch the program. The main Netscape (browser) window appears, and the Netscape home page starts loading.

3. Select Netscape News from the Window menu to display the main News window.

4. Select Show All Newsgroups from the Options menu. Netscape News displays a message box, shown in Figure 5-11, informing you that it may take a few minutes to save the list of all newsgroups.

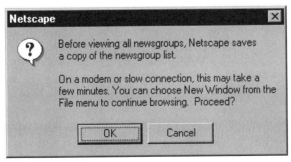

Figure 5-11: *Displaying the newsgroup list may take a few minutes.*

5. Click the OK button in the message box to proceed. Netscape Navigator 2.0 then retrieves from your news server a complete list of all newsgroups available via the server and displays this list in the newsgroup list pane of the News window, as shown in Figure 5-12.

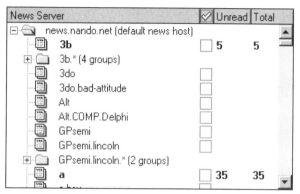

Figure 5-12: *The first page of all newsgroups available on the news.nando.net news server.*

Notice that Netscape News doesn't immediately show every available newsgroup in the newsgroup list pane. Using a screen design that resembles the Windows 95 Navigator (or Windows 3.1's File Manager), the list groups all newsgroups in folders by category. The first page of the list shown in Figure 5-12, for example, shows two categories of newsgroups: 3b.* and GPSemi.lincoln.*. The plus sign to the left of these folders indicates that each contains newsgroups that are not displayed. The number in parentheses (to the right of the folder's name) tells how many newsgroups there are in the folder.

Many newsgroups no longer contain active articles. When a newsgroup does contain active articles, Netscape News displays its name in a bold font and shows the number of unread articles and the total number of articles in this newsgroup in the Unread and Total columns, respectively.

To see a list of newsgroups in a category, scroll to the category and click the plus sign to the left of the category's folder icon.

Netscape News opens the folder and lists the newsgroups in the category. The major category may contain subcategories. In that case, Netscape News groups the subcategories into folders. Figure 5-13, for example, lists newsgroups in the news.* major category. This category contains several subcategories including news.admin.*, news.announce.*, and news.groups.*. Notice that we are already subscribed to the *news.answers* newsgroup.

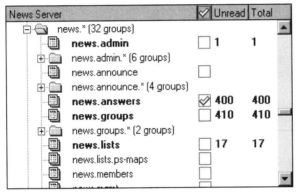

Figure 5-13: *The news.* category of newsgroups as listed in the newsgroup list pane of the News window.*

FINDING OUT ABOUT NEW NEWSGROUPS

If you completed the procedure described in the preceding section, you have discovered just how long it can take to display a complete list of all available newsgroups. Unless you enjoy watching grass grow, you probably don't want to download this list very often. But you probably do want to periodically find out about any new newsgroups that may have formed since the last time you checked. Here's how:

1. Make sure you are connected to the Internet, either directly or through a SLIP or PPP connection with your access provider, and launch Netscape Navigator 2.0. The main Netscape (browser) window appears, and the Netscape home page starts loading.

2. Select Netscape News from the Window menu to display the main News window.

3. Select Show New Newsgroups from the Options menu. Netscape News displays a message box, shown in Figure 5-14, telling you the number of newsgroups that have been added since you last checked. Netscape News adds the new newsgroups to the end of the list of subscribed newsgroups in the newsgroup list pane of the News window.

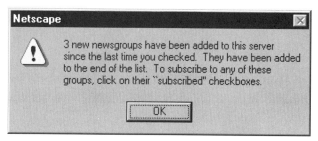

Figure 5-14: *A message about new newsgroups.*

Subscribing From the List

Once you have displayed a list of available newsgroups, it is very easy to subscribe to one. To subscribe, click the newsgroup's check box in the Subscribed column. Netscape News adds a subscribed (checkmark) icon to the check box.

Each time you open Netscape News, the program asks your news server to determine whether each of your subscribed newsgroups contains articles you haven't read. By default, Netscape News lists in the newsgroup list pane all subscribed newsgroups that contain unread articles. If you choose the Show Subscribed Newsgroups option from the Options menu, Netscape News will always list all newsgroups to which you have subscribed.

If you decide later that you're no longer interested in a particular newsgroup, just click the newsgroup's Sub column again to remove the subscribed icon. Netscape News will no longer list this newsgroup in the newsgroup list pane of the News window.

READING NEWS

Assuming that you have completed the steps described earlier in this chapter to configure Netscape News and to subscribe to newsgroups, you are ready to start reading news.

CHOOSING A GROUP

As you know, all network news articles are found in Usenet newsgroups, so before you can read the news, you need to choose a newsgroup. Follow these steps:

1. Make sure you are connected to the Internet, either directly or through a SLIP or PPP connection with your access provider. If you are using SLIP or PPP connection and are not currently connected, click the Dial-Up Connection icon for your access provider (or if you are not using the Windows 95 Internet software, click the icon you use to connect to your ISP).

   ■ If you are using Windows 3.1 rather than Windows 95, follow the instructions that came with your TCP/IP software for accessing the Internet.

2. If Netscape Navigator 2.0 isn't already running, click the Netscape Navigator 2.0 icon to launch the program. The main Netscape (browser) window appears and the Netscape home page starts loading.

3. Select Netscape News from the Window menu to display the main News window. By default, the News window lists all subscribed newsgroups that contain active articles, as shown in Figure 5-15.

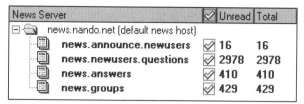

Figure 5-15: *The active newsgroups in the newsgroups list pane of the News window.*

4. Click one of the groups listed in the newsgroup list pane. Netscape News populates the message heading pane with the headings of all active articles in that group.

   In Figure 5-16, articles from the *news.groups* newsgroup are listed in the message heading pane. (**Note:** The message heading pane in Figure 5-16 is threaded and sorted by subject.)

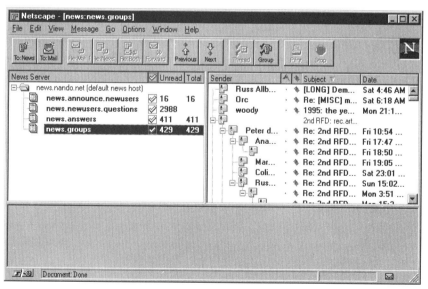

Figure 5-16: *The news.groups newsgroup contains 429 unread messages.*

READING AN ARTICLE

After all the effort you've expended to configure Netscape News, list available newsgroups, and subscribe to newsgroups, actually reading an article is so easy that its almost a letdown. To display the contents of an article, simply click the article's heading in the message heading pane. Netscape News displays the article's contents in the message pane. The message pane in Figure 5-17 shows the header information of an article from *news.groups*. Use your mouse and the vertical scroll bar or use the cursor keys to scroll the article into view.

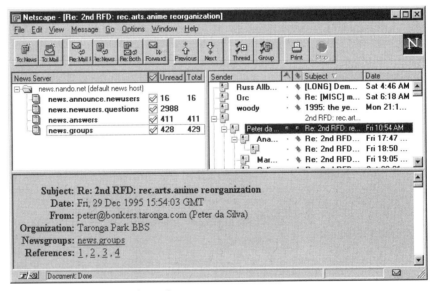

Figure 5-17: *An article from the news.groups newsgroup.*

By default, Netscape News displays the following article header information at the top of the News window message panel:

- **Subject**. Briefly describes the subject matter of the article. All articles in a thread have the same subject.

- **Date**. Gives the date the article was posted to the newsgroup.

- **From**. Provides the return e-mail address of the article's author.

- **Organization**. Identifies the author's organization (if any).

- **Newsgroups**. Lists hyperlinks to all the newsgroups to which the article was posted. You can go directly to a newsgroup by clicking on the newsgroup name.

- **References**. Identifies as hyperlinks other messages earlier in a thread: the numeral *1* denotes the original message in the thread; the numeral *2* denotes the second message; and so on. You can go directly to the referenced message by clicking on the numeral.

To cause any additional header information to also display at the top of the message panel, select the Show All Headers option on the Options menu. Here are a few of the more common header items that may appear:

- **Path**. Lists the complete Usenet path for this particular article, from the originating news server to your news server.

- **Reply-To**: Identifies the e-mail address to which replies should be addressed. This address is usually but not always the same as the address in the From field.

- **Lines**. Indicates the length of the message in lines.

- **Message-ID**. Specifies the article's unique message identification number.

- **References**. Identifies each of the other messages earlier in a thread by its message ID. You can still go directly to each message by clicking the hyperlink.

- **Supersedes.** References an article or articles that the current article supersedes.

- **Expires.** Gives the date and time after which the article should be removed from the newsgroup.

- **NNTP-Posting-Host**. Identifies the NNTP news server to which the article was originally posted.

- **X-Newsreader**. Identifies the program used to create and post the article.

- **Xref.** Cross-references other newsgroups.

When you display an article, Netscape News removes the diamond from the Read column to indicate that you have read the article. If you want the article to still be marked as *unread*, click the article's Read column to toggle on the diamond.

TIP

> *You can get another group of messages by selecting Get More Messages from the file menu in the Netscape News window.*

FOLLOWING A THREAD

By choosing to thread newsgroup headings (see the "Configuring Threading & Sorting" section earlier in this chapter), you can quickly read an entire series of related articles from beginning to end. Each subsequent article in a thread is listed, indented, in the message heading pane and just below the article to which it replies. Figure 5-18 shows a series of threaded messages from the *news.groups* newsgroup. To read the next article in the discussion, simply select the next article listed in the message heading pane. To read the preceding message in the thread, display the preceding message in the list.

At times, it may be convenient to maximize the size of the message pane in order to more easily read news articles. Since the message heading pane wouldn't be visible, Netscape News provides a couple of ways to move from one article to the next and back without displaying the message heading pane. When the threading feature is active, these navigation shortcuts move between articles in the same thread.

To read the next article, as it would appear in the message heading pane, either:

- Click the Next button in the toolbar; or
- Select Next Message from the Go menu.

To read the next unread article, either:

- Click the Next button in the toolbar; or
- Select Next Unread from the Go menu.

To read the preceding message in the message pane:

■ Select Previous Message from the Go menu.

To read the preceding unread article, either:

■ Click the Previous button in the toolbar; or,

■ Select Previous Unread from the Go menu.

As mentioned in the preceding section, you can also use the References field in the message header to move to previous articles in the current thread. Clicking a reference number displays an earlier article in the thread, but in the main Netscape Navigator 2.0 window (the window normally used to browse the World Wide Web), rather than in the News window. This behavior can be somewhat disorienting since newsgroup articles are normally displayed in the message pane of the News window.

FLAGGING ARTICLES TO BE READ LATER

Often it is convenient to attempt to identify articles of interest from the article headings. As you scroll through the headings list, flag articles that you want to read later by clicking the articles' Mark column. When all the articles you want to read are flagged, you can use the Next Flagged, Previous Flagged, and First Flagged options on the Go menu to move between flagged messages.

SAVING ARTICLES

From time to time as you are perusing the thousands of network news articles available on the Internet, you undoubtedly will want to save an article or two for future reference.

To save an article to a disk file:

1. With the article displayed, select Save As from the File menu. Netscape News displays the Save As dialog box.

2. Type a file name for the new file in the File Name text box.

3. Click the OK button. Netscape News saves the file to disk.

PRINTING ARTICLES

Printing a Usenet article is even easier than saving a copy. To print an article:

1. Make sure your printer has paper and other necessary supplies, is turned on, and is properly connected to your computer.

2. Click the Printer button on the toolbar. Netscape News displays the Print dialog box.

3. Make sure the printer settings are correct, and click the OK button. Netscape News sends the article to your printer.

OFFENSIVE MATERIAL

Unless you've been living on a mountaintop in Tibet, you are certainly aware of the Internet's reputation as a place where children can be exposed to offensive material. Most of the offensive material spoken of in the lurid headlines is found on Usenet. Network news is the First Amendment in action, at its best and at its worst. The same network that brings you uplifting information about health, religion, art, and education also can bring you (and your children) explicit sexually oriented conversations and graphic erotica. Although several state and federal lawmakers have already introduced legislation aimed at regulating the availability of pornographic material via the Internet, other less intrusive options are already available to protect impressionable young minds from electronic media intended for mature audiences. ➡

Fortunately, objectionable material tends to be found on a finite list of Internet sites. Several commercial software products are available that enable parents to in effect *block* these objectionable Internet sites, regardless of the type of site (Usenet, World Wide Web, Gopher, FTP, and so forth). The best-known brand of child protection software is SurfWatch. Surf-Watch is a subscription-based product, updated monthly, and is available in most major software outlets. Each month, the makers of SurfWatch scour the Internet for new sites that some parents may find objectionable and add these sites to the list of blocked Internet resources. The new blocked list is then encrypted and sent out to parents for installation to their SurfWatch-protected computer.

WRITING NEWS

You learned earlier in this chapter that lurking on Usenet newsgroups is considered acceptable behavior, but Usenet is fundamentally a collaborative medium of communication, a virtual community of sorts. When you get the urge to become an active member of this community, Netscape News is ready to assist you.

REPLYING TO AN ARTICLE

The easiest way to begin to participate in newsgroups is to reply to, or follow up on, an existing article. You don't have to worry about how to break the ice or what to type into the various header fields. Just join in the conversation. There are, however, several ways to reply: in public with a posted article; via e-mail directly to the author of the article to which you are replying; or both publicly and via e-mail.

IN PUBLIC

To reply to a news article publicly with a news article of your own:

1. While connected to the Internet, and with the original article displayed in the News window's message pane, either click the Re:News button in the toolbar (the one with the newspaper-clipping-and-arrow icon on it), or choose Post Reply from the Message menu. Netscape News displays the Compose window.

    For example, suppose you are displaying the article shown in Figure 5-18.

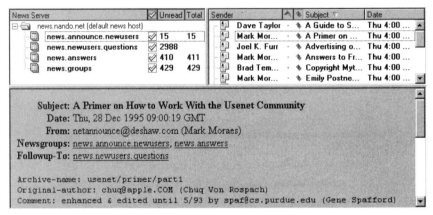

Figure 5-18: _The news article to which you are going to reply._

When you click the Re:News button in the toolbar, Netscape News displays the Compose window shown in Figure 5-19. Notice that the Subject and Newsgroups fields in the Compose window are already filled in. Netscape News repeated the subject of the original article and will post your new article to the newsgroup specified by the Followups-To field in the original article—the _news.newusers.questions_ newsgroup.

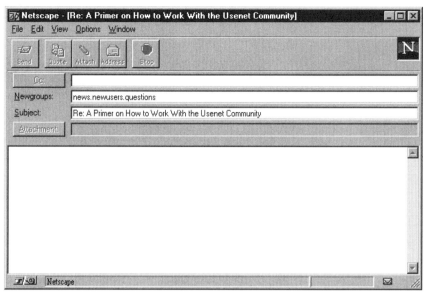

Figure 5-19: *The Compose window.*

2. Type your article and either click the Send button on the
   Toolbar or select Send Now from the File menu, or press
   Ctrl+Enter. Netscape News sends your article to your news
   server, which takes care of posting the article to the appro-
   priate newsgroup. Netscape News then returns you to the
   News window.

   For example, after reading the primer shown in the
   article in Figure 5-19, you might have a question about
   newsgroups. Type your message in the Compose window
   and post it to the *news.newusers.questions* newsgroup. You
   can then check back later in that newsgroup to see if
   anyone responded to your question.

   By default, the Compose window lists the following
   header fields:

   ■ **Cc.** Use this field to address a copy of your message to
     an e-mail address. If you have filled in an e-mail
     address in the News Messages field in the Composi-
     tion tab of the News and Mail Preferences dialog box,
     that address will appear here.

- **Newsgroups**. By default, this field contains the name of the same newsgroup to which the original article was posted, unless the header of the original article lists a different newsgroup in the Followup-To field.

- **Subject**. This field contains the subject of the thread.

- **Attachment**. If you attach a file to your article, the name of the attached file appears here.

You can optionally also display the following header fields by selecting the respective field name from the View menu (or by selecting Show All):

- **From**. By default, this field contains your name and return e-mail address, as entered in the Identity tab of the News and Mail Preferences dialog box.

- **Reply To**. Use this field if you want e-mail replies to your article to be sent to an e-mail address other than your standard From address.

- **Mail To**. Use this field to send the article to an e-mail address.

- **Mail Bcc**. Use this field to e-mail a blind copy. This field will not appear in the header of the message actually transmitted to the other recipients of the article/message.

- **Followups-To**. Use this field to specify the newsgroup to which followup articles should be posted. If you leave this field blank, followups will be posted to the newsgroup to which your article is posted.

VIA E-MAIL TO THE AUTHOR

If you would rather not post a followup to an article publicly—because what you have to say may not be of general interest, because your comments are of a personal nature, because you are shy, or for whatever reason—you can send an e-mail message instead to the author of the article.

To reply via e-mail:

1. While connected to the Internet, and with the original article displayed in the News window's message pane, either click the Re:Mail button in the toolbar (the one with the icon of an envelope and an arrow), or choose Mail Reply from the Message menu (or press Ctrl+R). Netscape News displays the Compose window.

2. Type your message and either click the Send button on the Toolbar or select Send Now from the File menu, or press Ctrl+Enter. Netscape News sends your message as e-mail to the author of the article to which you are replying. Netscape News then returns you to the News window.

TIP

You can add an author's e-mail address to your address book by selecting Add to Address Book from the Message menu. For more information on the Address Book, see Chapter 4, "Netscape Mail."

BOTH IN PUBLIC & TO THE AUTHOR

Occasionally, you may want to post an article in reply to an existing article and also send a copy to the article's author. To do so:

1. While connected to the Internet, and with the original article displayed in the News window's message pane, either click the Re:Both button in the toolbar (the one with the icons of both a newspaper *and* an envelope with an arrow), or choose Post and Mail Reply from the Message menu. Netscape News displays the Compose window.

2. Type your article and either click the Send button on the Toolbar or select Send Now from the File menu, or press Ctrl+Enter. Netscape News sends your article to your news server, which takes care of posting the article to the appropriate newsgroup. Netscape News also sends your message as e-mail to the author of the article to which you are replying. Netscape News then returns you to the News window.

POSTING A NEW ARTICLE

Starting your own thread in a newsgroup is really just as easy as replying to an existing article. You just have to come up with the subject line.

To post a new article:

1. While connected to the Internet, and while browsing in the newsgroup to which you want to post your article, either click the To:News button in the toolbar, or choose New News Message from the File menu. Netscape News displays the Compose window.

2. Netscape News automatically enters the name of the current newsgroup into the Newsgroups field. You can change the newsgroup and/or add other newsgroups as destinations for the article.

3. Type a subject for your article in the subject line. Try to be concise, but make your subject line descriptive. Remember that everyone else browsing the newsgroup will decide whether or not to read your article based on the subject line.

4. Type your article and either click the Send button on the Toolbar or select Send Now from the File menu (or press Ctrl+Enter). Netscape News sends your article to your news server, which takes care of posting the article to the appropriate newsgroup.

TIP

Just as with regular e-mail, you can also forward newsgroup posts to other recipients. Simply click the Forward button in the Netscape News window.

USENET ETIQUETTE

Even though your contact with Usenet is through your computer, the Usenet itself is really a VERY LARGE community of people. Always keep that fact in mind when you are reading and posting articles. Following is a summary of the article "A Primer on How to Work With the Usenet Community Newsgroups," which is periodically posted to the *news.announce.newusers* newsgroup. I highly recommend you read the full article as well.

"Never forget that the person on the other side is human. Don't blame system admins for their users' behavior. Never assume that a person is speaking for their organization. Be careful what you say about others. Be brief. Your postings reflect upon you; be proud of them. Use descriptive titles [subjects]. Think about your audience. Be careful with humor and sarcasm. Only post a message once. Please rotate [rot13] material with questionable content. Summarize what you are following up. Use mail, don't post a follow-up. Read all follow-ups and don't repeat what has already been said. Double-check follow-up newsgroups and distributions. Be careful about copyrights and licenses. Cite appropriate references. When summarizing, summarize. Mark or rotate [rot13] answers or spoilers. Spelling flames (i.e., criticism about misspellings) are considered harmful. Don't overdo signatures. Limit line length and avoid control characters. Please do not use Usenet as a resource for homework assignments. Please do not use Usenet as an advertising medium. Avoid posting to multiple newsgroups."

USING THE NEWS READER AS A PICTURE VIEWER

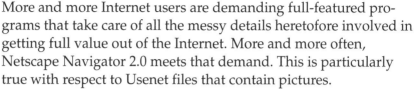

More and more Internet users are demanding full-featured programs that take care of all the messy details heretofore involved in getting full value out of the Internet. More and more often, Netscape Navigator 2.0 meets that demand. This is particularly true with respect to Usenet files that contain pictures.

One of the more popular pastimes unique to the Internet is the trading of digital pictures of all kinds—pictures of movie stars, animals, cartoons, heavenly bodies, you name it. While digital pictures can be made available on FTP sites or attached to electronic mail, Usenet has become a widely used method of sharing favorite electronic images. Most such files are posted in the newsgroups that have names beginning with *alt.binaries.pictures*.

Many image files on the Internet, including most images displayed on the World Wide Web, are stored as Graphics Interchange Format (GIF) files. The GIF standard was originally designed for use on CompuServe. GIF files can be displayed by Netscape Navigator 2.0 as inline images within a page of text and perhaps other pictures. Or a hyperlink could point to a GIF file that would display in a window by itself when you click the hyperlink.

Because of its high resolution and the relatively high data compression, the Joint Photographic Experts Group (JPEG) file format is the current favorite for storing digital pictures for transmission over the Internet.

For your convenience, Netscape Navigator 2.0 can display either JPEG or GIF files as inline images, embedded in the text of a news article or a World Wide Web home page. The program can also display both types of picture files in stand-alone windows.

If a network news article contains either a GIF file or a JPEG file, Netscape Navigator 2.0 will display the image, along with the rest of the article, in the message window.

Although Netscape Navigator 2.0 displays GIF and JPEG images contained in a news article, it does not enable you to save the images to disk in a viewable form. You can accomplish this task, however, with the help of some additional software and by using the following procedure:

1. Use the Save As option on the News window's File menu to save the article that contains the target GIF or JPEG image. Give the file name a UU extension (e.g., *dalmat.uu*) because this file has been encoded in a format known as *uuencoding*.

2. Use one of the decoder programs available on the Internet to decode the uuencoded file. One such program, freely available on the Internet, is named UUDeView. To use this program, just drag the uuencoded file from the Windows 95 Explorer (or Windows 3.x File Manager) to the UUDeView Launcher. The program automatically decodes and saves the image file to disk for you. There are a number of other decoder programs freely available on the Internet. You can get UUDeView at the following URL: http://www.uni-frankfurt.de/~fp/uudeview/

MULTIPART FILES

Many digital picture files are rather large, so many newsgroups limit the size of files that can be posted. As a consequence, it is sometimes necessary to break large picture files into smaller files. When someone posts files that have been split up in this fashion, you'll often see multiple related articles posted together to a newsgroup . The subject lines for the files include notations that each file is one of a set. For example, one article indicates that it is (1/3); the next article is (2/3); and the third article is (3/3).

Netscape Navigator 2.0 does not provide you the capability to put such files back together. You'll need to obtain other software for that purpose. One such program, freely available on the Internet, is named UUDeView. To use this program to put a GIF or JPEG file back together, first save to a disk file each news article that contains a piece of the digital image you want to reconstruct. Then drag and drop each of these files to UUDeView. The program will combine the pieces of the image and create a single file that can be viewed using Netscape Navigator 2.0 or a graphics program such as Paint Shop Pro.

MOVING ON

After reading this chapter and trying your hand at network news, you should now feel like a full citizen of Usenet. You have learned how to subscribe to newsgroups and are now able to read and respond to newsgroup articles and begin your own discussions. Move on next to Chapter 6, "Getting Files via FTP," to learn how easy it is to find and download from the Internet *tons* of useful software using FTP (File Transfer Protocol).

chapter six

Getting Files via FTP

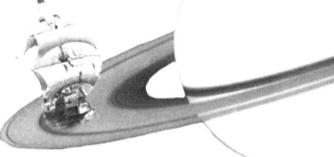

Hopefully by now you have found a few ways that Netscape Navigator 2.0 can simplify and enrich your life. Through its many easy-to-use features, you can access the Internet for sending and receiving e-mail; for viewing a wide variety of information, available from educational and government institutions as well as businesses and individuals; for reading the subject-specific information contained in newsgroups; and perhaps simply for relaxing and having some fun. But we haven't even touched on one of the oldest "classic" wonders of the Internet: the huge libraries of files that are available for you to download (copy to your computer) free of charge. The way you actually get these files is via a protocol known as *FTP*.

WHAT IS FTP?

FTP is one of the simplest and most obvious acronyms you'll come across on the Net: it simply stands for File Transfer Protocol. That sounds pretty generic, but every implementation of FTP follows the same very specific rules for sending and receiving data. The file must be broken up into pieces at one end and reassembled properly at the other; the data has to be checked for errors and stamped with the correct filename and date; and the FTP software has to enable users to navigate through the host system's directories to find the right file.

Throughout the Internet are scattered literally thousands of servers that provide files to users via FTP, and they all do their job in much the same way. Many of these sites are known as *anonymous* FTP sites, which means they allow any Internet user to log on specifically for the purpose of retrieving files. You don't need to be a registered user on the system. Typically, when logging in to anonymous sites, you specify *anonymous* as your username and your e-mail address as the password. With Netscape Navigator 2.0, you don't even have to do this, since the software takes care of the login process automatically. Are there FTP sites that are not anonymous? Sure! Many corporations, for instance, maintain non-anonymous FTP sites so that employees can trade work-related files while on the road. Of course, you need an account and a real password to access files on these FTP servers. But in this chapter, we'll be dealing primarily with anonymous sites.

WHAT'S OUT THERE?

So what kinds of files are available at these anonymous FTP sites? You name it! There are:

- Fully functional software programs, including spreadsheets, text editors, modem programs, databases, and a dazzling variety of utilities.

- Updates and patches to most major retail software programs.

- Electronic texts ranging from Shakespeare's complete works to David Letterman's latest Top Ten list.

- Thousands of images, sounds, video clips, and animations.

- Technical reports, journals, electronic magazines, news summaries, and archives of user messages.

- Books and tutorials like this one that will help you get started with just about any software task.

Figure 6-1 shows some of the directories at a well-known FTP site, the University of North Carolina SunSITE. We'll explore this site more thoroughly later in the chapter.

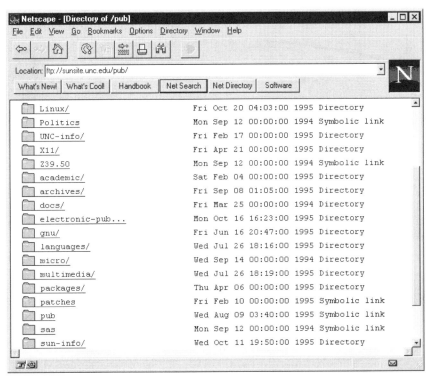

Figure 6-1: *Some of the directories of files at SunSITE.*

SENDING FILES

Grabbing files from anonymous FTP sites might be the most entertaining use of Netscape Navigator 2.0's built-in FTP facility, but there are other practical applications as well. For instance, when I finish writing this chapter, I will FTP it to Netscape Press, where an editor will massage the text and then place it back on the FTP server so I can look over her changes.

To send a file via FTP, navigate to the remote FTP site and directory you want, then select Upload File from the Navigator File menu. A dialog box appears letting you choose the file to send.

You should keep in mind, though, that Netscape Navigator 2.0 can be used only to transfer files to FTP servers that support anonymous login. In order to send files to an FTP site where you have a restricted account requiring a specific user name and password, you need a dedicated FTP program. There are many available on the Net, and if you have Windows 95 or Windows NT, you already have a simple text-based utility on your hard drive. Please see the Windows 95 or NT help files for further information.

And I can do whatever I want with all this stuff? I hear you asking. Well, yes and no. To understand why I'm waffling on this question, you need to understand that there are three broad categories of files on the Internet, and each of these categories has different rules and guidelines for usage.

PUBLIC DOMAIN

Public domain files are files that have no copyright, and there are no restrictions whatsoever on their usage. For instance, you can do whatever you want with Shakespeare's *Hamlet* or *A Winter's Tale*. Modern texts are sometimes released into the public domain as well, by authors who care more about wide distribution than about collecting any royalties or other fees. Many political polemics, for instance, are public domain.

But what about software? Sure, there's lots of public domain software on the Net. This has often been created by altruistic developers as a resource for the good of the community. The old adage "you get what you pay for" doesn't always hold true on the Net. For instance, until recently some of the very best Internet client software was public domain. Of course, there are developers who release unfinished or buggy programs into the public domain to collect feedback, as part of their development process or simply because they don't want to go through the process of refining their work. But programs like these are usually clearly marked, and in some situations they can provide a cost-effective way of dealing with very specific software tasks. And some public domain software is a true group effort: perhaps a programmer started a project years ago, and then somebody downloaded it and worked with it a bit more, then somebody else added new features, and so on. Since there are no restrictions on the redistribution or modification of public domain software, a program may evolve over the course of many years, forged as much by public scrutiny and feedback as by the work of any single designer.

FREEWARE

Freeware files are copyrighted, but there are no charges for using them. Let's say you write a program that you are very proud of, but you want to make sure anybody can use it for free. You place it on the Internet with a copyright notice and perhaps a text file explaining any restrictions on its use. For instance, you may want to make sure the software is always distributed in its original form, unmodified and bearing your name as the sole author. You may want to make it clear that nobody else may sell the software, but may only distribute it freely as you have.

Many people misunderstand freeware, confusing it with public domain files. No, they are very different. Freeware is free, but you have to play by the rules.

What About Viruses?

In spite of all the hype it gets, the Net is no utopia—it is more like a microcosm. Just as there is a slight chance you could get mugged on your way to the corner store, there is a slight chance that you will someday download a file that "crashes your hard drive" or otherwise messes with your system, causing you that peculiarly modern form of grief known as "restoring everything from backups." (That's assuming you bothered to keep an up-to-date backup like everyone told you to!)

How common are viruses? Certainly much less than sensationalistic mass media stories would have you believe, but there are some out there. The best defense, of course, is making sure that at any given moment you could restore everything you need from backup tape or disks. If this is not the case at your house, I'd suggest you put this book down and get busy backing up files.

There are other precautions you can take as well. Virus checking programs such as McAfee Associates's SCAN are available at most major FTP sites, and there are a number of excellent commercial products as well, such as Norton Anti-Virus. It's a good idea to check your entire system once in a while using one of these programs. If you do discover a problem, delete all infected files from your hard drive, or follow any instructions that came with your antivirus software. You will also probably need to completely restore your hard drive from backup.

Yes, this can be a serious inconvenience. But in the interest of alleviating some of the techno-paranoia that flares up whenever the news weeklies don't have a juicy enough scandal, let's debunk a few myths:

- Except in very rare cases, you cannot get viruses from text files or from most data files such as word processor documents. Generally speaking, something has to be *run* on your computer to infect it.

- **Most viruses do not destroy hardware, they only mess up your software so badly that it seems as though your hardware is faulty. Getting rid of all infected software and then completely restoring your system from backup will usually solve the problem.**

- **Viruses do not jump from disk to disk across your office.**

- **You won't catch any viruses by hanging around in particular Usenet newsgroups, though it can sometimes feel like you're coming down with something nasty!**

For more information about viruses, here are a couple of Web sites to check out:

- **The Frequently Asked Questions (FAQ) file for the VIRUS-L/comp.virus mailing list (http://www.cis.ohio-state.edu/hypertext/faq/usenet/computer-virus-faq/faq.html). This FAQ contains a lot of basic information about viruses, including common symptoms and how to proceed if your system is infected.**

- **Virus Information (http://csrc.ncsl.nist.gov/virus/). This page contains a comprehensive set of links to additional virus-oriented sites, as well as reviews of antivirus software.**

SHAREWARE

Shareware is a great marketing innovation that came into being almost concurrently with PCs. Shareware files or programs are distributed on a trial basis: you can download them and use them for free, but only for a short evaluation period. If you like the resource and want to keep using it, you must pay a fee (usually small) to the author or delete it from your machine. Generally it is OK to make copies for your friends to evaluate, but you, of course, can't charge.

Shareware files and programs are copyrighted. You must not copy them except as specifically allowed by the author, and you must abide by any restrictions detailed in the license or accompanying documentation. There has been plenty of litigation over misuse of shareware materials!

The advantages of shareware for the user are obvious: you get to try something out without spending a penny. But there are advantages for shareware authors as well. Distribution costs are kept to a minimum, and there are no middlemen to eat profits. The author also enjoys a direct relationship with the customer and often refines the product based on individual feedback rather than distributors' charts and graphs.

HOW TO KNOW WHAT YOU'RE GETTING

FTP sites are really just directories full of files, much like the directories on your own computer. The FTP protocol itself includes no provisions for describing the files or providing additional information, although it does let you view file details such as size, time, and date. So how do you know what all the files in an FTP directory really are? There are two ways:

- Many of the larger FTP sites have Web "front ends." In other words, you initially access them via a Web document that explains a little about the site and what it contains. When you're ready to download a file, you click on a link that fires up the actual FTP protocol, showing you lists of files and directories or going right ahead and transferring the file you want. Figure 6-2 shows an example of a Web front end to an FTP site, on the Netscape server itself.

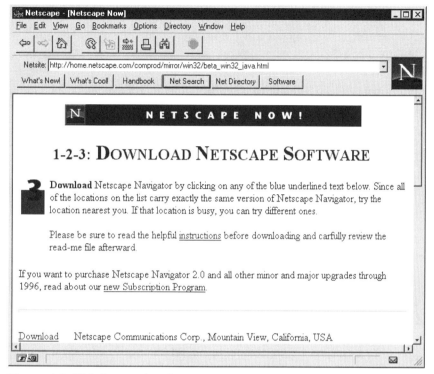

Figure 6-2: *Web front end to the Netscape FTP server.*

■ Most well-established FTP sites include informational files that describe the rest of the available files. These informational files are often named README or INDEX (sometimes in lowercase), or sometimes they have names that begin with a dot, as in .INDEX.

TIP

By default, Netscape Navigator 2.0 displays text files at FTP sites rather than automatically saving them to your hard drive. But what if you want to save a text file after viewing it? No problem. Just press Ctrl+S or select Save As from the File menu.

Now let's click the README file link at SunSITE to view its contents, shown in Figure 6-3.

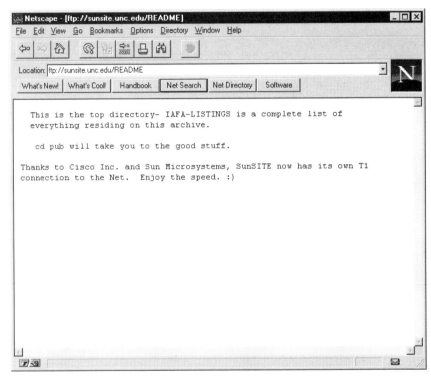

Figure 6-3: *The contents of the README file.*

As you can see, the README file contains information about the various files available at this site.

COMMON FILENAME EXTENSIONS

Knowing somebody's last name won't necessarily tell you anything about the person, but the few characters that compose the extension to a filename are packed with information. For instance, if a file ends with .TXT, you can be pretty sure it's an ASCII text file, readable on virtually any system by using a simple text viewing program. But not all extensions are so obvious, so I've compiled a table of some of the most common ones you'll come across. Table 6-1 is by no means complete, but it's a good reference to keep handy as you start exploring FTP sites.

Extension	Type of File
.TXT	Simple text file, readable using Notepad, WordPad, or even the DOS type command.
.ASC	Probably a simple ASCII text file as well.
.DOC	May be a text file or a Microsoft Word document.
.EXE	An executable file (DOS or Windows program) that can be run from the command line or from the Windows Run command (or by double-clicking the file's icon in Windows 95). Often it is a *self-extracting archive* file; when you run it, it is decompressed into several files.
.ZIP	An archive file that has been compressed using the PKZIP compression program. You can use PKUNZIP or WinZip to extract the separate files that are part of the archive (see "Understanding Compression" later in this chapter).
.HQX	A file that has been archived using the BinHex compression program; you must use BinHex to decompress it. This compression standard is more common in the Macintosh world, and chances are good that an .HQX file is really intended for Mac use.
.SIT	A compressed, or "stuffed," Macintosh file. Probably not useful on your PC, although if you need one of these files, several good PC unstuffers are available on the Net.
.ARJ	Another type of compressed file. Several compression and decompression programs such as WinZip and DRAG AND ZIP can handle these files.
.LHA	See note on .ARJ above.
.ARC	See note on .ARJ above.
.ZOO	See note on .ARJ above.
.Z	A file compressed using the UNIX Zip. You can use the program GZIP, or a general purpose utility such as WinZip or DRAG AND ZIP, to decompress it.
.GZ	A file compressed using the GNU Zip program for UNIX. See note on .Z above.
.TAR	An archive file that has been compressed using the UNIX tar facility. It may be decompressed using a PC version of tar or a general purpose utility such as WinZip or DRAG AND ZIP.

Table 6-1: *Common filename extensions on FTP sites.*

UNDERSTANDING COMPRESSION

You no doubt noticed that many of the notes in Table 6-1 refer to compression. When you look at the staggering number of files on the Internet (or, if you have Windows 95, at the staggering number of files on your hard drive!), it is clear that it's important to shrink files so that they are as small as you can possibly make them. And of course the smaller the file, the quicker it travels from one machine on the Internet to another, reducing overall transfer time and network traffic. But what exactly is file compression?

Think about the number 20,000,000,000,000,000,000,000. Now imagine trying to read this number to another person so that he or she can write it down. You *could* say "two zero zero zero zero zero zero zero zero zero zero zero zero zero zero zero zero zero zero zero zero," but that's the stupid way to do it. If you want to maintain your friend's respect, you'll probably say "two followed by 22 zeros." You have effectively compressed the information into fewer words, and your friend can decompress it by actually writing out the 22 zeros.

There are 256 different characters that may appear in a computer file in any order, or just half that number in the case of ASCII text files. In some files, there are no repeated characters and no repeated patterns of characters, but most are full of repetitions even if the repetitions are accidental. This means that most files can be compressed. Think of a database, for instance, in which there are lots of spaces that fill out fixed-length fields. It's easy to see how you can compress a file like this by indicating the space character and the number of times it should be repeated.

Of course, I'm oversimplifying. Compression techniques have become very sophisticated and use a variety of subtle approaches, or *algorithms*, that go far beyond merely tallying repeated characters. Some try to maximize the amount of saved disk space; others try to speed up the process of compressing and decompressing files. Most try for some sort of balance between these two aspects of the process.

You have to decompress most compressed files before they can be used; compressed files are good only for transferring and storing the information. The exceptions to this are compressed graphics and sound files, which you can view or listen to directly, without running any decompression software. In this case, Netscape Navigator 2.0 (or some other viewing program) is automatically decompressing the file for you.

SMALLER + SMALLER = BIGGER

As you travel around to different FTP sites, you'll notice that graphics files such as GIFs are never "zipped up" into archives; they're always left just as they are, with their original extension. Why?

Well, GIF files are *already* compressed. The graphics standard includes an algorithm for storing these files in as few bytes as possible. Images are obvious candidates for compression, since so many pixels are repeated. Think of the background, for instance, or large patches of color. If a graphics file contained position and color information for each individual pixel that appeared onscreen, it would be gigantic!

OK, so a GIF file is already compressed. But couldn't you make it even smaller by compressing it again? Nope. Curiously, by running a GIF file through a compression program such as PKZIP or WinZip, you actually make it *bigger*!

Kind of strange, huh? Well think about it: assuming that GIF compression is pretty tight (which it is), you're only going to eke out a few more bytes of space savings. But this added compression actually costs more space than it saves, for PKZIP has to add to the file the information about how to decompress it. In other words, it has to announce "this file has been compressed using PKZIP version *x*" as well as a bunch of other technical information. For this same reason, it may not always be worth compressing small files that are known to contain lots of nonrepeating information.

Clearly, you really need a compression program to deal with all the files you collect from the Net. In the next section, you'll kill two birds with one virtual stone: you'll learn how to use Netscape Navigator 2.0's FTP features as you download a copy of WinZip 6.0, one of the best compression/decompression programs available.

DOWNLOADING YOUR FIRST FILE

In this example, you'll access a Web page that serves as a front end for an FTP site. You will be able to download the WinZip 6.0 file simply by clicking a link on the Web page, without wading through the actual directories on the FTP server itself. Later in the chapter, you'll see how Netscape Navigator 2.0 displays this more "raw" FTP information.

To download WinZip 6.0 using Netscape Navigator 2.0's built-in FTP:

1. Make sure you are connected to the Internet, either directly or through a SLIP or PPP connection with your access provider. If you are using a SLIP or PPP connection and are not currently connected, double-click the Dial-Up Connection icon for your access provider.

    ■ If you are using Windows 3.1 rather than Windows 95, follow the instructions that came with your TCP/IP software for accessing the Internet.

2. Double-click the Netscape Navigator 2.0 icon to launch the program. The main window appears, and the Netscape home page starts loading as shown in Figure 6-4.

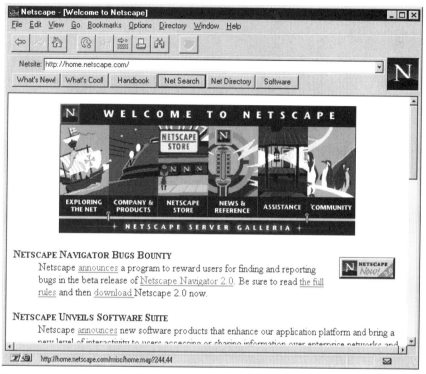

Figure 6-4: *The Netscape home page.*

3. Click your mouse inside the Location field at the top of the window to select the URL http://home.netscape.com/.

4. Replace this URL with the one for the WinZip home page by typing **http://www.winzip.com/**. Once you have typed in the new URL, press Enter. Netscape Navigator 2.0 retrieves the WinZip home page, as shown in Figure 6-5.

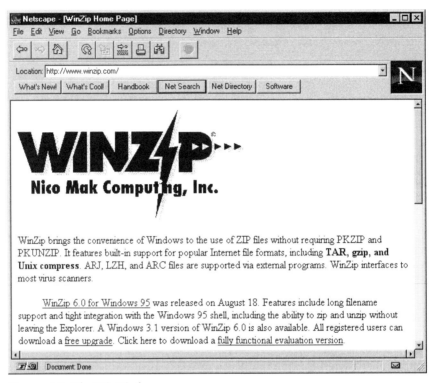

Figure 6-5: *The WinZip home page.*

5. You might want to take some time to look around the WinZip home page. When you are ready, scroll down the page and click the Download WinZip link. The Download WinZip page appears, as shown in Figure 6-6.

TIP

You can save FTP sites as Bookmarks just like any Web document. Select Add Bookmark from the Bookmarks menu, or simply press Ctrl+A. This is convenient if you don't have time to download a long file immediately, but want to be able to find it easily later on.

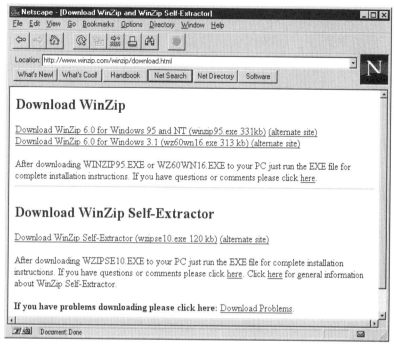

Figure 6-6: *The Download WinZip page.*

6. Now place your cursor over the top link on the page (don't click just yet). Notice that the status line indicates the URL pointed to by the link, ftp://ftp.winzip.com/winzip/winzip95.exe. The *ftp* at the beginning of the URL tells Netscape Navigator 2.0 to use the FTP protocol to connect with the site *ftp.winzip.com*, switch to the *winzip* directory, and download the file *winzip95.exe*.

7. Click one of the top two links, depending on whether you are using Windows 95 or Windows 3.1. After Netscape Navigator 2.0 has made contact with the remote FTP site, the Unknown File Type dialog box appears, as shown in Figure 6-7. This simply means that no special action or helper application (viewer) has been configured for this kind of file (.EXE), and you can choose what to do with it.

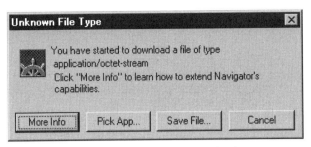

Figure 6-7: *The Unknown File Type dialog box.*

■ If you have already configured Netscape Navigator 2.0's Helpers tab so that there is a program or process associated with .EXE files, you won't get this message. Netscape Navigator 2.0 can, for instance, automatically run a file like this as soon as it has been received, or it can save it to disk automatically, without popping up this dialog box. To learn how to make these configuration changes, see "Helper Applications" later in this chapter or click on the More Info button to view a tutorial document at Netscape's own Web site.

TIP

You can click the Pick App button to configure an application to run once the file has been downloaded. For instance, if you are downloading a Microsoft Word document, you might want to run Word right away. Again, for more information on helper applications, see the "Helper Applications" section later in this chapter, or click the More Info button.

8. Click the Save File button. The Windows 95 or Windows 3.1 Save As dialog box appears.

9. Choose a location (such as your \TEMP directory) for the file, and then click the Save button. The Saving Location dialog box appears, showing you the progress of the file transfer. Once Netscape Navigator 2.0 has finished downloading the file, the Saving Location dialog box disappears.

TIP

Before Netscape Navigator 2.0 actually saves or runs a file you download, it may pop up a warning. You should read this message before continuing.

Congratulations! You've just downloaded your first file via FTP, and you now have an important tool for dealing with files you will download in the future. To install WinZip 6.0, simply run the executable file that you saved on your hard drive. You can run it from the DOS command line or using the Windows Run command. Be sure to read any informational files included with the program, and please remember that WinZip 6.0 is shareware: if you continue to use it, you must register it. The WinZip package contains complete information on how to do this.

Now let's visit an anonymous FTP site the more traditional way, without relying on a Web page as the front end.

FTP Traffic Jams

FTP sites are among the busiest resources on the Net. They may not get as many users as the most popular Web pages, but because of the way FTP works, there is a built-in traffic problem.

When you access a Web page, you quickly download the document and are off. Click a link on the page, and you bop back to the site, or to a different site. You flit from site to site, never staying longer than it takes to get the requested information. But with FTP, you remain logged in to the server while cruising and perusing directories at your own pace, and of course you remain logged in as you download files. The Web is like a fast-food joint, or like the old-fashioned automats where you walked around grabbing the dishes you wanted; FTP is like a real restaurant, with its share of customers who just never seem to stop eating!

➡

Because of this inherent traffic problem, you might sometimes get a message telling you that too many users are already logged on when you connect with an FTP site. Sometimes, however, you will simply be unable to connect at all, and Netscape Navigator 2.0 will just seem to be spinning its wheels. The solution to either of these problems is simple: try again later. In fact, try again *much* later, at a time when there are likely to be fewer info-junkies cruising the Net (3 A.M. works pretty well).

You say you like to sleep at night? Fortunately there is another solution. For many of the larger public FTP servers, there are also *mirror sites*, FTP servers that contain the exact same files and directory structure but may experience less traffic. These mirror sites are kept in sync with the original: anything you can get at the original you can get at its mirror, and you can be sure that you're downloading the same version. Often the "sorry, we're too busy" message you get when trying to log on to an FTP server includes a list of mirror sites.

NAVIGATING FTP SITES

For this tutorial, we'll return to a site we looked at briefly at the beginning of this chapter, the gigantic SunSITE FTP server at the University of North Carolina. This site houses literally thousands of files of interest to the Internet community, from casual Net surfers to seasoned experts. I use SunSITE as an example because it is fairly typical of some of the large public FTP sites scattered around the Net. To get to SunSITE:

1. Make sure you are connected to the Internet either directly or via your SLIP or PPP access provider. If Netscape Navigator 2.0 is not currently running, launch it by double-clicking its icon.

2. In the Location box at the top of the window, select the currently displayed URL and replace it with **ftp:// sunsite.unc.edu/**. Press Enter. After a few moments, the top-level directory at the SunSITE FTP site appears, as shown in Figure 6-8.

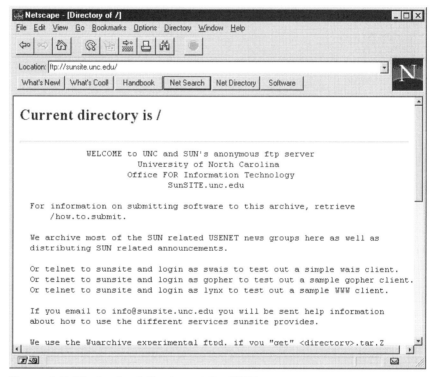

Figure 6-8: *The top-level directory at SunSITE.*

3. Read the information at the top of the page, and then scroll down to the bottom half. You can now see a list of files and several subdirectories of this top-level directory, as shown in Figure 6-9.

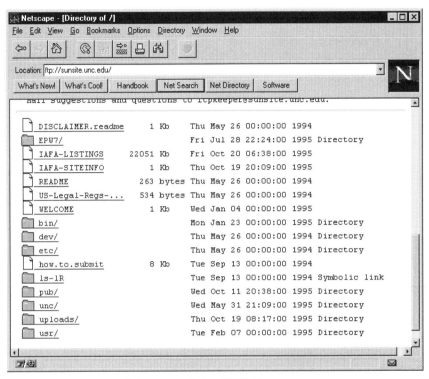

Figure 6-9: *Contents of the top-level SunSITE directory.*

■ Notice that Netscape Navigator 2.0 indicates directories
with a folder icon. The program also tries to determine,
based on extension, what kinds of files are located on
the remote server, and it displays appropriate icons for
the particular file types. In this case, the available files
do not have extensions, so Netscape Navigator 2.0
uses the generic blank file icon.

4. Click the DISCLAIMER.readme link. (It's a good idea to get in the habit of reading every file that has *readme* in its name, especially if you think it might contain legal restrictions or licensing information.) The text of the DISCLAIMER.readme file appears in your Netscape Navigator 2.0 window.

   ■ By default, Netscape Navigator 2.0 displays text files in its own window. If you want, you can configure the program so that it uses a different utility for displaying text. In fact, you can configure Netscape Navigator 2.0 so that it uses a wide range of "helper applications" to display or run different types of files. If you click on a Microsoft Word document, for example, you may want Netscape Navigator 2.0 to launch Word and immediately load the new file. Or you may want Netscape Navigator 2.0 to simply download all text and Word files instead of displaying them. For more information on changing these settings, see "Helper Applications" later in this chapter.

5. Once you've read the DISCLAIMER.readme file, click the Back button to return to the top-level directory. The README you read earlier in this chapter said that most of the good stuff was under the /pub directory, so let's go there. Scroll down and click the /pub link. (Directories named "pub" often contain files that are useful to the general public.) The /pub directory appears, as shown in Figure 6-10.

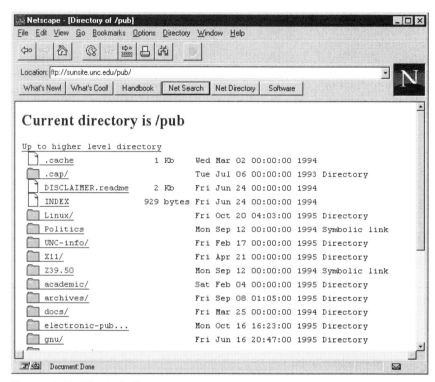

Figure 6-10: *The /pub directory.*

TIP

*If you know where you want to go on an FTP server, you can include the directory right in the URL. For instance, you could enter **ftp:// sunsite.unc.edu/pub/** right in the Location box in Netscape Navigator 2.0. And if you know what file you want to retrieve, you can even include the filename in the URL!*

From here you can cruise around on your own for a while—
Netscape Navigator 2.0 makes it so easy that you don't need me
to hold your virtual hand any more. If you're interested in programming languages, click the link to the languages/ directory;
if you're interested in multimedia, click multimedia/. You can
always back up a level using the Back button, or you can return to
any level you've already seen via the Go menu.

Some of the most useful files on SunSITE are the Windows
Internet client programs contained in the /pub/micro/pc-stuff/
ms-windows/winsock/apps/ directory. Since you're using
Netscape Navigator 2.0, you can already take care of most Internet
tasks without any supplemental programs, but as you get more
familiar with the Net, you may encounter some specialized service
that requires a very specialized tool. This is a good place to look.

You already know that you can get to the /pub/micro/pc-stuff/
ms-windows/winsock/apps/ directory by clicking your way
down, level by level. But since you already know how to navigate
this way, let's accelerate the process by taking a shortcut:

1. In the Location box near the top of the Netscape Navigator 2.0 window, edit the currently displayed URL so that
   it reads **ftp://sunsite.unc.edu/pub/micro/pc-stuff/
   ms-windows/winsock/apps/**.

   ■   A long URL like this is an excellent candidate for a
       bookmark. I, for one, don't want to type it again!

2. Press Enter. Netscape Navigator 2.0 automatically takes
   you to the correct directory, as shown in Figure 6-11.

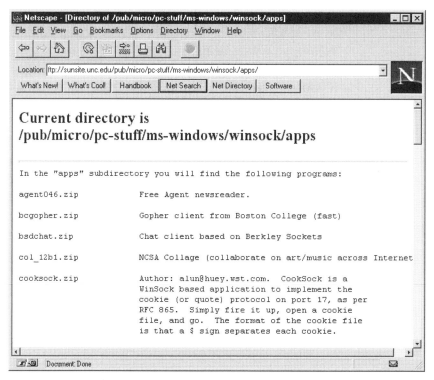

Figure 6-11: *The /pub/micro/pc-stuff/ms-windows/winsock/apps/ directory at SunSITE.*

The top section of the page contains capsule descriptions of a few files in this directory. This is a convenience you won't find at most FTP sites. More commonly, you need to view a file called something like INDEX or CONTENTS to get descriptive information.

Take a few moments to scroll down the list of files. Notice that Netscape Navigator 2.0 labels binary executable files (files with an .EXE extension) with a special icon that includes a binary number on it. This provides an easy way to see at a glance what kinds of files are available. All of the executables in this directory are actually self-extracting archives, just like the WinZip file you downloaded earlier. The other files in this directory have the extension

.ZIP, indicating that after retrieving them, you must decompress and extract their components using WinZip. If you want, you can have WinZip do this automatically as soon as any .ZIP file is retrieved; see "Helper Applications" later in this chapter.

WHAT ARE SYMBOLIC LINKS?

As you look around FTP sites, you'll notice that in any given directory there are files, subdirectories, and something called "symbolic links." What exactly are they?

A symbolic link is really just a nickname or, more exactly, a pointer to another directory or file. Imagine you are the administrator of an FTP site, and you just put a brand new evaluation version of Netscape Navigator in the directory /pub/pc/windows/win95/www/apps/netscape. That's buried pretty far down in the directory structure, and people are going to take quite a while navigating down to that level. In addition, if they type in the entire URL, they are likely to make mistakes, taking even more time and further adding to the traffic problem. You want to make sure that users get to the new Netscape file quickly and efficiently. What to do? Create a symbolic link in the top-level directory, and call it, for instance, new_netscape. When a user clicks new_netscape, he or she is automatically transported to the directory where the file *really* lives.

The administrators of FTP sites can create symbolic links to directories or to files. If you click a link that's associated with a directory, you "teleport" to that directory; if you click a link to a file, Netscape Navigator 2.0 views the file or begins the download process. Symbolic links make it quicker, and much more pleasant, to navigate FTP sites that have complex directory structures.

SEARCHING FOR FILES

FTP is great if you know what you're looking for and where to find it. But what if all you know is that you need a particular kind of program, let's say, and you have no idea where to start looking? Or what if you can only remember part of the name of a file you want? Fortunately, the Net offers a wide variety of services for locating files in the FTP haystack. One of the old standbys, and still one of the most useful tools on the Net, is a service known as Archie.

ARCHIE

Archie is an Internet service that lets you search indexes of most of the files available at anonymous FTP sites. These indexes are maintained on special Archie servers located around the world. To use Archie effectively, you need to know part of a file's name, or at least be able to make a reasonable guess about what characters might be in its name. For instance, let's say you want to find WinZip 6.0 but don't remember the exact name of its self-extracting archive file. Archie lets you specify a string of characters that appears anywhere in the name. It would be safe to guess that the string "winzip6" appears somewhere in the file name, so you can use that as your Archie search criterion and find the correct file even if its name is "latestwinzip600z.exe." For advanced users interested in specifying very precise search parameters, Archie even supports the full set of regular expressions that let you search for all kinds of patterns within filenames. For instance, you could look for a file that begins with a lowercase letter, followed by any number of digits, followed by the string "zsa-zsa," followed by a number greater than five, followed by an extension of either .TAR or .SH, followed by another extension of . . . . Well, you get the idea. It is beyond the scope of this book to provide a tutorial on regular expressions, but I like to think of them as wildcards on steroids. If you want more information, why not use some of the Internet search tools you've learned about so far?

OK, let's give Archie a try:

1. Make sure you are connected to the Internet either directly or via your SLIP or PPP access provider. If Netscape Navigator 2.0 is not currently running, launch it by double-clicking its icon.

2. In the Location box at the top of the Netscape Navigator 2.0 window, replace the currently displayed URL with **http:// www-ns.rutgers.edu/htbin/archie** and press Enter. In a few moments, the Rutgers University Archie Request Form page appears, as shown in Figure 6-12.

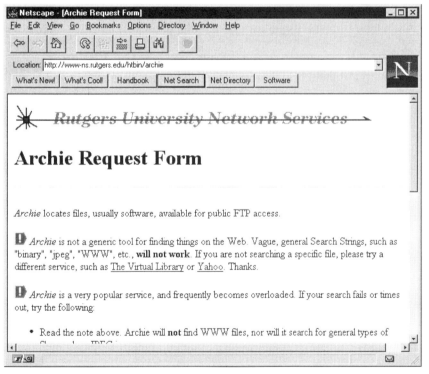

Figure 6-12: *The Archie Request Form page.*

3. Scroll down the page until you get to the search form itself. Fill it out as follows:

■ In the Search By section, click the top radio button, Looking for Search Term in File Names (Ignore UPPER/lowercase).

■ In the Search Term box, type **winzip6**.

■ Leave the other settings alone.

Your completed search form should look like Figure 6-13.

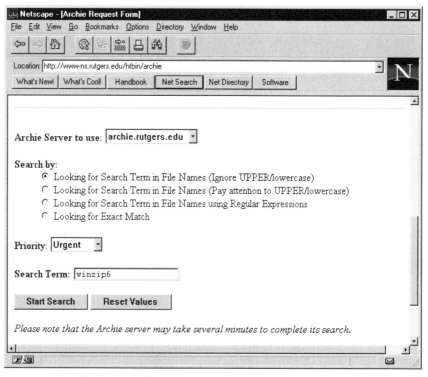

Figure 6-13: *The completed search request.*

4. Now click the Start Search button. In a few moments, the Archie Search Results page appears, as shown in Figure 6-14, providing you with links to a few different FTP sites where you can get WinZip 6.0.

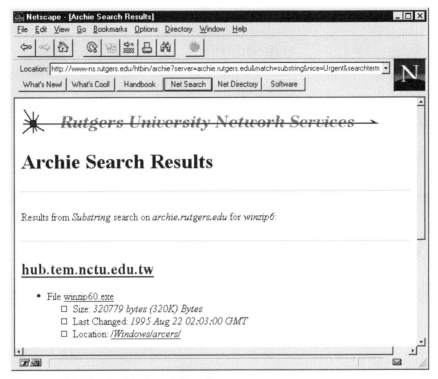

Figure 6-14: *The Archie Search Results page.*

As you can see, Archie is great if you know something—*any-thing*—about the name of the file you are looking for. But what if you're looking for a particular *kind* of file—a mortgage calculator, for instance—that could have any name at all? Luckily, the Internet provides search utilities for this situation as well. One of the best is the c|net Virtual Software Library.

THE C|NET VIRTUAL SOFTWARE LIBRARY

To get to the c|net Virtual Software Library:

1. Make sure you are connected to the Internet either directly or via your SLIP or PPP access provider. If Netscape Navigator 2.0 is not currently running, launch it by double-clicking its icon.

2. In the Location box at the top of the Netscape Navigator 2.0 window, replace the currently displayed URL with **http://vsl.cnet.com/** and press Enter. In a few moments, the Virtual Software Library home page appears, as shown in Figure 6-15.

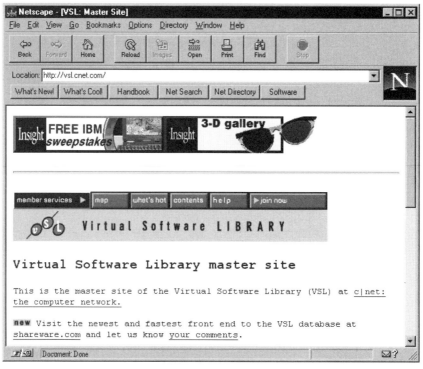

Figure 6-15: *The Virtual Software Library home page.*

3. After reading the introductory information on this page, click the Quick Search button under Search Options. The VSL Quick Search Form appears.

4. Since we are interested in mortgage calculators for Windows, leave the drop-down list of file categories set to MS-Windows. In the leftmost search word box, type **mortgage**. You can leave the other box empty. Your completed search form should look like Figure 6-16.

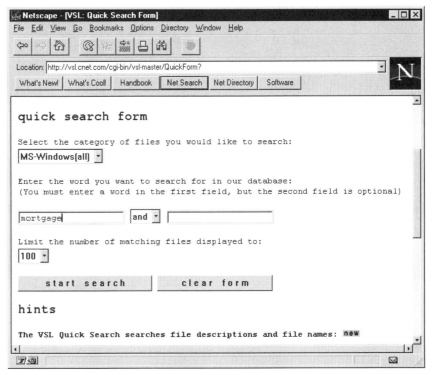

Figure 6-16: *Completed VSL quick search form.*

5. Click the Start Search button. In a few moments, the Search Results page appears as shown in Figure 6-17, with links to several different mortgage programs for Windows. You can click any one of these to retrieve the file from its FTP site.

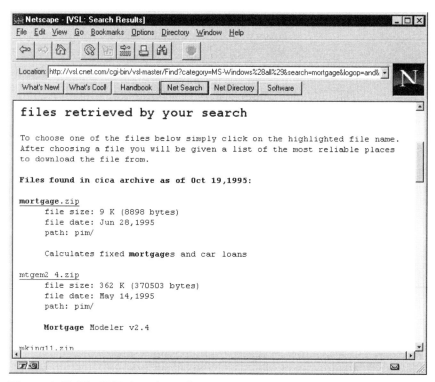

Figure 6-17: *The VSL Search results.*

The Virtual Software Library provides such a powerful search tool that you'll probably want to add it to your Bookmarks.

USING WEB TOOLS TO FIND FILES

While there are other specialized tools for finding files on FTP sites, you may not actually need them. The World Wide Web is becoming more and more prominent as a front end for FTP servers. This means that you can find many files without specialized FTP search services; you simply use the same search engines you use for locating other types of information on the Web itself. The best of these utilities are available by clicking the Netscape Navigator 2.0 Net Search button. While an InfoSeek search, for instance, may not get you directly to a particular file, it will probably take you to a Web page with a link to the file you're interested in. And of course, you can find lots of files by browsing through the dozens of categories that appear when you click the Net Directory button.

As I mentioned earlier, Netscape Navigator 2.0 does more than just go out and retrieve files for you—it can actually help you start working with them right away. In the next section, you'll learn how to take advantage of this powerful feature.

WHAT ARE RFCs?

Just when you thought we were done with acronyms!

RFC stands for Request for Comment, and that's exactly what it is: a document put out on a public FTP site so that other Net users can read it and comment on the content. But an RFC contains very specialized information, technical information about the Internet itself. In fact, many of the Internet standards that have developed over the years are the result of this RFC process.

Most RFC files are slow, tedious reading, and nobody's turned them into a musical yet. But they are invaluable to anybody wanting to learn more about the Net, and a few of them are even fun. (Well, if you're a geek like me.) RFC 1208, for example, is a large glossary of networking terminology, and RFC 1325 has lots of tips for new Internet users.

How do you know what the different RFC files cover? Here are two URLs:

- ftp://isi.edu/in-notes/rfc-retrieval.txt

- ftp://isi.edu/in-notes/rfc-index.txt

The first file provides instructions on locating and downloading RFCs, and the second contains short descriptions of all the RFCs that currently exist.

HELPER APPLICATIONS

You've already seen that when you click on a text file at an FTP site, Netscape Navigator 2.0 automatically displays the contents rather than simply downloading the file to your hard drive. But that's only a small example of the automation that's possible. To understand how all of this works, let's take a look at the Helpers tab under General Preferences.

1. Select General Preferences from the Netscape Navigator 2.0 Options menu. The Preferences dialog box pops up with the Appearance tab selected, as shown in Figure 6-18.

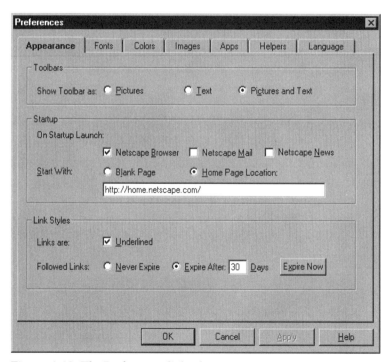

Figure 6-18: *The Preferences dialog box.*

2. Select the Helpers tab, as shown in Figure 6-19.

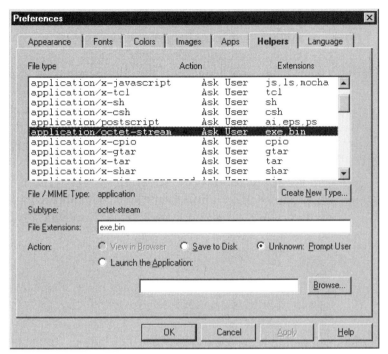

Figure 6-19: *The Helpers tab, with settings for the application/octet-stream file type.*

TIP

You can also select a helper application by clicking the Pick App button in the Unknown File Type dialog box that appears when you download a file (see Figure 6-7).

This looks like a fairly complicated dialog box at first, but once you understand the concepts, it's really pretty simple. The large scrolling list includes the names of different kinds of files you might encounter as you cruise the Net with Netscape Navigator 2.0. These file types are listed using a naming standard known as Multipurpose Internet Mail Extensions (MIME). In MIME nomenclature, for instance, files with an .EXE or .BIN extension are classified as applications, with a subtype designation of octet-stream. If you scroll down the list, you'll see many different types of files, some familiar and some unfamiliar. Usually the MIME designations make sense, as in the case of Graphics Interchange Format (GIF) files, which are classified as images with a subtype of gif.

Here's where it gets interesting. For each type of file it encounters on the Internet, Netscape Navigator 2.0 has a default action that's listed in the Action column of the list. For image/gif files, for example, you can see that the default action is Browser. This means that GIF graphics will be displayed automatically by Netscape Navigator 2.0 itself, right within the browser window. And for application/octet-stream files, the default is Ask User: when you click on a link to an .EXE or .BIN file, you will be asked what you want to do with the file, as shown earlier in Figure 6-7.

TIP

Settings in the Helpers tab also affect the way attached files are handled in Netscape Mail (see Chapter 4, "Netscape Mail").

But suppose you don't like Netscape Navigator 2.0's default action for a particular file type. Fortunately, it's very easy to change. In this example, we'll change the default action for PKZIP compressed files so that they are automatically saved to disk, without any "What do you want to do with this file?" dialog box popping up.

1. If you are not already in the Helpers tab, select General Preferences from the Netscape Navigator 2.0 Options menu. Click the Helpers tab.

2. Scroll down the list of file types until you find application/x-zip-compressed. Select this entry by clicking on it. The specific settings for the application/x-zip-compressed file type appear, as shown in Figure 6-20.

   ■ Notice that the Action column indicates Ask User for this file type.

3. In the Action section near the bottom of the dialog box, click the Save to Disk radio button. Now the word *Save* appears in the Action column.

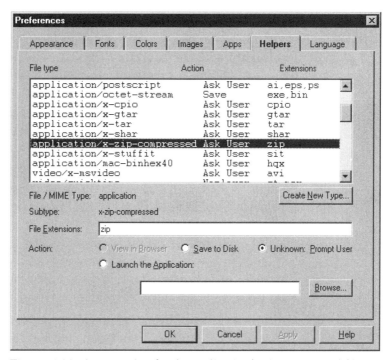

Figure 6-20: *A new action for the application/x-zip-compressed file type.*

4. Click OK to return to the main Netscape Navigator 2.0 window. If you want to save your changes for future sessions, make sure to select Save Options from the Options menu.

That's all there is to it! Now when you click on a link to a ZIP file, it will be saved to disk automatically.

TIP

Instead of selecting Save to Disk for ZIP files, you may want to select Launch the Application and enter the name of a decompression program such as PKUNZIP or WINZIP. That way, ZIP files will be decompressed automatically.

Let's take a closer look at the other possible actions that you can associate with a file type:

■ **View in Browser**. Netscape Navigator 2.0 can display several kinds of image and document files: ASCII text, Joint Photographic Experts Group (JPEG) and GIF graphics, and of course, HTML pages. Typically you'd leave these file types associated with the View in Browser action because it is the simplest and quickest way to view the information, but in some cases you may want Netscape Navigator 2.0 to launch a separate viewing or editing program as soon as the file is retrieved.

■ **Save to Disk**. This is obviously the most convenient option for binary files retrieved via FTP, but it can be useful in other situations as well. There are times, for instance, when I need to collect a lot of information directly from text files, but I don't want to view them right away. I temporarily set the Save to Disk option for text files, collecting them on my hard drive so I can view them later.

■ **Unknown: Prompt User**. When Netscape Navigator 2.0 encounters a file type that is associated with this action, it pops up the dialog box shown above in Figure 6-7. This option is useful for file types you might want to treat differently at different times. In the case of sound files, for instance, you might sometimes want to hear them right away, while at other times you might prefer to save them to disk.

■ **Launch the Application**. This is the most interesting and powerful action you can associate with a file type, and one of the most important features of Netscape Navigator 2.0. We are really talking about two different actions here:

   ■ If you select this radio button _without_ filling in the box just below it, Netscape Navigator 2.0 simply launches the associated file as an application. For instance, if you associate all .EXE files with the Launch the Application action, they will run as soon as they are retrieved (this is pretty dangerous—I wouldn't recommend it!).

   ■ If you select the radio button and enter the name of another helper application in the box, Netscape Navigator 2.0 will run the helper application as a viewer for the associated file. The word _viewer_ in this context is traditional but pretty misleading: the helper application might play the associated file rather than display it (in the case of a sound file) or even let you edit it (in the case of a Word document.) Take a look at the example in Figure 6-21, in which .AU and .SND audio files are associated with the Netscape-produced audio player, Naplayer.

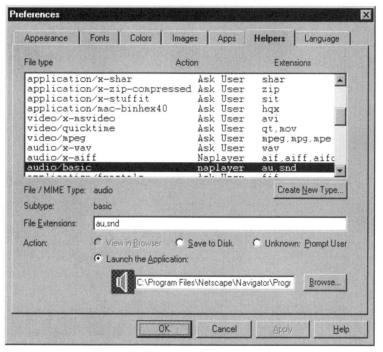

Figure 6-21: *Audio/basic files associated with Naplayer.*

- This means that whenever you click on an .AU or .SND file, Netscape Navigator 2.0 automatically plays the sound using this separate Naplayer utility.

TIP

Use the Browse button to find helper applications on your hard drive.

ADDING NEW EXTENSIONS

If you want to get really fancy, Netscape Navigator 2.0 even lets you add new extensions for particular file types. For instance, you might want to add the extension .ASC to the text/plain file type, since some systems use this extension to designate ASCII text files.

To make the change:

1. If you are not already in the Helpers tab, select General Preferences from the Netscape Navigator 2.0 Options menu. Click the Helpers tab.

2. Scroll down the list of file types until you find text/plain. Select this entry by clicking on it. The specific settings for the text/plain file type appear.

3. After the word *text* in the File Extensions box, type **,asc**. The tab should now look like Figure 6-22.

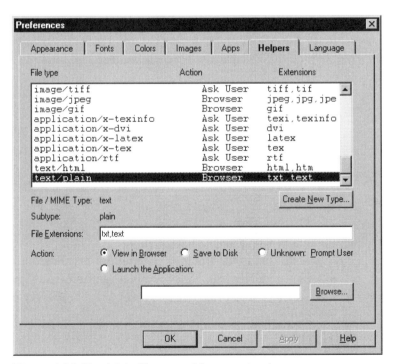

Figure 6-22: *Text/plain file type with new extension.*

4. Click OK to return to the main Netscape Navigator 2.0 window. If you want to save your changes for future sessions, make sure to select Save Options from the Options menu.

TIP

When adding a new extension, make sure it's not one that is commonly associated with any other file type. For instance, some text files have the extension .DOC, but you should not *add .DOC as an extension to the text/plain file type, because it is more commonly used to indicate MS-Word documents. If you do not heed my warning, you may start seeing blenderized* purée de Word *in your text viewer!*

ADDING NEW FILE TYPES

Now if you want to get *really* fancy, you can even add new file types and subtypes to Netscape Navigator 2.0's default list. However, this is truly a propeller-head option: you should not even be thinking about it except to add a new standardized MIME type, and unless you really know what you're doing. Assuming you have the proper geek credentials, though, it's pretty easy:

1. If you are not already in the Helpers tab, select General Preferences from the Netscape Navigator 2.0 Options menu. Click the Helpers tab.

2. Click the Create New Type button. The Configure New Mime Type dialog box pops up, as shown in Figure 6-23.

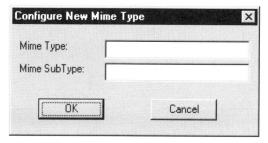

Figure 6-23: *The Configure New Mime Type dialog box.*

3. Enter the new MIME type and subtype in the appropriate fields and click OK.

Netscape Navigator 2.0's Helpers facility lets you deal efficiently with just about any file on any Internet FTP site. And if you want to further automate Netscape Navigator 2.0 with new viewers, sound players, editors, or any kind of helper application, guess how you get these programs? By FTP, of course!

MOVING ON

In this chapter, you've learned the basics of navigating FTP sites and downloading files. You've also learned some strategies for finding files on the Net by name or by subject area, and you've seen how Netscape Navigator 2.0 can be customized to help you deal with your new files more efficiently. Now all you need is a bigger hard drive!

You already have most of the Web basics down, and you could easily take off at this point and start exploring on your own. But before you do that, I'd like to show you two more extremely powerful tools that are old mainstays when it comes to exploring the Net. They are Gopher and Telnet.

chapter seven

Gopher & Telnet

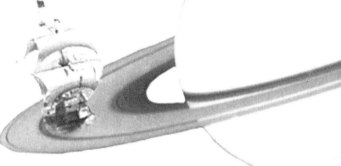

There is no question that the World Wide Web is one of the most exciting services available on the Net. It plunges you into an electronic world full of bright images and sounds, and it lets you jump around from link to link, blazing new information trails. Its hypermedia browsing facilities provide a whole new approach to research, an approach that's very different from the plodding linear methods we grew up with. Some say that hypermedia browsing more closely models the way our minds really work, encouraging us to integrate knowledge by associative leaps rather than by carefully planned logical stitching.

However, there are some research tasks that call for a more traditional approach to the great volume of data available on the Net; there are also some wonderful repositories of knowledge that have not yet been "Webified." Fortunately, Netscape Navigator 2.0 supports some of the older Internet services that are still very useful tools. The most important of these are *Gopher* and *Telnet*.

WHAT IS GOPHER?

What if you don't know exactly what you're looking for on the Net and want to refine your search carefully as you explore? What if you want to delve deeply into a particular area of interest, for instance, constitutional law? Typical Web sites may not help you, for often the links to other information are as arbitrary, whimsical, and wild as the imagination of the page's author.

Gopher servers, on the other hand, serve up information in tidy hierarchical menus and submenus, sticking to a subject and presenting it in top-down, outline format. Using World Wide Web documents, you leap rapidly from peak to peak. Using Gopher, you follow logically related information trails.

HOW DO THEY COME UP WITH THESE NAMES?

Most of the Internet services were developed not by commercial software companies, but by individuals in academia, often graduate students. This evolution is reflected in some of the jargon. If the marketing division of a software company had been involved, we'd probably be talking about Super UltraSearch Max Plus instead of Gopher. But the Golden Gopher is the mascot of the University of Minnesota, where this powerful tool was developed, and there were no people in suits calling the shots.

Once you name something "Gopher," you have to extend the metaphor. If you visit many Gopher sites, you'll discover that they are sometimes called Gopher *holes*. And avid Gopher users often talk about *burrowing* to other sites. It's all kind of quaint in this age of cyber this and surf that.

In addition to extending metaphors, computer people have a compulsive need to mix them, and so it is very common on the Net to talk about *Gopherspace*. (You can put yourself into an altered state trying to visualize that one.) Gopherspace is simply the total collection of hierarchically organized resources available to you via Gopher.

In the old days (before last year), Gopher servers were usually accessed with specialized Gopher client programs, but Netscape Navigator 2.0 makes extra software unnecessary. Netscape Navigator 2.0 can log you on to a Gopher server and then present you with the information so that it looks very much like any Web page. Menu items are colored like other Web links, and clicking on them brings up the appropriate submenus. Let's give it a try using the *WELL Gopher* as an example.

USING GOPHER

The WELL is a large information service known for the variety of its online forums and the lively interactions of its users. It also maintains a very interesting Gopher site that's accessible to anyone on the Net. To begin exploring it:

1. Make sure you are connected to the Internet, either directly or through a SLIP or PPP connection with your access provider. If you are using a SLIP or PPP connection and are not currently connected, double-click on the Dial-Up Connection icon for your access provider.

   ■ If you are using Windows 3.1 rather than Windows 95, or if you are using Windows 95 but are not using the Microsoft TCP/IP facility, follow the instructions that came with your TCP/IP software for accessing the Internet.

2. Double-click the Netscape Navigator 2.0 icon to launch the program. The main window appears, and the Netscape home page starts loading, as shown in Figure 7-1.

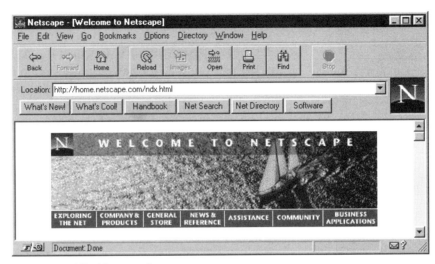

Figure 7-1: *The Netscape home page.*

3. Click your mouse inside the Netsite field at the top of the window to select the URL http://home.netscape.com/.

4. Replace this URL with the one for the WELL Gopher site by typing **gopher://gopher.well.com/**. Then press Enter. Netscape Navigator 2.0 retrieves the top-level WELL Gopher menu, as shown in Figure 7-2.

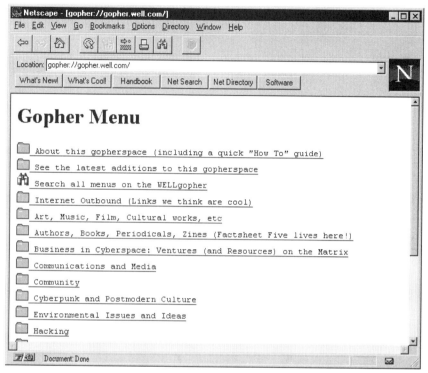

Figure 7-2: *The WELL Gopher.*

■ Notice that when you connect to a Gopher server, virtually all the text in the Netscape Navigator 2.0 window is composed of links. In the top level of the WELL Gopher, these are links to submenus rather than files, as indicated by the folder icons. The exception is the Search All Menus on the WELLgopher item, which brings up a searchable index of the entire Gopher server.

5. Click the top menu item, About This Gopherspace. A new submenu appears, as shown in Figure 7-3.

■ Notice that most of the links are to actual text files now, as indicated by the icons.

6. Click the top item, What Is This Place? (The Basic Story). This time a text file appears, as shown in Figure 7-4.

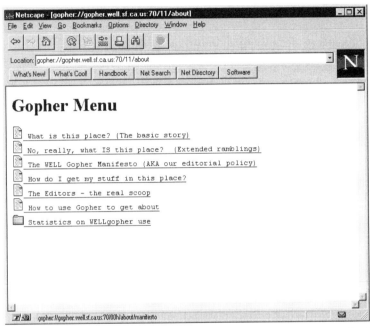

Figure 7-3: *The About This Gopherspace submenu on the WELL Gopher.*

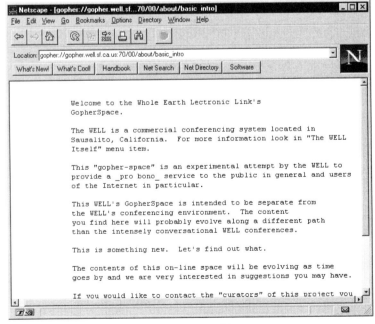

Figure 7-4: *The WELL Gopher welcome file.*

7. After reading the file, click Netscape Navigator 2.0's Back button to return to the About This Gopherspace menu. You might want to read some of the other articles here, such as "How to use Gopher to get about," or the "extended ramblings" version of the "What is this place?" file. (The WELL is famous for its extended ramblings.)

8. When you're done reading, click Back again to return to the top-level WELL Gopher menu. From there you can begin to explore many different areas. Feel free to browse. The WELL Gopher is especially known for its information on media, communications, cyberpunk literature . . . and the Grateful Dead.

TIP

Gopher menus can be saved, printed, copied, or made into Bookmarks and shortcuts just like any other kinds of pages. In most cases, you needn't pay attention to whether you're at a Web, Gopher, or File Transfer Protocol (FTP) site. If you can see it in Netscape Navigator 2.0, you can work with it using any of the techniques you learned in Chapter 3, "A Quick Look Around."

Although the hierarchy of all Gopher sites is similar, their content varies greatly. There are Gopher sites that specialize in just about any academic field you can think of, from art to astrophysics. In addition, there are Gopher sites that are just plain fun.

But the great thing about Gopher is that it allows a site to include on its menus links to other sites as well. In other words, you are not restricted to the information available on only that particular server. Gopher is really the precursor of the Web in letting sites link to one another in a vast information net.

As you start burrowing from one site to another, you are actually creating a customized hierarchical pathway for yourself, and you can move backward and forward along it to find the information you need. Let's see how this works.

STRETCHING GOPHERSPACE

To demonstrate how you can "stretch" Gopherspace, let's use the WELL Gopher site again as a starting point (if the WELL Gopher is already displayed in your Netscape Navigator 2.0 window, skip ahead to step 3 below):

1. Make sure you are connected to the Internet either directly or via your SLIP or PPP access provider. If Netscape Navigator 2.0 is not currently running, launch it by double-clicking its icon.

2. In the Location box at the top of the window, select the currently displayed URL and replace it with **gopher://gopher.well.com/**. Press Enter. After a few moments, the top-level menu at the WELL Gopher site appears, as shown above in Figure 7-2.

3. This time, click the Internet Outbound (Links We Think Are Cool) link. The Internet Outbound Gopher menu appears, as shown in Figure 7-5.

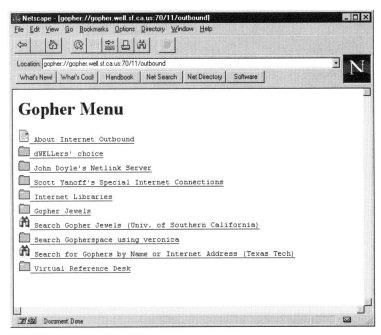

Figure 7-5: *The Internet Outbound Gopher menu on the WELL.*

4. All of the links on this menu provide useful starting points for Gopher burrowing. For this tutorial, click Scott Yanoff's Special Internet Connections. The Special Internet Connections Gopher menu appears, as shown in Figure 7-6.

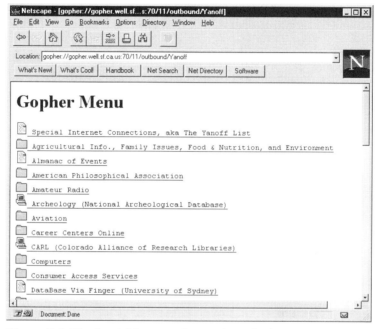

Figure 7-6: *The Special Internet Connections Gopher menu.*

■ Notice the icons depicting a computer terminal next to some of the links. This is how Netscape Navigator 2.0 indicates a Telnet connection. If you click on one of these links, Netscape Navigator 2.0 will launch a Telnet session with the host site. (More about Telnet later in this chapter.)

The Yanoff List, as it is sometimes known, offers you a wide variety of new jumping off points—or digging down points—for further Gopher burrowing. You should feel free to explore, and you might want to save this menu as a bookmark.

But before you descend into the Gopher tunnels, note that the Location box contains the URL gopher://gopher.well.sf.ca.us:70/11/outbound/Yanoff. *WELL* is still part of the site address because you've never really left the WELL; no matter how far or deep you burrow through the menus, *WELL* will still form the initial part of the URL. The URL provides a map of the path you took to get to the target information.

There are many ways to get to the Yanoff List, but you have constructed a tunnel that begins at the WELL and passes through the Internet Outbound menu. What this means is that you have a complete record of your travels, and in saving a particular URL as a Bookmark, you are actually saving a map of your entire journey. With this kind of hierarchical structure, there is really no way to get lost.

This is what I mean by stretching Gopherspace. With each new link you click, you are further extending a *customized* information pathway. You can see why Gopher is a useful research tool when you're trying to refine your quest for particular information.

The WELL is only one of many tunnel entrances. In the next section, I'll list some interesting Gopher sites to begin your explorations.

GREAT GOPHER HOLES I HAVE KNOWN

Table 7-1 lists a few of the best-known Gopher sites.

URL	Description
gopher://gopher.uis.itd.umich.edu/	University of Michigan archive
gopher://ashpool.micro.umn.edu/	University of Minnesota archive
gopher://wx.atmos.uiuc.edu/	Weather maps
gopher://gopher.eff.org/	Electronic Frontier Foundation archive
gopher://gopher.well.sf.ca.us/	Whole Earth 'Lectronic Link (WELL) archive
gopher://wiretap.spies.com/	The Internet Wiretap

URL	Description
gopher://siggraph.org/	Conference proceedings and materials from the graphics special interest group (SIGGRAPH) of the Association for Computing Machinery
gopher://gopher.cpsr.org:70/ 11/cpsr	Computer Professionals for Social Responsibility archive
gopher://akasha.tic.com/	Sample issues of John Quarterman's Matrix News Internet newsletter, several works from Bruce Sterling
gopher://gopher.echonyc.com	Interesting information about New York City and media

Table 7-1: *Some well-known Gopher sites.*

USING GOPHER TO FIND PEOPLE

One of the most important uses of Gopher is to find people. Yes, you can use Netscape Navigator 2.0 to burrow for your long-lost Uncle Waldo—provided he's been spending some of his lost years hanging out on the Net. In fact, Gopher provides the easiest-to-use interface for a wide range of search tools.

To find Waldo, start by going to the URL gopher:// gopher.micro.umn.edu/. From there, select Phone Books. Many options, including Whois searches, X.500 gateway searches, and phone books at other institutions, will appear. Searching for individuals on the Net requires that you know something about their "Net lifestyle"—where they hang out on the Net, and whether or not they are affiliated with any university or subscribe to Usenet newsgroups—so at this point, you're on your own. You may not find Waldo, but at least you'll have an easy time looking.

Now that you know something about Gopher, let's take a brief look at another faithful old workhorse of the Internet, Telnet.

WHAT IS TELNET?

The World Wide Web is the showroom of the Net. It's where you'll find information in all the latest styles and colors. If you want to show a newbie what the Net is all about, you'll almost certainly start with the Web.

But a fancy new car right off the showroom floor isn't always the best way to travel. Sometimes you need an all-terrain vehicle, a rugged tool that will take you places you can't access using the newer Web protocols. Telnet dates back to the days when the information superhighway was just a two-lane blacktop, and fortunately you can still take advantage of its raw power through Netscape Navigator 2.0.

Using Telnet, you log in to other computers on the Net interactively. Once you log in, the Telnet host presents you with a command line or with text-based menus; you type menu choices or commands. Typical public Telnet sites include library card catalogs, weather information services, and a variety of specialized databases. You can also Telnet to text-based online services such as the WELL or Echo. And if you have a UNIX account on another computer on the Net, you can use Telnet to log in and run any UNIX program available on the host machine.

MUDs & MOOs

It's great to be able to access vast libraries of esoteric information via the Internet, but at some point we have to step back and take stock again of what computers are really for: playing games!

Some of the most interesting games spawned by modern information technology are MUDs and MOOs. MUDs are *Multiple-User Dimensions*, real-time, interactive role-playing games. MOOs are the object-oriented version, in which users can create their own objects, such as new rooms or features of the landscape. There are also variants of MUDs known as MUCKs, MUSHes, and MUSEs. ➡

What all these games have in common is that several players at a time use the Internet to interact with one another as characters in a fictional world. Some of these text-based virtual worlds are full of magic and dragons, others are more like discussion forums, and some are meeting places for playing out group fantasies. Here are a couple of Web pages to get you started:

■ MUDs, MOOs, and Other Virtual Hangouts (http://jefferson.village.virginia.edu/iath/treport/mud.html). Lots of info about MUDs and MOOs, and links to several sites.

■ MUDs, MOOs, & MUSHes, "Hip-Waders in the CMC Swamp" (http://www.oise.on.ca/~jnolan/mud.html). Links to information and games.

Also check out the Usenet newsgroups under rec.games.mud. It's important to read the FAQs and whatever other information you can get before trying these games, as each has its own culture and rules of etiquette.

How does this remote login process work? Telnet is really a *terminal emulation* protocol. That means it makes your PC behave like a terminal that's directly connected to the host computer. What is a terminal? A terminal is a device that can't really do anything on its own, but when it is attached to a computer it provides users with a display screen and a keyboard. In other words, a terminal provides the user interface to a host computer. Normally, terminals are attached to the host by means of cable, but terminal emulation programs allow you to connect remotely using a PC and phone lines. With terminal emulation programs like PROCOMM PLUS and Telix, you dial directly into a host; with Telnet, you connect via the Internet.

Figure 7-7 shows a typical Telnet session. In this example, I am logged in to the Echo online service, and you can clearly see the interactive nature of this kind of connection.

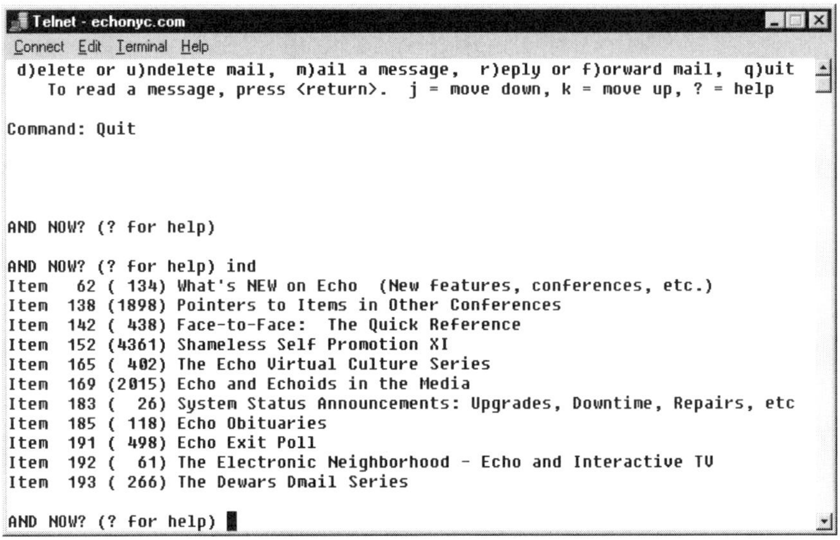

```
Telnet - echonyc.com                                    _ □ X
Connect  Edit  Terminal  Help
d)elete or u)ndelete mail,  m)ail a message,  r)eply or f)orward mail,  q)uit
    To read a message, press <return>.  j = move down, k = move up, ? = help

Command: Quit




AND NOW? (? for help)

AND NOW? (? for help) ind
Item   62 ( 134) What's NEW on Echo  (New features, conferences, etc.)
Item  138 (1898) Pointers to Items in Other Conferences
Item  142 ( 438) Face-to-Face:  The Quick Reference
Item  152 (4361) Shameless Self Promotion XI
Item  165 ( 402) The Echo Virtual Culture Series
Item  169 (2015) Echo and Echoids in the Media
Item  183 (  26) System Status Announcements: Upgrades, Downtime, Repairs, etc
Item  185 ( 118) Echo Obituaries
Item  191 ( 498) Echo Exit Poll
Item  192 (  61) The Electronic Neighborhood - Echo and Interactive TV
Item  193 ( 266) The Dewars Dmail Series

AND NOW? (? for help) █
```

Figure 7-7: *A Telnet session with Echo.*

TELNET & NETSCAPE NAVIGATOR 2.0

Let's see how observant you are: what's wrong with Figure 7-7?

That's right, it depicts some other software instead of Netscape Navigator 2.0. Instead of the usual toolbar and Netscape logo, you see a much simpler window. Did the author make a mistake? Did the editors miss it?

No. The fact is that Netscape Navigator 2.0 does not actually include built-in Telnet. Not only that, I don't know of any Web browser that *does* include built-in Telnet. Let me explain.

Terminal emulation programs and Web browsers are two very different kinds of software. Terminal emulation programs concentrate on interpreting ASCII character sequences on the fly, while Web browsers concentrate on displaying multimedia documents.

Since these two functions are not a good fit, the authors of most World Wide Web programs have decided to support Telnet by launching an external helper application when necessary. If you click a link that represents the URL for a Telnet connection, Netscape Navigator 2.0 launches your Telnet session by executing a separate program, passing to it the address of the site. As soon as you're finished with the Telnet session, you can return to the

Netscape Navigator 2.0 window and to whatever document was last displayed in it. In fact, you don't even have to wait. If you're the kind of person who likes to do several things at once, you can go back and forth between active Telnet sessions and the main Netscape Navigator 2.0 window.

But how does Netscape Navigator 2.0 know what Telnet program to use when you navigate to a Telnet URL? It requires a little bit of setup, but fortunately the setup is very sraightforward.

TN3270

Almost all public Telnet sites these days support the standard version of the protocol that uses the VT100 terminal emulation. However, there is a variant of Telnet known as *TN3270*. TN3270 sites require that you use a program that makes your PC act like an IBM 3270 terminal instead of a DEC VT100.

Your regular Telnet program probably does not include TN3270 capabilities. If you plan to connect to TN3270 sites, you'll need to download a special TN3270 program from the Net. Now that you've read Chapter 6 and know all about finding files on the Net, this should be no problem at all!

SETTING UP TELNET

Way back in Chapter 2, "Getting Started," we took a quick look at the Apps tab, which is where you tell Netscape Navigator 2.0 what program you want to use for Telnetting to remote sites. To get to the Apps tab:

1. In the main Netscape Navigator 2.0 window, select General Preferences from the Options menu. The General Preferences dialog box appears.

2. Click the Apps tab. The Apps tab includes fields where you can specify several supporting applications, including Telnet and TN3270, as shown below in Figure 7-8.

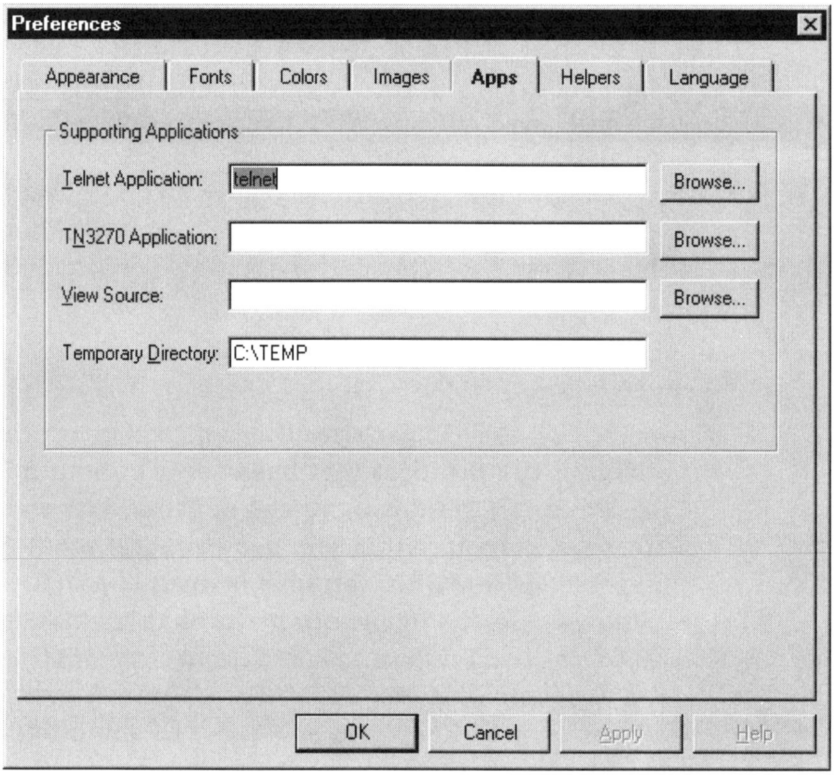

Figure 7-8: *The Apps tab.*

3. In the Telnet Application field, fill in the name of your Telnet application. Optionally, you can find the appropriate program on your hard drive using the Browse button.

TIP

*If you're using Windows 95, you can simply type **telnet** in the Telnet Application field.*

4. In the same way, complete the TN3270 Application field if you plan to use TN3270.

TIP

While you're in the Apps tab, you might also want to specify an application other than Netscape Navigator 2.0 to view or edit the HTML source of any Web documents displayed in the program. You can also tell Netscape Navigator 2.0 what work directory to use for storing temporary files.

    5. Click OK.

That's all there is to it! Now you're ready to start actually using Telnet.

USING TELNET

As with any other Internet service supported by Netscape Navigator 2.0, you can get to a Telnet site by any one of several methods. You can:

- Click a Telnet link in a Web document or at a Gopher site.

- Type a URL in Netscape Navigator 2.0's Location box.

- Select a Telnet link from Bookmarks.

- Double-click a desktop shortcut to a Telnet site.

Any one of these actions will have the same result: Netscape Navigator 2.0 launches your Telnet application, which then logs you in to the site specified in the URL.

Let's give it a try by going back to a Telnet link you may have noticed earlier in a Gopher menu, the National Archeological Database. You may not be the slightest bit interested in archeology, but I have chosen this site because it is very typical of research sites that are publicly accessible via Telnet.

For the sake of this tutorial, I'm assuming you're using the Windows 95 Telnet application. The basic instructions should be close to accurate even if you're using a different program:

    1. Make sure you are connected to the Internet either directly or via your SLIP or PPP access provider. If Netscape Navigator 2.0 is not currently running, launch it by double-clicking its icon.

2. In the Location box at the top of the window, select the currently displayed URL and replace it with **gopher:// gopher.well.sf.ca.us:70/11/outbound/Yanoff**. Press Enter. (Hey, if you'd saved the Yanoff menu as a bookmark, you wouldn't have to type in the URL again.)

3. Click the Archeology (National Archeological Database) link. After a few seconds, the Telnet application appears with a login prompt from the remote site, as shown in Figure 7-9.

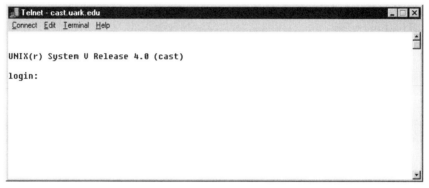

Figure 7-9: *Windows 95 Telnet program with login prompt from the National Archeological Database.*

In addition, a small message box pops up telling you to log in to this site as "nadb," as shown in Figure 7-10.

Figure 7-10: *Login information message box.*

TRAP

Not all sites supply you with login instructions like this, but many do. Depending on the exact timing of data received from the remote site, the Telnet window might cover the informational message box so that it is invisible to you. Before experimenting with different logins to see what will work, move or temporarily minimize the Telnet window to make sure you didn't miss an important message.

*If the remote system presents you with a login prompt but no information about what to enter, try typing **guest** and pressing Enter.*

4. Click OK in the message box. It disappears.

5. At the login prompt in the main Telnet window, type **nadb**. You are now logged in to the National Archeological Database, as shown in Figure 7-11.

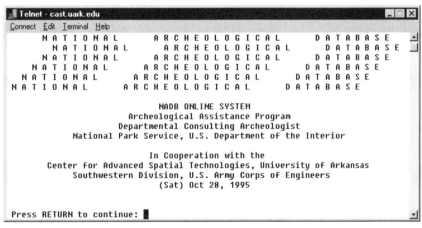

Figure 7-11: *You're logged in to the National Archeological Database via Telnet.*

6. As directed by the remote system, press Return (Enter) to continue. The NADB Connection Menu appears. Since you are connected via the Internet, select item 4, Internet to NADB, and press Return.

7. Continue following any directions that appear in the Telnet window. As is typical with research sites like this, you are asked to enter some information about yourself and to

choose an ID number. Once you've gotten through this process, the NADB Main Menu appears, as shown in Figure 7-12.

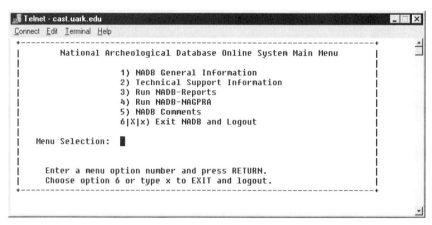

Figure 7-12: *The NADB Main Menu.*

TIP

Most Telnet programs let you copy text directly from the terminal window so that you can save it or paste it into other applications.

8. At this point, you can choose an item from the menu to get more information about the NADB or to access its search tools immediately. If you're interested in archeology, feel free to return to this site later, but for now let's select menu option 6 (or the letter *x*), Exit NADB and Logout. If you are using the Windows 95 Telnet program, a message box pops up explaining that your connection to the host has been lost, as shown in Figure 7-13.

Figure 7-13: *The Connection to Host Lost message.*

LOGGING OFF REMOTE SYSTEMS

Your Telnet program probably provides a way to disconnect from a remote site at any point, without even telling the remote host that you are leaving. In the Windows 95 Telnet program, you simply choose the Disconnect option from the Connect menu.

Whenever possible, however, you should end your session cleanly by logging out from the remote Telnet site, choosing the appropriate menu options, or following instructions for quitting. Otherwise, the software at the remote Telnet site may not immediately realize you are gone and may keep the connection open for several minutes, exacerbating Net traffic jams.

Unless you're having technical problems with the connection, disconnecting without logging out is considered poor online etiquette.

9. Once you are disconnected from the remote host, you can simply quit your Telnet program.

That's all there is to it. At first it may seem awkward that Netscape Navigator 2.0 needs to launch a separate helper application for Telnet access, but there are several advantages to this system. The most significant bonus is that you can use any Telnet application you want, including ones that are much more configurable and full-featured than the program included with Windows 95.

Speaking of configuration, let's take a quick look at some ways to tailor your Telnet application so that it works most efficiently for you.

CUSTOMIZING YOUR TELNET APPLICATION

Most Telnet applications offer a variety of options to make your online life easier and more productive. Since the Windows 95 Telnet program is typical of the simple applications that are available, we'll use it as an example. If you're using a different program, you may have to look around a little for the configuration options we're examining, but they should be there somewhere.

1. Launch Telnet by clicking its icon on the desktop or by using the Windows 95 Run command. The main Telnet window appears, as shown in Figure 7-14.

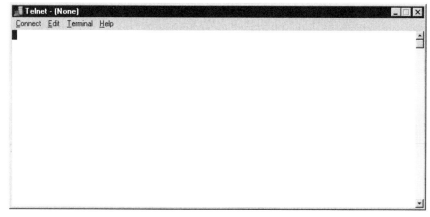

Figure 7-14: *The Windows 95 Telnet application.*

■ Most Telnet applications don't require you to be connected to the Net to change preferences or configuration options.

2. Select Preferences from the Terminal menu. The Terminal Preferences dialog box appears, as shown in Figure 7-15.

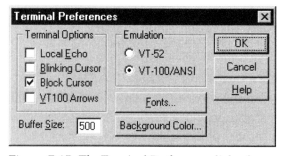

Figure 7-15: *The Terminal Preferences dialog box.*

The options in this dialog box are pretty typical of what's available in Telnet programs. Here are some tips for configuring these settings:

- **Local Echo**. Most remote Telnet sites echo back to you all the characters you type so that you can see what you are doing. Generally you should leave this check box unchecked; check it only if your typing is invisible to you.

- **Blinking Cursor**. Check this box if you want your cursor to blink while you are in Telnet. This can help you find the cursor on remote systems that include lots of lines or underscores in their screens.

- **Block Cursor**. Check this option if you want a block cursor instead of the usual cursor. This may be much easier to see on some systems.

- **VT100 Arrows**. The VT100 terminal emulation includes two different sets of character sequences ("mappings") that can be sent to the remote Telnet host when you press the arrow keys. Unless your arrow keys don't seem to be working properly at a particular site, leave this box unchecked. (For the propeller heads out there, unchecked means Keypad Application Mode, and checked means Keypad Cursor Mode. The remote site may send sequences that temporarily change your default setting.)

- **Buffer Size**. This option lets you specify how many lines you can scroll back to see text that has scrolled out of the Telnet window. Since the VT100 terminal displays 25 lines of text at one time, this option should be set to 25 or greater.

- **Emulation Options**. Unless a remote Telnet host explicitly requires VT52 emulation, you should keep this set to VT100/ANSI. Other Telnet programs may let you choose from a wider variety of terminal emulations, but VT100 is the most commonly supported one on publicly accessible sites.

- **Fonts**. Click this button to change the font of the text that appears in your Telnet window.

- **Background Color**. Click this button to change the background color of your Telnet window.

Once you have made your configuration changes, click OK to return to the main Telnet window.

MOVING ON

This has been the "back to basics" chapter—a quick look at some of the older workhorse Net services available through Netscape Navigator 2.0. Now we're going to go in the other direction and explore Netscape Navigator 2.0's multimedia capabilities. In its support of Gopher and Telnet, Netscape Navigator 2.0 provides you with a dependable off-road utility vehicle. But as you'll see in Chapter 8, its forward-looking integration of graphics and sound make it a true cyber-spaceship.

chapter eight

Sound & Graphics in Netscape Navigator 2.0

By now you have some idea what World Wide Web sites look like and have to offer. Unlike many other Internet services, the Web is not restricted to text. Web documents can contain images, sound, and now even 3D objects. As a Web user, you have at your fingertips a vast assortment of multimedia documents that virtually come to life when you view them. Netscape Navigator 2.0 enables you to interact with these multimedia documents in a variety of ways.

GRAPHICS ON THE WEB

Pictures play an important role in our lives: we hang them on our walls; we pay money to stand and look at them in museums; we take snapshots of our loved ones and favorite places. Just as pictures are a common form of communication in our society, they are an important part of the World Wide Web. In fact, much of the growth and popularity of the Web is a result of people like you and me having a new way to gather and disseminate information in a colorful and creative way.

In the following sections, you'll read about the types of graphics that are available on the Web and how you can view and download them with Netscape Navigator 2.0.

WHAT KINDS OF IMAGES ARE AVAILABLE?

Each month, thousands of new Web pages are created and placed online. Almost all of them contain some sort of graphic. Graphics can be small or large, colorful or black-and-white, tasteful or tasteless. You can probably find the exact image you're looking for on the Web if you look long enough. It may not be legally posted there, but it will be there (I discuss copyright infringement later in this chapter).

So what kinds of images can you expect to find on the Web? Almost anything. There are:

- Paintings by Renoir, Van Gogh, and little Jimmy from Ms. Wharton's first grade class.

- Publicity shots of your favorite movie and television stars, including Brad Pitt, Riki Lake, and Bill Gates.

- Detailed weather maps like the ones you see your local weather man pointing at on the 11 o'clock news.

- More *Star Trek* and *Deep Space Nine* photos than we care to know about.

- Business logos and advertisements, from IBM and Microsoft to Absolut and Ford Motor Company.

- Cartoons and animations.

- And yes, some pictures of naked people, if you look hard enough.

GRAPHICS IN NETSCAPE
NAVIGATOR 2.0—AN OVERVIEW

Fortunately for all you picture lovers, Netscape Navigator 2.0 includes features that let you view the majority of graphics on the Web. Graphics appear in a variety of sizes, shapes, and formats. In one way or another, Netscape Navigator 2.0 can either display them or provide an easy way for you to view them in another application. The best way to understand the types of graphics and how they display on Netscape Navigator 2.0 is to link to a fairly typical site.

To view a graphic in Netscape Navigator 2.0:

1. Make sure you are connected to the Internet, either directly or through a SLIP or PPP connection with your access provider. If you are using a SLIP or PPP connection and are not currently connected, double-click the Dial-Up Connection icon for your access provider.

   ■ If you are using Windows 3.1 rather than Windows 95, or if you are not using Windows 95's built-in networking, follow the instructions that came with your TCP/IP software for accessing the Internet.

2. Double-click the Netscape Navigator 2.0 icon to launch the program. The main window appears, and the Netscape home page starts loading.

3. Click your mouse inside the Location field at the top of the window to select the URL http://home.netscape.com/.

4. Replace the URL with the one for the Universal Pictures home page by typing **http://www.mca.com/ universal_pictures/index.html**. Then press Enter. Netscape Navigator 2.0 retrieves the Universal V/IP page, as shown in Figure 8-1.

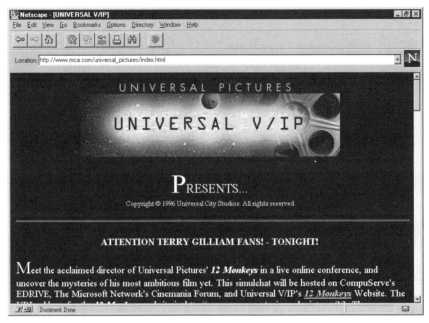

Figure 8-1: *The Universal Pictures Universal V/IP home page.*

HAVE I GOT THE ENTIRE DOCUMENT?

Many Web pages take some time to download to your computer. How can you be sure you've received the whole thing? Netscape Navigator 2.0 provides several clues.

First, you can look at the status line at the bottom of the Netscape Navigator 2.0 window. This area indicates the transfer progress of the Web document. On the left side of the status line is a readout that displays the size, percentage downloaded, and the rate at which Netscape Navigator 2.0 is retrieving the document. You might have a difficult time reading this line because it's constantly changing, but it will give some idea of how fast your modem is transferring data. At the far right of the status line is a small graphical bar that represents the data transfer. The bar expands to the right as the new page transfers. When the document has completely transferred, this area goes blank, which tells you that no more data is being sent.

Another way to tell if a Web page is completely transferred is to look at the Stop button on the Netscape Navigator 2.0 toolbar. If it displays a red stop sign (which you can click to stop the transfer), the document is still transferring.

But probably the coolest way to see if a document is still transferring is to watch the animated Netscape logo in the top right corner of the Netscape Navigator 2.0 window. As the document transfers, a meteor shower streams across the big Netscape *N*. When the shower ends, the document has finished downloading and all the graphics are displayed.

On a Web page like the one shown in Figure 8-1, you may see several different graphics and notice that they're used in a variety of ways. By far the most prevalent type of image you encounter in Web pages is an *inline graphic*. Inline graphics are part of the Web document itself, and not a separate file; they appear alongside the text. Inline graphics can include photos, buttons, icons, cartoons, and many other types of pictures. They are used for the following purposes:

- Logos
- Decorations
- Bullet points
- Illustrations
- Separators

Sometimes graphics are not inline, but exist only as a separate image file that you can download to your hard disk for later viewing, or one that you need to view in a separate application from Netscape Navigator 2.0. One common external viewer is

LView Pro, which was used to display the graphic shown in Figure 8-2. You'll learn more about these types of images and how to view them in the section entitled "Graphics on Demand," later in this chapter.

Figure 8-2: *A graphic displayed in LView Pro.*

When you connect to a site, such as http://www.vmedia.com (Ventana's Web site), the Web document begins to transfer to your computer and appears in Netscape Navigator 2.0. As the document displays, you usually see some text first, and then the graphics begin to appear. Depending on the speed of your connection, images may seem to flow in line by line or pop right up along with the text. It all has to do with the amount of data that your modem or phone line can transmit to your computer monitor. For example, high-speed connections, such as ISDN or T1 phone lines, can transmit more data per second than modem connections.

TIP

Tired of waiting for a document's images to display? Click the Stop button on the Netscape Navigator 2.0 toolbar to stop the transfer. If you want to complete the transfer later, click Reload.

Or turn off the automatic display of graphics entirely, as described later in this chapter under "Text-Only Mode."

To accommodate users with all kinds of connections, some sites now include two different versions of the same page. One page usually includes a lot of graphics that a typical modem user will not want to wait to download to his or her computer. The other usually has very few images and mostly text. When you link to a site that has these options, such as the Internet Underground Music Archive (IUMA), you must make a choice to view the page with a lot of images, or one that has been toned down a little to avoid unnecessary waiting.

Figure 8-3 shows what you'll see if you choose the pages with fewer graphics; Figure 8-4, on the other hand, shows you the same site when you choose to see the graphics-intensive pages. Running with a 14.4 kbps modem, the graphics-intensive page took more than 2 minutes to display. The "lite" version took only 12 seconds!

Figure 8-3: *The IUMA site with lots of graphics.*

Figure 8-4: *The IUMA site again, this time with very few graphics.*

Most sites include the same textual information in both their graphics version and their text-only pages—the only thing you'll miss is the images themselves.

You'll learn later how to optimize the display of graphics in Netscape Navigator 2.0, but let's first discuss a couple of special-purpose graphics often used on the World Wide Web: background images and icons.

BACKGROUND IMAGES

Background images do just what their name implies—they provide the background to the text and other graphics in a Web document. Background images typically are very small images (such as a picture of a small cloud) that are repeated again and again over the entire background. (This technique sometimes is referred to as *texture mapping* in graphics design programs.) The images can be solid colors, textures, pictures, patterns, or whatever the Web author comes up with. For example, the Graphion home page pictured in Figure 8-5 shows a gray granite background. Some other texture backgrounds you may encounter include marble, wood grain, metallic, and skin. (Yes, that's right. Skin.)

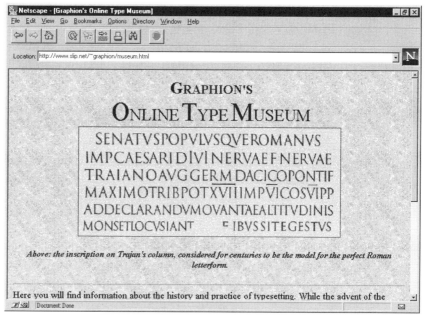

Figure 8-5: *Graphion's home page, showing gray granite background.*

When Web page authors create a page, they can enter HTML code (the language of Web pages) to include an image as the background. Not all Web sites use backgrounds (because of the extra burden of downloading them), but most do. Backgrounds offer the Web author a way to set a standard color, texture, or image for the entire Web site. This eliminates the need to rely on the Web browser to provide a color (using the Options | General Preferences | Colors properties) for the Web page.

ICONS

Icons are another type of graphic you'll encounter on almost all Web pages. Icons are small images or buttons, sometimes miniatures of larger images you can find at that site. Icons are used to highlight certain points on the page, lead you to another Web page or site, or let you view or download a larger image. Let's look at each of these uses.

In Figure 8-6, you see a set of icons to the left of some text on the Web page. These icons serve the same purpose that bullets do in a book or business document: to distinguish key points. Icons can also be used to highlight special text on a page, in much the same way that "Tips" in this book are delineated with small icons.

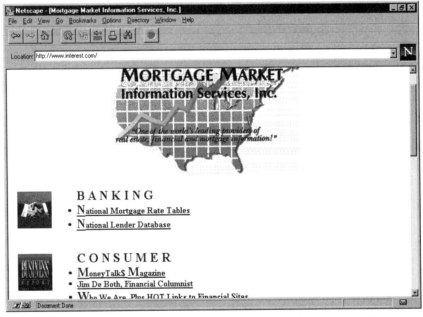

Figure 8-6: *Icons emphasize important text on the page (© Mortgage Market Information Services, Inc.).*

The second type of icon is actually a hotspot that links to another page or another site, sometimes to graphics of products or announcements. This type of icon works the same as linked text on a page—when you click on it, you connect to that other site or page. Icons of this type have a small blue border around them to indicate they are links. Figure 8-7 shows examples of icons that you click to advance to another related site.

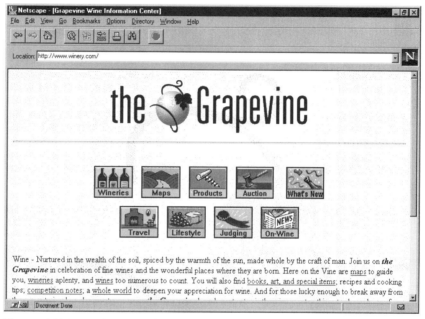

Figure 8-7: *Icons that provide links.*

WHAT IS THE NETSCAPE NOW ICON?

After your first 10 or 15 minutes on the Web, you're bound to run into a Web page that includes the Netscape Now icon (see Figure 8-8). Netscape provides this icon for Web page authors to include on pages designed especially for Netscape Navigator 2.0. This icon, or button, links the user to Netscape's home page so that users who don't have Netscape Navigator 2.0 installed can order or download a copy of it. For more information on obtaining permission to use this icon, see http://home.netscape.com/comprod/mirror/netscape_now_program.html.

Figure 8-8: *Web page authors can use the Netscape Now icon on pages designed for Netscape Navigator 2.0.*

Icons are also used as small "try-before-you-download" versions of larger graphics. Click this kind of icon (often called a *thumbnail*), and the larger image begins to transfer. The advantage of this approach is obvious: the smaller thumbnails transfer to your machine much more quickly than full images you may not even be interested in.

For example, the Web page in Figure 8-9 shows small icons of Renoir paintings (http://sunsite.unc.edu/wm/paint/auth/renoir/). You can scroll down the page and click the painting you'd like to see in full size. A larger painting displays in Netscape Navigator 2.0, as shown in Figure 8-10.

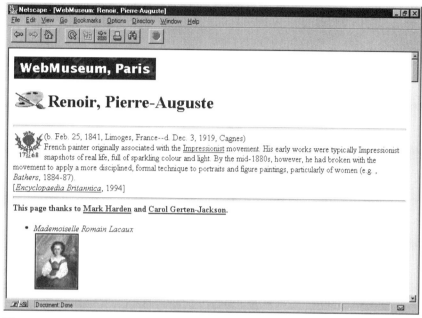

Figure 8-9: *Thumbnail of a painting.*

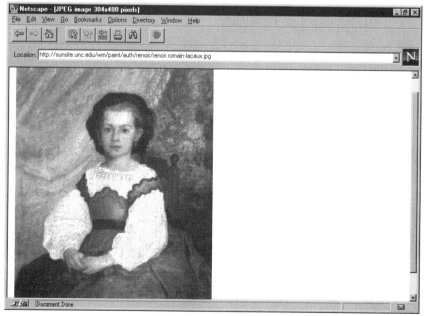

Figure 8-10: *Full view of the same painting.*

TIP

Conscientious Web page authors include file sizes and estimated transfer times next to icons. Use these estimations to guide you in determining if the wait is going to be worth it. When I am on these sites, I find the smallest file and download it first. If I don't like the quality, I probably will not download another one.

GRAPHICS FORMATS SUPPORTED BY NETSCAPE NAVIGATOR 2.0

The graphics in Web documents typically come in standard file formats that most Web browsers, such as Netscape Navigator 2.0, can understand and display on your computer. The standard file formats include Graphics Interchange Format (GIF), Joint Photographic Experts Group (JPEG), and XBM. GIF and JPEG are the most common graphics you'll encounter in Web pages. XBM is a UNIX graphics format and is more likely to be found at university or research areas that generally work with high-speed computing applications.

ANY OTHER FORMATS OUT THERE?

Many other types of graphics formats are available on the Web, including Macintosh PICT, BMP, PCX, TIFF, and encapsulated PostScript (EPS), but the most common image formats are GIF and JPEG.

Both GIF and JPEG files are compressed to save transmission time and to limit their storage size. It is beyond the scope of this book to get into the technical differences between JPEGs and GIFs, but the two formats excel in different areas. JPEG compression is often used for ultra-realistic photographic images, while GIF is used for colorful graphics. GIFs can start to display on your screen while they are still downloading, while with JPEG images you must wait for the entire image before it appears (although a new standard call "progressive JPEG" is emerging, which displays images while they are loading). GIF images may also be *transparent*. Transparent GIF images are graphic files that have been customized to eliminate the background color of the image. Thus they appear to "float" on top of the Web page instead of being stuck inside a rectangular prison.

TIP

JPEG files generally have an extension of .JPG; GIF files always have an extension of .GIF.

When authors create Web pages, they make sure the images they place as inline graphics can be displayed by the most popular Web browsers. Because Netscape Navigator is such a popular browser, Web authors almost always try to develop pages that are compatible with it. This means that they use GIFs and JPEGs. You should not have any problem viewing most Web pages.

GRAPHICS ON DEMAND

Some Web sites offer images you can download to your computer for subsequent viewing. These differ from inline graphics because they are not part of the text of the Web page display, but are only linked to in the document. You can still view many of these files in Netscape Navigator 2.0, using it simply as a file viewer instead of a Web browser. Or, if you want to edit the file or save it in a different format, you can view it in a stand-alone graphics application such as Paint Shop Pro.

At the Saturn Web site shown in Figure 8-11, for example, you can download a picture of one of the auto maker's new models and then view it in Netscape Navigator 2.0.

Figure 8-11: *The Saturn Web site.*

To download a picture:

1. Make sure you are connected to the Internet either directly or via your SLIP or PPP access provider. If Netscape Navigator 2.0 is not currently running, launch it by double-clicking its icon.

2. In the Location box at the top of the window, select the currently displayed URL and replace it with address for the Saturn Web site, which is **http://www.saturncars.com/ 96-models/SL/**, and press Enter.

3. After the Web document transfers to your computer and displays, click on a link to a full-size picture. These are listed underneath the picture of the car on the home page. The links describe the view of the image, such as Front View or Rear View. Next to a hot link is the approximate size of the image in kilobytes. The larger the image, the more time it takes to display.

4. Click on the "A picture of the car in motion" link. Notice that Netscape Navigator 2.0 opens a new page where the image will display. Figure 8-12 shows the completed version of this picture.

Figure 8-12: *The Saturn SL/SL1 in motion.*

Now that the image is onscreen, what can you do with it? Not much, at this point. Netscape Navigator 2.0 is not designed to be a graphics editor, but only a viewer of certain graphics types. What you can do is save the image to your hard disk for later viewing. If you enjoy a particular image and you've waited several minutes for it to transfer to your machine, you owe it to yourself to save it to disk.

To save an image to disk:

1. Select Save As from Netscape Navigator 2.0's File menu. The Save As dialog box appears, as shown in Figure 8-13.

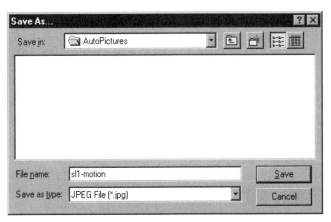

Figure 8-13: *The Save As dialog box.*

2. Choose a location for the file and then click the Save button. The Saving Location dialog box appears, showing the progress of the file transfer.

TIP

To save a graphic quickly, right click the image and select Save This Image As from the context menu.

■ Because the file already has been downloaded to your computer (but not saved to disk), it takes only a few seconds to save it to disk.

3. Click on the Back button to return to the previous Web page.

WHO OWNS THE IMAGE?

The easy answer to this question is "probably not you." Almost every image on the World Wide Web and the Internet is owned by someone or by a legal corporation. Don't think that just because you can download an image to your computer's hard disk, you own the rights to the file. In most cases, you do not. In fact, some images have been placed on the Web illegally, without permission from their owners. By downloading these images, you may also be breaking the law.

Fortunately most sites comply with International copyright laws and make available only those images they own or have legally licensed from another party. These images are protected by copyright laws and usually are provided for you to view but not reuse or sell in any form.

Some sites legally allow you to download graphics for use in commercial or noncommercial ways. Clip art images, for example, fall into this category. Many sites offer downloadable images that you can use in business documents, Web documents, and other sources. The caveat here is that you are still responsible for making sure that the images you download are indeed owned or licensed by the person owning the Web site and that you can reuse them.

Other sites require that you first pay a fee to acquire the rights to view and download images. Sites such as MTV, Sony, and Playboy offer repositories like this. Again, copyright laws restrict you from reselling these images as your own. You can only look at them, just as when you buy a magazine with an image of R.E.M., you can't make copies of the image and sell them to your friends. You own the physical magazine, but not the rights to the photographs within it.

CONFIGURING GRAPHICS SETTINGS IN NETSCAPE NAVIGATOR 2.0

As you've already seen, Netscape Navigator 2.0 comes ready to display GIF, JPEG, and XBM graphics. Netscape Navigator 2.0 also includes customization options to configure the way graphics are viewed. These options are necessary because not all video display hardware is created equal. For example, you may be able to display 256 colors, while your 12-year-old son has configured his hot rod machine to display 16 million. We all know that in carefully mixing his paints, Renoir used many more than 256 separate colors. So what does Netscape Navigator 2.0 do about images that were created with more colors than your machine can display? It uses two different approaches to solving the problem: *dithering* and *color substitution*.

Dithering is a process that arranges pixels (the little "dots" on your screen) of varying shades to achieve a visual effect, often a simulation of a different color. For instance, a pattern of black and white pixels can be used to simulate gray. By varying the ratio of white pixels to black pixels, you get different shades of gray. Since there is more information in this scenario, images that are displayed with dithering take slightly more time to display than images using simple color substitution.

Dithering often provides excellent approximations of colors that are not available on your display system. Sometimes, however, they can make an image look speckled, particularly at low resolutions. If you're not into the speckled look, try switching to color substitution.

Color substitution does what you'd expect. As Netscape Navigator 2.0 reads in a graphics file and encounters a color not available on your display, it substitutes a color that *is* available. Color substitution may make a graphic's look slightly "off," but they will be textured the same as the original.

Let's take a look at the color options:

1. From the Netscape Navigator 2.0 Options menu, select General Preferences. The Preferences dialog box appears, as shown in Figure 8-14.

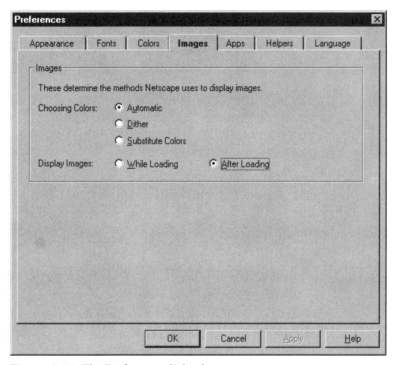

Figure 8-14: *The Preferences dialog box.*

2. Click the Images tab to display it.

3. At Choosing Colors, select the way Netscape Navigator 2.0 handles graphics.

   ■ **Automatic.** Lets Netscape Navigator 2.0 decide what colors to use when displaying a graphic. This is the default setting and should be OK for most users. With this setting selected, Netscape Navigator 2.0 makes up its own mind whether to dither or to substitute available colors.

- **Dither.** Tells Netscape Navigator 2.0 always to dither the computer's available colors to most closely match the image's colors. In Windows, JPEG images are dithered automatically.

- **Substitute Colors.** Instructs Netscape Navigator 2.0 to substitute an available color that most closely matches the image's colors.

TIP

By experimenting with these color settings, you can determine the best view for your system. Sometimes you may have to adjust a setting if your PC's monitor does not display an image properly.

There is one more setting in the Images tab. It specifies whether or not images will be displayed before they have been completely transferred. To change this setting, select from the following choices:

- **While Loading.** Instructs Netscape Navigator 2.0 to display partial images while they are being transferred. This is the default setting.

- **After Loading.** Tells Netscape Navigator 2.0 to wait until the entire image has transferred before displaying it. On very fast networks, this *may* be slightly faster than the other method, but I'm a child of the visual age and get anxious if I don't see something happening on my screen right away.

After you make changes to the Images tab, click OK to save them and return to the main Netscape Navigator 2.0 window. Or click Cancel if you want Netscape Navigator 2.0 to disregard any changes you have made.

TEXT-ONLY MODE

If you have a modem connection to the Web and have been following the various links in this chapter, you're probably growing tired of waiting for some of the documents to transfer. In fact, if you have a modem that operates at less than 28.8 kbps, you may already be working on next year's letter to Santa. But besides speeding up your Internet connection, there is another approach: you can bypass graphics altogether.

Netscape Navigator 2.0 gives you the option of turning off the automatic display of graphics by deselecting the Auto Load Images option on the Options menu (see Figure 8-15). When this option is turned off, a small icon appears as a placeholder wherever an image is supposed to display. Figure 8-16 shows a Web document in text-only mode, with several placeholders for graphics.

Auto Load Images option

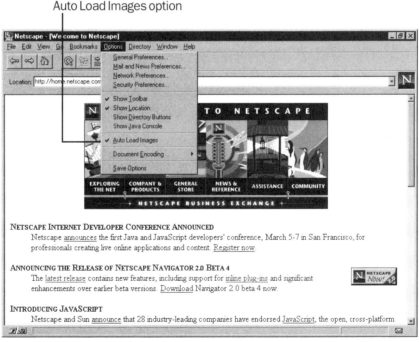

Figure 8-15: *The Auto Load Images option turns off the automatic display of graphics.*

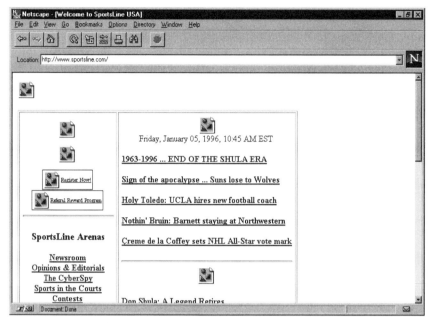

Figure 8-16: *A Web page with graphics turned off.*

If you then come across a particular document whose graphics you want to view, you can easily display them by clicking the Images button. This reloads the document with graphics displayed.

If you want to display graphics other than those supported directly by Netscape Navigator 2.0, there is one more configuration step: setting up helper applications.

SETTING UP HELPER APPLICATIONS

You read earlier in this chapter about how you can download images to view in another application, such as LView or Paint Shop Pro. When configured to work with Netscape Navigator 2.0, these applications are called *helper applications*. To make them work with Netscape Navigator 2.0, you must set them up manually using the Helpers tab of the General Preferences dialog box.

First, obtain a helper application and install it on your system. Applications that let you view or edit graphics are available from various sources, including third-party books, software stores, FTP and Gopher sites, and World Wide Web sites. Some of the applications that you might want to obtain are listed in the Table 8-1.

Viewer Name	Supports File Types
LView Pro	GIF JPEG/JPG, TIFF, BMP
Paint Shop Pro	GIF JPEG/JPG, TIFF, BMP
GhostView	PostScript

Table 8-1: *Some graphics viewers that can be used as helper applications.*

TIP

Virtually any *program that can run on your system can be used as a helper application in Netscape Navigator 2.0.*

Netscape Navigator 2.0 natively displays GIF and JPEG files, so unless you're interested in editing or format conversion you won't gain much with a helper application that supports only these formats. You need one that offers the capabilities to read those formats and others, such as TIFF and BMP. These file types are fairly common, and some Web sites may include these types of graphics in their documents or file archives.

Once you acquire and install a helper application on your system, use the following steps to configure it to work with Netscape Navigator 2.0 to display any TIFF files you encounter:

1. Select General Preferences from the Options menu. The Preferences dialog box appears.

2. Click the Helpers tab, shown in Figure 8-17. If you feel overwhelmed by this screen, see the sidebar "What Are All Those Funny Settings?" below.

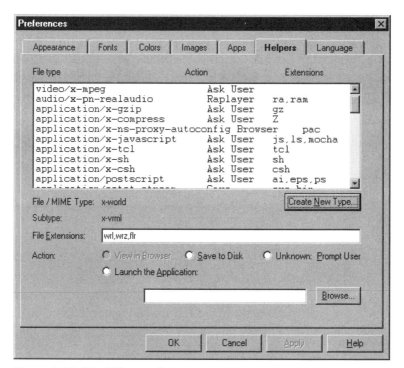

Figure 8-17: *The Helpers tab.*

WHAT ARE ALL THOSE FUNNY SETTINGS?

The Helpers tab looks fairly complicated at first, but once you understand the concepts, using it is really pretty simple. The large scrolling list includes the names of different kinds of files you might encounter as you cruise the Net with Netscape Navigator 2.0. These file types are listed using a naming standard known as *MIME*. In MIME nomenclature, for instance, files with an .EXE or .BIN extension are classified as applications, with a subtype designation of "octet-stream." If you scroll down the list you'll see many different types of files, some familiar and some unfamiliar. Usually the MIME designations make sense, as in the case of GIF files, which are classified as images with a subtype of gif.

Here's where it gets interesting. For each type of file it encounters on the Internet, Netscape Navigator 2.0 has a default action that's listed in the Action column of the list. For image/gif files, for example, you can see that the default action is Browser. This means that GIF graphics will be displayed automatically by Netscape Navigator 2.0 itself, right within the browser window. And for application/octet-stream files, the default is Save. When you click on a link to an .EXE or .BIN file, it will be saved to your disk.

3. In the long scrolling list at the top of the tab, scroll down until you see the image/tiff entry. Click it. Notice in the File Extensions text box that the extensions .TIFF and .TIF automatically appear. These are the extensions for TIFF images Netscape Navigator 2.0 will recognize. Netscape Navigator 2.0 can then launch the associated helper application and tell it to load the TIFF image.

4. Click the Launch the Application radio button, which is below the File Extension box. This tells Netscape Navigator 2.0 to launch your helper application when it encounters a TIFF image.

5. Now you need to tell Netscape Navigator 2.0 where on your computer to find the helper application. In the text box below the radio button you just clicked, enter the full path and file name of the helper application. If you are using LView Pro, for instance, this will be something like **C:\LVIEW\LVIEWP1A.EXE.**

TIP

Use the Browse button to find helper applications on your system.

6. Click OK to save your changes and return to the main Netscape Navigator 2.0 window.

Now when you encounter a site that includes TIFF images, Netscape Navigator 2.0 automatically starts the helper application and lets you view and manipulate the image.

The subject of graphics on the Internet is a very large one, and we've covered only the basics in this chapter. Chapter 9, "Advanced Netscape Navigator 2.0," will go into more advanced uses of graphics through Netscape Navigator 2.0 *plug-ins*, but for now let's see—or rather, hear—what's up with sound in Netscape Navigator 2.0.

VIDEO ON THE NET

Not only can you display static images with Netscape Navigator 2.0, you can also play video clips complete with motion and sound! Since there are several competing computer video standards, Netscape did not include a video player in the base Navigator product, but it is simple to add one. You follow the same procedures outlined earlier for adding any other kind of helper application. In addition, Netscape Navigator 2.0 supports what are known as *inline plug-ins*. Plug-ins are special purpose modules that can be added to Netscape Navigator 2.0 to extend its features. With inline plug-ins, video clips may be displayed right within the main browser window. You'll learn more about inline plug-ins in Chapter 9, "Advanced Netscape Navigator 2.0," and you can find links to further information on the Netscape home page.

SOUND ON THE WEB

Many computers you purchase today come with sound cards and speakers. This has fueled the growth of sound capabilities on the Web. Thousands of Web sites now include sound files that offer a new way to experience online content. Radio stations, public television stations, and network news shows are providing sites that feature sound recordings. Some sites even include *live* performances of rock bands or the play-by-play of weekly football games. As the Web matures, you'll be able to sit back and enjoy the pleasing sounds of the Internet as you work on that marketing proposal or college term paper. The history of technology is a history of distractions, and the good folks at Netscape are doing their best to distract you by including a sound player with Netscape Navigator 2.0.

AT WHAT COST SOUND?

If a picture is worth a thousand words, what's the value of the spoken word? It may or may not be worth the time it takes to download a file with sound it and listen to it.

Sound files have been available on the Internet and World Wide Web for years, but for the most part have been impractical to use. They are impractical because they are huge and offer only short segments of actual content. A 30-second sound recording may occupy over 5MB of disk space. In my book, that is just too much transmission time and disk space to waste for very little excitement.

A sound file I downloaded recently from the WTUE radio station site (http://www.arsdayton.com/wtue.html) contained a 1-minute sound clip of a Bush song (see Figure 8-18). This file ended up being 1.3MB in size.

Figure 8-18: *A sound clip that cost me 24 minutes of download time and provided only 60 seconds of entertainment.*

Sound on the Net has also been hampered until recently by the unavailability of PCs equipped with sound devices. Until several months ago, most computers did not include sound cards and speakers. This made it difficult for users to spend time downloading and listening to sound files on their system.

WHY CAN'T I USE MY PC'S SPEAKER?

You can, but you'll be disappointed with the results. Every PC comes equipped with a tiny speaker in it that you may hear beep every once in awhile. You'll hear it beep a few times, for instance, when you start up your computer. You can make this speaker play some of the sound files you find on the Internet by acquiring a speaker driver from Microsoft (called SPEAKE.EXE) and loading it on your system. You also need to acquire an application that plays different sound files. For many users, the reigning champion during the past year or so has been WPLANY.EXE, which is short for "We Play Anything." You can download WPLANY.EXE from ftp://ftp.cam.org/systems/ms-windows/slip-ppp/viewers/wplny09b.zip.

SPEAKE.EXE can be found at ftp://ftp.microsoft.com/Softlib/MSLFILES.

Not all the news is bad on the sound front, however. New applications are becoming available that allow you to listen to sound files *as they are transmitted* to your computer. That means you don't have to wait forever, racking up online charges, to see if you even like the thing. One of the packages that offers this incremental playing of sound files is called RealAudio, which is discussed later in this chapter. What these packages offer users is a sense of real-time interaction across the Internet. If you don't like what you hear, you can immediately stop the transmission of the sound file before you invest a lot of your time.

SUPPORTED SOUND FILES IN NETSCAPE NAVIGATOR 2.0

Netscape Navigator 2.0 includes built-in support for the following sound file formats: AU, SND, AIF, AIFF, and AIFC. It's not important to know what all these acronyms mean, but you *should* know that the two most popular sound types on the Web are AU and SND.

I said earlier that support for these file types is built right into Netscape Navigator 2.0. Well, I lied—but it was only a very small lie, one that would pass in Washington for shining unvarnished truth. Here's the deal: Netscape Navigator 2.0 plays sound files using a separate utility called the Netscape Audio Player, or simply Naplayer (see Figure 8-19). But Naplayer is already set up as a helper application, and if I hadn't told you about it, you might never have realized it wasn't part of the main Navigator executable. You never have to worry about configuring it. Of course, you may encounter sound files that Naplayer does not support. For these files, you can configure Netscape Navigator 2.0 to work with other helper applications that support these sounds. See "Other Audio File Types on the Web" later in this chapter for more information.

Figure 8-19: *Netscape's Naplayer application.*

LISTENING TO SOUND
IN NETSCAPE NAVIGATOR 2.0

When you connect to a Web site that contains sound files, you generally will see a speaker icon indicating that it is a sound file. If the sound file is of a type that Netscape Navigator 2.0 supports, you can click the icon. Netscape Navigator 2.0 automatically launches Naplayer and plays the file.

The following steps show you how to do this:

1. Make sure you are connected to the Internet either directly or via your SLIP or PPP access provider. If Netscape Navigator 2.0 is not currently running, launch it by double-clicking its icon.

2. In the Location box at the top of the window, select the currently displayed URL and replace it with **http://www.iuma.com**. Press Enter. After a few moments, the Internet Underground Music Archive (IUMA) appears.

TIP

If the IUMA site is busy, you can check out one of these two sites for sound files:
http://www.cnn.com
http://www.whitehouse.gov/White_House/html/pres-welcomes.html

The first URL is for the Cable News Network (CNN) home page. The second URL is for the White House home page. At the White House home page, you can listen to President Clinton welcome you to the Internet and tell you how much he's excited about all this technology.

3. Click on a link to a sound file, as shown in Figure 8-20. The Viewing Locations dialog box appears.

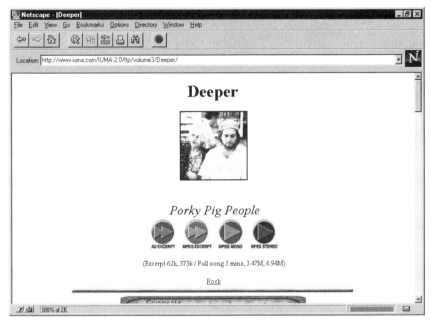

Figure 8-20: *Some sound file links at IUMA.*

■ For some of these links, you may have to go looking for the audio files. Some sites will not let you link directly to the sound file without passing through their "front door."

4. The entire file must be transferred to your system before it begins to play, so sit back and read *War and Peace*. (Just kidding. Reading the rest of this book should be about right.)

5. When the file has been transferred, Naplayer pops up on your screen and plays the sound file. All of this is done automatically. You needn't lift a finger.

In Naplayer, you can adjust the way the sound file plays by using the Controls menu items:

- **Beginning.** Starts the sound clip over.
- **Seek Back.** Rewinds the file.
- **Play.** Starts the sound clip.
- **Stop.** Stops the sound clip.
- **Seek Forward.** Fast-forwards the file.
- **End.** Moves to the end of the sound clip.

TIP

Use the Naplayer toolbar button to perform the same tasks as the Controls menu items.

When the sound file ends, it stops automatically and you can do one of two things: play the same sound clip over and over again, or get a life and close Naplayer. You'll notice that Naplayer does not give you the option to save the sound file to your disk. After waiting several minutes, or even hours for a large file, you might find this a little disappointing.

If you do want to save a sound file to disk, set up the Helpers tab so that Save to Disk is selected for this particular file type. Later you can play it in manually simply by launching Naplayer from the Windows Run command. Let's revisit the Helpers tab to see what I'm talking about:

1. Select General Preferences from the Netscape Navigator 2.0 Options menu.

2. In the Preferences dialog box, click on the Helpers tab.

3. Scroll down the long list of files until you reach audio/ x-aiff. Click it.

4. Click the Save to Disk radio button in the Action area.

5. Do the same with audio/basic. Again, this instructs Netscape Navigator 2.0 to save all AU and SND files straight to disk instead of using Naplayer to play them automatically

Now when you click a link to a sound file of one of these types, you are presented with the Save As dialog box. Enter a location and file name for the file and click Save. The Viewing Locations dialog box appears, updating you on the progress of the file.

After the file is stored on your disk, use the following steps to play in Naplayer:

1. Launch Naplayer, using the Run command from the Windows 95 Start menu or the Windows 3.1 File menu. Naplayer is usually located in the same directory as Netscape Navigator 2.0 itself, and unsurprisingly, the executable file is called NAPLAYER.EXE.

2. Once in Naplayer, select Open from the File menu. Then select the file you just downloaded.

3. Press the Play button on Naplayer. (It doesn't start automatically, as it did when Netscape Navigator 2.0 launched it.)

After the file plays, you can replay it or simply close Naplayer.

OTHER AUDIO FILE TYPES ON THE WEB

Just as with graphics files, several different types of sound files are available on the Web. One of the most popular is the WAV sound file format. WAV files are Microsoft Windows audio files. If you have Windows set up to play sound events, such as when you start or exit Windows, you've probably heard these types of files. Bleep, chlunk, ding, vreeeep—you and the irritated people you live with know what I'm talking about.

Because so many users access the World Wide Web with Windows, more and more sites are offering WAV as an alternative to AU or SND files. Netscape Navigator 2.0 does not natively support WAV, but you can configure a helper application to play back these files. Luckily, one such program, Media Player, is installed with Windows.

Media Player is usually is stored in the folder or directory where you installed Windows. To configure it as a helper application for all WAV files you encounter on the Web, follow these steps:

1. Select General Preferences from the Options menu.

2. In the Preferences dialog box, click the Helpers tab.

3. Scroll down the long list of files and click the item audio/ x-wav.

4. Click the Launch the Application radio button in the Action area. This instructs Netscape Navigator 2.0 to load a helper application when it encounters a WAV file.

5. In the text box below that radio button, enter the path and filename of Media Player (or use the Browse button to locate the file on your system). If, for instance, you have Media Player in the root folder under the Windows folder, your entry would look like this:
   C:\WINDOWS\MPLAYER.EXE

6. Click OK to save your changes.

Now whenever you encounter a WAV file on the Web, Netscape Navigator 2.0 will know to launch Media Player to play it.

USING REALAUDIO WITH NETSCAPE NAVIGATOR 2.0

You just read that the Web is full of sound files that you may want to ignore because of their large size and short content. But fortunately there is a utility that lets you listen to some audio files while they are being transferred. Using this utility can save you a lot of time.

Using the RealAudio player, which is available from the Progressive Networks Web site, you can hear news, sporting events, music and much more. The RealAudio format makes you feel as though you're listening to the radio, right on the Net (well, almost). Figure 8-21 shows the RealAudio player in action.

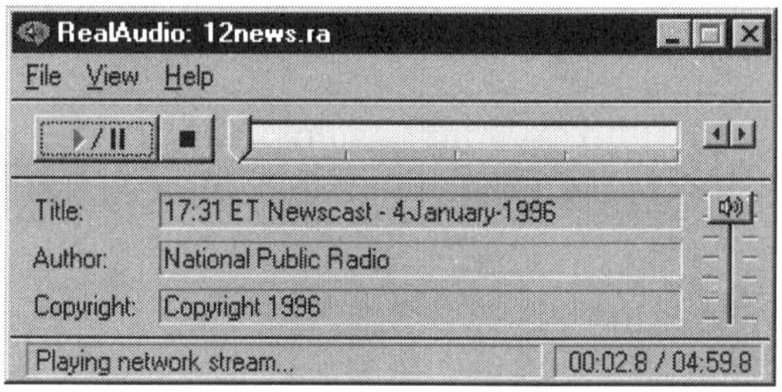

Figure 8-21: *The RealAudio player.*

REALAUDIO AS A NETSCAPE NAVIGATOR PLUG-IN
At the time of this writing, RealAudio 2.0 beta testing has begun. RealAudio 2.0 includes several new features, including high-quality audio output (FM radio–quality sound with 28.8 kbps modems), live audio, and most important, plug-in support for Netscape Navigator 2.0. You will learn about plug-ins in Chapter 10, "Commerce & Security on the Net," so for now we'll concentrate on the more established and tested version of the product. You can also get more information from the RealAudio 2.0 home page at http://www.realaudio.com/products/ra2.0/index.html.

WHAT IS REALAUDIO?

RealAudio consists of two pieces. The first piece is one you'll probably never have to use unless you become a Web site administrator. The RealAudio Server is the software that enables Web sites to offer RealAudio files. The server software is purchased by companies like ABC News and National Public Radio that wish to offer their news online in a format similar to broadcasting live reports. In fact, the same news reports you hear on the radio or television are saved as RealAudio files to disseminate online via the Web.

The other piece of the RealAudio puzzle is the client utility that enables users like you to listen to RealAudio recordings. When you install RealAudio on your system, it adds itself as a new helper application. Then when you encounter a RealAudio file, Netscape Navigator 2.0 automatically starts the RealAudio players and plays the file.

TRAP

RealAudio Player plays only RealAudio files. It does not play files in other audio formats!

OBTAINING REALAUDIO

The RealAudio client software, which is what you want to install on your system, is free of charge from the RealAudio site. To get a copy of RealAudio, connect to RealAudio's Web site (http://www.realaudio.com/) and download the software to your computer.

Before you take the time to download and configure RealAudio, read the list of system requirements to run the program. The requirements include 2MB of free disk space and a sound card with a Windows Sound driver. (The RealAudio Player is not compatible with the PC Speaker program or other software programs that emulate a sound card.)

Once you determine that your computer can run RealAudio, use the following steps to download it from the Progressive Network Web site:

1. Make sure you are connected to the Internet either directly or via your SLIP or PPP access provider. If Netscape Navigator 2.0 is not currently running, launch it by double-clicking its icon.

2. In the Location box at the top of the window, select the currently displayed URL and replace it with **http://www2.realaudio.com/release**. Press Enter. After a few moments, the RealAudio home page appears.

3. Click on the link to download the Windows version of RealAudio.

4. Unless you've preconfigured a helper application for EXE files, the Unknown File Type dialog box appears.

5. Click on the Save to Disk button. The Save As dialog box displays.

6. Enter a location for the file such as C:\TEMP\. (There is no need to change the filename.)

7. Click Save to save the file to your hard disk.

Now let's set up RealAudio so that it will work with Netscape Navigator 2.0.

INSTALLING & CONFIGURING REALAUDIO

RealAudio should now be on your computer and ready to install. Before you go any further, disconnect from your Internet provider and make sure that Netscape Navigator 2.0 is *NOT* running.

To install RealAudio, run the file you just downloaded by double-clicking it in the Windows Explorer (or in the File Manager if you are using Windows 3.1). RealAudio starts its installation program. Then simply follow the instructions that appear on your screen. At the conclusion of the setup process, the RealAudio player launches and plays a Welcome to RealAudio message. If the message sounds distorted, see the "Sound" section of the RealAudio Release Notes, which are stored on your system where you installed RealAudio.

TRYING OUT REALAUDIO

When you connect to sites that contain RealAudio links, you can listen to a link by clicking it. It's that easy. The RealAudio player first contacts the host computer that contains the audio file. After a few moments during which it downloads the initial section of the file, it starts to play it over your system speakers. You can adjust the volume of the playback by using the slider control on the right side of the player, as shown in Figure 8-22.

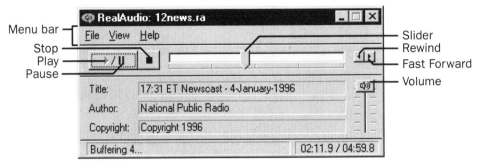

Figure 8-22: *The RealAudio player.*

So that you can try out RealAudio, Table 8-2 lists some sites that include RealAudio files. In the future, look for events such as football games, rock concerts, speeches, and the like to be simulcast as RealAudio events that you can listen to live.

Site Name	Address
National Public Radio	http://www.npr.org/
ABC Radio Network	http://www.abcradionet.com/
Delta Dream Vacations	http://pwr.com/LEISURE/ DELTA.html
Advanced Digital Services	http://206.65.169.39/
Grace Hour	http://www.smart.net/~ggwo/
Nightstand	http://www.nightstand.com/
Tabernacle Baptist Church	http://www.tabernacle.org/~tbc/
Toyota Motor	http://www.toyota.co.jp/
North Carolina News Network	http://www.capitolnet.com/ncnn/
QuikQuiz Stop Smoking	http://www.mindspring.com/ ~wbarnes/health/quikquiz.html
Adtek Web Services	http://www.adtek.com/
Tech Talk Radio Network	http://ttn.nai.net/
BBC Radio 3: Facing the Radio	http://www.bbc.co.uk/ftr/
Black Cat Radio	http://www.pulver.com:80/thecat/
MusicNet	http://www.man.net/~musicnet/
OneWorld	http://www.oneworld.org/ realaudio/index.html
I-Net LIVE!	http://www.pennet.net/inetlive/

Table 8-2: *Some sites that have RealAudio files.*

CAN I CREATE MY OWN REALAUDIO FILES?

Yes, you can, but you'll need some extra software. Specifically, you must download a copy of the RealAudio Encoder from the Progressive Networks Web site. Using Encoder, you start with a WAV or AU audio file and convert it to the RealAudio file format, with the extension .RA. Within the RealAudio file you can insert a name of the file, author, and copyright information. This information is displayed on the user's machine when he or she is playing it back. Of course, the file you've created doesn't do you much good unless you have a way to distribute it to the public. You must copy it to a site that has the RealAudio server software. For more information on RealAudio servers, see the RealAudio Web site at http://www.realaudio.com/.

INTRODUCING JAVA

The next chapter covers some of the exciting new multimedia technologies supported by Netscape Navigator 2.0, including Java. But let's get in the mood for this futuristic stuff by taking a quick look at Java now, since it is so often used to create graphical elements in Web pages.

Java applets are the hottest new eye-candy on the Web. And what are *applets*? They are simply small applications written in the Java programming language. Yes, Java is actually an entire programming language. (For the propeller-heads reading this, it's similar to C++ but without pointers.) Java lets developers create platform-independent multimedia applications for distribution on the Web. Web browsers that support these Java applets allow users to visit sites that include Java applets (or even full-blown applications) and actually run them. When integrated into Web pages, Java applets allow graphics rendering, real-time interaction with users, live information updating, and instant interaction with Web servers.

You can download Java applets and run them safely on any platform. Since Netscape was in the technological vanguard in supporting Java, you don't need a special helper application to interpret the Java code. And the same Java applets run on any operating system that supports Java, so you don't have to figure out which version of an applet to link to.

TIP

Java was designed to provide some level of security on the Internet, with several built-in safeguards against viruses, tampering, and other security threats. Until someone comes up with ways to include viruses with a Java applet, you should feel pretty safe downloading and running applets in Netscape Navigator 2.0. The time will come, however, when you'll probably need to rely on a virus checker that checks and cleans applets as they are transmitted to your system. Security-conscious users can block Java applets in Netscape Navigator 2.0 by selecting Disable Java in the General tab of Security Preferences.

Figure 8-23 shows an example of what a Java applet can do.

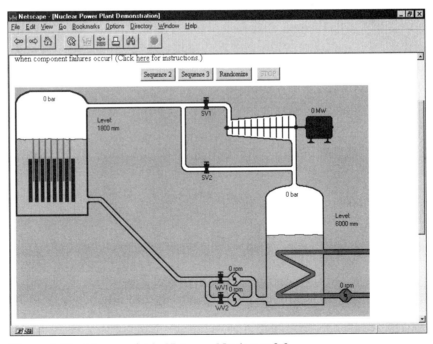

Figure 8-23: *A Java applet in Netscape Navigator 2.0.*

Some of the earliest Java applets available on the Web are relatively small and don't do much. Many are company logos that rotate on a center axis, displaying different lighting effects and textures. Although these efforts are primitive, anyone who sees these applets realizes the potential of the technology. Someday Java may be used to create entire virtual worlds in which users can interact with each other while navigating the World Wide Web.

TRAP

Java is built into the Windows 95/Windows NT version of Netscape Navigator 2.0, but it may not be included in the initial release for Windows 3.1. Please check the Readme file for the latest information.

MOVING ON

In this chapter, you've learned the basics of viewing graphics and listening to sound in Netscape Navigator 2.0. You've also learned how to overcome some of the limitations of static sound files on the Web by installing and using the RealAudio Player, and we've briefly mentioned Java.

Some of the more advanced features of Netscape Navigator 2.0 are covered in the next chapter. Read it to learn about image maps, proxy, the Netscape Navigator 2.0 LiveScript scripting language, and plug-ins. There, you also can find a brief introduction to creating your own Web page (it's very simple to do).

chapter nine

Advanced Netscape Navigator 2.0

You now have had some time to get acquainted with Netscape Navigator 2.0's basic features, such as bookmarks, viewing and saving graphics, and accessing remote files via FTP. You may now want to examine the more advanced features of Netscape Navigator 2.0. Some of these features are not exactly new to Netscape Navigator 2.0, but they offer a way for you to optimize and configure certain settings, such as proxies and cache. Other advanced Netscape Navigator 2.0 features are brand new. These include client-side image maps, inline plug-ins, Java support, and Netscape Navigator 2.0 JavaScript. These features are also covered in this chapter.

Let's start with Netscape Navigator 2.0's support for proxy gateways.

TIP

If you are connected to the Internet via a modem and SLIP or PPP connection, you don't have to worry about setting up proxies. Also, if you are not having problems connecting to the Web, you don't need to read the next section. You can skip to the section called "Understanding & Setting Cache Sizes."

Using Proxies in Netscape Navigator 2.0

Proxy gateways are a security feature deployed by many businesses. System administrators set up proxy gateways so that users on a LAN are not actually connected directly to the Internet. Instead, any Internet data they send or receive is handled by the proxy computer, which passes the information on. The proxy may be completely transparent, allowing all data in and out of the organization and simply monitoring activity, or it may be part of a *firewall* that restricts both inbound and outbound access in various ways. The proxy settings in Netscape Navigator 2.0 allow the program to pass on a network request (in the form of a URL) to an outside agent through a firewall, which performs the request for Netscape Navigator 2.0. The proxy agent then returns any Internet information to Netscape Navigator 2.0.

What Is a Firewall?

You've probably read horror stories about hackers who get online only to sabotage or destroy data. As the new information technologies mature, acts like these probably won't have the same thrill they used to, but cyber-criminals will never disappear completely. That's why businesses, universities, government agencies, and other sites that have sensitive data on their networks are forced to think of ways to keep these types of users away. Firewalls are software and hardware solutions that provide a layer or several layers of protection between the Internet and a network. These layers are designed to keep the bad guys out, but they also restrict users within a network from getting out on the Internet directly. For this reason, proxies were created to enable users to work through firewalls and access the outside world.

By the way, the term *firewall* comes from the days when brick walls were built between apartment buildings to keep fires from spreading from one building to the next. The metal between the engine and the passenger compartment of a car is also called a firewall.

Users of a Netscape Navigator 2.0 software client using a proxy gateway still think they are on the Internet even though they technically are not. Proxy gateways are implemented based on the type of service in use, such as FTP, Gopher, WAIS, news, and HTTP (the World Wide Web). Each URL access method can send its requests to a different proxy.

CONFIGURING PROXY SETTINGS

Your first task is to ask your system administrator if a proxy is even necessary or available. If you are running Netscape Navigator 2.0 on an internal network from behind a firewall, you then need to know the names and associated port numbers for the server running proxy software for each network service. You'll need this data so that you can fill out the Proxies tab in the Network Preferences page in Netscape Navigator 2.0, as shown in Figure 9-1.

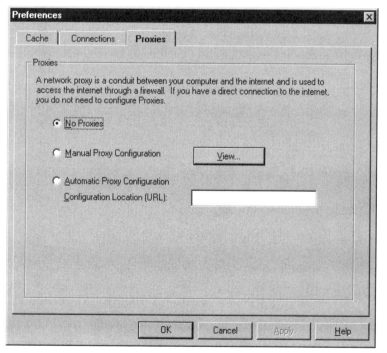

Figure 9-1: *The Proxies tab.*

The Proxies tab includes the following items:

■ **No Proxies**. Configures Netscape Navigator 2.0 to run without a proxy. This is the default setting.

■ **Manual Proxy Configuration**. This option allows the most flexible configuration of proxy gateways for each type of URL. If you want to configure the proxy settings yourself, use this option, as described below under "Configuring a Proxy Manually."

■ **Automatic Proxy Configuration**. Instructs Netscape Navigator 2.0 to configure your proxies automatically based on a configuration file designed expressly for your proxy server. Click the radio button and then provide the file's URL in the Configuration Location (URL) field.

CONFIGURING A PROXY MANUALLY

To set a proxy using the Manual Proxy Configuration choice, follow these steps:

1. Double-click the Netscape Navigator 2.0 icon to launch the program. The main window appears, and if you are using a starting page located on your hard drive it will display in the Netscape Navigator 2.0 window. Otherwise, you will see a blank window. This is because you are not yet connected to the World Wide Web (remember, that's what you're trying to establish by configuring the proxy settings). Click the Stop button to stop Navigator from looking for the home page it isn't going to find.

   ■ If a message box pops up telling you that Netscape Navigator 2.0 cannot find a domain, go ahead and click OK. This message box is telling you something you already know!

2. Select Network Preferences from the Options menu, then click the Proxies tab, shown above in Figure 9-1.

3. Click on the Manual Proxy Configuration radio button.

4. Click the View button to display the Manual Proxy Configuration tab, as shown in Figure 9-2.

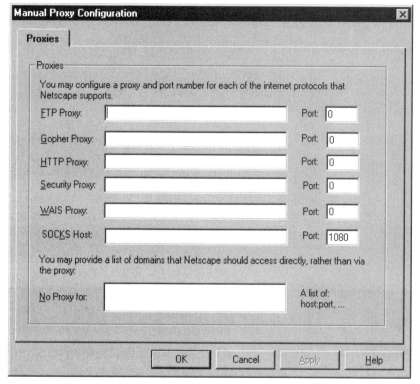

Figure 9-2: *The Manual Proxy Configuration tab.*

■ The long list of Proxies should be blank unless already configured by your network administrator. The Port settings will all have zeros in them, with the exception of the SOCKS host port, which should read 1080. If you see some other data already listed, stop and ask someone if these are the proper settings. If so, you're done.

5. Fill in each of the proxy fields with the following information:

TIP

You can put the Internet addresses for multiple hosts in each field. If your network administrator provides you with multiple proxy addresses for each protocol, they should be separated by commas. Do not use wildcards for multiple addresses!

- **FTP Proxy**. Enter the Internet address of the system running the proxy software and the port number for FTP protocol access. When set correctly, you'll be able to access anonymous FTP sites.

- **Gopher Proxy**. Enter the Internet address of the system running the proxy software and the port number for Gopher protocol access. When set correctly, you'll be able to access Gopher menus.

- **HTTP Proxy**. Enter the Internet address of the system running the proxy software and the port number for HTTP protocol access. When set correctly, you'll be able to access Web pages and sites.

- **Security Proxy**. Enter the information for your Secure Sockets Layer (SSL) protocol resource.

- **WAIS Proxy**. Enter the Internet address of the system running the proxy software and the port number for WAIS protocol access. When set correctly, you'll be able to access WAIS databases.

- **SOCKS Host**. If your network uses a SOCKS Host gateway as part of a firewall, enter its Internet address here.

6. Your network may be configured to allow you to access certain sites directly, without going through a proxy. If so, enter the addresses for these sites in the No Proxy For box. The format of these entries is the Internet address followed by the port number for the allowed protocol. For instance, the standard port number for Gopher is 70, so to allow direct access to the Gopher server at pjames.com you would enter **pjames.com:70**.

> **TIP**
>
> *Unless you have a photographic memory, take this book or page with you when you talk to your site administrator. Have him or her fill out the correct addresses and ports for each setting. Then enter them yourself in your copy of Netscape Navigator 2.0. Why? Because you need to make sure all these settings are perfect before trying to use Netscape Navigator 2.0. Otherwise you'll experience problems and won't be able to access anything on the Net.*

7. Click OK, then click OK again in the Proxies tab to return to the main Netscape Navigator 2.0 window.

Now that you've got this all set up, you should be able to connect to the Internet via your company's LAN. Give it a try by clicking the Home button. If it doesn't work, you'll need to talk once more to your network administrator. Every network is configured a little differently, so we can't give you any easy answers here.

UNDERSTANDING & SETTING CACHE SIZES

OK, so you've spent several hours on the World Wide Web and love it. The only problem is that you hate waiting for all the graphics to display, especially when you've already been to that same site and you know it hasn't changed yet. What can you do to speed things up a little?

First, buy a faster modem. Upgrading from a 14.4 kbps to a 28.8 kbps modem virtually doubles the amount of data you can download in a given period of time. If you can't do that right now, or you have already upgraded, set the cache size in Netscape Navigator 2.0 to increase the amount of data that is stored on your local computer and in your computer's memory while you use Netscape Navigator 2.0. Navigator accesses information from your hard disk and memory much faster than it does from the Internet.

WHAT IS A CACHE?

A *cache* (pronounced "cash") is a reserve area on your computer that houses information downloaded from the Internet as you navigate. You can think of it as a temporary holding area that Netscape Navigator 2.0 uses to store data between the time it is downloaded and the time it is displayed. If your cache is large enough, it can store entire Web pages and even graphics. That way, when you return to a previously visited site, Netscape Navigator 2.0 doesn't have to download the information all over again; it can simply grab it from the cache.

TIP

The Netscape Navigator 2.0 Refresh command (available from the View menu) redisplays the current document using information stored in the cache. The Reload button, on the other hand, actually goes back to the original document and reloads it from the Internet. If you think that a document may have changed since the last time you visited it during the current session, you should use the Reload button to view any updates.

SETTING CACHE SIZES

Netscape Navigator 2.0 enables you to set a memory cache and a hard disk cache. As you hit a Web site, information from that site is stored in both of these caches. When an item is in the memory cache, Navigator can access it more quickly than an item stored on the hard disk. Items stored in the memory cache are temporary and are emptied when you exit Netscape Navigator 2.0. The hard disk cache, on the other hand, stores the information even after you quit a Navigator session. The next time you start up Navigator, the information in the disk cache may be available.

There are advantages and disadvantages in setting high cache sizes for both types of caches. Even though memory caches are much quicker than disk caches, devoting more RAM to this type of cache can slow down your computer's overall performance. On the other hand, higher disk cache settings eat up your hard disk space. Another problem associated with high disk cache settings is the speed at which Netscape Navigator 2.0 shuts down when you exit the program. With a larger disk cache it takes more time for Netscape Navigator 2.0 to clean out any excess files from the cache upon exit. If you notice Netscape Navigator 2.0 takes a lot of time to close, you may want to reduce the size of the disk cache.

Follow these steps to change your settings for cache sizes:

1. Double-click the Netscape Navigator 2.0 icon to launch the program. The main window appears, and Navigator tries to load the Netscape home page. Click the Stop button.

2. Select Network Properties from the Netscape Navigator 2.0 Options menu. Click the Cache tab, shown in Figure 9-3.

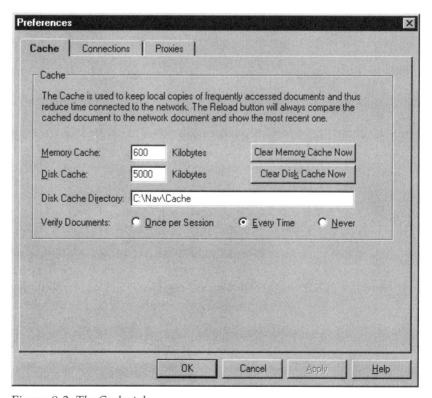

Figure 9-3: *The Cache tab.*

3. You can set the size of the memory cache in the Memory Cache field. The default setting is 600K of RAM (about .5MB of memory). Unless you have a large amount of memory on your system, such as 16MB or more, you may want to keep this setting where it is. Otherwise, you can try setting it at 1200K to see if your browsing speeds increase.

4. Set the amount of hard disk space that you want to reserve for a disk cache. This value is entered in the Disk Cache field; its default is set to 5000K (5M) or hard disk space. On most newer computers that come with hard disks of 450MB or more, you should have no problem reserving 5M or even 10MB for this cache.

TIP

Experiment with both the memory cache and hard disk cache sizes to determine the best settings for your system. If you tend to use Netscape Navigator 2.0 without other applications running at the same time, such as a word processor or spreadsheet, you can set the memory cache much higher to make Netscape Navigator 2.0 run quicker. If you tend to run Netscape Navigator 2.0 with other applications that need large amounts of memory, keep the memory cache low, around 600K. This ensures that each application running has ample RAM to run properly.

5. You can change the directory or folder in which Netscape Navigator 2.0 stores the cached items to disk by entering the name in the Disk Cache Directory field. By default, Netscape Navigator 2.0 creates a directory called CACHE in the Netscape Navigator 2.0 folder. Unless you have specific reasons for changing it, this location should be fine.

6. To clear the current content from your disk or memory caches, click Clear Memory Cache Now or Clear Disk Cache Now. When you click either of these buttons, the confirmation box shown in Figure 9-4 pops up, asking if you are sure you want to clear the selected cache. Click OK to confirm that you do; click Cancel if you change your mind.

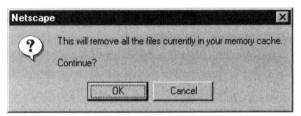

Figure 9-4: *The Clear Cache Now confirmation message.*

WHY WOULD I WANT TO CLEAR A CACHE?

Depending on how much navigating you do or how often you visit a site, you may want to periodically clear a cache setting. Having a cache decreases the time it takes to access sites that you've recently visited, but it does increase the strain on your local computer. When your memory cache is set to a high value, the amount of memory devoted to Netscape Navigator 2.0 cannot be used by other resources. This slows down your machine when you run these other applications. Also, you may want to clear the memory cache if you've been online for several hours and you feel your machine responding sluggishly to Netscape Navigator 2.0. After you clear the cache, you should notice an improvement in your PC's performance.

7. Click one of the radio buttons in the Verify Documents section. If a document stored in cache has been revised, you'll want to see the revision instead of the old document. These buttons specify how Netscape Navigator 2.0 checks the Web for document revisions:

- **Once Per Session.** Checks for page revisions only once during the time you start and quit Netscape Navigator 2.0. This is the default setting.

- **Every Time.** Checks for changes each time you request a Web document rather than relying on data stored in the cache. Because Netscape Navigator 2.0 is constantly checking the cached item against the Web page, you encounter a little performance degradation when you use this option.

- **Never.** Performs no verifications; a page available in cache is always brought from cache. Not a good selection if you want to see the latest-and-greatest offerings at a particular Web site.

8. Click OK to return to the main Netscape Navigator 2.0 window.

SETTING NETWORK CONNECTIONS

One way to speed up a connection to a site is to increase the number of connections to a specific server (a server is the computer that houses the Web page). With more than one connection to a server, Netscape Navigator 2.0 can bring in a page's text and multiple image files simultaneously. You can set this by clicking the Connections tab after selecting Network Preferences from the Options menu. By specifying a larger number of connections in the Number of Connections field (4 is the default), you are specifying more simultaneous connections. However, doing so can slow down the speed of each individual connection.

The other setting in this tab is the Network Buffer Size value. You can set the amount of data that your computer receives per transmission. The default is 32K. Larger values may speed things up, but they may also allow so much data through that your computer becomes saturated. This means it may slow down instead of speeding up. Unless you really know what you are doing, you should leave this setting as it is.

Now that we've looked at a few ways of optimizing Netscape Navigator 2.0's performance, we're ready to take a look at a few advanced features that really take advantage of that performance: Java, JavaScript, and new HTML 3.0 features.

JAVA!

When you get older and your grandchildren ask you about the good old days of the World Wide Web, you'll tell them about Java. You'll tell them that Java was the technology that got us one step closer to bringing real-time interaction between people on the Internet. Java is actually a programming language developed by Sun Microsystems, Inc. It enables software developers to create secure two-way Web applications very straightforwardly. These applications are called *Java applets*. With traditional Internet and World Wide Web content, the focus is mainly only one-way—from the server to the user. It's similar to the cable television that comes into your house. You can receive data from this cable, but you cannot transmit data back through it. We've seen that forms allow for some two-way interactivity, but Java really opens up the possibilities. When Java applets are integrated with a Web browser, such as Netscape Navigator 2.0, you can experience live information updating, interaction with other users, and instant interaction with Internet servers.

Java applets are embedded in Web pages (using the APPLET HTML tag) and automatically downloaded by Netscape Navigator 2.0 to your computer. A Java run-time application included in Netscape Navigator 2.0 executes the Java applet and enables you to interact with the applet. An example of a Java applet is shown in Figure 9-5.

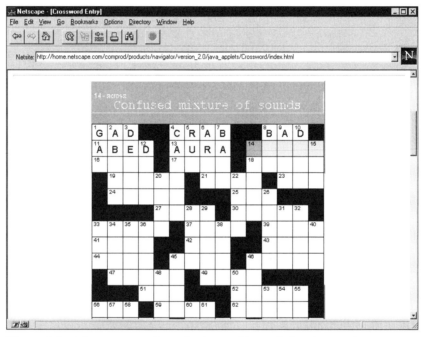

Figure 9-5: *A Java crossword puzzle that enables real-time interaction.*

WHY AREN'T JAVA APPLETS MORE INTERESTING?

As a society raised on motion pictures and television, we may think the Java applets available now are too crude to take seriously. Please remember that we are in the pioneering days of this technology, and in using it, you are one of the pioneers. Java applets are like sketches for all kinds of new applications that haven't been fully realized. They also are a major step in making online communication more than just text, pictures, and a lot of downloading.

How many times have you hit a site that includes a sound file or movie file that you were unable to view or listen to, either because of the required download time or because you didn't have the application that supported that file type? With Java applets, the code for the file that is available at the site can be interpreted by Java and then executed. You don't have to worry about having the correct executable loaded on your machine to access files. So Java developers can create applications without fear of incompatibilities. But for Java applets to become as plentiful as other applications on the Internet, they need some time to prosper and evolve.

As more and more developers acquire Java programming skills, and more and more people start using browsers (like Netscape Navigator 2.0) that support Java, Web sites will begin to include them. In fact, they may become as plentiful as graphics and other files you encounter on the Web now. For this reason, you need to know how to interact with Java applets when you encounter them.

INTERACTING WITH JAVA APPLETS

When you arrive at a site that includes a Java applet, you really don't have to do anything special. Netscape Navigator 2.0 does all the work. Once you click on a Java applet, you just wait for it to transfer to your computer. A complete download may take several minutes. Once the applet arrives on your machine, you interact with it per the individual applet's instructions.

Many sites offer a list of directions like these instructions from the Java applet site for the Crossword Puzzle applet shown in Figure 9-6:

```
How to play:
1) The current word you are working on is highlighted in
yellow.
2) The current letter is highlighted in cyan.
```

3) Click on any letter to move to that word.
4) <Spacebar> switches between across and down. It pivots around the current letter.
5) <Back space> erases the current letter.
6) Incorrect letters are drawn in red.

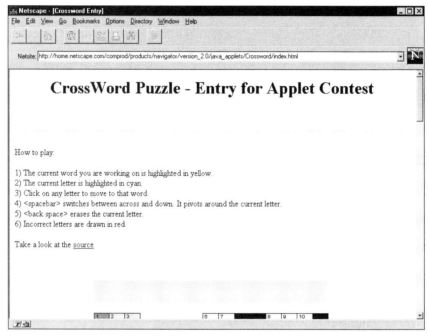

Figure 9-6: *Instructions for the Crossword Puzzle applet.*

The main difference between this type of application and one that has previously been on the Internet is that the Java applet lets you interact with it directly in Netscape Navigator 2.0. Previously you would have had to download a file (such as a crossword puzzle file to use in a word processor, for instance) that runs separately from Netscape Navigator 2.0. For this particular Java applet, you fill out the crossword puzzle while it displays in Netscape Navigator 2.0. You can type in letters, delete letters, and move from one box to another using your mouse and keyboard.

If you're interested in taking a look at some Java applets, you can do so by visiting one of the sites listed in Table 9-1. These sites include one or several applets that automatically display in the Netscape Navigator 2.0 window.

Applet	Where You Find It
Blinking Text	http://www.javasoft.com/applets/applets/Blink/example1.html
Curve	http://fas.sfu.ca:80/1/cs/people/GradStudents/heinrica/personal/curve.html
Crossword	http://home.netscape.com/comprod/products/navigator/version_2.0/java_applets/Crossword/index.html
Financial Portfolio Demo	http://www.javasoft.com/applets/applets/StockDemo/standalone.html
Imagemap	http://www.javasoft.com/applets/applets/ImageMap/example1.html
Modern Clock	http://www.wsrn.com/southern/java/DateClock.html
Pythagoras	http://home.netscape.com/comprod/products/navigator/version_2.0/java_applets/Pythagoras/index.html
Simple 3D Viewer	http://www.javasoft.com/applets/applets/WireFrame/example1.html
StarField	http://home.netscape.com/comprod/products/navigator/version_2.0/java_applets/StarField/index.html
Traditional Clock	http://www.javasoft.com/applets/applets/Clock/index.html

Table 9-1: *Java applets and where to find them.*

Another great resource that has sprung up over the past few months is the Gamelan Java Directory at http://www.gamelan.com/. This Web site is full of links and resources to Java sites and development news. If you're serious about Java, either as a developer or end user, you need to check out this site every so often to see what's new on the Java front.

ARE JAVA APPLETS SAFE?

Yes, for the most part. Java is similar to the C++ programming language but without pointers. *Pointers* enable programs to reference arbitrary memory locations on your computer. These memory locations might contain cached passwords. The developers of Java, Sun Microsystems, excluded pointers for this security reason (and to aid in error handling). This precaution does not guarantee, however, that a developer intent on breaking into your system can't do so. Applets are written in a Java language subset that is secure to avoid that possibility. Further, applets can't perform most file system access or file I/O routines.

Another form of security is in the Netscape Navigator 2.0 browser itself. Select Security Preferences from the Options menu and then click the General tab, shown below in Figure 9-7. Notice the Disable Java check box. Netscape Navigator 2.0 offers this option so that you can disable Java support for those times you want to download a Java applet to your machine but then cut off the network transactions *back* to the server (you also can disconnect from the Internet and run the applet locally). When you leave the option unchecked, this means you want full access to Java applet so you can initiate a two-way communication between your client and the server machine. By default, this setting is cleared to enable full Java access.

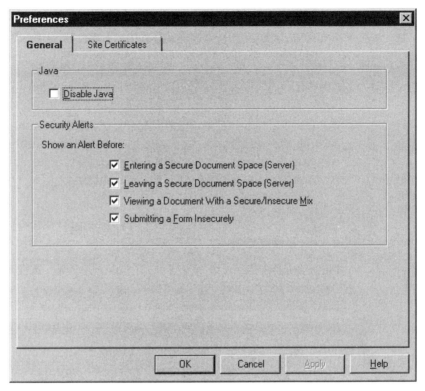

Figure 9-7: *The General tab.*

Instructions for Java applets are embedded in HTML documents using the <APPLET> tag. When you arrive at a Web site that includes a Java applet, Netscape Navigator 2.0 automatically downloads the applet and interprets it. For those interested in developing Java applets, you can obtain Sun's official documentation from its Web site, as well as download the Java API (application programming interface) for that site. To access that site, use this URL: http://java.sun.com/.

When you arrive at the Sun site, notice the small Java applet at the bottom of the Web page. It's an animated cup of steaming coffee (you know, hot java). The first place you'll probably want to visit at that site is the documentation area. This area includes a full introduction to Java and starts you on your way to understanding how to create your own applets.

Java is what's known in the computer industry as a "cool new feature." It's not just something that's needed to perform a particular task—it also looks toward the future and has a strong element of fun to it. It's the kind of feature that every programmer wants to work on. Unfortunately, it doesn't take that many developers just to incorporate Java into a browser, but Netscape has done something to please all those programmers they couldn't hire. Inline plug-ins, covered in the next section, allow third-party developers to actually extend Netscape Navigator 2.0 with new features, limited only by their imaginations.

EXAMINING INLINE PLUG-INS

Netscape Navigator 2.0 is a robust World Wide Web application that enables you to experience most of what is available on the Net. As the Web becomes more popular and the technology of browsers improves, more sophisticated multimedia content is becoming available. You just saw, for instance, how Java is adding new dimensions to Web content. Movies, three-dimensional objects, desktop-published documents, and video conferencing are slowly making their way onto the Web as well. Not only is this type of data putting strains on the infrastructure of the Internet, it also is forcing Web browsers to evolve from text and graphics displayers to real-time, interactive multimedia viewers.

Not to worry. Your investment in Netscape Navigator 2.0 is a good one. Netscape Navigator 2.0 supports several types of plug-in applications that enable you to experience most of what is available online. Plug-ins are applications that extend Netscape Navigator 2.0's capabilities to view and interpret various document and file types, such as Adobe Acrobat PDF (Portable Document Format) files, Macromedia Director movies, and virtual reality environments. Netscape Navigator 2.0 uses its new Live Objects technology to enable developers to create rich multimedia content for the Internet and let users view the content in Netscape Navigator 2.0 using plug-ins.

Up until Netscape Navigator 2.0, Web users were required to configure separate helper applications that work independently of their Web browsers to view and control most multimedia documents. When you download and configure plug-ins to work with Netscape Navigator 2.0, however, the plug-ins become part of the browser itself. Movies, sound events, virtual reality environments, and more display in the Netscape Navigator 2.0 window.

WHY DO I NEED A SPECIAL APPLICATION FOR MULTIMEDIA?

To make the experience worth your time, that's why. The biggest challenge for multimedia developers is the speed of the Internet. Most Web users dial in with modems operating at 14.4 kbps and 28.8 kbps. By one account, as many as 65 percent of all users access the Internet via a 14.4 kbps modem. At these rates, the user sees only about 1 to 2 kbps of effective throughput. If the Internet host is heavily loaded, or if there is unusual network congestion, this rate can drop even lower. Multimedia developers face the task of maximizing the impact of their productions while minimizing the time a user must wait to see them.

By using a plug-in with Netscape Navigator 2.0, such as Macromedia's Shockwave player to play Director movies, Web sites can transform static pages into dynamic productions without substantially increasing the amount of time a user waits. Many of the plug-ins are optimized to transfer data across slower Internet connections, such as 14.4 kbps and 28.8 kbps.

Now that you know a little about Netscape's inline plug-ins, let's take a look at how Netscape interacts with these helpful applications.

How Plug-ins Display in Netscape Navigator 2.0

When you use a plug-in with Netscape Navigator 2.0, it may not always be apparent that the plug-in is a separate application from Netscape Navigator 2.0. With helper applications, you always know when a graphics program or a media player starts because you see it display in a separate window. Plug-ins, however, can interact with Netscape Navigator 2.0 in one of three modes of operation:

■ **Full-screen plug-ins.** Full-screen plug-ins are just that—plug-ins that take up the entire Netscape Navigator 2.0 screen. An example of this type of plug-in is the WebFX viewer that displays when you encounter a VRML three-dimensional world file, such as the one shown in Figure 9-8.

Figure 9-8: *WebFX, a full-screen Navigator plug-in.*

■ **Embedded plug-ins.** Embedded plug-ins are referenced in HTML documents so that when a user clicks on the reference, the plug-in activates and displays the object. Although this is similar to the way in which other objects, such as embedded graphics, are handled, embedded plug-ins can respond to user events, including mouse motions. As a Web author, you specify embedded plug-ins by using the <EMBED> HTML tag, as shown in the following syntax:

```
<EMBED SRC="trailer.mpg", WIDTH=150, HEIGHT=250
CONTROLS=TRUE>
```

In the preceding example, when the user clicks on the plug-in reference on the Web page, an MPEG player activates and plays a film clip named "trailer.mpg."

■ **Hidden plug-ins.** Hidden plug-ins are ones that users cannot see or otherwise control, such as a plug-in that plays a MIDI sound file in the background.

To help you get a better idea of what a plug-in is and how it can extend Netscape Navigator 2.0's own capabilities, the next section provides a list of available plug-ins and shows how to find, install, and use two of the coolest plug-ins: WebFX and Shockwave.

GETTING PLUGGED IN

Some of the plug-ins that Netscape Navigator 2.0 supports are listed in Table 9-2. (Note that at the time of this writing, several of these plug-ins were not available. See the accompanying URL for updates.) These plug-ins display multimedia content in Netscape Navigator 2.0 without the need to activate separate helper applications or download the file and play it in a separate application.

Plug-in	What It Does
Macromedia Shockwave	Plays Macromedia Director 4.0 movies in Netscape Navigator 2.0. Director movies include animation, buttons users can click on, digital videos, and sound. For more information, see http://www.macromedia.com/.
Adobe Acrobat Plug-in	Enables Netscape Navigator 2.0 to display Acrobat PDF (Portable Document Format) files inside Netscape Navigator 2.0 windows. PDF documents are designed with specific font control and precise image placement, such as professional-quality desktop publishing documents, books, or magazines. PDF files also include hot links (URLs) that enable you to move to other Web sites. The URL for Adobe is http://www.adobe.com.
RealAudio	Plays real-time audio inside Netscape Navigator 2.0. See http://www.realaudio.com for the latest information on this Progessive Network product.
Iconovex AnchorPage	Automatically indexes, abstracts, and hyperlinks all HTML documents that you read in Netscape Navigator 2.0. See http://www.iconovex.com for the latest information on AnchorPage.
WebFX	Paper Software's VRML browser brings 3D objects to the Netscape Navigator 2.0 window. Very cool. According to Paper Software's Web page, you can "seamlessly fly through inter-connected 3D worlds" without leaving Netscape Navigator 2.0. See http://www.paperinc.com/.

Table 9-2: *Netscape Navigator 2.0 plug-ins.*

The rest of this section examines two exciting Netscape plug-ins in detail.

Using WebFX With
Netscape Navigator 2.0

One of the first plug-ins available for Netscape Navigator 2.0 in beta is a product that enables you to view virtual reality images (known as VRML files). Paper Software's WebFX is a plug-in for Netscape Navigator 2.0 for Windows 3.1 and Windows 95. The WebFX plug-in enables you to fly through interconnected three-dimensional worlds on the Internet completely within the familiar confines of the Netscape Navigator 2.0 interface. WebFX provides full VRML 1.0 compliance; progressive rendering; physics-based navigation; animated viewpoints; GIF, JPG, and BMP textures; 3D text; image backgrounds; and support for common Open Inventor nodes, so you can view as many 3D files on the Internet as possible.

What Is VRML?
VRML, pronounced "ver-mel," is a standard for creating three-dimensional computer environments. VRML is short for the Virtual Reality Modeling Language, which is the programming language you use to create VRML objects, such as spheres, cubes, and surfaces. There are several helpful documents available on the Internet if you're interested in the technical aspects of VRML, including Radiance Software's Web site at http://www.webcom.com/radiance/. You also can find the VRML specifications at http://www.clark.net/theme/vrml/.

To use WebFX with Netscape Navigator 2.0, you need to install it first. To do so:

1. Make sure you are connected to the Internet, either directly or through a SLIP or PPP connection with your access provider.

2. Double-click the Netscape Navigator 2.0 icon to launch the program. The main window appears, and the Netscape home page starts loading.

3. Click your mouse inside the Location field at the top of the window to select the URL http://home.netscape.com/.

4. Replace this URL with the one for the Paper Software home page by typing **http://www.paperinc.com/**. Once you have typed in the new URL, press Enter. Netscape Navigator 2.0 retrieves the Paper Software home page, as shown in Figure 9-9.

Figure 9-9: *Paper Software's home page.*

5. You might want to take some time to look around the Paper Software home page. Some things might have changed a little since this book was written, so Figure 9-9 may be outdated. When you are ready, click the link that enables you to download the WebFX program for your operating system. The WebFX Downloads page appears.

6. Follow all instructions for downloading the software, entering your correct operating system, the product you want (WebFX Plug-in for Netscape 2.0), and an FTP site to retrieve it from. Once you start the download, the Unknown File Type dialog box appears.

   ■ If you have already configured Netscape Navigator 2.0's Helper Apps tab so that there is a program or process associated with .EXE files, you won't get this message. Netscape Navigator 2.0 can, for instance, automatically run a file like this as soon as it has been received, or it can save it to disk automatically, without displaying this dialog box. To learn how to make these configuration changes, see "Helper Applications" in Chapter 6, "Getting Files via FTP."

7. Click the Save to Disk button. The Windows 95 or Windows 3.1 Save As dialog box appears.

8. Choose a location (such as your \TEMP directory) for the file and then click the Save button. The Saving Location dialog box appears, showing you the progress of the file transfer.

9. Once Netscape Navigator 2.0 has finished downloading the file, exit the program and close the connection to your Internet provider.

TIP

Any time you run a Setup program in Windows 3.1 or Windows 95, it's a good idea to exit all other programs (except Windows itself). This is particularly true when installing plug-in programs to Netscape Navigator 2.0. Unless otherwise stated, you need to exit Netscape Navigator 2.0 when installing a new plug-in, otherwise you may encounter problems when you use Netscape Navigator 2.0 the next time.

Now that you have the WebFX file on your system, let's go ahead and install it:

1. Find the file you've just downloaded using Windows 95 Explorer or Windows File Manager. When you find the file, double-click it. It decompresses automatically.

2. Double-click the SETUP.EXE file to start the installation program. The WebFX Setup screen appears, as shown in Figure 9-10. You may want to take some time to read the dialog box on this screen.

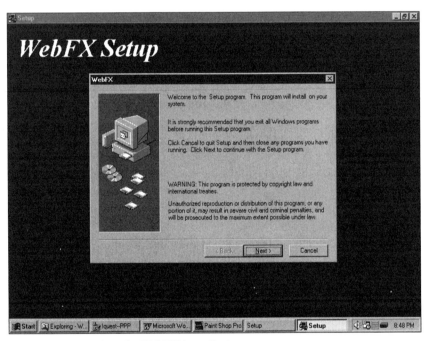

Figure 9-10: *Starting the WebFX installation program.*

3. Click the Next button to continue the installation. This displays the Netscape Program Directory dialog box, shown in Figure 9-11.

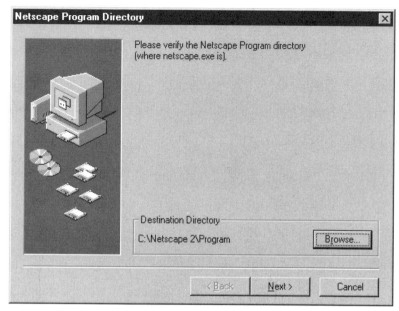

Figure 9-11: *The Netscape Program Directory dialog box.*

4. Confirm that the directory listed in the Destination Directory area is the correct path to Netscape Navigator 2.0. If this is not the correct directory, click the Browse button and select the appropriate path and filename.

5. Click Next. The Choose Destination Location dialog box appears, as shown in Figure 9-12. This is the directory in which you want to set up and store WebFX.

6. Confirm that the directory listed in the Destination Directory area is the correct directory. If you want to name a new directory in which to store WebFX, click the Browse button and enter a new location in the Browse dialog box.

7. Click Next. The Folder Selection dialog box appears, as shown in Figure 9-13. You can instruct the Setup program to place icons for WebFX in any Start menu folder you like (the default usually works just fine).

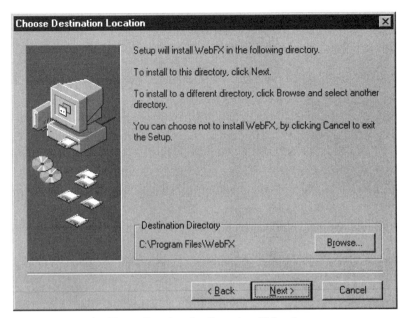

Figure 9-12: *The Choose Destination Location dialog box.*

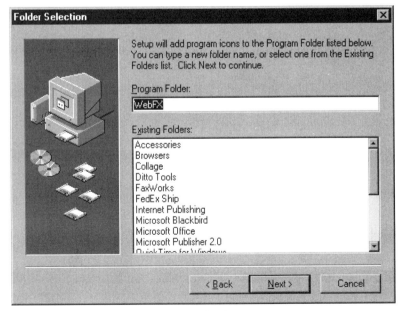

Figure 9-13: *The Folder Selection dialog box.*

8. Choose a folder from the list, or create a name for a new folder.

9. Click Next. The Setup program copies files to your disk. When it finishes, a message displays telling you that it has finished installing the program and that you can double-click on the program's icon to activate it.

10. Click OK. The folder in which WebFX is stored appears on your Windows desktop.

SHOULD I READ THE WEBFX READ ME FILE?
In most situations, you'll want to read these notes. Why? Because they contain last-minute changes to the software that may affect the way it works with Netscape Navigator 2.0. They may also contain special instructions on how to use WebFX with your operating system. If you don't read them now, keep them on your computer so you can refer to them later.

You now are ready to use WebFX with Netscape Navigator 2.0. The following steps start you on what might be the first trip you've ever made in a virtual reality world. Buckle up and have fun!
To use WebFX:

1. Double-click the WebFX Plugin for Netscape icon in the folder where you stored WebFX. This starts Netscape Navigator 2.0 and displays the WebFX Plug-in for Netscape page in the Netscape Navigator 2.0 window, as shown in Figure 9-14.

   ■ Don't mistake this page for a remote home page. It is actually a file stored locally on your hard disk. Look at the Location line on the Netscape Navigator 2.0 window to get the full path and filename.

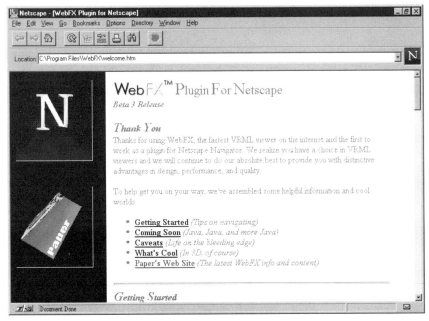

Figure 9-14: *The WebFX page in Netscape Navigator 2.0.*

2. Click the What's Cool link on the WebFX page. This displays the What's Cool screen, with two frames as shown in Figure 9-15.

   You have a few choices here. You can, for example, click on the big *N* in the right pane to access the Netscape Communications home page. Or you can click on one of the 3D demo worlds listed in the left pane. Let's immerse ourselves in one of these worlds:

3. Click the House of Immersion link. This displays a 3D house on your screen, as shown in Figure 9-16. You can now interact with this house using mouse and keyboard controls. Table 9-3 lists the various actions you can perform. Go ahead and experiment with these controls until you get a good idea of how 3D environments work. Don't panic— it takes a little while to get comfortable moving about in these worlds.

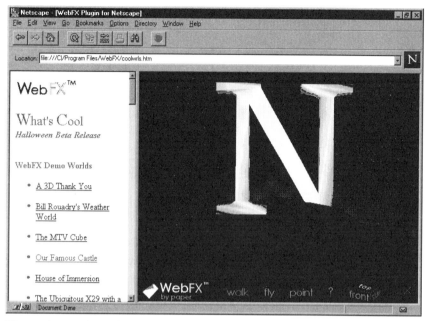

Figure 9-15: *The WebFX What's Cool page.*

Figure 9-16: *The House of Immersion 3D environment.*

Mouse Button	Action	Result
Left	Drag	Walks through the scene.
Left	Alt+Drag	Moves the scene.
Left	Click	Jumps to an attached Web site.
Left	Ctrl + Click	Automatically walks to where you clicked.
Right	Drag	Orbits about the scene.
Right	Click	Pops up the WebFX main menu.

Table 9-3: *Navigation in the House of Immersion.*

HELP! I DON'T KNOW WHERE I AM!

For many users just starting out with VRML and 3D environments, getting acclimated is difficult. It reminds me of what it must be like for newbie astronauts to experience weightlessness the first time. You can move around an object onscreen in any direction—up, down, below, through, and so on. If you get totally lost and disoriented, click the reset button at the bottom of the page. This returns you to the original display of the house.

4. When you finish navigating through one environment, click on another in the left pane, such as The MTV Cube, as shown in Figure 9-17. Or you can simply exit the program by selecting Exit from the File menu.

Figure 9-17: *The MTV Cube.*

SHOCKWAVE & NETSCAPE NAVIGATOR 2.0

Another plug-in that Netscape Navigator 2.0 supports is a product from Macromedia called Shockwave. Shockwave lets you view Macromedia Director movies (see Figure 9-18) and multimedia files in Netscape Navigator 2.0. Developers can include Director movies in HTML documents by using the <EMBED> tag. Documents can include more than one movie per HTML page.

Figure 9-18: *A Macromedia Director movie.*

■ Though you can't see it in this illustration, as you move your mouse pointer over each of these pictures, they disappear.

When you access a site that includes a Director file, you can scroll through the Web page even while the movie is playing. You can interact with the movie by clicking on the visible portions of the movie. You can also enter text from the keyboard into text fields in the movie. And the movie can access information from the Internet and open URLs.

To download a copy of Shockwave, enter **http://www.macromedia.com/Tools/Shockwave/shock.html** in the Netscape Navigator 2.0 Location field and press Enter. Next, click the link Get the Shockwave Plug-In for Your Browser. On the next page, click the link for your appropriate operating system, such as Windows 95. You now can download the file by clicking one of the links provided. The actual downloading process is similar to the way you downloaded the WebFX plug-in.

After you download the Shockwave Plug-In file, double-click the file named SW10B132.EXE (the actual name may differ depending on the file you download). This decompresses the files for Shockwave, including the SETUP.EXE file. Double-click SETUP to install Shockwave on your system. Again, you should close any Windows application that you have open prior to starting the Setup program.

Once Shockwave is installed, you can start Netscape Navigator 2.0 and test out the new plug-in. One site that uses a multimedia image to enhance its appeal is the Welcome To Netscape page for Shockwave. The URL for this page is: http://home.netscape.com/ comprod/products/navigator/version_2.0/plugins/ director_examples/director_example1.html. (Think they could have made that URL any longer?)

The interesting part of this page is that the normally static image at the top of Netscape's page is now animated. It includes a moving marquee, has hyperlinked buttons, and even highlights a button as you pass your mouse pointer over it.

You can see other uses of Shockwave at the Macromedia Shockwave Vanguard Gallery at http://www.macromedia.com/ Tools/Shockwave/Vanguard/index.html. Listed here are companies that are integrating Shockwave-compatible images into their Web sites, including Advertising Age, c I Net, and the American Cancer Society.

UNDERSTANDING SERVER PUSH & CLIENT PULL

Most Web pages require that you interact with them in some way. They usually include links to other pages, graphics to click, animation to view, or sound objects to download and listen to. All of these items are initiated in some way by the user, the person using the client application (Netscape Navigator 2.0, in this case).

Another type of HTML instruction enables Web authors to design pages that deliver an updated version of the page without interaction from the user. This technology is called *server push*.

Using server push, the server transmits Web page instructions and information to your system and displays them in Netscape Navigator 2.0. As you navigate to various Web sites that support server-push technology, the connection between you and the server on the other end remains open. The server can continue to "push" updated information and data to your computer continuously. The connection between you and the server closes when you leave the site.

An example of a Web site that supports server push is the Word site at http://www.word.com (see Figure 9-19). It uses server push in a variety of ways, often to display advertisements during the time you are moving from one page to another. The advertisement appears, gives you a few moments to read it, and then disappears so that you can continue on to the item that you originally selected.

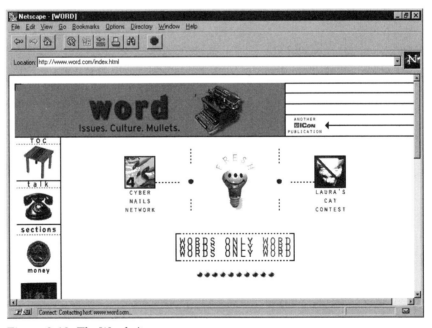

Figure 9-19: *The Word site.*

Throughout Word, there are clever icons that rely on server push for animation. There are all kinds of uses for server push. A sports site, for instance, can use server push to keep a scoreboard updated with the latest scores and team highlights.

In *client pull* the server transmits not only Web page information to your system, but also programming code. This code instructs Netscape Navigator 2.0 to perform a predefined action automatically; this action may be as simple as reloading a page after a set amount of time or loading a URL after a few minutes. At the time specified, Netscape Navigator 2.0 pulls updated Web pages to your computer as instructed.

CREATING YOUR OWN HOME PAGE

Now that you've seen a little bit of the Web, you may want to start creating your own Web pages. Why? Perhaps you've found a number of sites that you'd like to return to regularly. Wouldn't it be convenient to create a home page that not only contains links to those documents, but also descriptions and maybe even pictures? It is beyond the scope of this book to show you exactly how to do this, but we *can* give you a few hints to get you started. And for those of you who are already familiar with HTML coding, we've provided a little information about one of the cool new Netscape extensions: client-side image maps and frames.

All Web pages are written in a language called HTML (HyperText Markup Language), a subset of SGML (Standard Generalized Markup Language, a system designed for typesetting and document page description). HTML is simply ASCII text with embedded codes representing instructions for the proper display of that text. The most basic HTML commands instruct the Web browser client program regarding the display of the information (what size and style of type, and so forth). Other HTML commands define the links to different data types (video, graphics, and audio) and other servers.

I've found that the best way to start learning the HTML techniques for creating Web pages is to study the content and structure of the pages you visit. You can look at the source code for the page you're on simply by selecting Document Source from Netscape Navigator 2.0's View menu. You can even save the source under a different file name on your own system by choosing Save As from the File menu. You can then use it as a template for your new HTML file, which can be edited in Notepad or any other text editor. If you get really serious, you should pick up a copy of Netscape Navigator 2.0 Gold, which includes a specialized full-featured editor for Web pages.

HTML files on most Web servers have the extension .HTML. Since DOS and versions of Windows prior to Windows 95 do not support extensions of more than three characters, however, Windows HTML files end with the extension .HTM. If you do not use the .HTM extension, Netscape Navigator 2.0 will not recognize your files as valid HTML pages.

Netscape Navigator 2.0 lets you preview or test any HTML documents you create. To view a local HTML file, choose Open File from the File menu.

There are several excellent HTML reference areas online, as shown in Table 9-4. These pages will teach you the basics of HTML authoring.

Site	URL
HyperText Markup Language: Working and Background Materials	http://www.w3.org/hypertext/WWW/ MarkUp/MarkUp.html
Peter Flynn's "How to Write HTML"	http://kcgl1.eng.ohio-state.edu:80/ www/doc/htmldoc.html
Introduction to HTML Documentation	http://www.hprc.utoronto.ca/ HTMLdocs/NewHTML/intro.html

Table 9-4: *Popular HTML references.*

If you want to start with more general information regarding the World Wide Web (straight from the horse's mouth), the best resource is the W3 Consortium Web server (http://www.w3.org/). The European Laboratory for Particle Physics (CERN), the folks who developed the Web, created this site and recently handed the task of maintaining it over to the W3 Consortium. This is a great clearinghouse for software information.

But just to show you how simple HTML coding can be, here's a template for the beginning of a customized home page. Type the following text into any text editor such as Notepad:

```
<HTML>
<TITLE>My Favorites</TITLE>
<H1>My Favorite Sites</H1>
<UL>
<LI><A HREF="http://www.vmedia.com">Ventana Online</A>
<LI><A HREF="http://home.netscape.com/">Netscape</A>
</UL>
</HTML>
```

Save this file with an .HTM extension. For instance, you can call it FAVE.HTM. Then, next time you're in Netscape Navigator 2.0, select Open File from the File menu, select your new file in the File Open dialog box that appears, and click Open. Voilà, you're a Web author!

NETSCAPE'S PROPOSED HTML 3.0 FEATURES

Without going into a lot of detail about HTML features and how proposed features becomes "real" HTML features (the way a bill becomes a law in the federal government), this section examines a few of the HTML 3.0 proposals from Netscape Communications. Netscape is submitting these proposals to the IETF and W3O for consideration; they will probably be standard HTML features in the coming year.

WHO ARE IETF & W3?

IETF and W3 are the governing bodies of the Internet and World Wide Web. IETF is the Internet Engineering Task Force. W3O ("W3" is short for "World Wide Web") is the W3 Organization and is made up of CERN and the Laboratory for Computer Science at MIT. These groups approve specifications, such as HTML, HTTP, TCP/IP, and so on, so that a common standard is used by everyone. This makes it possible, for example, for millions of users to communicate via Internet e-mail all over the world. Of course, as new applications and technologies are created, the standards must change or evolve to allow for expansion. Many individuals, researchers, and companies submit proposals for consideration to these bodies in hopes that their specifications will become standards. You can find out more about the IETF by visiting http://www.ietf.cnri.reston.va.us/home.html.

You've already been introduced to some very basic HTML tags. What you'll see here are new specifications supported in Netscape Navigator 2.0. These include embedded objects, frames, client-side image maps, and targeted windows.

You read earlier about inline plug-ins. These are handled by the embedded objects specifications, particularly using the <EMBED> tag. (See the earlier section called "How Plug-ins Display in Netscape Navigator 2.0" for specifics on the types of objects to embed.

You also know a little about frames from way back in Chapter 3, "A Quick Look Around." Frames allow you to display different Web documents in different portions of the main Netscape Navigator 2.0 window. You can have a graphic in one frame and a text explanation in another, for instance. And the data in each frame can be manipulated as if it were the only contents of the display window. For example, you can print the contents of a single frame, or even include the contents of a single frame in an e-mail message, by selecting Mail Frame from the file menu.

But now let's take a closer look at just one of the exciting new features of Netscape Navigator 2.0 that will probably become part of the HTML 3.0 specification: *client-side image maps*.

UNDERSTANDING CLIENT-SIDE IMAGE MAPS

Many Web sites feature graphical maps you can click on to access different services or documents, such as the one shown in Figure 9-20. The graphic at the top of the Netscape Home Page is actually an image map that you can click on to move to different parts of the Netscape Web site.

Figure 9-20: *A typical image map.*

Image maps as they are written now are server-side maps. This means that the map stays on the server; when you click an area of the map, the request travels back to the server to be processed. As you might guess, it takes time just for the server to figure out where you want to go; then it has to process the transaction. This takes time that you would rather not spend when connected via a slow modem.

With client-side maps, however, the image map is embedded in the Web page and downloaded directly to Netscape Navigator 2.0.

TIP

If you're a Web developer, the new tags used to create client-side image maps are <MAP> and <AREA>. The basic syntax is as follows:
<MAP NAME="name"> <AREA [SHAPE="shape"]
COORDS="x,y,..." [HREF="reference"] [NOHREF] </MAP>

One of the problems associated with the current HTML map specifications is that they work only via the HTTP protocol. There is nothing wrong with this if you do all your transactions over the Web. But what if you want to access an image map on a local disk? The new client-side specifications take this into consideration and enable developers to look beyond just online transactions.

The potential for client-side maps is great. Developers can design image maps that are specified in only one file, such as the home page, and then reused by each document on that site. To update this type of map requires that only one file be changed, whereas server-side maps require a separate map for each page. Another place you may start seeing this HTML extension is on non-HTTP mediums such as CD-ROMs. CD-ROM developers could use the <MAP> and <AREA> tags to help locate archived data on their CDs.

WHAT ARE TARGETED WINDOWS?

In Netscape Navigator 2.0, browser windows can now have names associated with them. You can have a link in one window refer to another window by using its name. When you click on the link, the document appears in the named widow. If the named window is not open, Netscape Navigator 2.0 opens it and names if for you.

For HTML authors reading this, here's a sample of the syntax:

```
<A HREF "something.html" TARGET "TEST"> Click to open
the TEST window</A>
```

EXAMINING NETSCAPE NAVIGATOR 2.0 JAVASCRIPT

If you want more control over Netscape Navigator 2.0 without learning C++, you can study *JavaScript*. JavaScript is a new scripting language that enables developers to create programs to enhance and customize their Web pages. JavaScript gives developers ways to access different events, such as startups, exits, and users' mouse clicks. Based on the Java language, this Netscape scripting language extends Netscape Navigator 2.0 to a wide range of possibilities and is easy enough for anyone who can compose HTML. Developers also can use JavaScript to make their HTML documents work with inline plug-ins and Java applets.

JavaScript contains predefined event handlers that respond to user events. You can integrate these event handlers right into HTML pages. One of the ways you can use JavaScript in a Web page is to display messages to users who click on an object in your pages, such as an image. Another way to use JavaScript is to play a sound file or activate a Java applet when the user clicks on an item or leaves a Web page. This is done is by using the new <SCRIPT> tag in your HTML document. When a user accesses the Web page that includes a <SCRIPT> tag, Netscape Navigator 2.0 automatically processes it using its built-in JavaScript interpreter.

JavaScript uses *properties* such as "visible" and "color" to return your specified response. You might, for example, design a Web page that includes listings and descriptions of your products. Let's say you sell countertops, and each model of countertop comes in various styles, textures, and colors. Customers to your site may want to design a virtual kitchen by mixing and matching colors and textures with different countertops and other fixtures. With JavaScript, you can include a selector that enables users to adjust the colors and textures of specific countertops. You could create the entire site as a Java applet, but why not use Java only where necessary (such as for creating the virtual kitchen and countertop and the selector). Then use JavaScript to change the colors and textures of the countertop in the applet.

JavaScript is an object-oriented scripting environment made up of *objects*, *properties*, and *methods*. Objects comprise properties, such as colors, size, weight, model number, and so on. Properties themselves also can have properties. Methods are functions that are associated with an object.

The syntax for JavaScript includes the following items and attributes:

■ <SCRIPT> and </SCRIPT>. The text of a script is inserted between SCRIPT and its end tag. As soon as a page is read in by Netscape Navigator 2.0 and a JavaScript script is included, the script is evaluated or executed.

■ <SCRIPT LANGUAGE="JavaScript">. The LANGUAGE attribute is mandatory unless the SRC attribute is present (see next bullet point) and specifies the scripting language.

■ <SCRIPT SRC="http:common.JavaScript">. The SRC attribute is optional and, if given, specifies a URL that loads the text of a script.

■ <SCRIPT LANGUAGE="language" SRC=url>. Shows that both LANGUAGE and SRC attributes are included.

TIP

For a more comprehensive and up-to-date user reference on JavaScript, see the Netscape Navigator 2.0 reference at http://home.netscape.com/ comprod/products/navigator/version_2.0/script/script_info/ index.html. You can find the JavaScript Authoring Guide at that location.

An example of a script follows:

```
<HTML>
<HEAD>
<SCRIPT LANGUAGE="JavaScript">
<!- Begin to hide script contents from old browsers
  function square(i) {
    document.write("What number is to be squared: ",
i,"<BR>")
```

```
    return i * i
  }
  document.write("The result of this calculation is:
",square(2),".")
<!- End hiding here ->
</SCRIPT>
</HEAD>
<BODY>
<BR>
The script is all finished calculating the square.
</BODY>
</HTML>

What number is to be squared: 2
The result of this calculation is 4.
The script is all finished calculating the square.
```

In this example, a number (2 in this case) is squared by using the square function in JavaScript. The script then returns the result (4) and displays the message at the end of the example.

MOVING ON

In this chapter, you've learned some ways to configure Netscape Navigator 2.0 to run more efficiently on your computer. You've also learned how to set up network proxies if you need to access the World Wide Web from a local area network that has a firewall in place. The remainder of this chapter focused on some of the new and exciting features of Netscape Navigator 2.0, including plug-ins, support of Java, frames, and JavaScript.

The next chapter discusses the role of Netscape Navigator 2.0's built-in security features and how to conduct electronic commerce transactions on the Web. If you feel a little uneasy purchasing things from a Web site, be sure to read the next chapter. You may feel more comfortable afterward.

chapter ten

Commerce & Security on the Net

The Internet has had a colorful history. The military started it, the academic world helped to develop and refine it, and thousands of individuals began using it for everything from research to interactive games. But as with every other innovation, at some point somebody says, "Well that's just great, but how do I make a buck with it?"

Freed from past restrictions on commercial activity, the modern Internet provides countless ways to make—and to spend—a buck. Businesses large and small maintain Web pages that promote their products and services. And these are not just businesses that deal with software or computers. Virtually every type of major enterprise is represented with a Web page.

Many companies go beyond merely promoting themselves on the Net—they actually sell products. Yes, the Internet is the Home Shopping Network of the future. You no longer have to wander over to your couch to go shopping for that Hummel figurine or autographed baseball; you can do it right at your keyboard. And the variety of products available is staggering. You can buy everything from mouse pads to MIGs.

Let's take a quick look at how online commercial transactions work.

THE MECHANICS OF ONLINE TRANSACTIONS

Way back in Chapter 3, "A Quick Look Around," you saw an
example of a Web page that included various forms elements, or
forms widgets, as they are known to seasoned Web authors. These
are screen objects that accept input from you—push buttons, radio
buttons, check boxes, drop-down lists, and edit fields that you fill
in with information. You have seen objects like these in the preferences dialog boxes for virtually every Windows program, but the
forms widgets are different. Forms widgets are not really part of
Netscape Navigator 2.0 or of any other software; they are components of the Web document you're viewing. If you select By
Document Source from the Netscape Navigator 2.0 View menu,
you'll see that these fancy interactive objects are really just simple
HTML tags. Figure 10-1 shows a typical forms document, the
Rutgers University Archie Request Form you saw earlier in the
book, and Figure 10-2 shows its source.

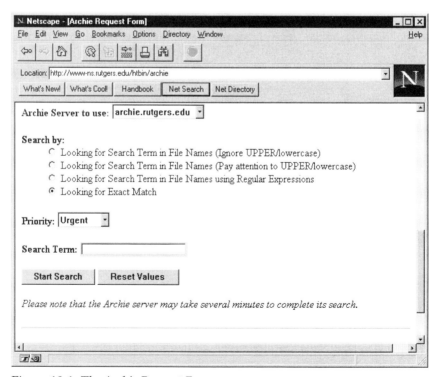

Figure 10-1: *The Archie Request Form.*

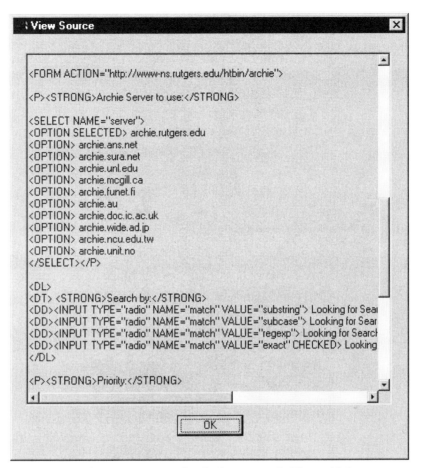

Figure 10-2: *The HTML source for the forms page in Figure 10-1.*

Almost every page that includes forms widgets also includes a button marked Submit or Send. When you click this button, all the information you've entered is sent out on the Net to a particular site specified in the Web document. Once it reaches this site, a special piece of server software known as a *Common Gateway Interface* (CGI) collects your data and processes it. Perhaps the gateway simply dumps your information into a database file, or perhaps it immediately starts checking your credit history. It may even send some new information back to you, such as an acknowledgment that it has received your order.

I know what you're thinking. The whole idea of sending addresses and phone numbers and especially credit card information across the Net to some distant company sounds risky. When you press the Submit button, your personal data goes bopping from computer to computer across the vast reaches of cyberspace. How can you be sure it gets to the right place, or that technically savvy criminals don't nab it en route?

And that brings us to the huge and controversial topic of security.

SECURITY ON THE NET

When I was a kid the mix of technology and commerce was already cause for panic. "Some companies encourage you to order products by telephone," complained the news media. "When you place your order, they'll try to get you to tell them your credit card number instead of mailing a check. Don't do it!" they warned. "Don't give *anyone* your credit card number over the phone!"

Twenty-something years later these fears seem quaint. The American public has become used to home shopping and 800 numbers and has clearly decided that convenience is worth a little risk. Did the nightmare scenarios come true? Did unscrupulous employees at companies all over the country steal thousands of credit card numbers and spend all your money at the track? Of course not. Most employees want to keep their jobs.

Security is about people, not technologies. No matter what methods you use to transfer information, somebody can steal it if he or she wants it badly enough. Germany under Hitler was home to some of the world's greatest cryptographers and information scientists, and yet the Allied powers were able to crack the secret codes. Hundreds or perhaps even thousands of workers—telephone sales agents, customer service representatives, data entry personnel, managers, bank tellers, system administrators—have access to your financial records or your credit card information. The operator could even listen in on your phone calls. And yet how often do you get ripped off?

The people who handle Internet transactions are really no different from the workers who already know or have access to your credit card numbers. Let's dispel a few myths:

- The Internet is *not* a den of hacker-thieves looking for a quick buck. There are easier ways to steal.

- Sending data across the Net does *not* give everyone on the Net access to that data.

- Most businesses set up shop on the Net because it offers a new, cost-effective point of sale, *not* because it enables them to collect more personal information about their customers.

- The Internet is *not* a leaky old boat full of giant security holes that can never be plugged.

That said, the security of information on the Net is still an important issue. Even though the biggest security hole is people rather than software or hardware, and even though abuses have been exaggerated by weekly magazines and so-called news shows, there's nothing wrong with making the Internet as secure a medium as possible for financial transactions. Netscape, recognizing from its inception as a company that commercial transactions were the Next Big Thing on the Net, has taken a lead in bolstering the security of transmitted data.

NETSCAPE & SECURITY: SSL

To understand what Netscape has done to address security issues, you have to understand the issues it is addressing. In other words, in what ways is it even possible to improve Internet security?

Information traveling between your computer and another machine, such as a Web server, is routed from Internet node to Internet node until it finally reaches its destination. It may pass through a handful or even dozens of computer systems. At any one of these sites, it is possible for a technically proficient but unscrupulous individual to access the stream of data for ulterior motives. Somebody could eavesdrop on you, collecting personal or financial information; somebody could copy your intellectual property, such as a great new idea for a patent; or somebody could even change your data before it reaches its destination, causing all kinds of mayhem. The Internet itself provides no built-in mechanism for preventing activities like these.

Netscape's response to this lack of security was to develop the *Secure Sockets Layer (SSL) protocol*. The SSL protocol enhances Internet security in three ways:

- It provides a mechanism for server authentication. This means that a Web site can make sure it's really dealing with you, not some cheap imitation.

- It provides privacy by using a powerful encryption technique on transmitted data.

- It provides data integrity, ensuring that the information you send arrives exactly as you sent it.

If you think about it for a moment, you'll realize that for SSL to work, both ends of the link—the client and the server—must run software that supports these features. If your Web browser encrypts your credit card information, for instance, the server you're talking to must be able to decrypt it. Currently SSL is supported by Netscape Navigator 2.0 and the Netscape Commerce Server, a Web server package that's rapidly becoming a standard for businesses on the Net.

How does SSL work? The Internet can be seen as a layered set of protocols. In Chapter 1, "The Net & the Web," you learned that everything rests on TCP/IP, the protocol suite that actually divides your data into packets and ships them out to the right destination. Above this there are application protocols such as Telnet, FTP, and HTTP. These are the support protocols for the various services available on the Net. SSL actually provides a new protocol layer, situating itself between TCP/IP and the application protocols. That way it is not dependent on any of these other protocols in order to do its job. Figure 10-3 is a diagram of how a message you type is processed by the various protocol layers, then travels across the Net to a Web server that "unprocesses" the information.

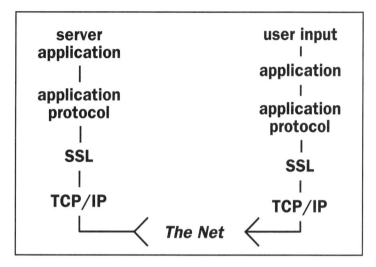

Figure 10-3: *A secure message sent to a Web server.*

SSL uses a powerful mechanism for protecting data known as *public key encryption*. Each Netscape Commerce server has its own unique pair of digital keys, which are really just long strings of random bytes. One of these keys is private and kept secret at the server site; the other is made public. When you send a message to a secure server, it is encrypted and automatically includes the public key for that site. The private key at the server end must be the one that "fits" this public key; otherwise, your data will not be decrypted and you will not be able to communicate. Since these pairs of keys are guaranteed to be unique, you can be certain that your information has reached the right destination before it is decrypted.

CERTIFICATES

Besides public key encryption, SSL offers another level of security called *digital certification*. Here's how it works:

In order to operate in secure mode and use the features of SSL, anyone who sets up a Netscape Commerce server must have requested and been sent a special digital certificate, a unique pattern of bytes that "unlocks" these features. RSA Certificate

Services, a division of RSA Data Security, Inc., handles the certification process. Before issuing a certificate (which of course is sent encrypted), RSA makes sure that the requesting organization is "for real." Digital certificates, in conjunction with public key encryption, help to protect you from fraud, pranks, and theft of intellectual property.

CAN'T SOME HACKER CRACK SSL?

Sure, hackers can break anything. It's just a matter of how much work it takes.

SSL uses authentication and encryption technology that was developed by RSA Data Security. The export version of Netscape Navigator 2.0, which is required by the United States Government to use a weaker version of encryption than the U.S.-only version, relies on what is known as RSA's "40-bit key RC4 algorithm." Even in this weaker implementation, the security is pretty impressive. Let's say your neighbor knows you are about to transmit your credit card number. He goes outside with a ladder and a bunch of equipment and manages to capture the encrypted data from your phone line. If you're a forgiving sort of person, you should go out and warn him that it takes an average of 64 MIPS-years to break the code. This means that if he gets a 64-MIPS computer to work round the clock on deciphering your information, he'll probably have the answer in about a year. By that time, your credit card will be maxed out anyway.

SSL IN ACTION

As I said, for Netscape's SSL security protocol to do its job, both the server and the client must support it. You already know that Netscape Navigator 2.0 supports it, so how do you know when you're connected to a secure server? Let's take a look:

1. Make sure you are connected to the Internet, either directly or through a SLIP or PPP connection with your access provider. If you are using a SLIP or PPP connection and are not currently connected, double-click the Dial-Up Connection icon for your access provider.

   ■ If you are running Windows 3.1 rather than Windows 95, or if you are running Windows 95 without using its built-in networking facilities, follow the instructions that came with your TCP/IP software for accessing the Internet.

2. Double-click the Netscape Navigator 2.0 icon to launch the program. The main window appears, and the Netscape home page starts loading as shown in Figure 10-4.

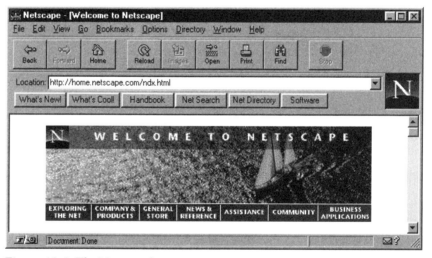

Figure 10-4: *The Netscape home page.*

3. Click your mouse inside the Netsite box at the top of the window to select the URL http://home.netscape.com/.

4. Replace this URL with **https://www.att.com/**, the URL for AT&T's secure home page. (No, that's not a typo. To access documents on secure servers, you type **https** instead of **http** in the protocol section of the URL.) A Security Information alert appears, as shown in Figure 10-5.

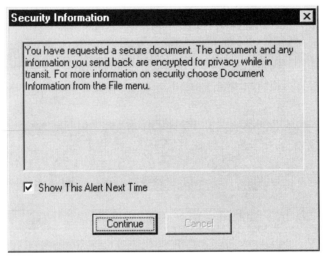

Figure 10-5: *Security Information alert.*

■ Whenever you are presented with a notification dialog box like this, you have the option of unchecking the Show This Alert Next Time check box. If you uncheck it, a corresponding check box is unchecked in the General tab of Netscape Navigator 2.0's Security Preferences. You can also change these options directly in the General tab. To learn how to do this, see the section below called "Security Preferences."

TIP

*News servers that use the Netscape Commerce Server also provide SSL security. The URL for a secure Usenet news site would begin with **snews:** instead of **news:**.*

5. After reading the Security Information alert, click Continue. The AT&T home page appears, as shown in Figure 10-6.

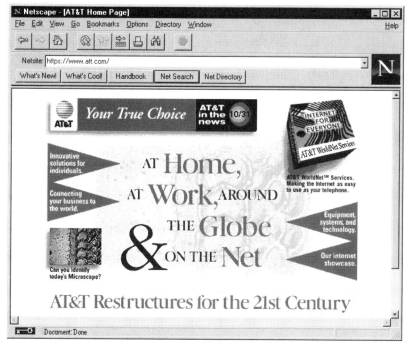

Figure 10-6: *The AT&T home page.*

There are some new details to notice in the Netscape Navigator 2.0 window:

- The security icon in the bottom left corner no longer depicts a broken key on a gray background, but an unbroken one on a blue background.

- There is a blue color bar across the top of the content area.

TIP

Check out the number of teeth on the key icon while displaying a secure document. If the key has two teeth, you are using high-grade encryption, the kind that cannot be exported from the United States to other countries. If it has one tooth, you are using the lower-grade encryption sanctioned by U.S. law for export.

These visual cues are great for letting you know that SSL security is in effect, but what if you want more detailed information about a particular secure document? Netscape Navigator 2.0 also provides a specific Document Information page for every site you visit. Let's take a look at the information that's available for the AT&T home page.

THE DOCUMENT INFORMATION PAGE

To view the Document Information page for the AT&T site:

1. With the AT&T home page still displayed in the Netscape Navigator 2.0 window (as shown above in Figure 10-6), select By Document Info from the View menu. The Document Info page appears, as shown in Figure 10-7.

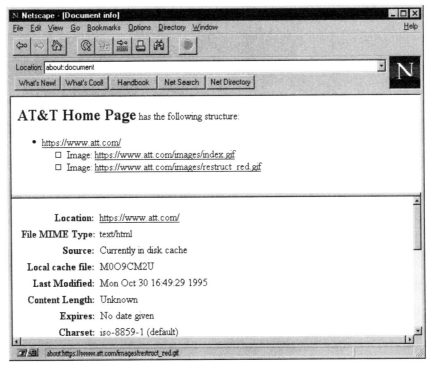

Figure 10-7: *Document information for the AT&T home page.*

■ The top panel of the Document Info page identifies the actual documents currently displayed in the Netscape

Navigator 2.0 window, including the URLs for the HTML file itself and for any inline graphics.

- The bottom panel is comprised of a miscellany of information about the document, including security information.

2. Scroll through the bottom panel to view information about the AT&T home page. Not all of this information is directly related to security issues, but even the more general items can help you determine the authenticity of a document. Here's a list of the fields and their meanings:

- **Location**. This is simply the URL of the document. Obviously, this should be the same as the URL you entered or the link you clicked.

- **File MIME type**. Since this is an HTML file, the MIME type is text/html.

- **Source**. This tells you how Netscape Navigator 2.0 is currently accessing the HTML source for the document. In this case, it has been cached to disk, and Netscape Navigator 2.0 is reading the cached version.

- **Local cache file**. This is the name of the file on your local hard drive that contains the source for the cached document.

- **Content length**. This is simply the size of the file, if available.

- **Expires**. This indicates when the cache file expires, based on your Preferences settings.

- **Charset**. This indicates the character set used by the document. In most cases the Charset will be iso-8859-1, which is the technical name for ISO-Latin (the character set used for Western European languges).

- **Security**. This field indicates the type of security used for this document. In this case, it's the medium-grade RSA algorithm.

Next there are several items specifically about the digital certificate issued to the server site:

- **Version**. This indicates the version of the digital certificate issued to AT&T.

- **This Certificate belongs to**. RSA requires that each applicant for a certificate submit a registered organization name and a variety of other identifying information. Obviously if you think you're at an AT&T site, but the owner of the DigitalID is not AT&T, you may have found a security problem.

- **This Certificate was issued by**. For now, this field should indicate that the certificate was issued by RSA. Other organizations might be involved in the certification process in the future, but if this field reads something like "Hacker d00d," you probably shouldn't submit your credit card number.

- **This Certificate is valid from**. As an added protection, digital certificates are issued for set lengths of time. This field indicates when the current certificate expires.

- **Certificate fingerprint:** This is a special digital signature that helps assure the authority of the certificate.

You shouldn't need to access this information very often, but if you suspect a security problem, the Document Information page offers you ample opportunity to play digital detective.

MIXED SECURITY DOCUMENTS

The SSL protocol allows for Web documents that contain a combination of secure and insecure information. When you access such a document using **https** in the URL, the insecure information is hidden and replaced by a special mixed security icon. If you want to access the insecure information, you should try connecting to the same address, but using **http** instead of **https** in your URL.

In addition, when you submit forms information in a secure or mixed document by pressing a Submit button or activating some other widget, Netscape Navigator 2.0 can pop up a message letting you know about the security of the submission process itself. This message is similar to the Security Information alert shown above in Figure 10-5, and you'll learn how to configure this option in the next section, "Security Preferences." With this added step, you can always know whether or not the information you want to send will be protected by SSL.

SECURITY PREFERENCES

Netscape Navigator 2.0 includes several options for customizing its security features. These can be accessed by clicking Security Preferences from the Options menu. Let's begin by looking at the General security preferences.

GENERAL SECURITY PREFERENCES

To access the general security preferences, simply select Security from the Options menu. The General tab appears, as shown in Figure 10-8.

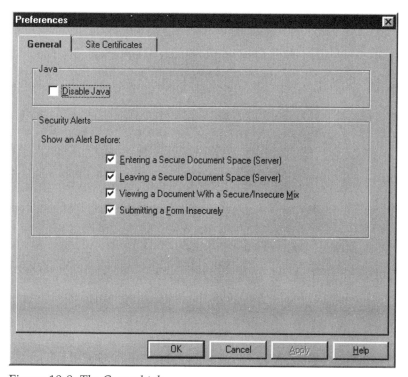

Figure 10-8: *The General tab.*

As you can see, there are two sections in this tab: Java and Security Alerts. Checking the Disable Java check box prevents Netscape Navigator 2.0 from running any Java programs. Why would you want to do this? Well, it's possible for Java programs to access information on your hard drive or even to infect your system with viruses or worms—unlikely, but possible. If you have any doubts about a particular site, you might want to temporarily disable Java by checking this box.

Earlier in the chapter, you saw that Netscape Navigator 2.0 pops up special security alert messages to inform you of changes in the security status of your connection. It's a good idea to leave these alerts enabled, but the Security Alerts section of the General tab lets you turn off any that you don't want to see. Here are the results of unchecking each of these boxes:

■ **Entering a Secure Document Space (Server).** Unchecking this box means that you will not receive notification when you are about to access a document on a secure server. If you spend a lot of time on secure servers and know what you are doing, you might want to uncheck this box.

■ **Leaving a Secure Document Space (Server).** Unchecking this box means that you will not be notified when you are about to *leave* a secure server and access a document that is not secure.

■ **Viewing a Document With a Secure/Insecure Mix.** Unchecking this box means that you will not receive an alert when you are about to access a document that contains both secure and insecure information.

■ **Submitting a Form Insecurely.** Unchecking this box means that you will not receive notification when you are about to submit information insecurely over the Net. If you do a lot of online shopping and are concerned about credit card fraud, I would not recommend unchecking this item.

SITE CERTIFICATES

Now select the other tab available in the Security Preferences dialog box, the one labeled Site Certificates. Figure 10-9 shows what you should see.

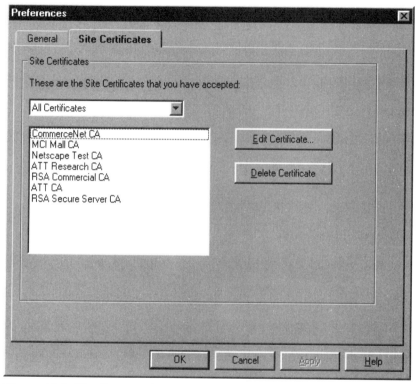

Figure 10-9: *The Site Certificates tab.*

To operate in secure mode, a Web server site must obtain a special certificate, and you are sent a copy of the certificate information when you connect using SSL. The Site Certificates tab lets you view this information to verify that any data you send goes only to the certificate owner. In addition, this tab lets you specify whether or not to allow connections to the owners of specific site certificates or to sites that have been certified by particular certifying authorities.

Let's take a closer look:

1. In the Site Certificates tab, make sure that All Certificates is selected in the drop-down list near the top.

2. From the list of certificates, select RSA Secure Server CA and click the Edit Certificate button. The certificate information for the Secure Server Certification Authority appears, as shown in Figure 10-10.

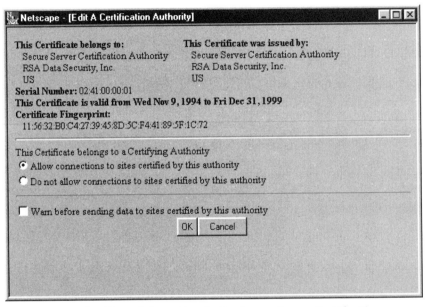

Figure 10-10: *Certificate information for the Secure Server Certification Authority.*

- This is the identifying information for a certifying authority rather than for a single site.

3. If you wish to allow connections to sites certified by the RSA Secure Server Certification Authority, leave the "Allow connections to sites certified by this authority" radio button checked. If you don't want to connect to sites certified by RSA, select the "Do not allow connections to sites certified by this authority" radio button.

- If you check the "Do not allow" radio button, you will be eliminating your ability to connect securely to any site certified by RSA, including the Netscape site itself!

4. If you want a warning to pop up before you send data to sites certified by RSA, check the "Warn before sending data to sites certified by this authority" check box.

5. When you're finished, click the OK or Cancel button.

You can also delete a certificate from the Site Certificates tab by selecting it and clicking the Delete Certificate button.

THE MOST POWERFUL SECURITY: COMMON SENSE

There is no question that Netscape Navigator 2.0, when used in conjunction with the Netscape Commerce Servers that are springing up all over the Net, provides very powerful protection from theft, fraud, and abuse of sensitive electronic information. I applaud Netscape for working so diligently toward making online commerce a safe and sensible option. It wouldn't surprise me if electronic transactions become the norm a few years from now. Enhanced security such as SSL is paving the way for this new way of doing business.

But you already possess a powerful security tool, more powerful than even the 128-bit key RC4 version of RSA's stream encryption algorithm: your common sense. I hate to get Forrest Gumpish on you, but here are a few things your mama should have always said:

- If you don't know anything about a company, don't send it your money. If you need more information, what better place for doing the research than the Net?

- Don't send sensitive information if the document doesn't include an e-mail address or a phone number you can use to get back in touch if there are problems.

- Expect some sort of acknowledgment of the transaction. If you don't receive one, get in touch with the company right away.

- Read the fine font.

- Disorganized Web pages could indicate sloppy business practices as well.

- If something looks like a scam, it just may *be* a scam.

Add these truisms to SSL, and you've got *real* security.

MOVING ON

By now you know how to cruise the Net pretty well using Netscape Navigator 2.0. You know how to jump from document to document on the Web, how to send and receive e-mail, how to read and post Usenet news, how to get files, and how to tap the power of hypermedia. In this last chapter, you learned a little about commerce on the Web, and how Netscape Navigator 2.0 provides security for online transactions.

Armed with all this information, you're ready to go wild exploring the Net. The best launching pads for cyberspace exploration are accessible right from the Netscape site: the What's New and What's Cool lists, the Yahoo directory, and the search engines on the Net Search page. Because of the way the Web works, from here you can branch out to any publicly available resources on the Net. But it always helps to have a few pointers, so in the next and last chapter of this book, I'll tell you about some of *my* favorite sites.

chapter eleven

Our Favorite Net Resources

Now that you can use Netscape Navigator 2.0 effectively, it's time to get out there and discover some really cool sites! You already know the best ways to get started:

- Netscape's own What's Cool page.
- Netscape's What's New page.
- The Yahoo directory, accessible from Netscape Navigator 2.0's Net Directory button.

These are great resources. But we thought we'd let you in on some of our own favorite pages and hangouts. This is a very personal list. It is by no means exhaustive, as that would be impossible, nor have we attempted to cover a broad range of topic areas. These are sites that we've found useful, instructive, inspiring, amusing, or just a bit peculiar. We've divided the entries into categories and listed them in alphabetical order, from Art to Windows 95. But hypermedia tends to defy categorization. If you don't find a site you're looking for under one category, try a related one. And if you have purchased the version of this book that comes with a CD-ROM in the back cover, you can browse an electronic version of this chapter, clicking on links to go directly to sites that interest you.

Except for e-mail and newsgroup resources, we've included an address in the standard URL format so that you can use it directly in Netscape Navigator 2.0. For many of the Gopher sites listed, we've also included path information. This path simply guides you to the appropriate area by following the Gopher's menu system.

A word of warning: The Internet is constantly under construction. A site that was there yesterday may have outgrown its current server and moved, or the person maintaining the site may have decided it was too much trouble and closed it down. All of the addresses included were accurate when we wrote the chapter, but it wouldn't surprise me if some sites had moved or closed down while the book was being printed. Yes, the Internet really *is* that changeable! In many cases, if a site has moved, you'll be able to get to the new location through a link that's kept at the old location. And you can always try looking for the site using Navigator's Net Search page. But if a site's gone, sometimes it's just plain gone. The best advice is simply to move on. There are plenty more out there!

TIP

Don't forget to create bookmarks or desktop shortcuts for your favorite sites.

The beauty of the Net is that you can't get too lost, so feel free to follow paths that lead away from our suggestions. With Netscape Navigator 2.0 and a willingness to explore, you'll soon be discovering all sorts of wonders that we've never even heard of!

ART: VISUAL

@art

Type: WWW

Address: http://gertrude.art.uiuc.edu/@art/gallery.html

Summary: An interesting "gallery" of new visual art that explores some of the possibilities inherent in the Web. This site is a must-see for electronic artists as well as anyone interested in visual information and Web design.

The Andy Warhol Museum

Type: WWW

Address: http://www.usaor.net/warhol/

Summary: Tour the Andy Warhol Museum in Pittsburgh, Pennsylvania.

Arts Online

Type: FTP

Address: ftp://nic.funet.fi/pub/doc/library/artbase.txt.Z

Summary: A list of arts-related resources on the Net.

Australian National University Art History Server

Type: WWW

Address: http://rubens.anu.edu.au/imageserve/

Summary: Michael Greenhalgh, Professor of Art History at Australian National University, compiled this collection of over 2,800 print images from the 15th to 19th centuries and another 6,000 images of classical and European architecture and architectural sculpture. Some highlights: a tutorial on the Palace of Diocletian at Split, a survey of the architecture of Islam, and a tour of classical sites in Turkey.

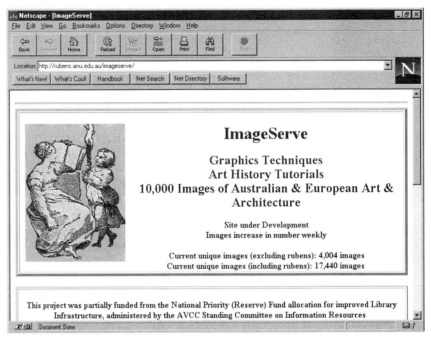

The Australian National University Art History Server.

Carlos' Coloring Book

Type: WWW

Address: http://robot0.ge.uiuc.edu/~carlosp/color/

Summary: A fun site, especially for younger kids, though they will need lots of help from an adult. By pointing and clicking you can choose virtual crayons and color in any one of several pictures. This is great for artistically challenged people like me, because there is no way to color outside the lines. After your masterpiece is finished, you can download it.

The FIGLET Site

Type: WWW

Address: http://www.inf.utfsm.cl/cgi-bin/figlet

Summary: Another site that brings out the artist in you, or at least makes it possible for you to create something artistic even if you have no talent or skill whatsoever. You type in your name or any word you want, choose a style, and a program immediately generates a "banner" made of ASCII characters. Great for creating an attractive signature for your e-mail messages or USENET posts.

Fractals

Type: FTP

Address: ftp://csus.edu/pub/alt.fractals.pictures/

Summary: Tons of fractal images in GIF format. They're arranged in directories by date; as of this writing, the latest is 1991, but there's a lot of cool stuff.

Fractals Fractals Fractals . . .

Type: WWW

Address: http://www.fishnet.net/~ayb/

Summary: Yes, another fractals page. I never get tired of them, and so this is a favorite site. Here you can find over 500 beautiful computer-generated graphics as well as links to other fractal sites. Enjoy.

Art Baker Fractal Images.

Gallery of Interactive On-Line Geometry

Type: WWW

Address: http://www.geom.umn.edu/apps/gallery.html

Summary: Use Kali to learn about the 17 crystallographic symmetry groups of the plane. This work is similar to that seen in some of M. C. Escher's woodcuts. Play a pinball-style game to explore the effects of negatively curved space. Much more involving symmetry groups and angle geometries. This page is maintained by The Geometry Center at the University of Minnesota.

Images, Icons, and Flags

Type: WWW

Address: http://white.nosc.mil/images.html

Summary: Links to lots of image sites and servers including NASA, space, travel, and medical images. Comprehensive icon and flag archives.

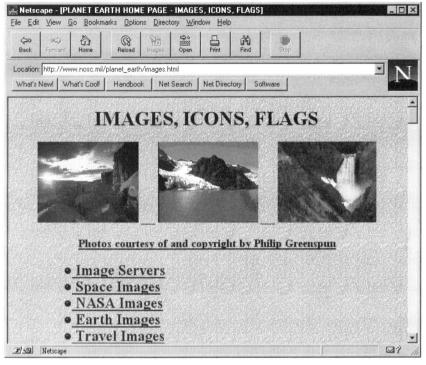

Images, Icons and Flags.

Institute of Egyptian Art and Archaeology

Type: WWW

Address: http://www.memst.edu/egypt/main.html

Summary: Take a color tour of Egypt or view the exhibit of Egyptian artifacts at the University of Memphis. The Institute of Egyptian Art and Archaeology is part of the Department of Art at the University of Memphis.

Kaleidospace

Type: WWW

Address: http://kspace.com

Summary: A commercial site, but well worth looking at. Independent artists gather here to display and sell their work.

Kaleidospace.

Kodak's Sample Digital Images Page

Type: WWW

Address: http://www.kodak.com/digitalImaging/samples/samples.shtml

Summary: Beautiful photographs, slickly presented. There's also valuable information on how the images were prepared.

Origami

Type: FTP

Address: ftp://nstn.ns.ca/listserv/origami-l/*

Summary: Learn new folding techniques, get display ideas, tips, and bibliographies. Subscribe to mailing list by sending e-mail to origami-l-request@ntsn.ns.ca.

The Planet Earth Home Page

Type: WWW

Address: http://white.nosc.mil/info_modern.html

Summary: Another good index to what's out there on the Web, with an excellent Getting Started page for novices.

Strange Interactions

Type: WWW

Address: http://amanda.physics.wisc.edu/show.html

Summary: An online art exhibit by John Jacobsen. From his artist's statement, "My work is an attempt to give a concrete aspect to the subconscious." Definitely worth checking out!

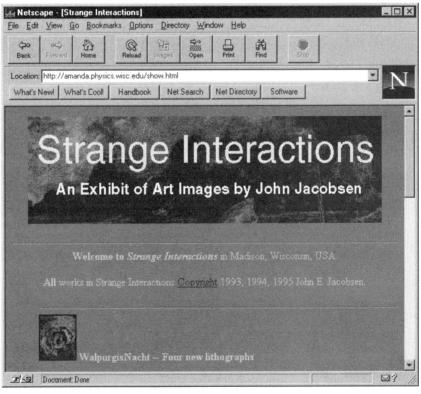

Strange Interactions.

WebMuseum

Type: WWW

Address: http://mistral.enst.fr/

Summary: Great art classics right on your computer screen! It takes a while to download some of the paintings, but it's still quicker and cheaper than flying to Paris.

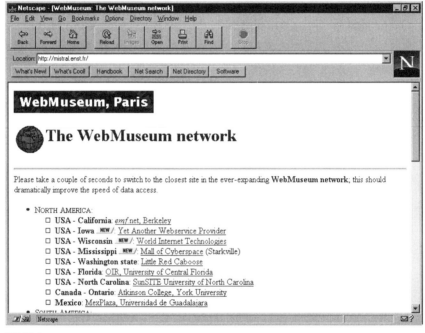

WebMuseum.

Some Related Newsgroups

alt.artcom

alt.postmodern

rec.arts.fine

rec.arts.misc

sci.fractals

ARTS: MULTIDISCIPLINARY

The Fluxus Page

Type: WWW

Address: http://www.panix.com/fluxus/

Summary: A grab-bag of art, music, and writing by the Fluxus pioneers of the early sixties (George Maciunas, Wolf Vostell, LaMonte Young, Yoko Ono, Philip Corner, etc.) and by later neo-Fluxus artists. A must-visit site for anybody interested in the history of contemporary art or interested in forms of expression that are innovative and fun at the same time.

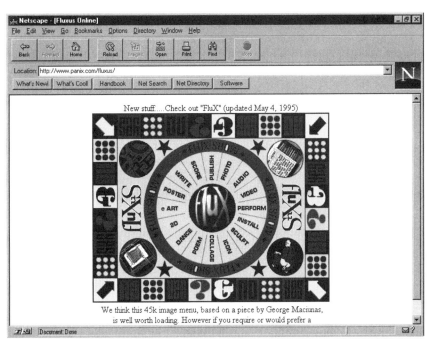

Fluxus Online.

IAMfree

Type: WWW

Address: http://www.rahul.net/iamfree/

Summary: This "Internet Arts Museum for free" offers interesting art, music, and literature in a virtual museum setting. All of the work included was specifically intended for this form of free Internet distribution.

Internet Arts Museum.

Life With Father

Type: WWW

Address: http://www.art.uiuc.edu/ludgate/the/place/ stories/life_with_father/myfather.html

Summary: This is a poetic, autobiographical story-with-pictures by the artist Joseph Squiers. It shows some of the possibilities for highly personal and highly professional artwork on the Web.

Megadeth, Arizona

Type: WWW

Address: http://caprec.com/Megadeth/megadeth.html

Summary: A well-designed and media-rich site maintained by the band Megadeth. Some of the highlights include a "HorrorScopes" service and a set of links to peculiar freeware programs. This is a good site for those who like their entertainment slightly spooky.

Megadeth, Arizona.

Postmodern Culture

Type: WWW

Address: http://jefferson.village.Virginia.EDU/pmc/

Summary: Postmodern Culture is an interesting, heady e-zine exploring recent developments in culture and the arts. It includes some poetry and fiction as well as essays.

The Singapore Graffiti Page

Type: WWW

Address: http://davinci.technet.sg/BOG/

Summary: This is an odd one. Remember Michael Fay, the American boy who was caned for scrawling graffiti in Singapore? This Web site, apparently sponsored in part by the Singapore government, lets you spray-paint *virtual* walls to your heart's content. (I didn't play around for too long, though, because I don't like even virtual spankings.)

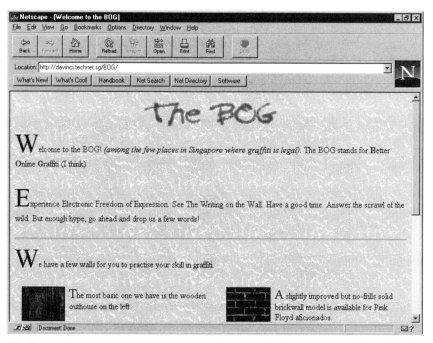

The Bog.

■ BOOKS, LITERATURE & ZINES

Alternative-X

Type: WWW

Address: http://www.altx.com/althome2.html

Summary: This is *the* place to visit if you want to catch up on recent trends in literary fiction, especially the so-called "avant-pop" phenomenon. This site includes stories and polemics by such great, innovative writers as Derek Pell, Euridice, and Harold Jaffe. Rather than playing with the visual possibilities of HTML, Alt-X serves up prose by the bucket-load, so if you're a literary type, there's an excellent bang/buck ratio.

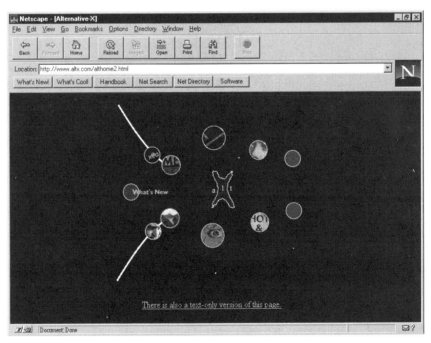

Alternative-X.

The Asylum

Type: WWW

Address: http://www.galcit.caltech.edu/~ta/cgi-bin/
asylhome-ta

Summary: This adventurous site exploits the interactive
possibilities of the Web. It includes collaborative
stories and poems that you can add to as well as a
"lite brite" that lets you exercise your imagination
by creating pictures out of little circles of color.

Basement Full of Books

Type: FTP or WWW

Address: ftp://greyware.com/pub/literature/bfob/
basement_full_of_books

http://www.greyware.com/bfob/default.html

Summary: Get autographed books (with personal inscrip-
tions) directly from their authors. Lots of science
fiction authors like Ursula K. Le Guin, Harlan
Ellison, David Brin, and Joe Haldeman. The list is
updated every month. You get a short synopsis of
each book, along with ordering information.

You can also get this list by sending an e-mail
message to mail-server@rtfm.mit.edu. Put "send
usenet/news.answers/books/basement-full-of-
books" (without the quotes) in the body of the
message.

Book FAQs and Info

Type: FTP

Address: ftp://quartz.rutgers.edu/pub/books/

Summary: Bookstore lists, book reviews, reading lists, and
other literary resources.

You can also Gopher to this site: gopher://
quartz.rutgers.edu. Choose Book FAQs and Info.

Bookstore List

Type: WWW

Address: http://www.cis.ohio-state.edu/hypertext/faq/ usenet/books/stores/top.html

Summary: This site presents, in hypertext form, lists of the best bookstores around the world. (They are taken from Usenet FAQs.)

Bordeaux and Prague

Type: WWW

Address: http://www.freedonia.com/~carl/bp/

Summary: Carl Steadman, the creator of the Bordeaux and Prague page, is a story writer and artist whose unusual work was influenced by postmodern French thought and Situationism. He uses the richness of HTML to present complex works effectively and with humor. This material is not everybody's cup of espresso, but I love it!

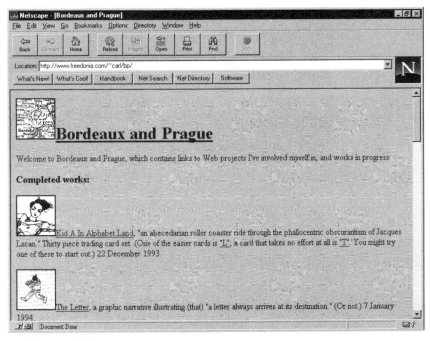

Bordeaux and Prague.

Delirium

Type: WWW

Address: http://pathfinder.com/@@X*hPJuE08wMAQG+P/
twep/Features/Old-Delirium/Delirium1.html

Summary: *Delirium*—a novel that utilizes the interactivity of
the Web—is an interesting example of hypermedia
in a literary context. Worth checking out if you're
interested in how technology creates new possibilities for the arts.

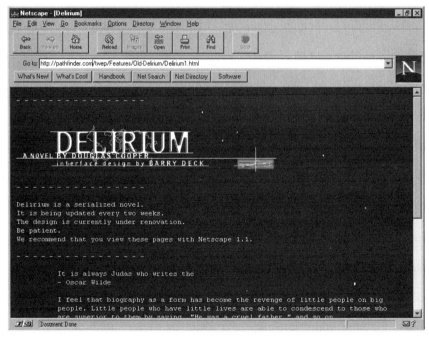

Delirium.

The Hypertext Fiction Page

Type: WWW

Address: http://www.ugcs.caltech.edu/~benedett/
hyper.html

Summary: A good introduction to the theory and practice of hypertext fiction, including a few interesting examples. This page is maintained by students at Caltech.

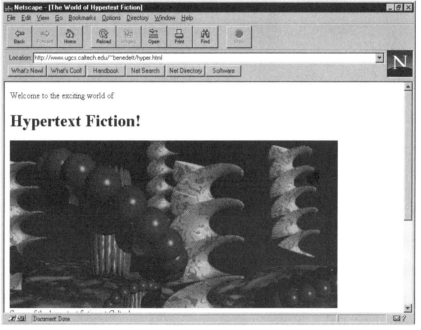

Hypertext Fiction.

John Labovitz's E-ZINE LIST

Type: WWW

Address: http://www.meer.net/~johnl/e-zine-list/
index.html

Summary: A directory of over 175 zines available on the Net.

Contact: John Labovitz
johnl@meer.net

Libido Magazine

Type: WWW

Address: http://www.indra.com/libido/cover3.html

Summary: In its print version, *Libido* is one of the best and "classiest" magazines that focuses on erotic art, photography, and writing. The electronic version is just as good. This is erotica for people who are not afraid to think.

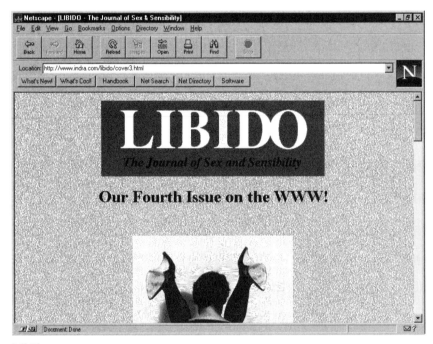

Libido.

The Nancy Drew Page

Type: WWW

Address: http://sunsite.unc.edu/cheryb/nancy.drew/ktitle.html

Summary: I love this site! Nancy Drew from a historical perspective. From a psychological perspective. From a sociological perspective. From an artistic perspective. This is pay dirt for pop culture fans and deconstructionists. By the time you're done here, you'll know Nancy better than you know yourself.

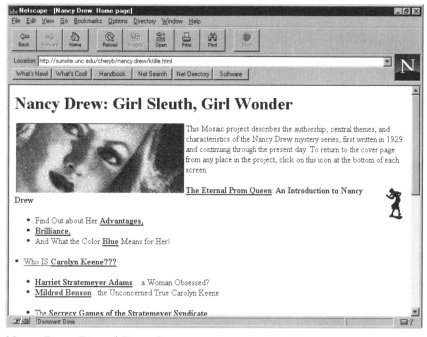

Nancy Drew, Eternal Prom Queen.

Online Fairy Tales

Type: FTP

Address: ftp://info.umd.edu/inforM/EdRes/ ReadingRoom/Fiction/FairyTales

Summary: I always enjoyed telling my kids stories when I put them to bed, but quite often I couldn't re-member exactly how a particular fairy tale went and ended up improvising my own bizarre plots. If only I'd had Internet access I could have FTPed to this site and quickly brushed up on any of the almost 100 tales provided!

Urban Desires

Type: WWW

Address: http://desires.com/

Summary: An *excellent* and intelligent zine full of provocative articles, interviews, reviews, and artwork. The masthead says it all: "An Interactive Magazine of Metropolitan Passions."

Word Magazine

Type: WWW

Address: http://www.word.com/

Summary: No, this has nothing to do with Microsoft Word. It's a big, intelligent New York–based zine that emphasizes high-quality writing and colorful graphics. It's sort of an East Coast HotWired, but with more of an emphasis on the arts and pop culture and less of an emphasis on things cyber. Definitely worth a look!

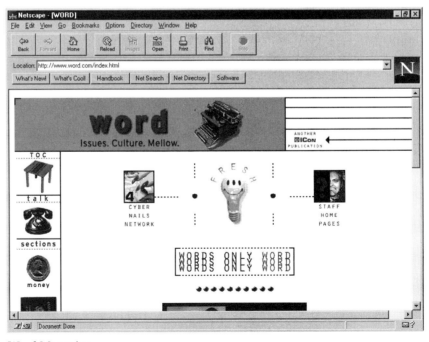

Word Magazine.

Some Related Newsgroups

alt.books.reviews	bit.listserv.literary
alt.books.technical	misc.writing
alt.etext	rec.arts.poems
alt.mythology	rec.arts.prose
alt.usage.english	rec.mag
alt.zines	

BUSINESS

Doing Business With Hong Kong

Type: WWW
Address: http://www.hk.super.net/~rlowe/bizhk/bhhome.html
Summary: Basic trade information, a trade contacts service, and a list of companies by trade.

Downtown Anywhere

Type: WWW
Address: http://www.awa.com/
Summary: Businesses can establish a Net presence in this virtual community. But it's not all business. Lots of Net and general reference info. Check out the library and newsstand, museums, the financial district, the sports arena and, of course, Main Street.

Marshall Space Flight Center Procurement Home Page

Type: WWW
Address: http://procure.msfc.nasa.gov
Summary: Advanced procurement information and small business assistance documents. Learn about federal streamlining initiatives. Pointers to other federal procurement sites such as the Johnson Space Center and Kennedy Space Center home pages.

Contact: Jim Bradford
GP01/Procurement Office
NASA/Marshall Space Flight Center
Huntsville, AL 35812
205/544-0306
jim.bradford@msfc.nasa.gov

Multilevel Marketing

Type: FTP
Address: ftp://rtfm.mit.edu/pub/usenet-by-group/
alt.answers/mim-faq
Summary: A FAQ that discusses different aspects of multi-
level marketing.

STO's Internet Patent Search System

Type: WWW
Address: http://sunsite.unc.edu/patents/intropat.html
Summary: Do a title search through all U.S. patents issued
since 1970.

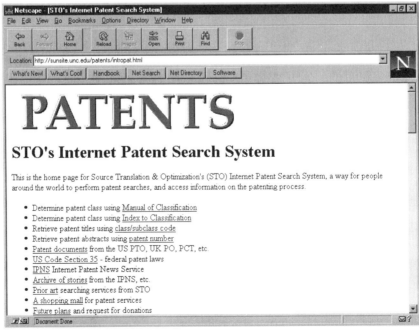

Patent Search System.

Strategy Web

Type: WWW

Address: http://www.onramp.net/~atw_dhw/home.htm

Summary: Question-and-answer hyperbook interactions with experts in business strategy. Check out the 60-second CyberCircuit for a brief "brain-training" session.

Some Related Newsgroups

alt.business.misc
alt.business.multi-level
misc.entrepreneurs

COMPUTING

Free On-Line Dictionary of Computing

Type: WWW

Address: http://wombat.doc.ic.ac.uk/

Summary: Searchable dictionary that includes terms related to general computing, programming languages, networks, domain theory, acronyms, computing history, and just about anything else that has to do with computers.

Global Monitor

Type: WWW

Address: http://nccr.monitor.ca:80/monitor/

Summary: A cool electronic mag loaded with computer-related info.

Global Monitor Magazine.

PC's and Macintoshes

Type: Gopher

Address: gopher://wiretap.spies.com

Path: Wiretap Online Library / Technical Information / PC's and Macintoshes

Summary: Lots of articles and tips for both PC and Mac users.

Toll-Free Numbers

Type: FTP

Address: ftp://oak.oakland.edu/pub/misc/telephone/ tollfree.num

Summary: Toll-free numbers for a bunch of computer companies.

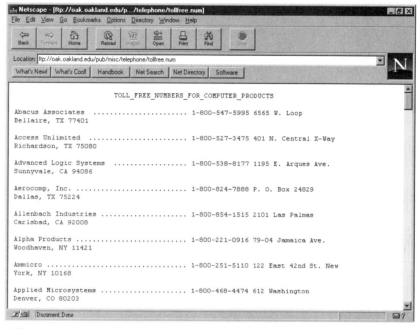

Toll-free number index.

UNB Graphic Services Desktop Publishing Resource Base

Type: WWW

Address: http://degaulle.hil.unb.ca/UNB_G_Services/ GSHomePage.html

Summary: Plenty of plugs for UNB's services, but enough pointers to clip art collections, font banks and other DTP resources to make it a valuable site.

Virus Information

Type: FTP

Address: ftp://oak.oakland.edu/pub/misc/virus

Summary: Technical information about most known viruses. Includes DOS and Mac data.

Some Related Newsgroups

alt.cad.autocad
alt.cyberpunk.tech
alt.privacy
clari.nb.general
comp.misc
comp.theory
comp.virus
comp.sys.misc

CULTURE & DIVERSITY

American Memory From the Library of Congress

Type: WWW

Address: http://rs6.loc.gov/amhome.html

Summary: A nicely done glimpse of America's past, including collections of photographs, text, and even sound recordings. Lots of material on American culture and history, most of it from special collections of the Library of Congress.

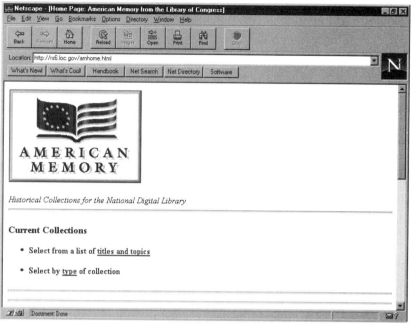

American Memory.

Native American Net Server

Type: Gopher

Address: gopher://alpha1.csd.uwm.edu

Path: UWM Information, Native American Net Server

Summary: Articles and cases on Indian law, book reviews, job openings, education, Native American newsletters, even Native American fonts.

Contact: Michael Wilson
University of Wisconsin at Milwaukee
mwilson@alpha2.csd.uwm.edu

Resources for Diversity

Type: WWW

Address: http://www.nova.edu/Inter-Links/diversity.html

Summary: This page has links to the African Studies Web, Chicano-LatinoNet, Disability Information,

Diversity at the University of Michigan, the Inter-Tribal Network for Native Americans, the Latin American Network Information Center, Minority Online Service (MOLIS), Omni-Cultural Academic Resource, Gay/Lesbian Resources, and Women's Studies at the University of Maryland.

Women's Resources Project

Type: WWW

Address: http://sunsite.unc.edu/cheryb/women/wshome.html

Summary: *Women's studies:* Pointers to women's studies programs at several colleges and universities. *Women and literature:* Bios of female authors from Harriet Beecher Stowe to Marge Piercy, from Jane Austen to Maya Angelou. A guide to women's resources on the Net.

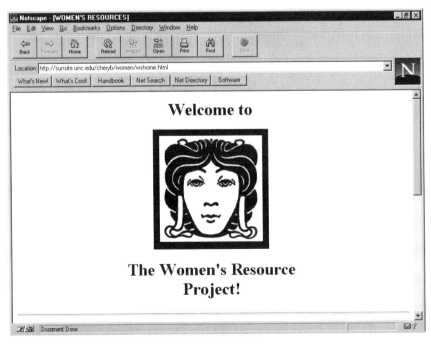

Women's Resources.

Some Related Newsgroups

alt.discrimination
soc.culture.african.american
soc.women

EDUCATION

Higher Education Resources and Opportunities
Type: Telnet
Address: telnet://fedix.fie.com
Login: new
Summary: The Minority On-Line Information Service is an online database service with all sorts of information about scholarships, grants, fellowships, conferences, research opportunities, and other opportunities for minorities and women.

Hillside Elementary School
Type: WWW
Address: http://hillside.coled.umn.edu/
Summary: Every student in Mrs. Collins' sixth grade class has created his or her own home page. Lots more planned for this site, a joint project of Hillside Elementary School in Cottage Grove, Minnesota, and the University of Minnesota College of Education.

Reading Disabilities
Type: FTP
Address: ftp://ftp.spies.com/Library/Article/Misc/disable.rd
Summary: Extremely clear and well-written paper, "Neuro-psychological Bases of Educational Disabilities," by Robert Zenhausern, Ph.D., Professor of

Psychology at St. John's University. It's a scholarly paper, but its style makes it accessible to the lay public.

Schoolnet Resource Manual

Type: FTP

Address: ftp://schoolnet.carleton.capub/schoolnet/manuals/Resource.txt

Summary: This is a huge file with about a kazillion pointers to science, technology, and education resources on the Net.

The manual's directory is full of Net information. Check out the Big Dummy's Guide to the Internet, Electric Mystic Guide to Internet, FTP Introduction, E-Mail Intro, Gopher.FAQ, Internet Basics, and Guidelines—Netiquette.

U.S. Department of Education

Type: WWW

Address: http://inet.ed.gov/

Summary: Get press releases and information about funding opportunities, speeches prepared for the U.S. Secretary of Education, Teachers' and Researchers' Guides to the U.S. Department of Education, and links to other educational resources.

ENTERTAINMENT

eye magazine

Type: WWW

Address: http://gold.interlog.com/eye/

Summary: This is Toronto's premier arts-listings weekly. Not only does it inform you of what's going on in Toronto, it also presents interesting features on musicians and other artists. This is a well-thought-out Web page.

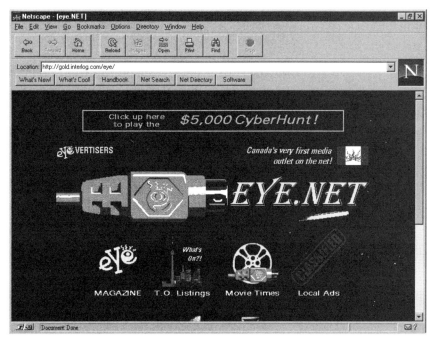

Interlog EYE.NET.

ENVIRONMENT

Ask-a-Geologist

Type: e-mail

Address: ask-a-geologist@octopus.wr.usgs.gov

Summary: Ever wonder what kind of rock is the most common in your area? How the mountains were formed? When the next earthquake is likely to hit your town? I'm not sure how the U.S. Geological Survey has time for this, but if you send your question to the address above you'll receive an answer within a couple of days. And since this service is free, you won't lose your chert. (Sorry about that.)

Cascades Volcano Observatory Home Page

Type: WWW

Address: http://vulcan.wr.usgs.gov/home.html

Summary: Arm yourself with information about volcanoes and other natural hazards. Get hazard assessments and warnings during volcano crises. Find out about the International Volcano Disaster Assistance Program. Links to Alaska and Hawaii volcano observatories.

The EnviroLink Network

Type: Gopher

Address: gopher://envirolink.org

Summary: As you'd guess, this site is full of information about ecology, environmental groups, endangered species, and environmental law.

The Forest

Type: Gopher

Address: gopher://cln.etc.bc.ca

Path: The Community Learning Network / Special Projects for the CLN / The Forest (Online Reference Materials)

Summary: Everything you ever wanted to know about forest environments and forest-related industries.

Institute for Global Communications (IGC)

Type: Gopher

Address: gopher://gopher.igc.apc.org

Summary: From the welcome message: "IGC runs four computer networks known as PeaceNet(TM), EcoNet(TM), ConflictNet, and LaborNet. IGC is the U.S. member of the Association for Progressive Communications, a 16-country association of computer networks working for peace, human rights, environmental protection, social justice, and sustainability."

TIOTS! (This is one terrific site!)

Contact: Institute for Global Communications
18 De Boom St.
San Francisco, CA 94107
415/442-0220
igc-info@igc.apc.org

Linkages Home Page

Type: WWW

Address: http://portal.mbnet.mb.ca/linkage/

Summary: Provided by the International Institute for Sustainable Development, publishers of the Earth Negotiations Bulletin. Links to information about international environment and development meetings such as the World Summit for Social Development, the International Conference on Population & Development, and the Earth Negotiations Bulletin.

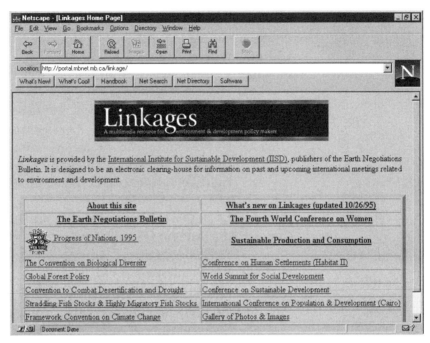

Linkages.

Ozone Depletion

Type: FTP

Address: ftp://rtfm.mit.edu/pub/usenet/news.answers/ozone-depletion/

Summary: FAQ files about the depletion of the ozone layer are posted monthly. There's a special section for the Antarctic ozone hole.

Students for the Exploration and Development of Space

Type: Gopher

Address: gopher://seds.lpl.arizona.edu

Summary: This site includes the latest information about celestial events as well as a wealth of material related to space exploration.

The Virtual Desert

Type: WWW

Address: http://www.well.com/user/vegas/desert/Top/index.html

Summary: If you love the American desert as much as I do, you'll love this Web page.

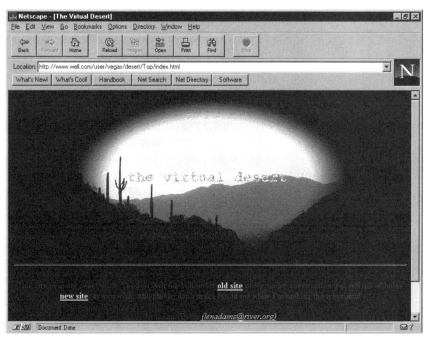

The Virtual Desert.

Some Related Newsgroups

bit.listserv.biosph-1
sci.environment

FINANCE

Credit Info

Type: FTP

Address: ftp://rtfm.mit.edu/pub/usenet/news.answers/consumer-credit-faq/

Summary: Is Mastercard better than Visa? What is a secured card? Do I want a fixed-rate or floating-rate card? Why is a discount better than a rebate? The answers to these and many other burning consumer questions can be found in the consumer credit FAQ, which was compiled from questions asked on the misc.consumers newsgroup.

Economics

Type: Gopher

Address: gopher://nysernet.org

Path: Special Collections:Business and Economic Development

Summary: If the world of business is your world, have a blast exploring these resources. Among them: a FAQ on advertising on the Internet, the Basic Guide to Exporting, Commerce Business Daily, and a U.S. Patent database.

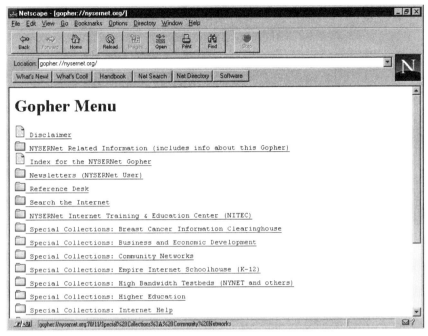

NYSE Gopher.

Foreign Exchange Rates

Type: Gopher

Address: gopher://una.hh.lib.umich.edu

Path: ebb /monetary statistics/ FRB foreign exchange rates

Summary: These figures from the Federal Reserve Bank of New York are updated weekly.

Koblas Currency Converter

Type: WWW

Address: http://bin.gnn.com/cgi-bin/gnn/currency

Summary: This page is updated weekly. By default, the page shows the currency rates of over 50 countries relative to U.S. currency (e.g., 1 U.S. dollar is worth 1.3605 dollars in Australia). To get currency rates relative to another country, just click the country you want.

Some Related Newsgroups

clari.biz.currencies.us_dollar
clari.biz.finance
clari.biz.economy.world

 ## FOOD & DRINK

The Chocolate Lovers' Page

Type: WWW
Address: http://bc.emanon.net/chocolate/
Summary: Lots of links to information about everybody's favorite designer drug.

Food Recipes Database

Type: Gopher
Address: gopher://gopher.aecom.yu.edu
Path: Internet Resources / Miscellaneous / Search the Food Recipes Database
Summary: Huge searchable recipe list.

HOT HOT HOT

Type: WWW
Address: http://www.hot.presence.com/g/p/H3/
Summary: No, it's not another one of those virtual sex sites you keep reading about. This one's a highly organized list of hot sauces from around the world. If you like your food spicy, check this out!

HOT HOT HOT.

Over the Coffee

Type: WWW

Address: www.cappuccino.com/

Summary: If you're a coffee lover, it's all here. Coffee trivia and factoids, a travelers' guide to coffee houses, a list of coffee-related USENET groups, a coffee recipe collection, lists of coffee (and tea) books, a glossary of coffee terminology, and resources for coffee professionals.

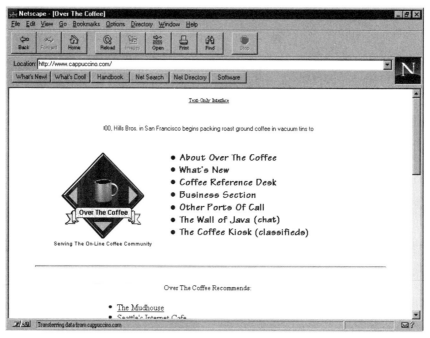

Over the Coffee.

Patriots' Trail Girl Scout Council

Type: WWW

Address: http://www.ptgirlscouts.org/ptgirlscouts.html

Summary: I've listed this Boston-area scouting page with other food-related Web sites because it lets you order your cookies online! Of course, the Scouts advise that you should support your local troop first, but if nobody comes knocking on your door and you've got a Thin Mints jones that just won't go away . . .

The Real Beer Site

Type: WWW

Address: http://realbeer.com/

Summary: If you want to hear about Coors and Anheuser-Busch products, watch football; if you want to find out about micro-breweries and carefully hand-crafted beers, check out this Web page. The emphasis here is on old-fashioned *quality*, and there is a wealth of information about beers from all areas of the country.

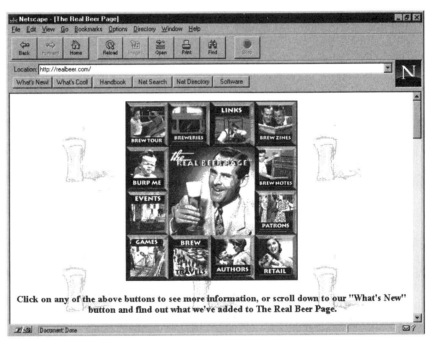

Real Beer.

Recipes

Type: FTP
Address: ftp://gatekeeper.dec.com/pub/recipes
Summary: A collection of over 500 recipes.

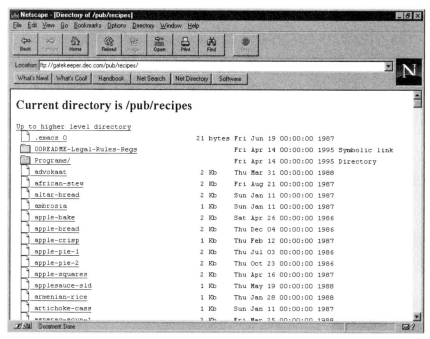

Recipes.

The Recipes Folder

Type: WWW
Address: http://english-www.hss.cmu.edu/recipes.html
Summary: If you're a vegetarian, you'll feel right at home here. If you're a flesh eater, you'll have to put up with the following subject headings: "Vegetarian Stuff," "Dead Animals" and "Things Possibly Involving Dead Animals and Possibly Not." Whatever your culinary predilections, this is a terrific list of recipe sources.

The Single Malt Page

Type: WWW

Address: http://www.dcs.ed.ac.uk/home/jhb/whisky/

Summary: I hate to admit it, but I've spent a lot of time at this site. Here you can learn everything there is to know about fine, single malt Scotch whiskey, or *whisky*, as they say over there. This is a serious, professionally designed Web page that includes a clickable map of the different whiskey-producing regions and even an Excel spreadsheet! As a concession to the nonpurists of the drinking world, there is even some recently added information on blended whiskeys.

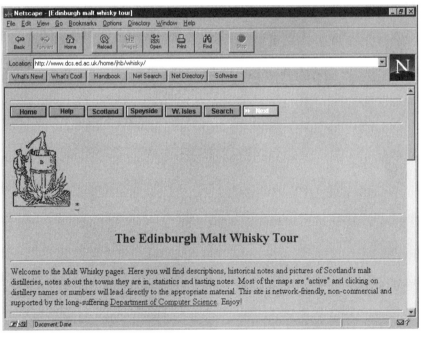

Whisky!

Vegetarianism

Type: FTP

Address: ftp://flubber.cs.umd.edu/other/tms/veg

Summary: All kinds of info for vegetarians and would-be vegetarians—FAQs, recipes, and so on. Another vegetarian resource to check out is the rec.food.veg newsgroup.

Veggies Unite!

Type: WWW

Address: http://www.honors.indiana.edu/~veggie/recipes.cgi/

Summary: A searchable index of over 900 vegetarian recipes. Links to other nutrition and health sites.

Some Related Newsgroups

alt.college.food
alt.folklore.herbs
alt.food.fat-free
alt.gourmand
alt.support.diet
rec.crafts.winemaking
rec.food.cooking
rec.food.historic
rec.food.recipes
rec.food.restaurants
rec.food.sourdough
rec.food.veg
sci.med.nutrition

FUN & GAMES

All About Blimps

Type: WWW

Address: http://www.iag.net/~zim/airship.html

Summary: This site is a great example of how the Web can provide very specialized information in a pleasant, well-designed, nonacademic format featuring clear text and excellent illustrations. If you want to learn about blimps, I wouldn't know where else to send you.

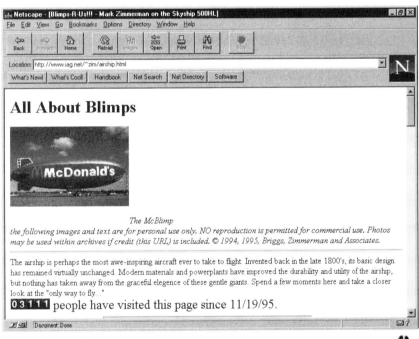

Blimps-R-Us!!!

The Beavis and Butthead Home Page

Type: WWW

Address: http://calvin.hsc.colorado.edu/

Summary: Heh—heh heh heh—heh heh—.

Chiba Woo

Type: WWW

Address: http://sensemedia.net/sprawl/

Summary: What do you get when you cross a MOO with a Web document? A WOO, of course. As you may know, a MOO is an interactive online game with object-oriented extensions. This site is an interesting experiment in extending MOOing to the Web. It also contains some excellent links to other sites.

Ferret Central

Type: WWW

Address: http://www.optics.rochester.edu:8080/users/pgreene/central.html

Summary: I keep threatening to get one of these wonderful animals, and after browsing this site, which includes a thorough FAQ, beautiful photos, and links to other ferret-related sites, you might want one too. Remember: *They are not rodents!*

Fly With Us!

Type: WWW

Address: http://www.interedu.com/mig29/

Summary: Have you ever wanted to climb into the cockpit of a MiG-29, roar down the runway and then fly at supersonic speeds to the edge of space? We're not talking virtual reality here, this is the real thing! For a price—make that a *hefty* price—Fly With Us!, Inc., offers you a first-class vacation in Russia that includes a flight with a "co-pilot" who hopefully knows more about the aircraft than you do. The Web site provides you with a description of the various vacation packages and even an in-flight video clip. I dare you to do this!

Fly With Us.

Games Domain

Type: WWW

Address: http://www.gamesdomain.com/

Summary: If you have any interest in games, check out this page. It has links to Usenet groups and games FAQs, a Walkthroughs link that can get you unstuck from several popular games, and over 100 links to games-related Web pages and FTP sites.

The Gardening Encyclopedia

Type: WWW

Address: http://www.timeinc.com/vg/TimeLife/CG/ vg-search.html

Summary: Want to start a garden but don't know what will grow in your back yard? Just enter some information about where you live, how sunny or shady your yard is, and what kind of soil you have;

you'll get back a list of appropriate plants and growing tips. This is another fine example of interactive applications on the Web.

Hollywood Online

Type: WWW

Address: http://www.hollywood.com/

Summary: This is the place to find out about the latest Hollywood movies. Not only does it include listings and discussion boards, it exploits the multimedia power of the Web by offering up sound clips and video trailers.

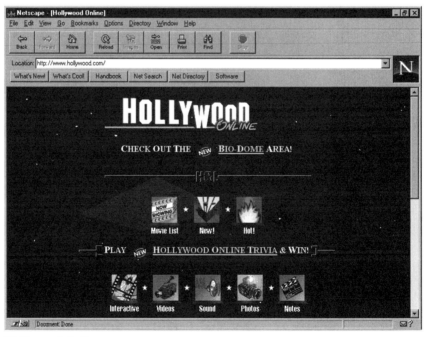

Hollywood Online.

Killer List of Video Games

Type: Gopher

Address: gopher://wiretap.spies.com

Path: Wiretap Online Library / Mass Media / Games and Video Games / The Killer List of Video Games

Summary: Get the inside scoop on your favorite games through files like Definitive Arcade Video Cheats, SEGA Genesis Secrets, Killer List of Video Games, Home Video Games History, and (yes, this is for real) The Rules of Tiddlywinks.

Roller Coasters

Type: FTP

Address: ftp://gboro.rowan.edu/pub/Coasters/*

Summary: FAQs, reviews of parks and coasters, animations, JPG and GIF images.

Sony

Type: WWW

Address: http://www.sony.com

Summary: As you would expect, this is a large, well-done, slick site that includes lots of information on movies, CDs, concerts, electronic equipment, and so on. It's a nice mall to visit.

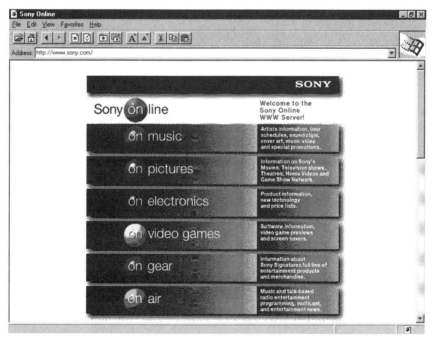

Sony (no baloney).

TV Net

Type: WWW

Address: http://tvnet.com/TVnet.html

Summary: Want to find out what's on tonight? TV Net can tell you! This page also includes a wealth of TV-related information and links to other sites. Put your computer near the couch and you'll never have to get up again.

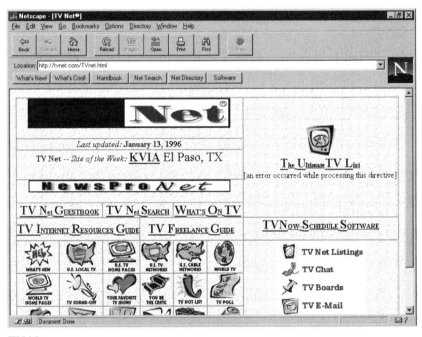

TV Net.

TV2NITE

Type: e-mail

Address: listserv@necom.com (type **subscribe tv2nite-l** in message)

Summary: You're at work, but you can't keep your mind off what you're going to do when you get home. *Baywatch* . . . *Melrose Place* . . . a new miniseries about OJ . . . Wait a minute, was that tonight or tomorrow? Better check. But why should you have to get up from your desk just to find out what's on TV tonight? There's really no reason to work so hard at work—now you can have tonight's TV lineup e-mailed to you every day. Tip: If you work at home, you can avoid trudging over to your desk by keeping a laptop PC right by the couch!

Virtual Vegas

Type: WWW

Address: http://www.virtualvegas.com/vvhome.html

Summary: Lost Wages is one of those love-it-or-hate-it cities. Since this site does a nice job of capturing all the gaudiness and tackiness, I suspect it may be one of those love-it-or-hate-it Web pages. There are layers of annoying registration forms to get through, and the process is made even slower by traffic (Virtual Vegas has received some mass-media attention). Once you're there, though, you'll see a well-crafted piece of glitzy Americana.

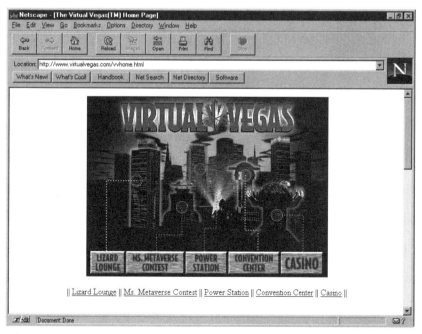

Viva Las Virtual Vegas.

WebMind Crosswords

Type: FTP
Address: ftp://rtfm.mit.edu/pub/usenet/news.answers/crossword-faq/
Summary: Crossword aficionado heaven. Guides, dictionaries, solution tips, software info, and so on.

Also try /pub/usenet/news.answers/puzzles/faq for a collection of mindbenders.

Zarf's List of Interactive Games on the Web

Type: WWW
Address: http://www.cs.cmu.edu/afs/andrew/org/kgb/www/zarf/games.html
Summary: Just what it sounds like. A good hotlist.

HEALTH, MEDICINE & RECOVERY

AIDS

Type: Gopher
Address: gopher://selway.umt.edu:700
Path: Sexuality / Acquired Immune Deficiency Syndrome (AIDS)
Summary: Lots of statistics and resources, as well as the full text of *Aids Treatment News.*

Americans With Disabilities Act

Type: Gopher
Address: gopher://scilibx.ucsc.edu
Path: The Library / Electronic Books and Other Texts
Summary: Get the full text of the 1990 Americans with Disabilities Act.

Cornucopia of Disability Information (CODI)

Type: Gopher

Address: gopher://val-dor.cc.buffalo.edu

Summary: A great resource for those with disabilities and health professionals. Lots of digests, info on legal issues and assistance, college guides, independent living centers, and employment resources.

Dr. Greenson's Gastrointestinal and Liver Pathology Home Page

Type: WWW

Address: http://www.pds.med.umich.edu/users/greenson/

Summary: Just what you've been waiting for! It even includes pictures of a GI Case of the Month and an Infectious Case of the Month. I'm thinking of making a musical of this page.

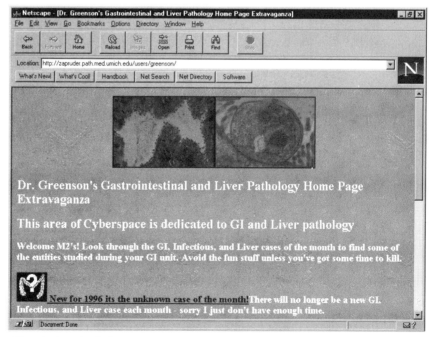

GI and Liver Pathology.

Forensic Medicine

Type: Gopher
Address: gopher://gopher.vifp.monash.edu.au
Path: Medical / Forensic Medicine
Summary: Lots of articles concerning how medicine and the law interact.

The Heart Page

Type: WWW
Address: http://sln.fi.edu/tfi/preview/heartpreview.html
Summary: All kinds of physiological information about the human heart, with great illustrations. No, you won't learn how to keep people from breaking it. . . .

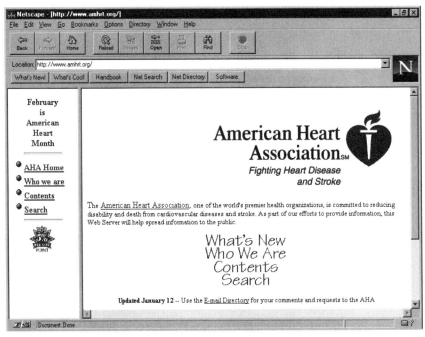

Preview the Heart.

Insomnia (Healthline Information Database)

Type: Gopher

Address: gopher://wilcox.umt.edu:700/1

Path: General Health Information / Antidepressants and Sleep Disorders

Summary: Hey, it's 3 A.M. and I'm ready to start another chapter!

Institute for Molecular Virology

Type: WWW

Address: http://www.bocklabs.wisc.edu/

Summary: Info about the AIDS virus, 3D images and animations of virus structures, 2D electron micrographs of viruses, online virology course material, phone book of virologists on the Net, and virology-related journal articles.

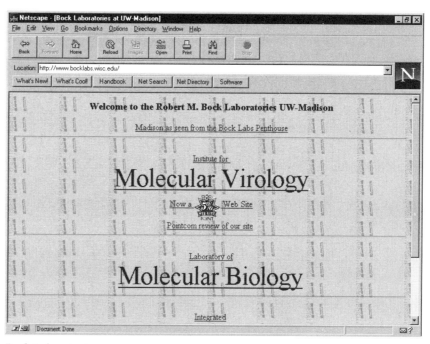

Bock Laboratories.

Midwifery and Birth Information Page

Type: WWW
Address: http://www.efn.org/~djz/birth/birthindex.html
Summary: This is my wife's favorite Web site. It includes articles on midwifery as well as prenatal and postnatal care. This is not a flashy site, but it's full of valuable information that can't be obtained elsewhere.

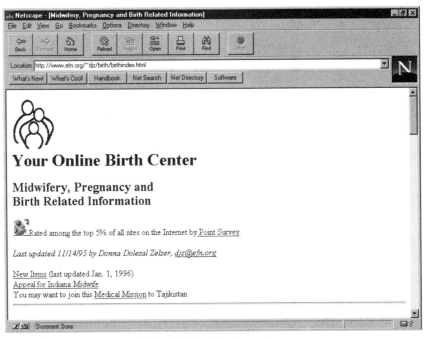

Midwifery, Pregnancy and Birth-Related Information

National Toxicology Program (NTP) Home Page

Type: WWW

Address: http://ntp-server.niehs.nih.gov/

Summary: Established by the Secretary of Health and Human Services "to coordinate toxicology research and testing activities within the Department, to provide information about potentially toxic chemicals to regulatory and research agencies and the public, and to strengthen the science base in toxicology. In its 16 years, the NTP has become the world's leader in designing, conducting, and interpreting animal assays for toxicity." The annual plan describes current work being done in carcinogenesis, toxicology, genetic toxicology, and chemical disposition.

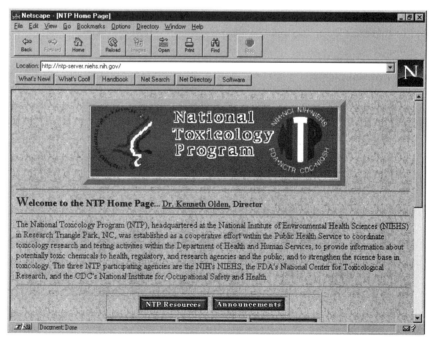

National Toxicology Program.

New York State Breast Cancer Information Clearinghouse

Type: Gopher

Address: gopher://nysernet.org/

Path: Special Collections: Breast Cancer Information Clearinghouse

Summary: A great resource for breast cancer patients, family members, and health professionals. Lots of info on treatment and rehabilitation, a list of names and phone numbers of support groups throughout the United States and pointers to other cancer resources.

Psycoloquy

Type: WWW

Address: http://www.w3.org/hypertext/DataSources/bySubject/Psychology/Psycoloquy.html

Summary: An electronic journal sponsored by the American Psychological Association. Contains reports on new ideas and findings in all areas of psychology. Contributors solicit peer feedback, and contributions are refereed by members of Psycoloquy's Editorial Board.

　　USENET: sci.psychology.digest

　　Or, to get articles automatically, send e-mail to listserv@pucc.bitnet or listserv@pucc.princeton.edu. Leave the Subject line blank and put the following in the body of the message: **sub psyc** *Firstname Lastname* (where *Firstname* and *Lastname* are your own names, *not* your Internet address).

Sexual Assault Recovery Service

Type: Gopher

Address: gopher://wilcox.umt.edu

Summary: Documents and discussions on dealing with sexual assault experiences and prevention.

　　You can also Telnet to selway.umt.edu and use the login *health*.

12-Step

Type: e-mail
Address: muller@camp.rutgers.edu
Summary: The purpose of this group is to share experiences about 12-step programs.

The Wellness List

Type: mailing list
Address: majordomo@wellnessmart.com
Summary: This list includes discussions of health, nutrition, wellness and life expectancy. Lots of healthy recipes, nutrition- and fitness-related product announcements, book reviews, and nutrition-related position papers.

To subscribe, send the following one-line message in e-mail: **subscribe wellnesslist** *your name* (where *your name* is your full name, *not* your e-mail address).

Some Related Newsgroups

alt.folklore.herbs
alt.health.ayurveda
alt.med.cfs
alt.support.diet
bit.listserv.c+health
clari.tw.health.misc
clari.tw.health.aids
misc.fitness.misc
misc.health.diabetes
talk.politics.medicine
sci.med.aids
sci.med.pharmacy

HISTORY

The History Resources Page

Type: WWW

Address: http://history.cc.ukans.edu/history/
WWW_history_main.html

Summary: The University of Kansas maintains this excellent collection of links to history resources around the Net. If you can't find out about it starting from here, it might not have happened.

History Sources

Type: FTP

Address: ftp://byrd.mu.wvnet.edu/pub/history

Summary: The directories are broken down by topic: diplomatic, general, maritime, military, and so on. The files include everything from Roosevelt's Inaugural Addresses to a paper on psych operations in the Gulf War to a Civil War bibliography. Sponsored by Marshall University Department of History.

Contact: Michael J. McCarthy
mmccarth@muvm6.wvnet.edu

MEDEIV-L

Type: mailing list

Address: listserv@ukanvm.cc.ukans.edu (send message with **SUBSCRIBE** in body)

Summary: This mailing list is for discussing all aspects of the middle ages.

Contact: Jeff Gardner jgardner@ukanvm.ukans.edu

Time's Man of the Year

Type: WWW

Address: http://pathfinder.com/time/special/moy/ moy.html

Summary: Each year since 1927, *Time* magazine has chosen somebody to appear on the cover as Man of the Year. Can you guess who was chosen in 1984? That's right, Peter Ueberroth. How about 1955? You guessed it, General Motors president Harlow Hubert Curtice. Once you get past the overwhelming male bias, this is actually a pretty interesting stroll down memory lane. While the articles about the individuals are informative, this site really says more about our values, about what types of achievement we have considered important over the course of recent history.

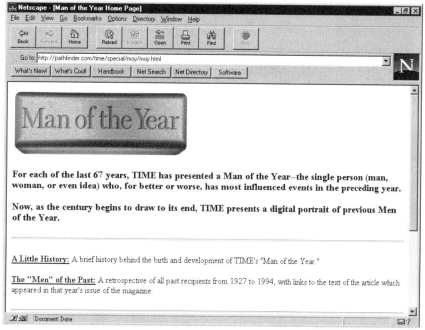

Man of the Year Home Page.

Some Related Newsgroups

alt.history.what-if
alt.revisionism
alt.war
alt.war.civil.usa
bit.listserv.history
soc.history

 HUMOR

Brettnews

Type: WWW

Address: http://pathfinder.com/vibe/vibeart/brettnews/index.html

Summary: *Brettnews* is a well-done, idiosyncratic personal humor zine. It always makes me laugh, and sometimes it even makes me think.

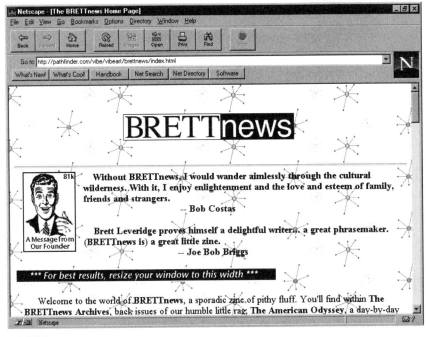

BRETTnews.

Cartoons

Type: Usenet
Address: alt.toon-pics
Summary: Download pictures of your favorite cartoon characters.

The Comic Book and Comic-Strip Page

Type: WWW
Address: http://dragon.acadiau.ca/~860099w/comics/comics.html
Summary: Links to lots of comic book and comic strip pages, comics conventions, reviews, lots of mailing lists you can subscribe to. A few related newsgroups are rec.arts.comics.misc, rec.arts.comics.strips, and alt.comics.alternative.

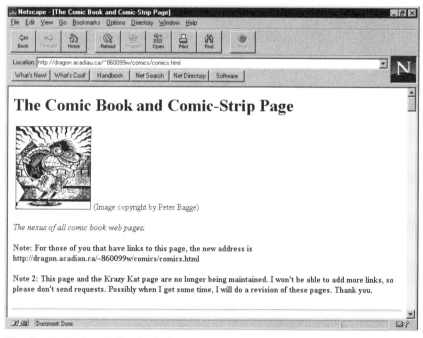

The Comic Book and Comic-Strip Page.

The Doctor Fun Page

Type: WWW

Address: http://www.unitedmedia.com/comics/drfun/

Summary: A new cartoon every day. Also available via FTP and Usenet.

Type: FTP

Address: sunsite.unc.edu

Path: /pub/electronic-publications/Dr-Fun

Type: Usenet

Address: alt.binaries.pictures.misc

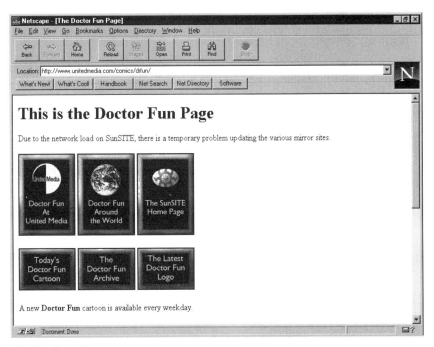

The Dr. Fun Page.

Funny Guys

Type: FTP

Address: ftp://cathouse.org/pub/cathouse/humor *then* /quotes *or* /standup

Summary: In the quotes and standup directories you'll find quotes and funnies from such notable laugh inducers (depending on your taste) as Woody Allen, Oscar Wilde, W.C. Fields, Andrew Dice Clay, Lenny Bruce, Rodney Dangerfield, Groucho Marx, and Mark Twain. One of my favorites is the british.humor directory. That's where Monty Python and Peter Cook reside. And check out the sports directory for Yogi Berra quotes and a selection of golf, racquetball, and bowling humor.

Mini-Annals of Improbable Research (mini-AIR)

Type: Gopher

Address: gopher://saturn.soils.umn.edu:70

Path: email-lists / mjir / mAir

Summary: AIR is a new science humor magazine, edited by Marc Abrahams, the father of the annual Ig Nobel Prize Ceremony, which "honors people whose achievements cannot or should not be reproduced." I must forewarn you, however. The following is a direct quote from the mini-AIR FAQ. Question: "Do you promise that there will be a minimum of puns involving the nickname 'AIR'?" Answer: "No."

Netwit

Type: mailing list

Address: help@netwit.cmhnet.org

Summary: If stupid Internet humor is your thing, send a message with your Internet address in the body of the message.

The Unofficial Tank Girl WWW Site

Type: WWW

Address: http://www.dcs.qmw.ac.uk/~bob/stuff/tg/index.html

Summary: Tank Girl is a creation of Jamie Hewlett and Alan Martin. On this page, you'll find a gallery of Tank Girl pictures, a Tank Girl FAQ, and everything else you need to be Tank Girl–literate.

Tank Girl.

Some Related Newsgroups

alt.comedy.british
alt.comics.buffalo-roam
alt.comics.superman
alt.fan.firesign-theatre
alt.fan.wodehouse
alt.fan.tank-girl
alt.folklore.college
alt.humor.best-of-usenet
clari.feature.foxtrot
rec.arts.comics.marketplace
rec.arts.comics.strips
rec.humor.d
rec.humor.funny

INDEXES, HOTLISTS & SEARCH TOOLS

Archie Request Form

Type: WWW
Address: http://hoohoo.ncsa.uiuc.edu/archie.html
Summary: Archie is a utility for locating files at anonymous FTP sites. You used to need your own Archie client to connect with an Archie host, or alternatively you could Telnet to a site that provided a text-based UNIX client. Now it's much simpler. This site lets you specify your request in a simple Web form and then does the rest of the work for you.

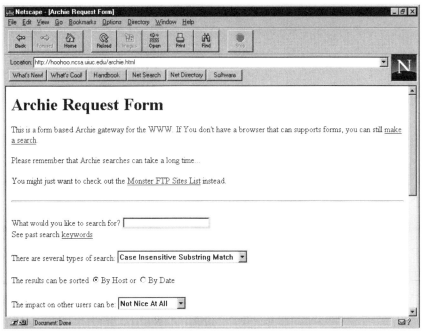

Archie Request Form.

ARGUS ClearingHouse for Subject-Oriented Resource Guides

Type: WWW

Address: http://www.lib.umich.edu/chhome.html

Summary: A well-organized collection of hotlinks, grouped by subject area.

Best of the Net

Type: WWW

Address: http://gnn.com/wic/botn/index.html

Summary: Part of the excellent GNN site, this document includes hotlinks to a variety of interesting Web pages.

Best of the Net.

Best of the Web

Type: WWW

Address: http://wings.buffalo.edu/contest/

Summary: This is the Academy Awards for Web pages, voted on by thousands of Internet users. There are a variety of categories, and you can jump right over to the winners via the provided hotlinks.

CityLink

Type: WWW

Address: http://www.usacitylink.com/

Summary: More and more city governments and civic organizations are establishing a presence on the Web. CityLink points you to many of these. It also includes a wide range of information that may be important to travelers. For instance, the New York link includes a brief guide to treating gunshot wounds.

The USA CityLink Project.

Comprehensive List of Sites

Type: WWW

Address: http://www.netgen.com/cgi/comprehensive

Summary: Comprehensive is right! This is an index to over 85,000 Web sites around the world!

Comprehensive List of Sites.

Cool Site of the Day

Type: WWW

Address: http://cool.infi.net/

Summary: On the Web, as in "real life," there's always someone who's willing to tell you where to go. This home page includes a new link each day to a particularly interesting and original site. There are also links to previously chosen cool sites.

Cool Site of the Day.

Cool Sites to Visit

Type: WWW

Address: http://kells.vmedia.com:80/alternate/vvc/onlcomp/mosaicqtw/hyperguide/CoolSite4.html

Summary: Ventana's own collection of cool stuff. The home page has a list and descriptions of current cool happenings. Go to General Net Resources (from the TOC page) for a terrific collection of information about the Net.

CUI W3 Catalog

Type: WWW

Address: http://cuiwww.unige.ch/w3catalog

Summary: This site, administered by the University of Geneva, provides a searchable front-end for several excellent Internet catalogs.

ECHO!

Type: WWW
Address: http://www.echonyc.com/
Summary: This is a collection of interesting home pages by members of the Echo online service. The documents vary from technology hotlists to experimental art.

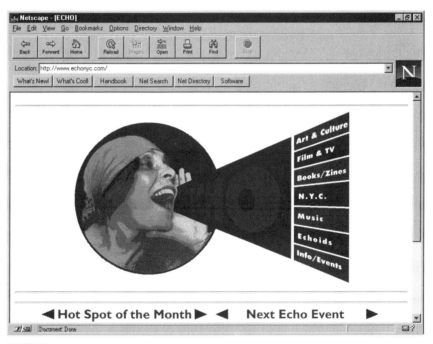

ECHO!

The EINet Galaxy

Type: WWW
Address: http://www.einet.com
Summary: EINet Galaxy is an easy-to-use and thorough hotlist. A good starting point for Web novices.

E-ZINE LIST

Type: WWW

Address: http://www.meer.net/~johnl/e-zine-list/

Summary: John Labovitz maintains the most thorough and up-to-date list of electronic zines currently available.

451f

Type: WWW

Address: http://hakatai.mcli.dist.maricopa.edu/451f/index.html

Summary: Another great collection of Web links.

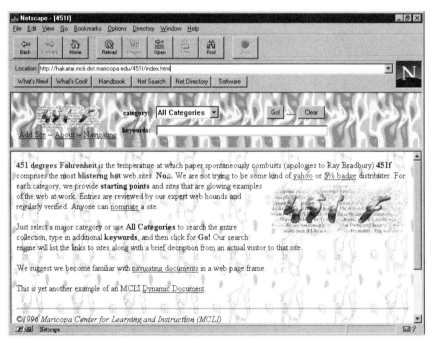

451f.

Harvest

Type: WWW

Address: http://harvest.cs.colorado.edu/

Summary: This is one of the best Web "search engines," including indexes of home pages, public domain software, newsgroups, and so on. It is easy to use and thorough, one of the best places to go when you want to "harvest" specific information.

Index Librorum Liberorum

Type: WWW

Address: http://www.fourmilab.ch/

Summary: John Walker has amassed a large, interesting collection of public domain electronic texts, technical papers and programs. Not only does he make these materials available to you, he has organized them so that it's easy to find what you're looking for.

Infomine

Type: WWW

Address: http://lib-www.ucr.edu/govpub/

Summary: Links to a variety of federal government Web sites.

InfoSeek

Type: WWW

Address: http://www.infoseek.com/

Summary: This claims to be the largest set of searchable indexes to WWW pages and to USENET newsgroups. After a quick look around I have no reason to doubt it. InfoSeek also maintains indexes to over 80 computer periodicals. A great place to start your research.

InfoSeek.

Inter-Active Yellow Pages

Type: WWW

Address: http://netcenter.com/yellows/index.html

Summary: Commercial products and services on the Net. Everything from consumer electronics to travel to "The World's First Totally Useless 900#s." There's also a Windows Hot Tip of the Month.

Internet Resources Meta-Index

Type: WWW

Address: http://www.ncsa.uiuc.edu/SDG/Software/ Mosaic/MetaIndex.html

Summary: This page has links to most of the resource directories and indexes on the Net.

The Internet Services List

Type: WWW

Address: http://www.uwm.edu/Mirror/ inet.services.html

Summary: This is Scott Yanoff's absolutely huge list of World Wide Web hotlinks. It is well-organized and updated regularly. Another great place to start browsing!

InterNIC Directory

Type: WWW

Address: http://ds.internic.net/

Summary: InterNIC provides several very large searchable databases of Internet resources. Definitely worth checking out.

JumpStation Front Page

Type: WWW

Address: http://www.stir.ac.uk/jsbin/js

Summary: Query the JumpStation database and get a set of links that correspond to your criteria.

JumpStation II

Type: WWW

Address: http://www.stir.ac.uk/jsbin/jsii

Summary: JumpStation II is a catalog of sites that lets you search by URL, title, header, or subject. It also includes a facility for locating particular servers if you only know a part of their address.

Justin's Links From the Underground

Type: WWW

Address: http://raptor.swarthmore.edu/jahall/

Summary: This is an almost legendary hotlist of interesting and unusual Internet sites.

List of American Universities

Type: WWW
Address: http://www.clas.ufl.edu/CLAS/ american-universities.html
Summary: Many major colleges and universities now have Web pages, and this site provides links to over 150 of them.

TILE.NET/*LISTSERV*

Type: WWW
Address: http://www.tile.net/tile/listserv/index.html
Summary: There are hundreds of special-interest e-mail lists, but how do you find them? This site provides an organized overview of what's available.

Lycos

Type: WWW
Address: http://www.lycos.com/
Summary: Lycos lets you search for specific Web documents based on keywords you enter. It maintains a database of over 800,000 URLs. There are some other interesting resources here as well, including a list of the frequency of over six million words used on the Web. Lycos is one of those facilities that's almost too good, presenting you with more information than you really need, but it's a great resource if you use it carefully to narrow down your search.

Lycos search engine.

Marius Watz' WWW Pages

Type: WWW

Address: http://www.uio.no/~mwatz/

Summary: Links that focus on philosophy, the avant-garde, cyberculture, and the computer underground. Check out his NEXUS project.

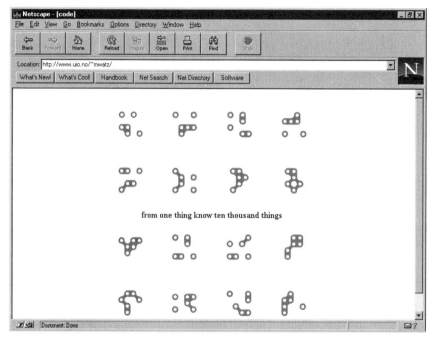

Marius Watz' WWW Pages.

Mirsky's Worst of the Web

Type: WWW

Address: http://turnpike.net/metro/mirsky/Worst.html

Summary: Not all of us have the time to cruise around the Web each day looking for the worst sites we can find. Fortunately, Mirsky does. Actually, some of his award winners I found more interesting than atrocious. I wonder what that says about me?

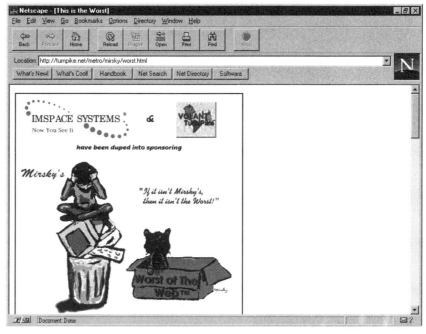

Mirsky's Worst of the Web.

The Mother-of-all BBS

Type: WWW

Address: http://wwwmbb.cs.colorado.edu/mbb

Summary: Links to just about everything on the Web. You can perform a WAIS search on the Bulletin Board.

NetManage WWW Starting Points

Type: WWW

Address: http://www.netmanage.com/netmanage/nm11.html

Summary: Yet another set of links organized by subject.

Nexor Public Services

Type: WWW

Address: http://web.nexor.co.uk/public/welcome.html

Summary: Yet another good search tool, letting you find information on the Web by keyword.

Open Market's Commercial Sites Index

Type: WWW

Address: http://www.directory.net

Summary: Businesses of all sizes are flocking to the Web to promote and even sell products and services. This site contains literally thousands of links to commercial sites; it also includes links to government and not-for-profit Web pages.

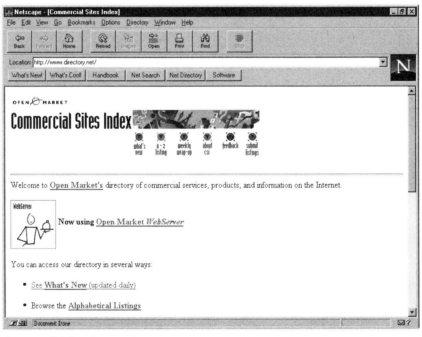

Commercial Services on the Net.

The Rumor Mill

Type: WWW

Address: http://www.galcit.caltech.edu/~ta/rmill.html

Summary: A small, highly selective collection of fun and bizarre hotlinks.

The SenseMedia Surfer

Type: WWW

Address: http://www.picosof.com:8080/html/scott.html

Summary: This is one of my favorite hotlists. It includes links to hundreds of different sites in many different categories. A great place to begin a day of Web surfing.

The Source

Type: WWW

Address: http://hakatai.mcli.dist.maricopa.edu/smc/ml/ source.html

Summary: A great selection of philosophy, religion, and psychology resources.

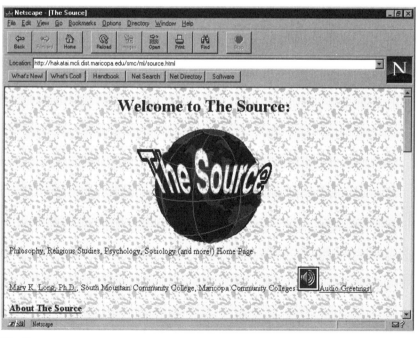

The Source.

Special Internet Connections

Type: FTP

Address: ftp://ftp.csd.uwm.edu/pub/inet.services.txt

Summary: A *huge* list of Internet resources, updated regularly. Better than a lot of other resource lists because it gives descriptions of each site. Print it out and start browsing—there's enough to keep you busy at least until the next edition of this book comes out.

Also available by mailing list by sending a subscription request to yanoff@csd4.csd.uwm.edu. The list is also posted regularly to several Usenet newsgroups including biz.comp.services and alt.internet.services.

Spider's Pick of the Day

Type: WWW

Address: http://gagme.wwa.com/~boba/pick.html

Summary: This is another "Cool Site of the Day"-type page, giving you yet another starting point each morning for wasting your precious work time on self-betterment and frivolity.

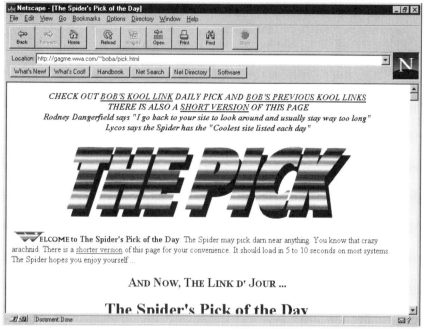

Spider's Pick of the Day.

The Internet Town Hall

Type: WWW

Address: http://town.hall.org/

Summary: This is a real grab-bag of electronic information and interesting links, a good starting point for a leisurely stroll around the Web.

The UCMP Subway

Type: WWW

Address: http://ucmp1.berkeley.edu/subway.html

Summary: A large hotlist of interesting sites, presented in a slightly unusual way: "The subway will take you to many virtual destinations throughout the Internet. Below you will see a map. Please touch a place on the map and you will receive a seat on the next train." Yes, yet another travel metaphor for browsing the Web!

UNC-CH Heliocentric Information Map

Type: WWW

Address: http://sunsite.unc.edu/heliocentric.html

Summary: I'll bet you didn't know that the University of North Carolina, with its SunSITE, is the center of the information universe—or at least the information solar system. Check out this interesting example of Web design, which provides lots of valuable information as well.

URouLette

Type: WWW

Address: http://www.uroulette.com:8000/

Summary: Overwhelmed by the sheer number of sites on the Web? Can't decide where to go next? You need the Web Roulette Server. Click on a roulette wheel and God knows where you'll end up. Given the nature of the Web, chances are it will be somewhere strange and fascinating, perhaps the home page of a nine-year-old particle physicist who likes cha cha music.

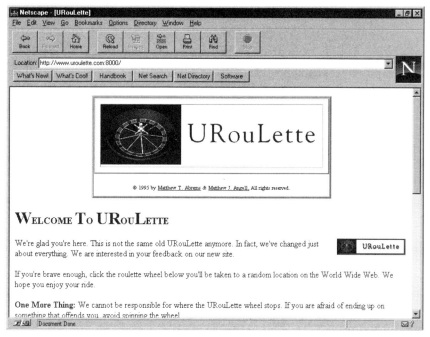

URouLette.

Usenet Launchpad

Type: Telnet

Address: launchpad.unc.edu

Summary: Not everybody has access to a good Usenet news server. Perhaps your service provider doesn't provide one as part of your account. Perhaps it is difficult to access due to traffic. Or perhaps it only includes a limited set of hand-picked "tasteful" newsgroups so that you can't post to some of your favorites such as alt.sex.bestiality.barney. Launchpad provides you a temporary shell account that you can use to launch one of the text-based UNIX newsreaders such as rn. You can also send e-mail and connect to Gopher or WAIS servers.

Vibe's World Map

Type: WWW

Address: http://pathfinder.com/vibe/vibeworld/ worldmap.html

Summary: While this seems to be mainly an ad for Timex, it is actually a pretty useful page. Click on any area of a world map and you will be presented with a comprehensive list of Web sites in that area. Since it's Timex, you also get the local time.

Vibe's World Map.

Virtual Town

Type: WWW

Address: http://wwwcsif.cs.ucdavis.edu/virt-town/ welcome.html

Summary: Plenty of good Web links presented in the form of a virtual town. You click on the area that you want to visit.

net.Genesis Wandex

Type: WWW

Address: http://www.netgen.com/cgi/wandex

Summary: Wandex is the World Wide Web Wanderer Index. This magic wand lets you enter a keyword and then locates the appropriate Web documents for you. Wandex has indexed over 27,000 Web documents from more than 12,000 sites.

Washington & Lee University's Netlink Server

Type: WWW

Address: http://honor.uc.wlu.edu:1020/

Summary: Links to high-level Internet sources, database of links to public login Telnet sites, WWW servers, WAIS servers—tons of stuff!

WebAnnounce

Type: WWW

Address: http://wwwac.org/WebAnnounce/

Summary: Once you've created your own Web page, you probably want to announce it to the online world. Many large public hotlists let you add your site, but it's inconvenient to keep track of all these promotional venues. That's where WebAnnounce comes in: now you can do all your self-publicizing from one page. This is a great time-saving utility!

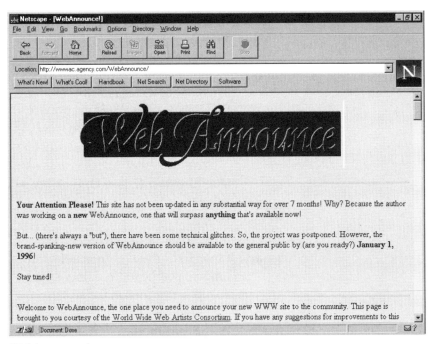

WebAnnounce!

The Webcrawler

Type: WWW

Address: http://www.webcrawler.com/

Summary: This excellent search engine indexes the contents of Web documents, so you can find pages that contain a particular word or phrase.

The Web's Edge

Type: WWW

Address: http://kzsu.stanford.edu/uwi.html

Summary: "UnderWorld Industries' Cultural Playground." Lots of alternative stuff. Check out "Stream of Conscience," an art/poetry Web-zine.

What's Hot and Cool on the Web

Type: WWW
Address: http://kzsu.stanford.edu/uwi/reviews.html
Summary: Lots of cool (and hot) alternative-type stuff.

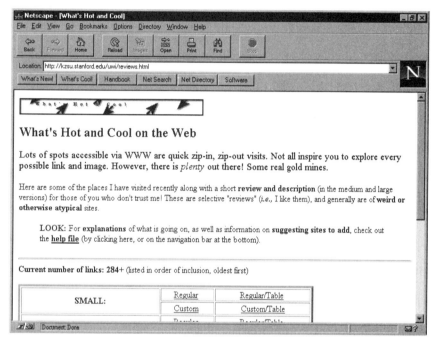

What's Hot and Cool.

NCSA What's New

Type: WWW
Address: http://www.ncsa.uiuc.edu/SDG/Software/
Mosaic/Docs/whats-new.html
Summary: Get the latest Web info here. Descriptions of and
links to new home pages.

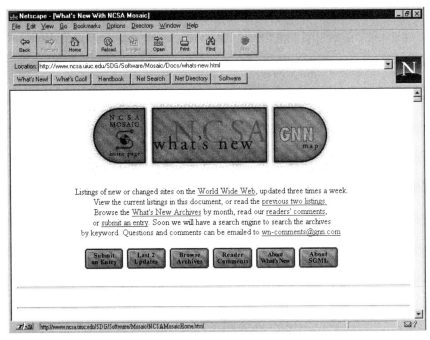

NCSA What's New.

The Whole Internet Catalog

Type: WWW

Address: http://gnn.com/wic/wics/index.html

Summary: Another giant hotlist organized into dozens of categories. It's worth checking out the ever-changing What's New section once in a while.

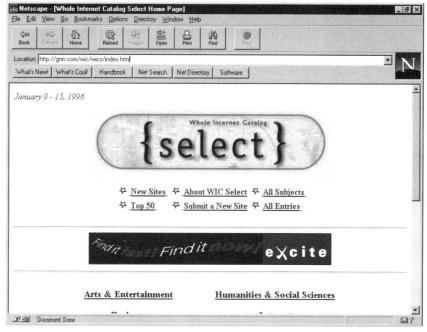

The Whole Internet Catalog.

Women's Web

Type: WWW

Address: http://sfgate.com/new/examiner/ womensweb.html

Summary: This page includes a very thorough hotlist of other women-centered sites. A great jumping-off place if you want to research women in computing, women's health, or dozens of other topic areas.

World Birthday Web

Type: WWW

Address: http://sunsite.unc.edu/btbin/birthday

Summary: Andy Warhol said that in the future everybody will be famous for 15 minutes. Well if you're a Web traveler, you can be famous for at least an entire day. Enter your name and birthday here and you will appear in the birthday list on that day. If you enter a URL for your home page, a hotlink to that site will be included as well.

The World Wide Web Consortium

Type: WWW

Address: http://www.w3.org/pub/WWW/

Summary: This is one of the best starting points for exploring the Web, although the sheer volume of information can be overwhelming.

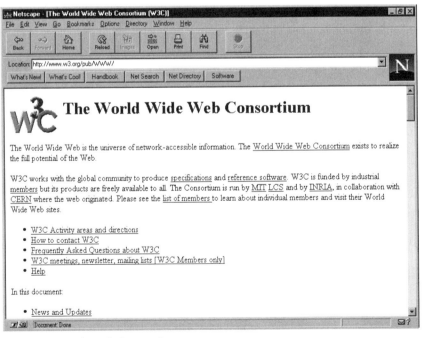

The World Wide Web Consortium.

World-Wide Web Worm

Type: WWW

Address: http://www.cs.colorado.edu/wwww

Summary: The "WWWW" is becoming one of the most popular tools for searching the Web. It is extremely flexible, allowing regular expression searches on URL, subject, and content. In spite of its flexibility, it's not difficult to use, and the site even includes a straightforward tutorial.

The World Wide Yellow Pages

Type: WWW

Address: http://www.yellow.com/

Summary: This is exactly what it sounds like—a directory of businesses that have home pages on the Web. What makes this different from the kind of yellow pages we're used to is that it is constantly updated, and you can even add entries yourself. A very useful tool.

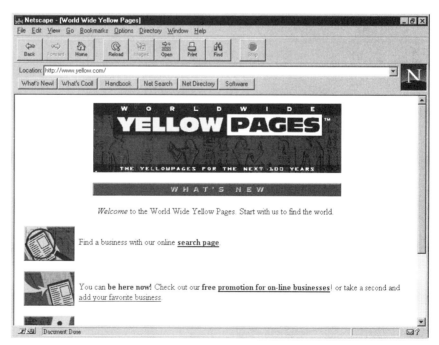

World Wide Yellow Pages.

Yahoo

Type: WWW

Address: http://www.yahoo.com (or Net Directory button)

Summary: Yahoo may be the best-known of the large public hotlists sprinkled around the Web. It includes a good search facility, and since it allows users to enter new sites it is always up-to-date. This is an excellent place to start exploring.

INTERNET STUFF

Acceptable Use Policies

Type: FTP

Address: ftp://nic.merit.edu/acceptable.use.policies/*.txt

Summary: Acceptable Use Policies for several networks that are part of the Internet. Policies are available for CICnet, CREN, JVNCnet, MICHnet, NorthWestNet, NSFnet, OARnet, and SURAnet.

A Beginner's Guide to HTML

Type: WWW

Address: http://www.ncsa.uiuc.edu/demoweb/html-primer.html

Summary: Learn to create HTML documents that can be placed on the Web.

Community Computer Networks: Building Electronic Greenbelts

Type: FTP

Address: ftp://ftp.apple.com/alug/communet/

Summary: Steve Cisler's excellent overview of community networks examining what kinds of information and services can be found on these systems, what groups are running community networks and cost aspects. The essay discusses current models for community networks and the impact these networks have on their local (physical) environment.

Contact: Steve Cisler
Apple Library
4 Infinite Loop
MS 304-2A
Cupertino, CA 95014
408/974-3258
sac@apple.com

Good Internet Books

Type: Gopher
Address: gopher://nysernet.org
Path: Special Collections: Internet Help / Good Books About the Internet
Summary: A great list of books about the Net. There's a short summary, the ISBN number and the price.

Internet Society

Type: WWW
Address: http://info.isoc.org/home.html
Summary: The Internet Society was created in 1991 to be the international organization that promotes global cooperation and coordination for the Internet and its technologies. Individuals and organizations can join. There's a great general info Internet FAQ.
Contact: Internet Society
org-membership@isoc.org
800/468-9507 (U.S. only)
703/648-9888

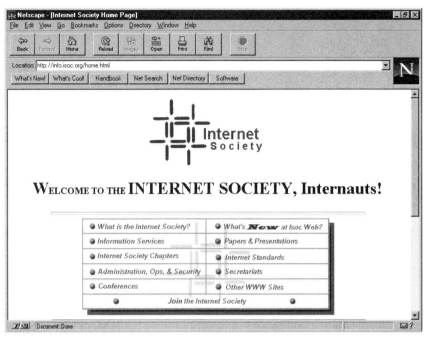

Internet Society.

Internet Web Text

Type: WWW

Address: http://www.rpi.edu/Internet/Guides/decemj/
text.html

Summary: Created in spring of 1994 (but updated since) by
John December for a course in Computer-Medi-
ated Communication at Rensselaer Polytechnic
Institute. His goal: to create an interface students
could use to familiarize themselves with the
Internet—how to use it, how to find information,
how to connect with people. He makes use of
icons to create memory aids to remembering
sources. This page also has links to lots of online
Internet guides and resources, such as *Zen and the
Art of the Internet*.

Contact: John December
decemj@rpi.edu

IRC Thesis

Type: FTP
Address: ftp://ftp.spies.com/Library/Cyber/electrop.txt
Summary: This honors thesis by E. M. Reid, "Electropolis: Communication and Community on IRC," explores the culture of Internet Relay Chat.

List of New Mailing Lists

Type: mailing list
Address: request-NEW-LIST@VM1.NoDak.EDU
Summary: Subscribe to this list and you'll always be on top of the latest mailing list info. Whenever a new mailing list is formed or an old one is updated, you'll receive a message describing the additions or changes.

    To subscribe, send the following one-line message in e-mail: **subscribe New-list** *your name* (where *your name* is your full name—*not* your e-mail address).

NCSA Mosaic

Type: WWW
Address: http://www.ncsa.uiuc.edu/SDG/Software/Mosaic/NCSAMosaicHome.html
Summary: Download the latest release of NCSA Mosaic, get installation and configuration instructions, info about bugs and bug fixes, FAQ,s and an online users' manual. Also get graphics viewers, HTML editors, Pkunzip, and winsocks.

Net Savvy

Type: FTP
Address: ftp://ftp.gsfc.nasa.gov/pub/old/internet/general-info
Summary: An Archie manual, basic TCP/IP commands, a guide to finding stuff on the Internet, LAN and ethernet FAQs, an FTP site list, and much more.

Netnews Filtering Service

Type: e-mail

Address: netnews@db.stanford.edu

Summary: Sign up with this Stanford service to help you zero in on the Internet stuff you want. You send a profile to the service, and they send you relevant news articles.

Send an e-mail message with the command HELP in the body of the message to get more information.

Why Are Internet Resources Free?

Type: Gopher

Address: gopher://wiretap.spies.com

Path: Wiretap Online Library / Cyberspace / Why are Internet Resources Free?

Summary: Ever wondered why you can get to most of the stuff on the Net without having to pay? This article explains it all for you.

Some Related Newsgroups

alt.answers
alt.culture.internet
alt.culture.usenet
alt.newbie
alt.online-service
alt.security.pgp
bit.listserv.new-list
misc.answers
misc.legal.computing
news.software.readers

Federal Jobs

Type: Gopher

Address: gopher://gopher.Dartmouth.EDU:70/11/careers

Path: Job Openings in the Federal Government

Summary: Lists of federal job opportunities and information that'll help you apply for a federal job.

Online Career Center

Type: Gopher

Address: gopher://msen.com

Path: The Msen Career Center/The Online Career Center

Summary: You can post your resume and search job lists at no charge, get career counseling, and connect with recruiting agencies.

Contact: occ@mail.msen.com

Some Related Newsgroups

bionet.jobs
bionet.women-in-bio
biz.jobs.offered
info.wisenet
misc.jobs.contract
misc.jobs.misc
misc.jobs.offered
misc.jobs.offered.entry
misc.jobs.resumes

JOURNALS & ZINES

Boardwatch Magazine

Type: WWW
Address: http://www.boardwatch.com/
Summary: A taste of what's in the print version of this wide-ranging monthly about BBSing and the Internet.

Boardwatch Magazine.

Career Magazine

Type: WWW
Address: http://www.careermag.com/careermag/
Summary: Tired of cruising the Net and want to get a job instead? Need money to support your online addiction? About to get fired for playing games on the Web instead of selling widgets? You need to check out this site quickly.

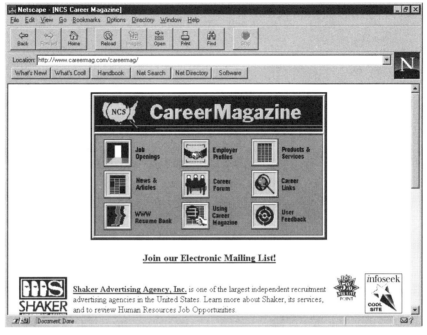

Career Magazine.

Computer Mediated Communication Magazine

Type: WWW

Address: http://www.december.com/cmc/mag/current/toc.html

Summary: An interesting electronic magazine filled with information and opinion about the technology and culture of the Internet.

dimFLASH

Type: WWW

Address: http://www.well.com/user/futrelle/dflash.html

Summary: An interesting zine with excellent graphics and hotlinks to other peculiar sites.

Editor & Publisher Interactive

Type: WWW

Address: http://www.mediainfo.com/edpub/

Summary: This is an extensive and constantly changing list of newspapers that offer online services. The list only covers large mass-media papers, not zines or electronic newsletters.

Editor & Publisher Home Page.

The Fiore Report

Type: mailing list

Address: sept4yu@ix.netcom.com
(send e-mail saying you want to subscribe)

Summary: Sex therapist Tony Fiore writes this monthly electronic newsletter that offers advice on improving or enhancing your sex life.

Fringeware

Type: WWW

Address: http://www.fringeware.com/

Summary: Fringeware is an interesting bunch of people in Austin who offer cutting-edge cyberinfo, cyber-art, and cyberproducts. This is the place to go when *Wired* looks tired.

HotWired

Type: WWW

Address: http://www.hotwired.com/

Summary: This is one of the biggest tourist attractions on the Internet, a sort of new-media Disney World for plugged in twenty-somethings. You'll find a little of everything here, though most of the material focuses on various aspects of cyberspace itself.

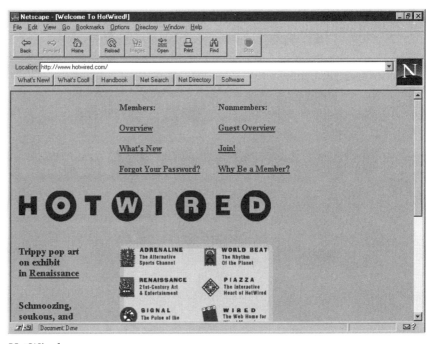

HotWired.

HYPE Electrazine

Type: WWW

Address: http://www.phantom.com/~giant/hype.html

Summary: A popular and well-done zine that features sound files. Worth a visit just for the bright colors!

iWorld

Type: WWW

Address: http://www.mecklerweb.com/

Summary: This is the Web home of Mecklermedia, the folks who publish *Internet World*. Here you can find a special hypermedia version of the magazine.

iWorld.

Link Digital Campus

Type: WWW

Address: http://www.linkmag.com/

Summary: In addition to the interesting Link zine, this site contains a thorough index to student publications from universities around the country. A valuable resource!

Link Digital Campus.

Mediamatic

Type: WWW

Address: http://www.mediamatic.nl/home.html

Summary: This is an interesting Dutch magazine about interactive media and its cultural implications. Well written and well produced.

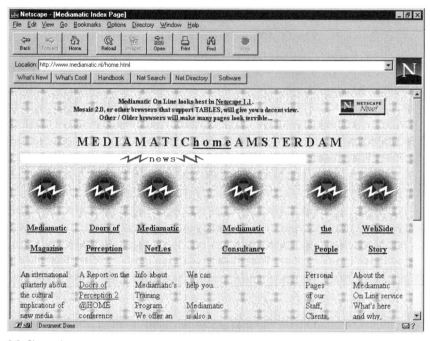

Mediamatic.

Melvin

Type: WWW

Address: http://www.melvin.com/

Summary: A lively, humorous zine full of commentary and colorful buttons.

Mercury Center

Type: WWW

Address: http://www.sjmercury.com

Summary: Many newspapers now offer electronic versions. This is one of the best, developed by *San Jose Mercury News*.

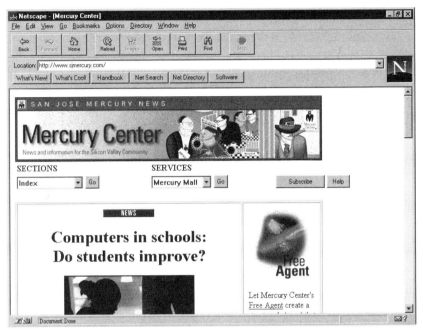

Mercury Center.

Netsurfer Digest

Type: WWW

Address: http://www.netsurf.com/nsd/index.html

Summary: This is an interesting electronic zine about the Net and interactive communications. Zines like this are popping up daily, but this one has more substance than most.

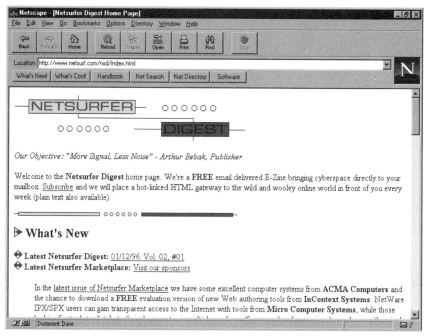

Netsurfer Digest.

Ziff-Davis Publishing

Type: WWW

Address: http://www.ziff.com

Summary: Ziff-Davis is the General Motors of computer magazine publishing. This site lets you access *PC Magazine* and eight others.

 KIDS

The Cisco Educational Archives

Type: WWW

Address: http://sunsite.unc.edu/cisco/cisco-home.html

Summary: Lots of hotlinks to Web pages of interest to school-age kids as well as teachers.

Explora-Net

Type: WWW

Address: http://www.exploratorium.edu/

Summary: This is the home page for the Exploratorium, a fascinating hands-on science museum in San Francisco. It includes areas of interest to both children and adults.

Global Show-n-Tell

Type: WWW

Address: http://www.manymedia.com/show-n-tell/

Summary: It is difficult to find good sites for younger children on the Web, but this is one of the best. It's an interactive exhibition of children's art; everything on display was created by kids and e-mailed in. I'd like to see more ideas like this!

Global Show-n-Tell.

Interesting Places for Kids

Type: WWW
Address: http://www.crc.ricoh.com/people/steve/kids.html
Summary: This Web page includes links to literally hundreds of entertaining and educational sites for children. Don't stick them in front of the TV, drop them off here!

IPL Youth

Type: WWW
Address: http://ipl.sils.umich.edu/youth/
Summary: This is the kids' section of the University of Michigan's Internet Public Library, and it's a wonderful site. Kids can submit their own stories to a contest, check out a book, explore math and science, chat about books they like, even submit questions to authors.

 LANGUAGES

Esperanto-English Dictionary

Type: Gopher
Address: gopher://wiretap.spies.com
Path: Wiretap Online Library / Articles / Language / Esperanto English Dictionary
Summary: Next time your boss tells you what to do, why not answer in Esperanto!

Foreign Language Resources

Type: WWW
Address: http://www.itp.berkeley.edu/~thorne/HumanResources.html
Summary: This is a large collection of links to sites that can help you learn a foreign language.

Human-Languages Page

Type: WWW

Address: http://www.willamette.edu/~tjones/ Language-Page.html

Summary: This page currently contains more than 100 links to over 40 different languages. Tutorials, dictionaries, software, and literature.

Japanese/English Dictionary–Gateway

Type: WWW

Address: http://www.wg.omron.co.jp/cgi-bin/j-e

Summary: This page is also available in Japanese. The dictionary entries can be viewed with text-based browsers or with Japanese text sent as images.

Travelers' Japanese with Voice

Type: WWW

Address: http://www.ntt.jp/japan/japanese/

Summary: Learn some simple Japanese before that next business trip.

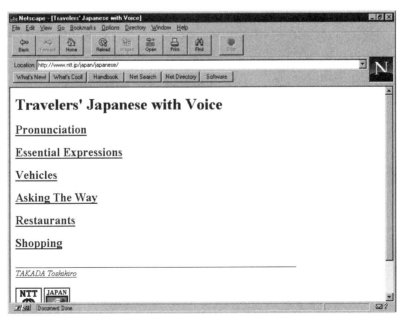

Travelers' Japanese with Voice.

Web Italian Lessons by Lucio Chiappetti

Type: WWW
Address: http://www.willamette.edu/~tjones/languages/Italian/Italian-lesson.html
Summary: Lessons are available as PostScript files, as well as in HTML format.

Some Related Newsgroups

alt.chinese.text
alt.japanese.text
k12.lang.francais
k12.lang.russian
sci.lang
soc.culture.esperanto
soc.culture.french

LAW

Advertising Law Internet Site

Type: WWW
Address: http://www.webcom.com/~lewrose/home.html
Summary: Legal aspects of marketing. Stuff about infomercials, home shopping, and 900 number regulations. You can also get FTC guides and consumer advisories.

American Civil Liberties Union (ACLU)

Type: Gopher
Address: gopher://aclu.org:6601/1
Summary: As of this writing, a lot of stuff in this Gopher is still under construction. Right now you can join the ACLU and check out the ACLU free reading room. Coming soon: legislative alerts and Congressional testimony, info about Supreme Court cases in which the ACLU is involved, and much more.

Criminal Justice Country Profiles

Type: Gopher
Address: gopher://uacsc2.albany.edu
Path: United Nations Justice Network / U.N. Criminal Justice Country Profiles
Summary: Find out how the criminal justice system works in different countries.

Legal Information Institute

Type: WWW
Address: http://www.law.cornell.edu/
Summary: Get information about recent Supreme Court decisions, search an e-mail address directory of faculty and staff at U.S. law schools. Lots of link to other law-related stuff.

West's Legal Directory (WLD)

Type: Gopher
Address: gopher://wld.westlaw.com
Path: West's Legal Directory via WAIS
Summary: Search for attorneys or law firms by specialty in any area in the United States or Canada. Profiles include information on such things as years of practice and offices held. You can also search for former students of law schools. E-mail questions to wldhelp@research.westlaw.com. Phone 800/777-7089.

Some Related Newsgroups

bit.listserv.lawsch-l
clari.news.usa.law
misc.int-property
mis.legal
misc.legal.computing

MISCELLANY: UNCLASSIFIABLE WONDERS

The Advanced Nerdity Test

Type: WWW

Address: http://gonzo.tamu.edu/nerd-backwards.html

Summary: If you're reading this book instead of *Proceedings of the ACM* you're probably not a total nerd. On the other hand, if you're reading this book at all, you're probably a little bit of one. Find out just how nerdy you really are.

Animals

Type: FTP

Address: ftp://rtfm.mit.edu/pub/usenet/news.answers

Summary: You'll find all sorts of animal stuff here. A few of the subdirectories to check out:

cats-faq
pets-birds-faq
fleas-ticks
dogs-faq

Blue Dog

Type: WWW

Address: http://kao.ini.cmu.edu:5550/bdf.html

Summary: This one's a lot of fun. Enter an arithmetic problem and Blue Dog barks the result. (You need to have support for .AU sound files.) You can have fun messing Blue Dog up by typing in problems that have fractional results.

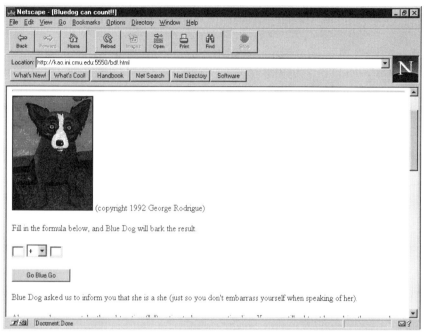

Arf! Blue Dog can count!!

The Digital Confession Booth

Type: WWW

Address: http://anther.learning.cs.cmu.edu/priest.html

Summary: It's so much easier this way. And, you can scroll through everybody else's sins, too!

Find-the-Spam

Type: WWW

Address: http://sp1.berkeley.edu/findthespam.html

Summary: Some people have too much time on their hands, and I'm glad they do. This is by far the goofiest, stupidest Web page I've come across. I love it.

F.N.O.R.D.

Type: WWW

Address: http://io.com/user/blade/fnord.html

Summary: F.N.O.R.D stands for the Foundation for Neo-Cognitive and Ontological Research and Development. Don't worry, that doesn't really mean anything. This creative "disorganization" is really dedicated to . . . nothing.

The Froggy Page

Type: WWW

Address: http://www.cs.yale.edu/HTML/YALE/CS/HyPlans/loosemore-sandra/froggy.html

Summary: This is one of my favorite sites. It includes many beautiful photographs of frogs as well as a variety of frog-related information. From the Froggy Page you might also want to jump to Sandra Loosemore's home page, which contains some other interesting links.

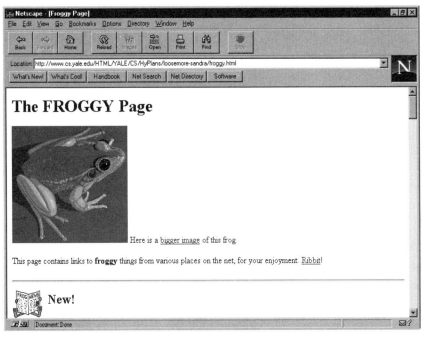

The Froggy Page.

The Grouchy Café

Type: WWW

Address: http://www.echonyc.com/~cafephrk/cafe.html

Summary: This is a warm friendly hangout with a real sense of *place*. Cafephreak, the proprietor, serves up recipes, anecdotes, information on coffee, a list of angst-ridden teenage books, fun artwork, and the memorable advice "Never fall in love with a lesbian who read Sartre instead of Judy Blume. She will rip out your heart."

Hacker Barbie

Type: WWW

Address: http://www.catalog.com/mrm/barbe/barbe.html

Summary: An amusing and interesting home page focusing on a transformed and far more interesting version of Mattel's Barbie doll. Not for everybody, but I really enjoyed this site.

Mr. Edible Starchy Tuber Head

Type: WWW

Address: http://winnie.acsu.buffalo.edu/potatoe/

Summary: Yes, this is what it sounds like. You add various features to a potato-shaped outline, coming up with "hilarious" distorted faces. This is where you come to relive a vital part of your 1960s childhood.

The MIT Gallery of Hacks

Type: WWW

Address: http://fishwrap.mit.edu/Hacks/Gallery.html

Summary: At MIT the word "hack" means a clever prank such as putting a phony police car on top of the Great Dome (Building 10) on the last day of classes. Many descriptions of hacks are accompanied by photographs. This site is an inspiration to college students everywhere.

Paul Haas' Appliances

Type: WWW

Address: http://hamjudo.com/

Summary: Paul Haas is a UNIX consultant. He also maintains a Web page that includes constantly updated information on his refrigerator (temperature, contents) and hot tub (temperature, contents). This is the age of information. Can you really afford to miss any?

The Really Big Button That Doesn't Do Anything

Type: WWW

Address: http://www.wam.umd.edu/~twoflowr/button.htm

Summary: This is another one of those useless sites, a giant push button that does not respond to your clicks. It includes, however, numerous philosophical musings on the nature of the button, and it allows you to add your own. A great site to visit if you've already figured out every other way to waste time.

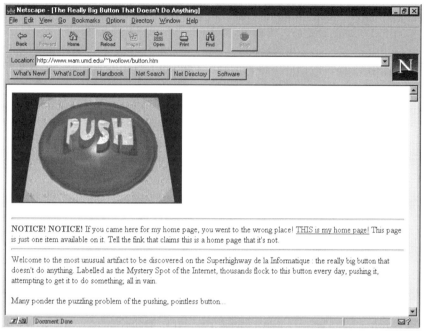

The Really Big Button.

Revenge

Type: FTP

Address: ftp://paradox1.denver.colorado.edu/Anony-mous/Textfiles/Revenge

Summary: This is a public FTP site that highlights postings from the alt.revenge Usenet newsgroup. The included files will give you hundreds of methods for getting even with your enemies or imagined enemies. I certainly don't recommend that any-body actually try these, but they do make for amusing reading and fun fantasy.

SCHWA™

Type: WWW

Address: http://fringeware.com/SchwaRoot/Schwa.html

Summary: I've always felt that the Internet wouldn't really be the same without Schwa. This crazy alien conspiracy think-tank typifies the wide range of viewpoints available to Netsurfers. Crackpots are one of America's greatest products, and I'm glad they have a voice on the Web.

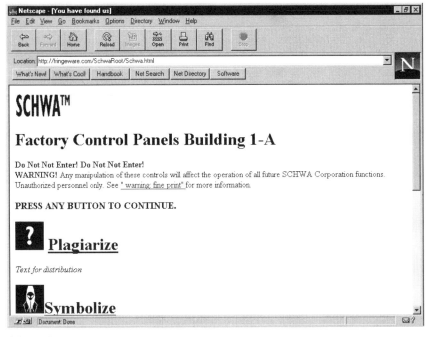

SCHWA.

SteveC's Pages

Type: WWW

Address: http://ftp.std.com/homepages/stevec/index1.html

Summary: Inspired silliness, including the Sofasphere II Project ("How will mankind absorb 500 channels?") and a collection of Stephen Hawking's favorite pick-up lines.

The Surrealist Compliment Generator

Type: WWW

Address: http://pharmdec.wustl.edu/cgi-bin/jardin_scripts/SCG

Summary: This Web page presents you with a unique randomly generated compliment each time you reload it. For instance, the first time I visited it told me, "Sound barricades into rolls of peanut butter when you speak." It was the nicest thing anybody had said to me all day, so I decided to try again. This time I got, "Ever so slightly, you remind me of a staircase falling exotically into a sea of spilled macaroni." There is also a slightly more serious side to this site, as it includes lots of fascinating information on the Surrealist Movement in the arts.

The TiReD-WiReD Server

Type: WWW

Address: http://www.cs.odu.edu/~bianco/bin/tired-wired.cgi

Summary: Every month devoted members of the *cyber-hipoisie* thumb as quickly as they can to *Wired* magazine's TiReD-WiReD list to find out what's cool to be talking about this month and what's oh-so-five-minutes-ago. This site offers an amusing take off on this cyberculture chestnut, an almost Dadaist list generated by some secret mathematical formula. Good clean fun.

The Wall O' Shame

Type: WWW
Address: http://www.milk.com/wall-o-shame/
Summary: A fun but humbling look at humankind, the Wall O' Shame presents examples of stupidity and inanity culled from newspapers, magazines, even the Net. This is not fiction; it's way too strange.

MULTIMEDIA

Index to Multimedia Information Sources

Type: WWW
Address: http://viswiz.gmd.de/MultimediaInfo
Summary: Links to film and video resources, media archives, MPC specs, cable regulations, desktop publishing, art, music, zines, publishers, MIDI, MPEG, satellite TV, Nielsen ratings, the Billboard chart, hypertext and hypermedia, multimedia software, newsgroups, and about a zillion other multimedia-related resources. Multimedia FAQ heaven and lots of conference announcements.

Silicon Graphics' Serious Fun Page

Type: WWW
Address: http://www.sgi.com/Fun/fun.html
Summary: As you would expect from this pioneering high-tech company, this site is loaded with fascinating computer-generated images and video clips.

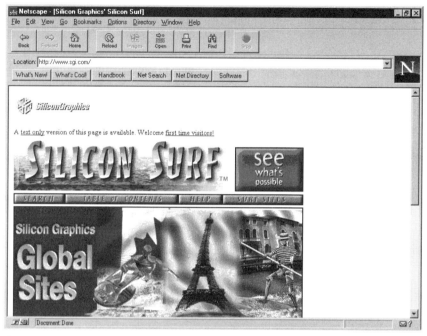

Serious Fun with SGI.

Music

Captain Beefheart
Type: WWW
Address: http://129.21.21.53/hpr.html
Summary: Lots of pictures, unreleased recordings, concert materials, artwork (done under his real identity as Donald Van Vliet), sound bites and info on Gerry Pratt's Beefheart fanzine.

Classical Music
Type: USENET
Address: rec.music.classical.performing
Summary: Lots of interesting and serious discussions (low garbage ratio).

The Death of Rock 'n' Roll

Type: WWW

Address: http://alfred1.u.washington.edu:8080/~jlks/
pike/DeathRR.html

Summary: *The Death of Rock 'n' Roll: Untimely Demises,
Morbid Preoccupations and Premature Forecasts of
Doom in Pop Music,* by Jeff Pike, was published by
Faber & Faber in 1993. This site contains lots of
samples from the book. They're meant to entice
you to buy the book, but you'll find plenty of info
about your favorite dead rock stars even if you
don't plan to make a purchase.

Contact: Faber & Faber
800/666-2211

Digital Tradition Folk Song Database

Type: WWW

Address: http://pubweb.parc.xerox.com/digitrad

Summary: A searchable database containing words and
music to thousands of folk songs collected by
Dick Greenhaus and friends.

Hyperreal—the Techno/Ambient/Rave Archive

Type: WWW

Address: http://hyperreal.com/

Summary: The Rave Archive will take you to the alt.rave
FAQ, The List of Rave Lists, and pointers to tons
of rave home pages.

Contact: Brian Behlendorf, founder of the SFRaves
mailing list
brian@hyperreal.com

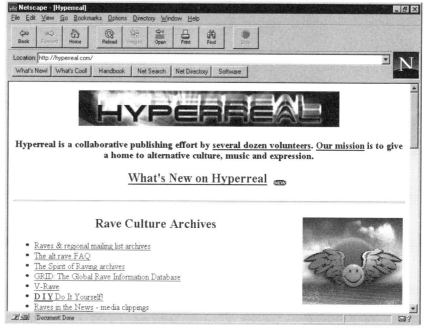

Hyperreal.

Internet Underground Music Archive (IUMA)

Type: WWW

Address: http://sunsite.unc.edu/IUMA/
or
http://www.iuma.com/IUMA/

Summary: IUMA is a huge catalog of artists, albums, and songs, including reviews and many MPEG samples. This site keeps getting bigger and better. It was founded by Rob Lord and Jeff Patterson to showcase unsigned musicians. Listen to clips from over 140 independent rock bands.

List of Coordinators

Type: WWW

Address: http://www.update.uu.se/pub/cathouse/
lyrics/Coordinator.html

Summary: Reviews and tech info about coordinators (a piece
of equipment which can be used to control and/
or program the performance of either an internal
or an external sound source. Some coordinators:
drum machines, sequencers, bass machines, MIDI
arpeggiators. A major site for electronic music
aficionados. Specifications, performance notes,
and personal reflections concerning the catego-
rized equipment. Regularly updated.

Lyrics

Type: FTP

Address: ftp://cathouse.org/lyrics

Summary: Forgotten the words to "Poisoning Pigeons in the
Park" or "The Vatican Rag"? Can't remember the
refrain to "Honky Tonk Woman"? Your kid
insists on hearing "It's Not Easy Being Green"
with the *correct* words? Never fear. This site has
lyrics for all of Tom Lehrer's, the Stones', and the
Muppets' songs, as well as over 50 other musical
groups and artists.

Random Band Names

Type: WWW

Address: http://www.terranet.ab.ca/~aaron/
band_names.html

Summary: Everyone who has started a band, except maybe
Courtney Love, has struggled with the difficulty
of coming up with a good name. Should you be
"Stuck Pig" or would "Timex Junk-Monkies"
make more sense? This site solves the problem by
offering you a unique randomly generated band
name. If you're not musical, you could probably
use it as your handle on AOL or some other
information service.

The Ultimate Band List

Type: WWW

Address: http://american.recordings.com/wwwofmusic/ubl/ubl.shtml

Summary: Want to find the Nick Cave Web site? This claims to be the largest listing of Internet resources for specific bands, and I have no reason to doubt it. What makes this a great site is that it can be updated by users and that it includes not just Web links but links to all kinds of resources: lyric files, newsgroups, mailing lists, digitized songs, and so on.

VANGELIS—The Man and the Music

Type: WWW

Address: http://bau2.uibk.ac.at/perki/Vangelis.html

Summary: Pictures, sounds, and digitized film sequences. Biographical information, as well as info about his solo and collaborative works, including motion picture scores.

Violin and Bow Makers

Type: WWW

Address: http://www.eskimo.com/~dvz/violin-makers.html

Summary: Get a regularly updated list of e-mail addresses for bowed stringed instrument makers throughout the United States. There's a short bio for each person. This site also includes info about The American Federation of Violin and Bow Makers.

The Voodoo Lounge: Rolling Stones Web Site

Type: WWW

Address: http://www.stones.com/

Summary: Be the first on your block with a "black polar fleece ear warmer with embroidered tongue." Yes, folks, this is where you'll find the official Stones merchandise catalog. Also tour schedules, music clips, picture collections, and interviews.

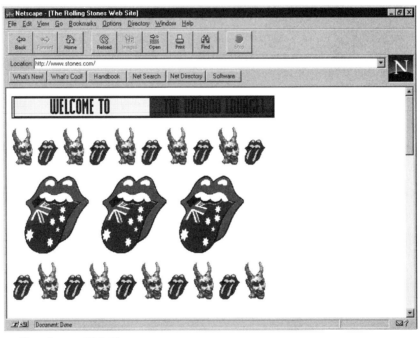

Rolling Stones Web Site.

WNUR-FM Jazz Information Server (The Jazz Web)

Type: WWW

Address: http://www.acns.nwu.edu/jazz/

Summary: Discographies, jazz media info (radio stations, etc.). History of jazz, live performance schedules, biographical info on artists, FAQ, lots of info on other jazz resources.

Woodstock '94 Internet Multimedia Center

Type: WWW

Address: http://www.well.com/woodstock/

Summary: Woodstock '94 is immortalized in this site. Everything in here was created during Woodstock by on-site participants and the Internet community. Over 300 pages of pictures, sounds, and text. Peace, dude.

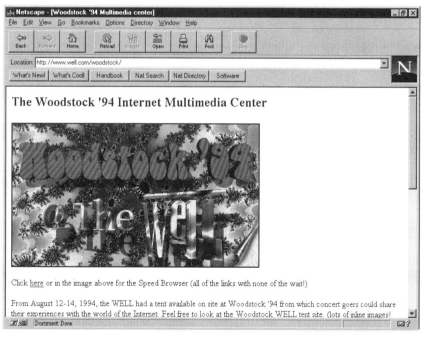

Woodstock '94.

Some Related Newsgroups

alt.emusic
alt.guitar.tab
alt.music.a-cappella
alt.music.filk
alt.music.jewish
alt.rock-n-roll.hard
alt.rock-n-roll.metal
rec.music.afro-latin
rec.music.bluenote
rec.music.celtic
rec.music.christian
rec.music.classical
rec.music.country.western
rec.music.funky
rec.music.indian.misc
rec.music.marketplace.cd

NEWS

Commercial News Services on the World Wide Web

Type: WWW
Address: http://www.jou.ufl.edu/commres/webjou.htm
Summary: Links to all the newspapers on the Net, campus as well as commercial, and to other newspaper and journalism-related resources.

Internet Talk Radio

Type: WWW
Address: http://juggler.lanl.gov:80/itr.html
Summary: Internet Talk Radio is modeled on National Public Radio. Its goal is to provide in-depth technical information to the Internet community through a series of audio files. "Geek of the Week" features interviews with key Net personalities.

The New South Polar Times

Type: WWW
Address: http://139.132.40.31/NSPT/NSPThomePage.html
Summary: Do you ever wake up wondering what's going on at the South Pole right now? Before this Web site opened its virtual doors it wasn't very easy to get the latest news from the bottom of the world, but it's fascinating stuff. You won't read about OJ, Newt, or Whitewater; instead, it's scientific research and life in one of the most beautiful and difficult environments. In more ways than one, this is a truly cool site.

OCCULT

Dark Side of the Net

Type: mailing list
Address: carriec@eskimo.com
Summary: Subscribe to this list if you want to find out about all sorts of occult-related resources, including stuff about vampires.

To subscribe, send the following one-line message in e-mail: **subscribe dark side of the net** *your name* (where *your name* is your full name— *not* your e-mail address).

Freud's Studies of the Occult

Type: FTP
Address: ftp://ftp.spies.com/Library/Fringe/Occult/freud.occ
Summary: Freud actually dug into paranormal studies, and this paper gives all the spooky details.

Occult

Type: FTP

Address: ftp://ftp.funet.fi/pub/doc/occult/

Summary: Lots of pictures and documents—everything from astrology to wicca to magic.

ONLINE SERVICES

Echo

Type: WWW

Address: http://www.echonyc.com/

Summary: Echo, an online service in New York structured somewhat like the WELL, has often been compared to a salon where artists and media professionals gather for stimulating conversation. This is not far from the truth. Echo has its own unique style and culture, "very New York" according to some users and certainly very different from most Internet forums. The Web site gives you a small taste of this uniqueness.

The WELL

Type: WWW

Address: http://www.well.com/

Summary: The WELL is a large West Coast online service that for many years has provided users with some of the most stimulating conferences in cyberspace. The Web page is like a snapshot, giving you a good picture of the unique WELL culture. This site is full of fascinating information and links, definitely worth a visit.

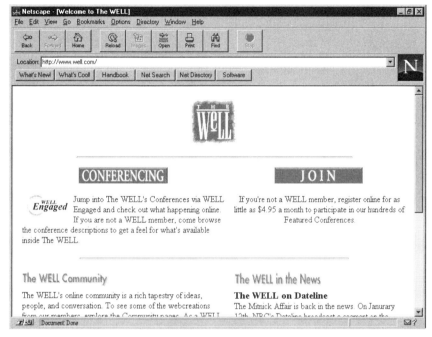

The WELL.

PHILOSOPHY

The American Philosophical Association

Type: Gopher

Address: gopher://apa.oxy.edu

Summary: Lots of philosophy stuff. Check out the International Philosophical Preprint Exchange, a collegial gathering of philosophers circulating prepublication drafts of their work and commenting on the work of others.

POLITICS, GOVERNMENT & SOCIAL ISSUES

Amnesty International

Type: WWW

Address: http://www.io.org/amnesty/overview.html

Summary: Contains the full text of the Universal Declaration of Human Rights, which was adopted by the General Assembly of the United Nations on December 10, 1948.

Contact: Hilary Naylor
AIUSA PeaceNet Coordinator
hnaylor@igc.apc.org
Amnesty International USA
500 Sansome St. #615
San Francisco, CA 94111
415/291-9233

Amnesty International.

Anarchist Electronic Contact List

Type: WWW
Address: http://www.cwi.nl/cwi/people/Jack.Jansen/
spunk/Spunk_Resources.html
Summary: Spunk Press maintains this collection of anarchist
and alternative resources. Newsgroups such as
alt.society.anarchy, alt.society.revolution, and
misc.activism.progressive. A Marx and Engels
Gopher hole. Alternative literature and mailing
lists.

Bibliography of Senate Hearings

Type: FTP
Address: ftp://ftp.ncsu.edu/pub/ncsu/senate/
Summary: Monthly bibliographies of Senate hearings.

The California State Senate

Type: WWW
Address: http://www.sen.ca.gov
Summary: As you would expect from the most computer
literate state in the nation, California has done a
great job making important government information available to the public. Here you can search
for pending bills in a particular area of interest,
view the actual content including proposed
changes, get updates on the bill's status, and so
on . If you leave an e-mail address you will be
notified automatically when the bill's status
changes. It would be nice if every state provided
this service!

Censorship

Type: FTP
Address: ftp://ftp.spies.com/Library/Article/Rights/
censored.bk
Summary: A list of books that have been banned, burned or
otherwise challenged in the last 15 years.

Center for Civic Networking

Type: FTP

Address: ftp://ftp.std.com

Summary: Choose /associations/civicnet

The CIA

Type: WWW

Address: http://www.odci.gov

Summary: Yes, they're here too. The World Fact Book, included at this site, is an excellent reference for general information on specific countries.

Declassified DOE Documents

Type: WWW

Address: http://www.doe.gov

Summary: The Federal government recently declassified hundreds of Department of Energy documents, including those dealing with nuclear experiments and the possible exposure of American citizens. Not only has the DOE made these documents available to professional researchers, they've put them up on the Web with an online index. Now you can find out the *real* reason you have three arms.

DIANA: An International Human Rights Database

Type: WWW

Address: http://www.law.uc.edu:80/Diana/

Summary: This site is dedicated to "completing the pioneering work in human rights information of Diana Vincent-Davis." It's a searchable database of human rights and law-related resources. As of this writing, there were over 10,000 pages available, with the volume increasing daily.

The FBI

Type: WWW

Address: http://www.fbi.gov/

Summary: Now that J. Edgar Hoover's gone they might not be everywhere anymore, but they do have their own presence on the Web. This is a surprisingly interesting home page. Of course there's a long warning not to copy their opening logo.

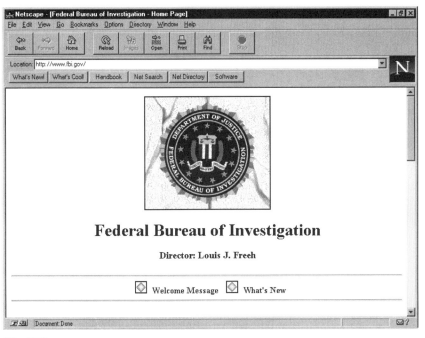

The FBI.

Fedworld

Type: WWW

Address: http://www.fedworld.gov/

Summary: Fedworld serves as a clearinghouse for information on federal agencies. It also contains links to dozens of government sponsored information servers. An important resource.

Government Documents

Type: Gopher

Address: gopher://wiretap.spies.com

Path: Government Docs (US: World)

Summary: Get full text files of government acts such as the Americans with Disabilities Act, the Brady bill and the Fair Credit Reporting Act. This area also has world constitutions, as well as NATO and White House press releases.

The MoJo Wire: Mother Jones Interactive

Type: WWW

Address: http://www.mojones.com/mojo_interactive/mojo_interactive.html

Summary: The Mother Jones Interactive page is organized into ten "campaign" areas such as Making Our Democracy Work, Waging Peace, Curbing Violence in America, Fostering Diversity and Community, Improving Our Nation's Education, and Keeping the Media Honest. You'll find articles from *Mother Jones Magazine*, resource guide listings, and "chat" rooms.

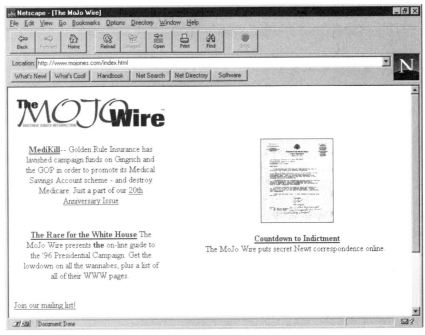

Get yer MoJo workin'.

National Child Rights Alliance

Type: WWW

Address: http://www.ai.mit.edu/people/ellens/NCRA/ ncra.html

Summary: A collection of documents about the NCRA and issues pertaining to child abuse.

Contact: Jim Senter
JIMSENTER@delphi.com

Silent Witness

Type: WWW

Address: http://gn2.getnet.com:80/silent/

Summary: Wanted Posters go interactive! This site is not tremendously relevant unless you live in Phoenix, but it demonstrates an interesting new use of the Web. Police reports are presented with photographs, sketches, and lots of information. Viewers are encouraged to call in anonymous tips if they have any information about the particular crime or missing person. I suspect this idea will spread to other cities.

United Nations

Type: Gopher

Address: gopher://nywork1.undp.org:70

Summary: Info about UN conferences, session highlights and press releases, UN System directories, UN Development Programme documents, links to other UN and related Gophers.

United States Department of Justice Home Page

Type: WWW

Address: http://www.usdoj.gov

Summary: Links to several Justice Department organizations concerning litigation, investigatory, and law enforcement offices. Also pages for various DOJ issues and links to other Federal government and criminal justice information sources.

U.S. Bureau of the Census

Type: WWW

Address: http://www.census.gov/

Summary: Census Bureau news releases, population information and projections, tips on genealogy, financial data for state and local governments and schools, and summarized demographic data.

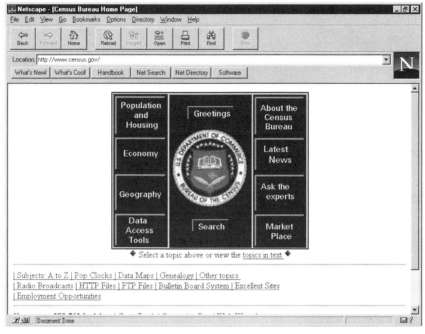

The Census Bureau.

The U.S. Constitution

Type: WWW

Address: http://www.law.cornell.edu/constitution/constitution.overview.html

Summary: Yep, just what it sounds like. See it while it lasts.

U.S. Department of Health and Human Services

Type: WWW

Address: http://www.os.dhhs.gov/

Summary: A starting point for accessing DHHS organizations. Cancer and AIDS related information, NIH grants and contracts, molecular biology databases, poverty guidelines, and links to other federal government resources.

U.S. Government Today

Type: Gopher
Address: gopher://wiretap.spies.com
Path: Government Docs (US & World) / US Government Today
Summary: Current membership lists for the House and Senate, phone and fax numbers for members of Congress.

Voice of America (VOA)

Type: Gopher
Address: gopher://gopher.voa.gov
Summary: Check out the International News and English Broadcasts radio newswire reports. You'll get daily reports, features, and documentaries on worldwide news events.
Contact: Chris Kern
202/619-2020
ck@voa.gov

Welcome to the White House

Type: WWW
Address: http://www.whitehouse.gov
Summary: As of the writing of this book, this is still where Bill and Hillary live. Tour the White House, check out Al Gore's favorite political cartoons, download a picture of Socks, read the electronic citizens' handbook, get detailed info about Cabinet-level and independent agencies, daily press releases, briefings on economic and environmental policy, information on government funded child care and disaster assistance, and lots more.

Some Related Newsgroups

alt.activism
alt.censorship
alt.politics.greens
alt.politics.libertarian
alt.politics.media
alt.save.the.earth
alt.society.conservatism
alt.society.revolution
bit.listserv.politics
bit.org.peace-corps
talk.politics.soviet
talk.politics.theory

PRIVACY

PRIVACY Forum

Type: WWW
Address: http://www.vortex.com/privacy.htm
Summary: Discussions of privacy in the information age. This directory includes all issues of the Privacy Forum Digest, as well as lots of related reports and materials.

The home page gives complete instruction for subscribing to the PRIVACY Forum.

Type: FTP
Address: ftp://ftp.vortex.com/privacy
Type: Gopher
Address: gopher://cv.vortex.com
Path: *** PRIVACY Forum ***

Privacy Information

Type: WWW
Address: http://www.eff.org/
Summary: The latest information on personal privacy online from the Electronic Frontier Foundation.

The Electronic Frontier Foundation.

■ REFERENCE

loQtus

Type: WWW

Address: http://pubweb.ucdavis.edu/Documents/
Quotations/homepage.html

Summary: Jason Newquist at the University of California at
Davis has put together a comprehensive quota-
tions resource. It includes his own quotations list
and pointers to a whole bunch of other quotations sources.

Contact: Jason Newquist
jmnewquist@ucdavis.edu

On-line reference works

Type: WWW

Address: http://www.cs.cmu.edu:8001/Web/ references.html

Summary: A great collection of links to dictionaries, geographical information, legal and governmental references, phone books, and other reference resources.

RELIGION & SPIRITUALITY

The Bhagavad Gita

Type: WWW

Address: http://www.cc.gatech.edu/gvu/people/Phd/ Rakesh.Mullick/gita/gita.html

Summary: The Hindu scripture in the original Sanskrit. Each chapter is a separate PostScript document. An English translation and a summary are also available from this page.

Buddhist Studies

Type: WWW

Address: http://coombs.anu.edu.au/WWWVL-Buddhism.html

Summary: Buddhist organizations, several Buddhist studies databases, links to Gopher and Web resources. A good place to start. From here, you should be able to find out whatever you want about Buddhism. This page also contains links to other religion resources.

Catholic Resources on the Net

Type: WWW

Address: http://www.cs.cmu.edu/Web/People/spok/catholic.html

Summary: Some of the sections: Liturgy and Worship, Scripture, Writings from the early Church, Vatican II documents (1962-1965), selected papal encyclicals and pronouncements, History and Culture, and related resources.

Full text of several books such as *Confessions of St. Augustine, The Imitation of Christ,* and *The Practice of the Presence of God*.

Electric Mystics

Type: Gopher

Address: gopher://wiretap.spies.com

Path: OO/Library/Article/Religion

Summary: Complete bibliography of online religious studies resources. Electronic documents, conferences, serials, software, and archives.

Hindu Names

Type: FTP

Address: ftp://ftp.spies.com/Library/Article/Language/hindu.nam

Israel Project

Type: FTP

Address: ftp://israel.nysernet.org/israel

Summary: Information about all aspects of Judaism and the state of Israel.

Never forget. Change to the /israel/holocaust directory for a wealth of information, including data, on the neo-Nazi movement.

Spirituality & Consciousness

Type: WWW

Address: http://zeta.cs.adfa.oz.au/Spirituality.html

Summary: Pointers to info about channeling, meditation, yoga, Veda, Theosophy, astrology, Bhakti-Yoga, Free Daism, paranormal phenomena, and lots more having to do with metaphysical and alternative views.

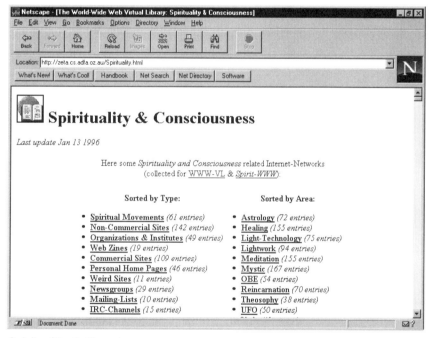

Spirituality & Consciousness.

SCIENCE

Alfred Wegener Institute for Polar and Marine Research

Type: WWW

Address: http://www.awi-bremerhaven.de/

Summary: The Alfred Wegener Institute has laboratories in Bremerhaven and Potsdam, bases in the Arctic and Antarctic, and research ships and aircraft. Lots of GIFs, maps, and charts of the polar region. Includes a detailed hydrographic atlas of the Southern Ocean. There's a database of polar and marine related docs on the Web, pointers to other WWW servers related to polar, marine, and global change research.

AMSAT: The Radio Amateur Satellite Corporation

Type: WWW

Address: http://www.qualcomm.com/amsat/ AmsatHome.html

Summary: If you're one of those people who makes and launches satellites in your backyard, this is *the* site for you.

Avion Online

Type: WWW

Address: http://avion.db.erau.edu/avion/ avionhome.html

Summary: The first online aviation/aerospace newspaper. The Space Technology section covers activity at Kennedy Space Center, including shuttle launches and landings. The Aeronautica section routinely covers activity in the aviation and aeronautics industry, including aviation trade news and special flying events.

Biological Sciences Resources

Type: FTP
Address: ftp://ksuvxa.kent.edu/library/acadlist.file5
Summary: This is a list of a whole bunch of mailing lists that have to do with the biological sciences.

Center for Coastal Studies

Type: WWW
Address: http://www-ccs.ucsd.edu/
Summary: The Center for Coastal Studies is a research unit of UC San Diego's Scripps Institution of Oceanography. You'll find all sorts of studies on subjects like global warming, long-term climate change, earthquake prediction, coastal protection, and sediment management.
Type: Gopher
Address: gopher://gopher-ccs.ucsd.edu

Comet Shoemaker-Levy 9

Type: WWW
Address: http://newproducts.jpl.nasa.gov/sl9/sl9.html
Summary: When Comet Shoemaker-Levy 9 collided with Jupiter in July 1994, it was the first time the collision of two major solar system bodies was observed and recorded. This page contains lots of background information and animations, and takes you to photo files from NASA and worldwide observatories. There's a whole section full of links to other Comet Shoemaker-Levy home pages (currently there are seven).

Lunar Institute of Technology

Type: WWW

Address: http://sunsite.unc.edu/lunar/index.html

Summary: The Lunar Institute of Technology was established in 2032, and its School of Starship Design is renowned throughout the Solar System. If you are one of the lucky few to attend this prestigious institution, you will participate in the design of a manned interstellar vehicle. Pick a specialty—Mission/Operations, Structure/Shielding, Payload/Sciences—and become part of the design team.

My description may be somewhat tongue-in-cheek, but you'll find some serious science here.

The Mercury Project

Type: WWW

Address: http://cwis.usc.edu/dept/raiders/

Summary: Ever since the first text-based adventure games computers we have been the masters of virtual worlds, engaging in all kinds of exciting activities from the comfort of our desk chairs. But no matter how deeply we immersed ourselves in these alternate realities, a part of us always knew they weren't really real. What if you could type something on your keyboard and have an immediate effect on a robot made of wires and metal, not just electronic information? Well the Mercury Project lets you do just that. In real-time you control the movements of a robot arm that's busy excavating an actual physical site as part of some academic research. Not exactly Star Wars, but it's a fascinating project that demonstrates the power of the Internet and makes you feel like a you're driving a big electronic bulldozer.

The Myers-Briggs Test—Kiersey Temperament Sorter

Type: WWW

Address: http://sunsite.unc.edu/jembin/mb.pl

Summary: Take this short psychological test to determine what makes you tick or tock. For instance, I found out that I'm the same kind of guy as Socrates, Gerald Ford, and Henry Mancini.

The NASA Newsroom

Type: WWW

Address: http://www.gsfc.nasa.gov/hqpao/ newsroom.html

Summary: All sorts of NASA press releases, press kits, status reports, fact sheets, and official statements.

NASA Online Information

Type: WWW

Address: http://mosaic.larc.nasa.gov/nasaonline/ nasaonline.html

Summary: NASA's home page, huge and full of interesting information. It includes links to specialized FTP sites, Gopher sites, and much much more.

Numerical Aerodynamic Simulation: The NASA Supercomputer

Type: WWW

Address: http://www.nas.nasa.gov/

Summary: This is the ultimate computer geek page, full of information on the NAS large-scale super-computing system used by NASA and other agencies. It is a rich and fascinating site.

Periodic Table

Type: FTP

Address: ftp://freebsd.cdrom.com/.12/games/msdos/educate/periodic.zip

Summary: Graphical DOS program that shows periodic table of the elements. Get detailed information about any element by moving to it and pressing Enter.

Primate Info Net

Type: Gopher

Address: gopher://night.primate.wisc.edu:70/11/

Summary: This entire gopher is devoted to primate biology. You'll find stuff about animal welfare legislation and behavioral patterns. Lots of newsletters and discussions.

Smithsonian Institution's Natural History Gopher

Type: Gopher

Address: gopher://nmnhgoph.si.edu

Summary: This Gopher contains newsletters, projects, and lots of pointers to other natural history resources. If you're interested in botany, vertebrate zoology, biodiversity, biological conservation, global volcanism, or anything else involving natural history, check out this cool site.

Space Movie Archive

Type: WWW

Address: http://www.univ-rennes1.fr/ASTRO/anim-e.html

Summary: We're not talking science fiction here. We're talking solar eclipses, meteorology, and space exploration. (With some science fiction thrown into the mix for good measure.) Tons of animations and instructions for getting animation viewers if you don't already have one.

Also available via FTP at the following address.

Type: FTP
Address: ftp://ftp.univ-rennes1.fr/pub/Images/ASTRO/
anim

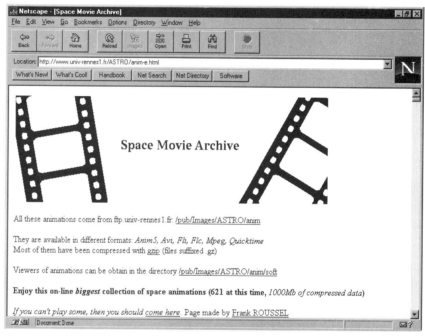

Space Movie Archive.

Stephen Hawking's Black Hole Theory

Type: Gopher
Address: gopher://wx.atmos.uiuc.edu
Path: Documents / fun / hawking.black.holes
Summary: The full text of Hawking's 1988 presentation,
"Baby Universes, Children of Black Holes."

United States Geological Survey

Type: WWW
Address: http://info.er.usgs.gov/
Summary: Geologic map of the United States and information about public issues, education, and environmental research.

Visual Interface for Space and Terrestrial Analysis (VISTA)

Type: WWW
Address: http://msx.nrl.navy.mil
Summary: A GUI system developed at the Backgrounds Data Center in Washington D.C. to "bring visualization to its databases of multiple remote sensing platforms." Users can query, visualize, and analyze geophysical and celestial data and metadata.

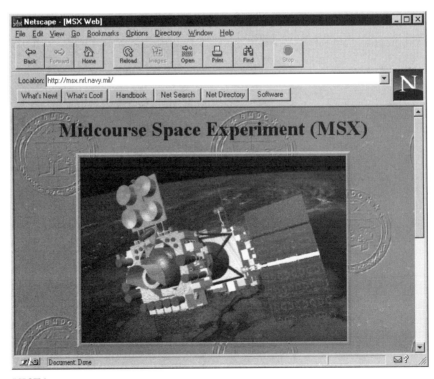

VISTA.

Some Related Newsgroups

alt.sci.planetary
bionet.genome.arabidopsis
bionet.genome.chromosome
bionet.molbio.ageing
bionet.plants
bionet.photosynthesis
bionet.population-bio
bionet.women-in-bio
sci.astro
sci.astro.hubble
sci.bio.ecolog
sci.astro.planetarium
sci.bio.technology
sci.engr.chem

SCIENCE FICTION

Isaac Asimov FAQ

Type: WWW
Address: http://www.lightside.com/SpecialInterest/
asimov/asimov-faq.html
Summary: This FAQ is full of fascinating stuff about the
master and his works.

J. R. R. Tolkien Information Page

Type: WWW
Address: http://csclub.uwaterloo.ca/u/relipper/tolkien/
rootpage.html
Summary: This page, put together by Eric Lippert, is an
amazingly complete Tolkien resource. In addition
to FAQs, book lists, Newsgroups, language
resources, info about the Tolkien Society, a
Middle-Earth map, Noldor and Great Houses
family trees. There are several query tools.
Contact: Eric Lippert
relippert@descartes.uwaterloo.ca

The Klingon Language Institute

Type: WWW

Address: http://www.abdn.ac.uk/~u06rmm/ homepage.html

Summary: In learning most foreign languages, there is no substitute for visiting the actual country. If you want to learn Klingon, however, there is no substitute for the Web pages maintained by the Klingon Language Institute. Even if you're not a *Star Trek* fan you'll get a kick out of this site, a labor of love for some very dedicated Klingon enthusiasts.

The MIT Science Fiction Library Pinkdex

Type: WWW

Address: http://www.mit.edu:8001/pinkdex

Summary: This is a thorough catalog of science fiction books that lets you search by keyword.

Science Fiction Resource Guide

Type: FTP

Address: ftp://gandalf.rutgers.edu/pub/sfl/sf-resource. guide.html

Summary: From the SF-Lovers Archives at Rutgers University. The ultimate SF link. It's all here—authors, awards, bookstores, fandom, fiction, movies, zines, conventions, and more.

Speculative Fiction Clearing House

Type: WWW

Address: http://thule.mt.cs.cmu.edu:8001/sf-clearing-house/

Summary: Science fiction, fantasy and horror archives, authors, awards, conventions, zines, and newsletters. Also resources for SF writers.

Unofficial Xanth Page

Type: WWW

Address: http://www.best.com/~wooldri/awooldri/
Xanth.html

Summary: For fans of Piers Anthony's Xanth world novels.
Some highlights: a cheat list for Companions of
Xanth, a Qbasic program that allows you to
generate Xanth-like talents, the Piers Anthony
FAQ, a Xanth family tree, the Xanth calendar,
and a color image of Piers and his dog.
Newsgroup: alt.fan.piers-anthony

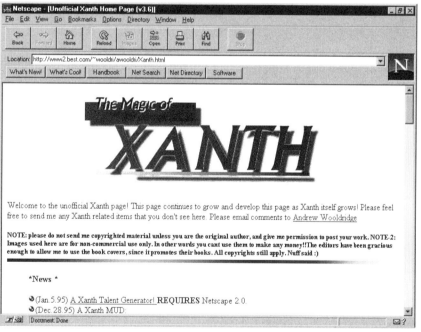

The Magic of Xanth.

SHOPPING

Aircraft Shopper Online

Type: WWW

Address: http://aso.solid.com/

Summary: Looking for a P51 Mustang fighter? Or is an old DC-3 more your style? Or do you want to sell your rusting 172 and upgrade to something a bit newer? Whether you want to buy or sell a plane, this is the best place on the Web to get started.

The Classified Advertising Page

Type: WWW

Address: http://www.imall.com/ads/ads.html

Summary: Whether you're looking for a computer, a job, or a date (or even if you're looking for all three), this is the site to visit. The listings, many of them links to USENET newsgroup announcements, are well organized and current.

The Future Fantasy Bookstore

Type: WWW

Address: http://futfan.com/

Summary: Digital maintains this excellent online book catalog full of SF and fantasy titles. This is probably the best Web source for this kind of material.

Hall of Malls

Type: WWW

Address: http://nsns.com/MouseTracks/ HallofMalls.html

Summary: I *hate* malls! Malls fall somewhere between rats and taxes on my list of the 10 Worst Things in the World. But I have to admit that electronic malls on the Web aren't *quite* so annoying—at least you're not bombarded with endlessly repeating muzak versions of "Little Drummer Boy."

If there's something you can't get online, it's probably pretty hard to get any other way. Malls are springing up all over the Web. And because there are so many malls, the Web has generated a new kind of virtual hell: the meta-mall, somewhere you can go to choose which mall you want to visit. Here it is, a glimpse of the Jetsonesque future. Shop till your hard drive drops.

Offworld Metaplex

Type: WWW

Address: http://offworld.wwa.com/

Summary: Oh no, a cyber *theme* mall! Let the mysterious Mr. Sin lead you through a "unique shopping experience." There's actually some pretty neat stuff here if you're in a consumerist mood.

The Virtual MeetMarket(sm)

Type: WWW

Address: http://vmm.ravenna.com/

Summary: "Wild and crazy netsurfer dude seeks female UNIX tigress for some fun with a SUN." That sort of thing.

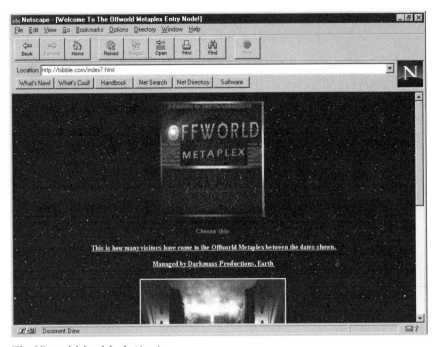

The Virtual MeetMarket(sm).

SHOWBIZ

Elvis Lives!

Type: WWW

Address: http://128.194.15.32/~ahb2188/elvishom.html

Summary: Created by superfan Andrea Berman to "honor his cultural and musical legacy." Take a tour of Graceland, inspect Elvis's shopping list, and check out the results of an online seance conducted in January 1994.

Gossip

Type: Usenet

Address: alt.showbiz.gossip

Summary: Don't get bogged down with the facts—this is pure unadulterated gossip.

SOFTWARE

Sandra's Clip Art Server

Type: WWW
Address: http://www.cs.yale.edu/homes/sjl/clipart.html
Summary: Tons of clip art from her own collection and other archive sites. You can also FTP to this site:
Type: FTP
Address: www.cs.yale.edu
Path: WWW/HTML/YALE/CS/HyPlans/loosemore-sandra/clipart/

SPORTS

Aquanaut

Type: WWW
Address: http://bighorn.terra.net/aquanaut
Summary: Everything scuba—a database of diveable shipwrecks, reviews of dive gear and equipment, reviews of popular dive destinations, and underwater pictures.
Newsgroup: rec.scuba

The Art of FENCING

Type: WWW
Address: http://www.ii.uib.no/~arild/fencing.html
Summary: Articles, fencing clubs and associations, events lists, the Internet Fencing Encyclopedia (a collection of links to pages about fencing).

Footbag WorldWide

Type: WWW

Address: http://www.cup.hp.com:80/~footbag/

Summary: Footbag is a new sport, similar to the game of Hacky Sack. Get tournament results, equipment information, images, and video clips of footbag action.

To join the mailing list and chat with other players at all levels, send e-mail to ba-footbag-request@cup.hp.com (include your first and last name somewhere in the message).

George Ferguson's Ultimate Page

Type: WWW

Address: http://www.cs.rochester.edu/u/ferguson/ultimate/

Summary: Ultimate Frisbee is a non-contact team sport. Get the official rules and tournament handbook here.

Hawaii's NHL Home Page

Type: WWW

Address: http://maxwell.uhh.hawaii.edu/hockey/hockey.html

Summary: Welcome to the world of hockey. From here, you can get to all of the NHL team home pages, the NHL Statserver, game schedules, and Stanley Cup info. Currently, there are plans to provide daily statistical updates on teams and players.

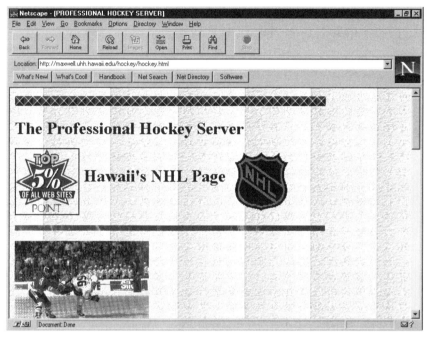

Professional Hockey Server (Author: Richard Crowe, The University of Hawaii at Hilo).

Korfball

Type: WWW
Address: http://www.earth.ox.ac.uk:80/~geoff/
Summary: Korfball is a mixed team sport that's kind of like basketball, but without backboards or dribbling. Get the latest information about this rapidly growing sport.

Mountain Biking

Type: WWW
Address: http://xenon.stanford.edu/~rsf/mtn-bike.html
Summary: Info about biking trails in various parts of the United States, as well as a link to a mountain bike page in the U.K.

Orienteering and Rogaining Home Page

Type: WWW

Address: http://www2.aos.Princeton.EDU:80/rdslater/orienteering/

Summary: Get out your old scout compass and hit the road. Announcements about these two popular sports, federation and club information, and links to related pages.

The Running Page

Type: WWW

Address: http://sunsite.unc.edu/drears/running/running.html

Summary: Info about upcoming races, race results, places to run, running related products, and running publications.

   Check out the Exercise Trails Network. Members of the American Running and Fitness Association have been contributing maps of their favorite running and exercise trails. You can get a free map by contributing one of your own, even if you're not a member. Otherwise, maps cost $1.

Speleology Information Server

Type: WWW

Address: http://speleology.cs.yale.edu/

Summary: For the uninitiated, speleology means hanging around in caves in a serious way. Newsletters, cave studies, caving clip-art and cartoons, and speleological societies around the world.

Sports World BBS

Type: WWW

Address: http://debussy.media.mit.edu/dbecker/docs/swbbs.html

Summary: Stats for NHL, NFL, NBA, and Major League baseball pools.

Volleyball World Wide Service

Type: WWW

Address: http://www.volleyball.org/

Summary: This page was created by Tom Jack, a software design engineer who coaches volleyball in his spare time, as a way of centralizing information about the sport. You'll find FAQs, info about the volleyball newsgroup, equipment, TV coverage, and coverage of Olympic and professional teams. Because Tom lives in Cupertino, California, there's lots of info about classes, clubs, tournaments and such in the San Jose/San Francisco area. Links to volleyball sites throughout the United States.

Contact: Tom Jack
taj@cup.hp.com
408/447-4239

STAR TREK

Star Trek Files

Type: FTP

Address: ftp://ftp.spies.com/Library/Media/Trek

Summary: Tons of Trek-related files, including a Klingon vocabulary and a *Deep Space Nine* bibliography.

British Starfleet Confederacy

Type: WWW

Address: http://deeptht.armory.com/~bsc/

Summary: If you join the British Starfleet Confederacy, you'll get a certificate of commission, officers' manual, identity card, stardate calendar, and six bimonthly newsletters and chapter bulletins. Even if you don't want to join the fleet, this page contains comprehensive links to all things Trek.

Contact: starfleet@subspace.demon.co.uk

Klingon Language Institute

Type: WWW

Address: http://www.kli.org/

Summary: The Klingon Language Institute was founded in 1992 "to promote, foster, and develop the Klingon language, and to bring together Klingon language enthusiasts from around the world." You'll find sound files, information about their postal course and how to subscribe to the mailing list, and a fascinating background on the development of the language (it's one of the few artificial alien languages actually developed by a trained linguist).

Klingon spoken here.

Strange Usenet Newsgroups

alt.angst
alt.barney.dinosaur.die.die.die
alt.buddha.short.fat.guy
alt.flame.roommate
alt.food.sugar-cereals
alt.geek
alt.happy.birthday.to.me
alt.pantyhose
alt.religion.santaism
alt.spam
alt.tasteless
alt.wesley.crusher.die.die.die
talk.bizarre

Technology

Telecom Information Resources on the Internet

Type: WWW

Address: http://www.ipps.lsa.umich.edu/telecom-info.html

Summary: A plenitude of pointers to telecommunications Net resources. It's all here—voice, data, video, wired, wireless, cable TV, satellite. You can find info about aspects of telecom issues, from technical to public policy, from economic to social impacts.

Contact: Jeff MacKie-Mason
jmm@umich.edu

THEATRE & FILM

Drama

Type: Gopher

Address: gopher://english-server.hss.cmu.edu

Path: Drama

Summary: Play scripts, drama-related materials, reviews, Shakespeare info. Follow path to Shakespeare-Glossary for glossary of Shakespearean terms.

Home Page of Theatre

Type: WWW

Address: http://www.cs.fsu.edu/projects/group4/theatre.html

Summary: Follow the links on this page to find myriad theatre resources. Some highlights: Ray Bradbury's Theatre Episode Guide, ruins of the Roman Theatre, The Fire Sign Theatre, and Computers in Theatre.

Internet Movie Database

Type: WWW

Address: http://www.msstate.edu/Movies/

Summary: This is the Web's most complete searchable database of of films. If you're a movie buff, don't miss this site!

Screenwriters' and Playwrights' Home Page

Type: WWW

Address: http://www.teleport.com/~cdeemer/scrwriter.html

Summary: As of this writing, this page is still under construction, but there are already lots of resources for screenwriters and playwrights. There's a guide to screenplay structure, scripts, discussion groups and tips from the pros.

Weird Movie List

Type: FTP

Address: ftp://ftp.spies.com/Library/Media/Film/weird.movi

Summary: Alphabetical list of weird movies, with descriptions. You can also get this list via Gopher. The address is wiretap.spies.com, then choose Wiretap Online Library / Mass Media / Film and Movies / Weird Movie List.

TRAVEL

City.Net

Type: WWW

Address: http://www.city.net

Summary: Good information on the largest and best-known cities around the world.

Clothing Optional

Type: FTP

Address: ftp://rtfm.mit.edu/pub/usenet/rec.answers/nude-faq/beaches

Summary: Get naked! Lists of clothing-optional beaches, hot springs, parks, and resorts worldwide.

Downwind

Type: Telnet

Address: telnet://downwind.sprl.umich.edu 3000

Summary: Traveling? Why not check out the current weather and the forecast for your destination city.

The Global Network Navigator/Koblas Currency Converter

Type: WWW

Address: http://bin.gnn.com/cgi-bin/gnn/currency

Summary: This page is updated weekly. By default, the page shows the currency rates of over 50 countries relative to U.S. currency (e.g., one U.S. dollar is worth 1.3605 dollars in Australia). To get currency rates relative to another country, just click the country you want.

GNN TC Internet Resources — Planning & Research

Type: WWW

Address: http://nearnet.gnn.com/gnn/meta/travel/res/planning.html

Summary: Even if the longest trip you ever take is from your computer to your printer, check out this page. It'll take you to all sorts of travel-related resources. You'll find U.S. Army Area Handbooks on Egypt, Indonesia, Israel, Japan, the Philippines, Singapore, Somalia, South Korea, and Yugoslavia. And get an inside peek at the documents the State Department gives its people before they travel to a country. Get the latest U.S. State Department travel warnings and consular information sheets. A few more highlights: The Internet Guide to Hostelling; Travel Health—Staying Healthy in Asia, Africa, and Latin America; the CIA World Factbook; Travel Tips for Less Developed Countries; and the Worldwide Telephone Codes list, which is a searchable list of area codes for the entire world.

The Hawaiian Islands

Type: WWW

Address: http://www2.hawaii.edu/visitors/
visit.hawaii.html

Summary: This one's maintained by the Hawaii Visitors
Center. There's a link to each of the islands.

The Jerusalem Mosaic

Type: WWW

Address: http://www1.cc.huji.ac.il/jeru/

Summary: Listen to the song of Jerusalem, view Jerusalem
from the sky, read about events in the history of
Jerusalem.

Local Times Around the World

Type: Gopher

Address: gopher://austin.unimelb.edu.au

Path: General Information and Resources / Local
Times Around the World

Summary: Connect to computers in cities around the world
to get local time reports.

PCTravel

Type: Telnet

Address: telnet://pctravel.com

Summary: PCTravel makes it easy for you to view and select
schedules and fares for all major airlines. All you
need to know is where and when you are going.
You can even buy your tickets online.

The Perry-Castañeda Map Collection

Type: WWW

Address: http://www.lib.utexas.edu/Libs/PCL/
Map_collection/Map_collection.html

Summary: This is a great collection of electronic maps from the Perry Castañeda Library at UT. It even includes National Park maps and a map of the South Pole. Needless to say, there are maps of Texas, too.

The Rec.Travel Library

Type: WWW

Address: http://rec-travel.digimark.net/

Summary: The rec.travel USENET newsgroups have always been a great source of travel information, but far from convenient when it comes to tracking down the facts you need. This Web site serves up a tremendous amount of up-to-date information on destinations, transportation, and even travel agents. It also includes links to other travel-related pages.

Subway Maps

Type: Gopher

Address: gopher://vishnu.jussieu.fr

Path: Indicateur des metros (don't worry, there's a file in English too)

Summary: Download color maps of the Paris and Lyon subways.

UT-LANIC

Type: Gopher

Address: gopher://lanic.utexas.edu

Summary: This is the University of Texas Latin American Network Information Center. Here you can access a wealth of information about Latin America, including catalogs, databases, FTP archives, other gopher sites, and so on.

Virtual Paris

Type: WWW
Address: http://www.paris.org/
Summary: Well, it's not quite the real thing, but it's a lot cheaper.

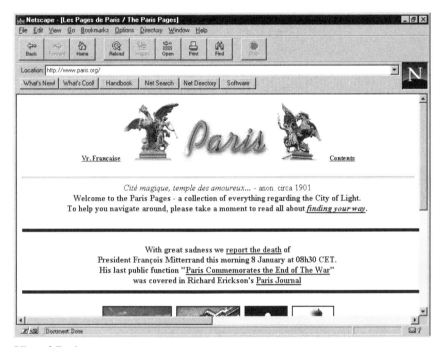

Virtual Paris.

Virtually Hawaii

Type: WWW
Address: http://www.satlab.hawaii.edu/space/hawaii/
Summary: This is a NASA site that includes lots of remote sensing satellite and aircraft images of Hawaii. It also provides real-time satellite data and links to several related pages. While it's not exactly the same as sunning on a beach in Maui, this is a great educational site.

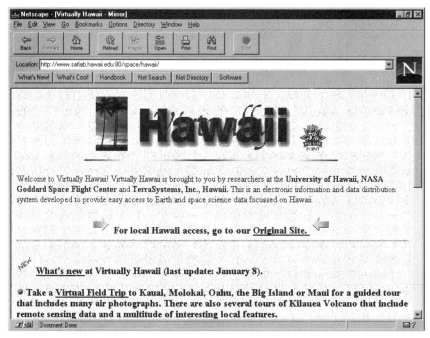

Virtually Hawaii.

Welcome to Eurogopher

Type: WWW

Address: http://www.sunet.se/eurogopher/eg.html

Summary: This is a great starting point for information about Europe.

A Related Newsgroup

rec.travel.marketplace

UTILITIES & SPECIALIZED INFORMATION

The AT&T 800-Number Directory

Type: WWW

Address: http://www.tollfree.att.net

Summary: This is a wonderful convenience that I use all the time. Simply type in the name of a company and you will be presented with the 800 number much more quickly than you could look it up in a phone book.

Electric Postcard

Type: WWW

Address: http://persona.www.media.mit.edu/Postcards/

Summary: This is a great idea, really exploiting the interactive possibilities of the Web. You choose from a large collection of "postcards," beautiful and interesting graphics files, and address one to a friend. Your friend can then log into this site and based on a tracking number pick up the postcard you "sent."

FedEx

Type: WWW

Address: http://www.fedex.com/

Summary: This site is about as sexy and inspiring as the U.S. Senate, but it lets you find out where your package is.

The Global Network Navigator/Koblas Currency Converter

Type: WWW

Address: http://bin.gnn.com/cgi-bin/gnn/currency

Summary: Find out what your dollar's worth in many major nations. An excellent tool for business travelers.

The IRS

Type: WWW

Address: http://www.irs.ustreas.gov/prod/

Summary And you thought you could get away from them on the Web! Actually this is a very useful site that provides forms, instructions, and answers to common questions. ("Do I really have to give you my money?" "Yes.")

The Jargon File

Type: WWW

Address: http://www.phil.uni-sb.de/fun/jargon/index.html

Summary: This is a huge index of jargon, especially tech-speak. After a few hours here you'll sound like you know what you're talking about.

The Mortgage Calculator

Type: WWW

Address: http://ibc.wustl.edu/mort.html

Summary: Back in the days when text-based DOS programs ruled the PC world like primitive insects, I had a utility for everything. In fact, I sometimes had several different programs for the same job. Then Windows came along, and disk space became as precious to me as Manhattan real estate. Thanks to behemoth programs like Word and Excel, not to mention Windows itself, there was no longer room for directories full of little one-job tools. Fortunately a wealth of simple utilities is available on the Net, and this flexible mortgage calculator is a good example. I find it quicker to click over to this URL via a bookmark than to load up a local copy of Excel!

NewsHound

Type:	e-mail
Address:	newshound-support@sjmercury.com
	(send a message requesting information)
Summary:	This is an electronic version of a clipping service. You tell them what you're interested in, and NewsHound keeps an eye out for articles that match your search criteria. It then sends you the information via e-mail. There is a monthly charge for the service.

Stanford Netnews Filtering Service

Type:	WWW
Address:	http://woodstock.stanford.edu:2000
Summary:	This is an interesting service for those who don't have access to a USENET news server or who don't want to weed through the thousands of newsgroups looking for what they want. The Stanford Netnews Filtering Service lets you specify areas of interest; it then sends you USENET postings, via e-mail, based on those criteria.

Taxing Times

Type:	WWW
Address:	http://www.scubed.com/tax/tax.html
Summary:	The only things that are certain in life are death, hard disk crashes, and taxes. This site can help you with one of those.

Xerox PARC Map Viewer

Type: WWW

Address: http://pubweb.parc.xerox.com/map

Summary: Another great example of how hypermedia can be used effectively on the Web. You are presented with a map of the world. Click on an area and it zooms in. Click again and it zooms in some more. You can also search by keyword. This is a well-designed tool that's great for putting geography in perspective.

 ## WEATHER

National Weather Service Forecasts

Type: Gopher

Address: gopher://wx.atmos.uiuc.edu

Summary: Weather reports by geographical region as well as by weather type.

[More] National Weather Forecasts

Type: Gopher

Address: gopher://downwind.sprl.umich.edu

Path: Weather Text, U.S. City Forecasts

Summary: Daily weather information for cities all over the country. Pick a state, then a city.

WEB INFO

A Beginner's Guide to HTML

Type: WWW

Address: http://www.ncsa.uiuc.edu/General/Internet/ WWW/HTMLPrimer.html

Summary: Once I started cruising the Web, it wasn't long before I wanted to start putting up my own pages. The HTML markup language that's used to create Web documents is not at all difficult, especially with some of the specialized editing tools. And to help you get started, NCSA provides an excellent hypermedia tutorial. You'll be creating simple documents in a matter of hours.

Advertising on the Web

Type: WWW

Address: http://www.eunet.ch:80/werbal.ch/

Summary: This is an experimental Web document demonstrating how advertising on the Web must differ from print advertising in order to be effective. This is worth checking out not just for those creating commercial Web pages, but for all who are interested in the evolution of the Net.

Building a Corporate Web

Type: WWW

Address: http://www.webcom.com/~wordmark/ sem_1.html#home

Summary: Wordmark Associates has put together this informative and well-thought-out hypermedia seminar for corporations wanting to establish a presence on the Web. I recommend that you read this information *before* designing your commercial Web pages.

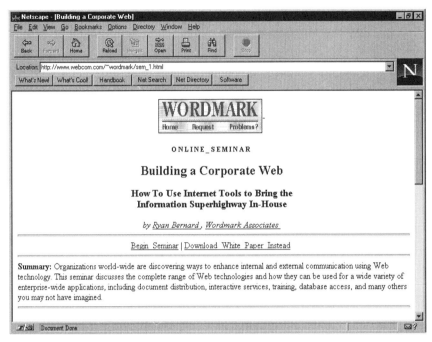

Building a Corporate Web.

The CGI Page

Type: WWW

Address: http://www.yahoo.com/Computers/
World_Wide_Web/
CGI_Common_Gateway_Interface

Summary: CGI scripts are programs on a Web server that process or manipulate data transmitted by a Web user via forms in an HTML document. Often written in PERL, CGI scripts are useful for many commercial applications on the Web, from collecting demographic information to selling products; they can also be used for more fun applications like presenting the user with a randomly selected fortune. This is a good starting place for learning about CGI.

Imagemaps Made Simple

Type: WWW
Address: http://www.ccsf.caltech.edu/clickmap.html
Summary: If you've explored the Web for more than half an hour, you've probably encountered imagemaps. These are pictures that can launch you to other documents depending where you click. If you've already learned the basics of creating Web pages, this is the best place to get information on developing your own clickable imagemaps.

The PERL Page

Type: WWW
Address: http://www.cis.ufl.edu/cgi-bin/plindex
Summary: PERL stands for Practical Extraction and Report Language. It is a flexible and fairly easy-to-use programming language that's especially suited to manipulating text. It is often used for developing CGI gateways on Web servers. This site will get you started on creating your own PERL scripts.

Talker

Type: WWW
Address: http://www2.infi.net:80/talker/
Summary: For those of you who can't get enough of yaking online, here's another interesting Web-based chat program. Looks interesting.

Useless Pages

Type: WWW
Address: http://www.primus.com/staff/paulp/ useless.html
Summary: You've seen how useful the Web can be for research, education, and publishing. Care to see how useless it can be? This site has nothing to recommend it other than the fact it has nothing to recommend it. It is highly successful in accomplishing its goal, and it even lets you add your own useless pages.

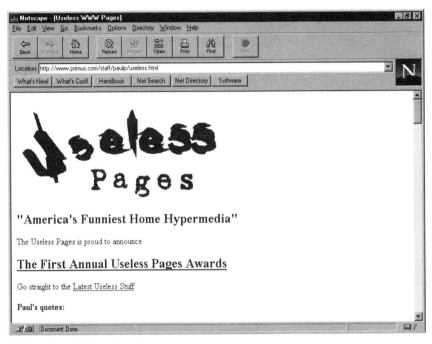

Useless.

Virtual "Separator Bar" Collection

Type: WWW

Address: http://inls.ucsd.edu/y/OhBoy/bars.html

Summary: No, this is not a hotlist of virtual drinking establishments. The bars we are talking about here are the horizontal rules that most HTML authors use to break up sections of their document. Instead of letting Web browsers display their default plain-vanilla line when you specify an <hr> tag in your page, why not ship a colorful, interesting, beautiful graphic bar instead? This site includes more horizontal rules than you'll ever use.

The Webaholics Home Page

Type: WWW

Address: http://www.cs.ohiou.edu/~rbarrett/webaholics/ver2//index.html

Summary: If you have tried more than fifty of the links suggested in this chapter, this is the one to try next. Hurry, it may not be too late.

WebChat

Type: WWW

Address: http://www.irsociety.com/webchat.html

Summary: WebChat is an exciting new Web-based facility for live conferencing or chatting. You can see a .GIF picture of the person you are chatting with, and you can place .GIFs and Web hotlinks in your messages.

Web Page Design and Layout

Type: WWW

Address: http://www.yahoo.com/Computers/World_Wide_Web/Page_Design_and_Layout

Summary: This is a great place to start if you're looking for ideas and advice on designing your own HTML home page.

The Worst Web Page

Type: WWW

Address: http://www.panix.com/~clays/biff/

Summary: With a little bit of design sense and a willingness to learn, almost anybody can create a decent home page. It takes a special talent, though, to create a truly hideous one. The author of this page has taken many of the annoying interface problems found in typical Web pages and thrown them all together into one ugly mess. While this site is very funny, it is actually more useful than it sounds. As you start designing your own Web documents it's a great place to learn what *not* to do.

Wow, The Web is BIG

Type: WWW

Address: http://www.mit.edu:8001/afs/sipb/user/ mkgray/ht/wow-its-big.html

Summary: This site offers frequently updated statistics on the size of the World Wide Web, based mainly on the flow of traffic. You'll be surprised at how popular the Web really is!

The WWW FAQ

Type: WWW

Address: http://www.boutell.com/faq/

Summary: This list of frequently asked questions is one of the best places to start learning about the Web. It is thorough, well-organized, and updated frequently. A good place to visit if you feel lost or confused or if you simply want a fuller understanding of how the Web works.

WINDOWS 95 PAGES

The Best Windows 95 Software

Type: WWW

Address: http://biology.queensu.ca/~jonesp/win95/ software/software.html

Summary: "I am attempting to keep this software archive as an 'elite' archive. This means that the freeware/ shareware that you will find here has been personally checked out by myself and deemed to be useful for most Win95 users. All of the applications that you'll find here will be 32-bit Windows 95 apps. There are many software archives out there, but I will keep this one relatively small with only the most useful apps."

Dylan Greene's Original Windows 95 Home Page

Type: WWW

Address: http://cville-srv.wam.umd.edu/~dylan/win95.html

Summary: "In addition to my other sources of timely information, I have been selected to become a ClubWin WebMaster. This means that I will be receiving periodic updates on new content and information from the Windows 95 team. For you, that means you will always be able to find the most recent information here, at Dylan's Windows 95 Pages."

Randy's Windows 95 Resource Center

Type: WWW

Address: http://www.cris.com/~randybrg/win95.html

Summary: Another excellent Windows 95 site. As a Microsoft ClubWin WebMaster site, Randy will always have the most up-to-date info straight from the horse's…uh…mouth.

Win 95 Net

Type: WWW

Address: http://www.pcix.com/win95/win95home.html

Summary: FAQs for Windows 95 and Plus!, links to other Windows 95 sites, a Win 95-Net discussion board, software archives.

Win 95-L Windows 95 FAQ

Type: WWW

Address: http://www.primenet.com/~markd/win95faq.html

Summary: "These questions and answers were compiled from responses to newsgroup posts and from the two mailing lists forums: WIN95-L, a general discussion group and WIN95-NET, a networking issues group."

Windows 95 InterNetworking Headquarters

Type: WWW

Address: http://www.windows95.com/

Summary: This site was featured in PC World's September 95 issue as "The Site To See" about Windows 95.

The Windows 95 Page

Type: WWW

Address: http://biology.queensu.ca/~jonesp/

Summary: "Here you will find the latest news about Windows 95, as well as finding all of the latest news concerning 32 bit shareware/freeware products, commercial software, and updates for Windows 95!!" You can get PC Computing's list of 1001 keyboard shortcuts for Windows 95, Microsoft's hardware and software compatibility lists in Windows Help format, the latest versions of Internet software and utilities, and, of course, the inevitable-but-always-useful links to other Win 95 sites. There's even a section of links to publications that have Win 95 info, like *InfoWorld, PC Week, The Computer Paper, Windows Sources* and *Windows Magazine.* (Be sure to check out the links in the Humour section.)

The Windows 95 QAID

Type: WWW

Address: http://www.whidbey.net/~mdixon/win40001.htm

Summary: QAID is an acronym for Question Answer Information Database, and it more than fulfills its promise. According to Mike Dixon, who compiled these pages, "The QAID Pages contain tons useful information, both documented and un-documented—comments from users of the QAID—Tips & Tricks—News and rumors—Dozens and Dozens of Questions and Answers and Information and instructions listed by topic."

Windows 95 Tips

Type: WWW

Address: http://www.process.com/Win95/win95tip.htm

Summary: A terrific and growing set of tips to help you work with and customize Windows 95.

Appendix A:
About the Online Companion

Information is power! Along with Netscape's popular Internet browser, the *Netscape Navigator 2.0 Online Companion* is all you need to be connected to the best Internet information and Netscape resources. It aids you with understanding the Internet and Netscape's role in the technology.

After installing the Netscape Navigator 2.0 software, you can access the special Web site for purchasers of Netscape Press products at **http://www.netscapepress.com**. Some of the valuable features of this special site include information on other Netscape Press titles, Netscape news, and valuable links to other Internet sites of value.

The *Netscape Navigator 2.0 Online Companion* also links you to the Netscape Press catalog, where you will find useful press and jacket infomation on a variety of Netscape Press offerings. Plus, you have access to a wide selection of exciting new releases and coming attractions. In addition, the catalog allows you to order online the books you want without leaving home.

The online companion represents Netscape Press's ongoing commitment to offering the most dynamic and exciting products possible. And soon netscapepress.com will be adding more services, including more multimedia supplements, searchable indexes, and sections of the book reproduced and hyperlinked to the Internet resources they reference.

Free voice technical support is offered but is limited to installation-related issues; this free support is available for 30 days from the date you register your copy of the book. After the initial 30 days and for non-installation-related questions, please send all technical support questions via Internet e-mail to help@vmedia.com. Our technical support staff will research your question and respond promptly via e-mail.

Appendix B:

If You Have the Companion CD-ROM

If you purchased the version of this book that includes a CD-ROM in the back cover, you'll find on the CD-ROM the official Netscape Navigator 2.0 software. In fact, as part of a line of official Netscape Press titles, this book is one of the selected few that do include the software. The CD contains Netscape Navigator 2.0 software for both Windows 95 and Windows 3.1. And it includes an electronic version of Chapter 11, "Our Favorite Net Resources," which you can browse electronically, simply clicking the links to visit sites that interest you.

Loading the CD-ROM is simple. If you are using Windows 3.1, insert the CD in your CD-ROM drive and, with Windows running, select File | Run from the Program Manager. Then type **D:\VIEWER** (where D: is your CD-ROM drive) in the command-line box and press Enter. You'll see a menu screen offering several choices.

If you are running Windows 95, insert the CD in the CD-ROM drive and double-click on the My Computer icon. Double-click the Companion CD icon and then the Viewer icon. You'll see a welcome screen that introduces the CD.

Your choices for navigating the CD appear at the bottom of this welcome screen. You can Exit from the CD, get help on navigating, browse the site listings in Chapter 11, learn more about Netscape Press, or view the Hot New Releases.

Click on **Our Favorite Net Resources**, and your Netscape Navigator 2.0 software will pop up a fully hyperlinked electronic version of Chapter 11. You can read descriptions and view images from the listed sites. Then, when you're ready to actually visit a site, simply click on the URL, and you'll be launched onto the Internet and be able to visit and view the sites with your Netscape Navigator 2.0 software.

By clicking the **Hot New Releases** button, you can see a bookshelf that displays other Netscape Press titles. Click on a specific book to learn about the other Netscape Press books that might be of interest to you.

After you finish, you can return to the main screen by clicking Menu. If you click on the **Netscape Press** button, you can learn more about the products and services that Netscape offers. Simply move the mouse over the icons to learn more about the individual products. Return to the main screen by clicking Menu.

Glossary

access privileges—A user's rights on a host. Typically users are allowed to create or edit files only in their home directories, though they can run programs from public directories.

acronym—A word made up of the first letters of the words in a phrase, such as **ROM** (read-only memory).

activate—To make a window the active one by clicking on it.

active window—The window with the highlighted title bar, where the user is currently interacting with a program.

ACU—*Automatic Call Unit.* Fancy word for a modem.

addressing—The assignment of unique names or numbers to every node on a network so that information doesn't get misdelivered.

algorithm—The step-by-step process a software program uses to produce its results.

alias—An alternate name used in place of a "real" one. Rather than using your real name to log in to a system, you probably use a shorter alias. Commands can also have aliases. For instance, you can create command files on a UNIX system so that instead of typing in **ls -al** to see all the files in your directory, you could just type **dir**.

American Standard Code for Information Interchange—*See* **ASCII**.

anchor—In HTML, the target of a link. It is sometimes also used to mean any link.

Archie—A network service used for locating files available at **FTP** sites that accept anonymous logins.

ARP—*Address Resolution Protocol.* Protocol used on a network for mapping Ethernet addresses to IP addresses.

ARPAnet—A wide area network developed in the 1960s by the Advanced Research Projects Agency of the U.S. Department of Defense. It linked government and academic networks around the world.

ASCII—*American Standard Code for Information Interchange.* This standard assigns a binary value to common text and control characters. ASCII is used for manipulating text in a program and for transmitting text to other devices or systems.

assigned numbers—The usual port numbers for well-known Internet services such as **Telnet**, **FTP**, and so on. For instance, hosts usually wait for Telnet connections on TCP port 23, for World Wide Web connections on port 80, and for Usenet News connections on port 119. These assigned port numbers are how the host knows what kind of connection is being requested.

asynchronous transmission—The transmission of data without special timing information. Each character you transmit is made up of several bits of information. In asynchronous communications, the characters are "packaged," usually by special start and stop bits, so that the receiving hardware or software knows when it has received an entire character. This way, the interval *between* characters doesn't have to be fixed, and information can arrive at any time. *See also* **synchronous transmission**.

attribute (text)—The display characteristics of text. Text attributes include bold, italic, underlined, and so on. In **World Wide Web** documents, text may be tagged with a wide variety of attributes using **HTML**.

authentication—The process of identifying a user to determine if he or she should have access to a particular computer system. Name and password prompts are a form of authentication.

bandwidth—The range of frequencies that can be transmitted over a network, limited by the hardware. Higher bandwidth allows more information on the network at one time.

baud rate—The number of signal changes per second as data is transmitted from one device to another. For instance, 110 transitions per second from a high frequency to a low frequency on a phone line would be 110 baud. Each signal change may signify one bit of data (for instance, high frequency to low could signify 1, low to high could signify 0); if a signal changes in multiple ways (frequency, amplitude, etc.), it may signify multiple bits of data. In the first case, baud rate would equal **bits per second**; in the second case, bits per second would be higher than the baud rate. The difference between baud rate and bits per second is a common icebreaker at nerd parties.

BBS—*See* **bulletin board system**.

binary—Numbers composed of combinations of two different digits, specifically 1 and 0. In the context of this book, binary data means information that may contain the full range of combinations of binary digits in a **byte**, as opposed to information that contains only the limited range of information that is displayable as text. Bytes of **ASCII** text contain only seven significant **data bits**, as in 1011001, while programs, graphics, spreadsheet files, and so on contain eight significant data bits per byte, as in 10011011. Any files that cannot be read as text are considered binary files.

BIND—*Berkeley Internet Name Domain* server. This is the DNS server on BSD and related UNIX systems. *See also* **DNS**.

BinHex—A file format, used mainly in the Macintosh world, for storing and transmitting binary data as **ASCII** text. This format is useful for transferring 8-bit data over 7-bit networks or data paths, or for including binary files as part of mail messages. Among UNIX and PC users, **UUENCODING** is more common.

bit—A *bi*nary dig*it*, the smallest piece of information that a computer can hold. A bit is always one of two values, written as 1 or 0 and corresponding to the on/off state of a digital switch or the high/low of electrical impulses. Combinations of bits are used to represent more complex information, such as **ASCII** text or commands to the computer.

bitmap—A representation of an image as an array of bits.

bit rate—The rate at which bits are transmitted, usually expressed as a certain number of **bits per second**, or bps. *See also* **baud rate**.

bits per second—*See* **bit rate**.

bookmarks—In Netscape Navigator 2.0, a means of permanently storing the **URL**s for sites you want to revisit.

bridge—(1) A device or a combination of hardware and software for connecting networks together. (2) Something that goes over troubled water. *See also* **internet**.

bulletin board system (BBS)—An electronic version of the old cork bulletin board—a place to leave and collect messages and files. A modern BBS is really like a whole collection of bulletin boards, with different sections covering different areas of interest. Users can generally exchange public as well as private messages, and many BBSes include extensive areas for distributing shareware or public domain software.

byte—A combination of **bits** used to represent a single character. In the world of personal computers, a byte is eight bits long.

cable—A bundle of wires or fiber strands wrapped with insulation and used to connect devices.

cache—An area of memory or a file used to store frequently accessed instructions or data. A memory cache is used to reduce hard disk access time. Memory and file caches are also used by Web browsers and other online programs to store images or data that rarely change; thus, a large home page does not have to be re-sent each time a connection is established.

carrier—A steady background signal on a communication channel used to indicate that the system is ready for the transmission of data. The carrier is then modified to represent the data transmitted.

CCITT—*Consultative Committee on International Telegraphy and Telephony.* This is an international standards-setting body that makes recommendations for international communications technologies.

CGI—*Common Gateway Interface.* A standardized technique that lets Web clients pass information to Web servers, and then on to other programs that process the information. When a Web site accepts the information you enter into a form, it is using CGI.

character entities—In HTML, special symbols that stand for other characters. Character entities begin with an ampersand (&) and end with a semicolon (;). For example, *&gt*; in an HTML document would appear on your screen as > (greater than).

check box—A Windows 95 control that lets you choose a particular option by clicking. Once you click, a check mark appears in the check box; click again and it is cleared.

CIX—*Commercial Internet Exchange.* CIX is an agreement among Internet service providers allowing them to make the Internet available to commercial traffic.

Clear To Send—A signal from a **DCE** to a **DTE** indicating that circuits are ready for data transmission. *See also* **DCE; DTE.**

clickable image—In a Web page, an image you can click in order to access a different URL. *See also* **imagemap.**

client—A computer or a software program that can access particular services on a network. The machine or the software that provides the service for a client is called a **server.** For instance, an e-mail client would request received mail from an e-mail server.

client pull—A method specific to Netscape products whereby a Web client can request the Web server to send it a particular set of data. *See also* **server push.**

client/server architecture—A system in which a **client** program establishes a connection with a **server** and then requests information or services. *See also* **client; server.**

Clipboard or **clipboard**—An area of memory where objects (data) are placed when a user carries out a Cut or Copy command or chooses a menu option. This data can then be passed to another program.

column heading—A Windows 95 control that displays data in a multicolumn list.

combo box—A standard Windows 95 control that combines a text box and a list box.

command button—A control used to initiate a command; also known as a push button.

command prompt—A set of characters or a symbol that indicates where you type in commands. The DOS C:\ prompt is an example of a command prompt.

connect time—The amount of time you're connected to a host or to a service provider.

connection—A link between two computers for the purpose of transferring or sharing information.

container—Any screen object that holds other objects, for instance, a folder.

content-type—The MIME name for particular types of files to be transferred by e-mail or the Web. For instance, the content-type for a GIF file is **image/gif**. *See also* **MIME**.

control—Any window object that lets you interact with a program by selecting an action, inputting data, and so on.

Control menu—The menu that pops up when you click the icon at the top left of a program's main window. It contains commands such as Move, Size, Maximize, Minimize, and Close.

crawler—*See* **spider**.

CSLIP—A common variant of the SLIP protocol that uses compressed IP headers. *See also* **SLIP**.

cyberspace—A slightly dated term referring to the entire world of online information and services. It was originally coined by the writer William Gibson.

daemon—UNIX-speak for a program that's always running on a server machine, waiting for requests for a particular service. For instance, an FTP server daemon sits and waits for an FTP client to connect and request files.

data—Information used or processed by a software program.

data bits—Bits that carry actual information as opposed to control information. For example, the bits in the middle of a **byte** might signify a text character and are, therefore, data bits, while the bits at the beginning and end of the byte merely mark the beginning and end of the data.

Data Carrier Detect (DCD or CD)—A signal from a **DCE**, such as a modem, to a **DTE**, such as a PC, indicating that a communication channel has been established with a remote device. *See also* **DCE; DTE.**

data-file object—An object representing a data file (spreadsheet, document, image, sound clip, etc.) in the file system.

Data Terminal Ready (DTR)—A signal from a DTE to a DCE indicating that it's ready to receive and transmit data. Usually, a modem keeps DTR high as long as it's turned on. *See also* **DCE; DTE.**

DCE—*Data Communication Equipment*. A device used by a **DTE** to transmit and receive information. Your modem is a DCE.

default—In software, the "out of the box" value of a configuration option. The software will use this value unless the user explicitly indicates a different one in a setup program, property sheet, or .INI file.

desktop—The visual work area that fills your screen and holds the objects you interact with, such as icons, the task bar, and so on. The desktop is a container (or folder) that can also be used as a convenient place to access files.

device driver—A program used by the system to access devices such as video cards, printers, and mice.

dialog box—In Windows 95, a box that appears on your screen requesting your input; it engages you in a *dialogue* with the software. It may contain edit fields, check boxes, list boxes, radio buttons, and so on, and it stays on your screen until you click its Cancel or OK button.

dial-up networking—A facility built into Windows 95 that allows users to link to a network or to the Internet using phone lines.

direct connection—A permanent connection between a computer and the Internet as opposed to a temporary dial-up or **SLIP/PPP** connection.

DNS—*Domain Name Service*, an Internet service that returns the appropriate **IP address** when queried with a **domain-name address**.

dock—To configure a toolbar so that it no longer floats, but lines up with the edge of a window or pane.

document (World Wide Web)—On the **World Wide Web**, a file or set of related files that can be transferred from a **Web server** to a Web **client.** The document may contain text, graphics, sound, or hyperlinks to other documents.

document window—A window that lets you view the contents of a document.

domain—A collection of associated computers on the Internet, given a specific domain name that is used as part of the Internet address.

domain-name address—The "plain English" address of a computer on the Internet, as opposed to its numeric **IP address**. For instance, www.echonyc.com is a domain-name address.

download—To get a file or files from a remote computer; the opposite of **upload**.

drag—To move a mouse while pressing and holding one of its buttons. Dragging is used to move or resize objects on the screen.

drop-down combo box—A Windows 95 control that combines a text box with a drop-down list box.

drop-down list box—A Windows 95 control that displays a current text selection, but that can be opened to display the entire list of choices.

drop-down menu—A menu that is displayed from a menu bar.

DTE—*Data Terminal Equipment*. A device that serves as the originating point or the final destination of information. Typically, a computer or a terminal is a DTE.

dynamic data exchange (DDE)—The exchange of data between programs such that any change in the data in one program affects that same data in the other program. For instance, if spreadsheet data are shared via DDE by Word and Excel, any changes made to the data in Excel will also appear in the Word document.

edit field—*See* **text box**.

electronic mail—A network service for transmitting messages from one computer to another. Also called *e-mail*.

ellipsis—The "..." added to a menu item or button label to show that the command needs more information to be completed. When you choose a command with an ellipsis, a dialog box appears so you can enter additional information.

encoding—The technique used for storing or expressing data. For instance, text may be stored via ASCII encoding or some form of encoding that uses compression (such as ZIP).

encryption—A method of **encoding** information for secure transmission. The data can be read in its original form only after it has been decoded. *See also* **public-key encryption**.

Ethernet—A hardware system and a protocol that is commonly used to connect computers on a LAN.

external viewer—A separate program used by a **World Wide Web** browser to display graphics or to play sound or video files. After downloading a particular media file, the Web browser launches the external viewer program appropriate to the type of file. In order for this to work, you must configure your Web browser with the names of the external viewer programs you have on your system. Another term for external viewer is **helper application**.

e-zine—A zine, or small non-mass-market magazine in electronic format. Some e-zines are text files distributed via electronic mail or posted on a BBS; others are Web pages with extensive graphics and even sounds.

FAQ—Abbreviation for *frequently asked question*. FAQs are lists of frequently asked questions (and their answers) in a particular topic area. For instance, a Windows 95 FAQ would help users understand the basics of using Windows 95 by providing answers to common questions. Most mailing lists and network newsgroups regularly provide updated FAQs. It is important to read the FAQ for a particular newsgroup before beginning to post messages.

file—A named collection of **ASCII** or **binary** information stored on a disk or other storage device. Files include text, programs, databases, spreadsheets, graphics, and so on.

file server—A computer that provides storage space for files and applications that may be shared by network users.

file transfer protocol—Any **protocol** for transferring files from one computer to another. A file transfer protocol usually includes provisions for making sure the data was transferred without errors and for resending any blocks of information that were corrupt.

finger—A UNIX program that lets you retrieve basic information about an Internet user or host. Finger is available via the Web at various sites.

flag—A characteristic of a file that may restrict its use in particular ways. A file may be flagged read-only, for instance.

flame—A public message on any electronic forum, such as a **BBS** or online service, that personally attacks another user. Usually a flame is in response to an earlier message. If the user who has been flamed responds with another flame, or if other users jump into the fray, a "flame war" ensues. Flaming, though common in **Usenet** newsgroups, is generally considered an obnoxious waste of other users' time and of network bandwidth.

folder—A container that holds and organizes objects, typically files or other folders. On the desktop, a folder may represent a directory in the file system; other folders within it are equivalent to subdirectories.

font—A particular style for displayed or printed characters, including the shape, weight, slant, and so on.

font size—The size of a **font**; typically represented in units of measurement called *points*.

FQDN—*Fully Qualified Domain Name.* The full domain name of a computer on the Internet, including both the hostname and the domain name. *See also* **domain-name address**.

FTP—Abbreviation for *File Transfer Protocol*, a particular file transfer protocol that is common on the Internet. It is also used as a verb, as in, "FTP me that file, wouldya?"

full duplex—A communications link in which both ends can transmit data simultaneously, as in a telephone conversation. In situations where you are working interactively online, full duplex communication lets a remote host echo back to you each character you type so that you can see what you're writing as you work. *See also* **half duplex**.

FYI—*For Your Information.* A series of technical documents on various Internet-related topics, available at many public FTP sites. *See also* **RFC**.

gateway—A device or the software that links networks that use different protocols. For instance, a Novell network might have an Internet gateway that "packages" information into the **TCP/IP** packets required for Internet communication. The term *gateway* is also used in a very specialized sense to mean a program on a **World Wide Web** host that accepts and processes information sent by a Web client. For instance, a document on a **Web server** might display a form in which you can type your name; the gateway program would then enter your name in a database.

GIF—(Pronounced "jiff.") Abbreviation for *Graphic Interchange Format*. This is a format for compressed graphic files developed by CompuServe and Unisys.

Gopher—A menu-based client/server system for exploring information resources on the Internet. A Gopher client is seamlessly built into Web browsers, so you don't need a separate Gopher client program.

Gopherspace—All of the information presented by a **Gopher** server, in the form of directory and file menus.

half duplex—A communications link in which both ends can transmit and receive data, but not at the same time. Half duplex communication is like two-way radio or CB, where only one person speaks at a time. In situations where you are working interactively online in half duplex, you will not see characters you type echoed to the screen unless you set your communications program to echo them locally. *See also* **full duplex**.

handle—An interface element added to an object to enable the user to move, resize, or reshape it.

handshaking—The initial negotiation and the exchange of control information between a **DCE** and a **DTE** or between two DTEs in a communications link. Handshaking is necessary to make sure both devices are ready to transfer data and can "understand" each other. *See also* **Data Carrier Detect; Data Terminal Ready; XOFF; XON**.

hardware handshake—A protocol whereby a **DTE** tells the connected computer to start or stop sending data. Typically hardware handshaking is implemented by raising and lowering the voltage on the DTR (**Data Terminal Ready**) line in the cable that connects the **DTE** and DCE. *See also* **XOFF; XON**.

helper applications—Programs that a Web browser such as Netscape Navigator 2.0 uses to perform tasks such as displaying particular types of graphics, playing sounds, or initiating Telnet sessions.

highlight—To emphasize text or some other display element, usually by selecting it with the mouse.

history list—In Netscape Navigator 2.0, the list of Web documents you've displayed during the current session.

home page—The **HTML** document you choose to display when you open a **Web browser** such as Netscape Navigator 2.0. It may be located on your own hard drive or on a remote **Web server**. Home page can also refer to the top-level document at a particular Web site.

host computer—A computer that a user can connect to in order to access information or run programs. A user may log in locally using a **terminal** or remotely using a computer and phone lines or the Internet.

hotlist—In a **Web browser**, a user-built list of frequently accessed **World Wide Web** sites. Also, an **HTML** document consisting of hotlinks to Web sites or other Internet resources.

HTML—Abbreviation for *Hypertext Markup Language*. A "markup language" for indicating attributes and links in a Web document. An HTML **tag** may tell a Web browser program how to display a piece of text or a graphic, or it may direct the browser to another file or document.

HTTP—The **protocol** that World Wide Web **clients** and **servers** use to communicate with each other.

hypermedia—**Hypertext** that also includes nontext information such as graphics, video, or sound.

hypertext—Text that is organized by means of links, or jumps, from one piece of information to another. The reader can move among related topics following his or her own associative pathways simply by clicking on specially tagged words or phrases. The Windows 95 Help system is a good example of hypertext, as are **World Wide Web** documents.

icon—An image used to represent an object such as a file or program.

imagemap—A graphic in a Web document that lets you click on certain portions in order to activate particular **URL**s. It has an associated map file that identifies these hot spots. *See also* **clickable image**.

inactive window—A window that you are not currently interacting with. Its title bar is not highlighted, and it receives no keyboard or mouse input. *See also* **active window**.

inline images—Graphic images contained within **World Wide Web** documents. An inline image displays automatically as part of a document when it is retrieved; a non-inline image must be retrieved by clicking on a **hotlink**.

internet—A larger network made up of two or more connected LANs (**local area networks**) or WANs (**wide area networks**).

Internet—The huge worldwide internet made up of cooperative networks and using **TCP/IP** protocols to offer a variety of services.

Internet access provider—A business or organization that provides Internet access to consumers, often via dial-up **SLIP** or **PPP** connections.

Internet address—*See* **IP address**.

IP address—Also called *Internet address*. The unique address for each computer on the Internet. The IP address appears as a set of four numbers separated by periods; the numbers indicate the **domain**, the **network**, the subnetwork, and the actual host machine. It may be translated into human-readable form, as in *bigcat.missouri.edu*, which indicates the machine *bigcat* in the University of Missouri domain, which is within the *edu* (education) top-level domain. In this form, it is usually referred to as the Internet address or **domain-name address** rather than the IP address.

ISP—*Internet Service Provider*. Another term for an **Internet access provider**.

Java—An object-oriented programming language developed by Sun Microsystems. It allows developers to create applications that may be run from within Web browsers such as Netscape Navigator 2.0.

JPEG—A format for compressed graphics files. JPEG graphics are commonly used as part of **World Wide Web** documents.

kbyte—*See* **kilobyte**.

kilobyte (K)—1024 (2^{10}) **bytes** of data. Thus, a 64K file consists of 65,536 bytes.

knowbot—A piece of software that can retrieve information from a variety of electronic sources when you give it a set of search parameters.

LAN—*See* **local area network**.

link—A special hidden **tag** in an HTML document on the Web. It includes the **URL** for another file or document, or for another anchor point within the same document. When you click a word, phrase, or graphic that's tagged as a link, Netscape Navigator 2.0 automatically retrieves the appropriate target.

list box—A control that displays a scrollable list of choices.

local area network (LAN)—A group of computers connected together by cable or wireless transceivers so that users can share resources such as database files, programs, printers, and so on. *See also* **wide area network**.

log in—To identify yourself to a remote system or network by typing in your login name and password.

login name—The name you use for security verification when you call into a remote system.

login prompt—The prompt (usually *login:* or *name:*) a remote host uses to tell you it's ready for you to type in your login name.

log off—To tell a remote host system or a network, using the appropriate commands, that you are terminating interaction. In many cases, logging off will also break the communications link to the remote machine.

log on—To tell a remote system or network, using the appropriate commands, that you are initiating a session.

maximize—To expand a window to its maximum size. *See also* **minimize**.

maximize button—The button used to maximize a window. In Windows 95, it is the second button from the right in the title bar.

megabyte (MB)—1024 **kilobytes**, or 1,048,576 bytes.

menu bar—A horizontal bar at the top of a window (between the title bar and the rest of the window) that contains menu choices. *See also* **drop-down menu**.

menu button—A command button that displays a menu.

menu item—A choice on a menu.

message box—A window that appears to inform you of something, for instance that a connection has been established or that an error has occurred.

MIME—Abbreviation for *Multipurpose Internet Mail Extensions*. MIME is a convention for identifying different types of **binary** information, such as images or sounds, and thereby indicating the appropriate programs for viewing or playing this information. MIME is used in attaching binary files to e-mail messages so that they can be displayed or played automatically when received.

minimize—To minimize the size of a window; in some cases, this means to hide the window. *See also* **maximize**.

minimize button—The button used to minimize a window.

modem—Short for *modulator/demodulator*. A hardware device that connects your computer to other computers using analog telephone lines.

modem command—An instruction, typed from the keyboard or transmitted automatically by a software program, that tells a modem to perform some action. For instance, the command ATH0 tells a modem to hang up the line.

Mozilla—This word stands for "Mosaic meets Godzilla." It is the name for the early Netscape products and for the Netscape-specific extensions to the HTML language. It has also become the Netscape mascot. The word and the associated image appear frequently in Netscape products.

MPEG—Abbreviation for *Moving Pictures Expert Group*. MPEG is a standard format for compressed video files, sometimes known as "desktop movies." MPEG files may be part of **World Wide Web** documents, but they require a special **helper application** for viewing.

MUDs and **MOOs**—Text-based multiuser interactive games, accessed using specialized software or via **Telnet**.

multiple selection list box—A special list box that's used for multiple independent selections.

multiuser system—An operating system, such as UNIX, that lets more than one user at a time access services.

My Computer—A Windows 95 object (icon) that represents all of your local data storage.

NCSA—*National Center for Supercomputing Applications*. NCSA is the department of the University of Illinois where the Web browser Mosaic was developed. Mosaic was the forerunner of all modern graphically based Web browsers.

network—A collection of interconnected computers. Each attached computer runs its own software processes, whereas in an unnetworked **multiuser system**, users run all processes on the central host computer and use terminals simply to interact. A network lets users share information as well as devices such as printers, disks, and modems.

network administrator—In an organization, the individual who is responsible for configuring and maintaining the network. This is the person to talk to if you have problems with a direct "hardwired" connection to the Internet.

Network Neighborhood—A Windows 95 folder that includes objects stored on a network file system.

NFS—Abbreviation for *Network File System*. NFS is a set of protocols developed by Sun Microsystems for allowing computers running different operating systems to share files and disk storage.

NIC—Abbreviation for *Network Information Center*, the organization responsible for supplying information about the Internet.

node—Any computer or other device on a network that has its own unique network address.

object—An entity that you manipulate in some way to perform a task. (Is that vague enough?) Typical objects are **icons** or **folders** on the **desktop**.

offline—Not currently connected to a remote computer.

online—Currently connected to a remote computer.

option button—A control that allows a user to select one choice from a set of mutually exclusive choices (also known as a *radio button*). *Compare* **check box**.

packet—A block of information that has been "packaged" with address information, error-checking information, and so on, for transmission on a **network** or on the **Internet**.

parameter—A variable that affects the results of a command. For instance, in the command *dir /p*, /p is a parameter.

parity—A crude system of error-checking used in data communications. For most scenarios these days, your communications software should be set to "no parity."

Perl—A programming language first developed by Larry Wall for UNIX systems. Because of its power in pattern matching and in handling strings, it is often the language of choice for creating **CGI** programs.

pixel—The smallest unit of graphic information on a computer screen. Graphic images are usually measured in pixels, and a pair of pixel coordinates can indicate an exact point within an image.

POP—*Point of Presence*. The local dial-up node an Internet access provider makes available for its customers.

POP3—*Post Office Protocol, version 3*. The protocol used by Netscape Navigator 2.0 and other e-mail programs to retrieve messages from your e-mail server. *See also* SMTP.

pop-up menu—A menu that appears right at the location of a selected object (sometimes called a *shortcut menu*). The menu contains items related to the selection.

pop-up window—A window with no title bar that appears next to an object and provides information about that object.

port—(1) A hardware connector on the back panel of a computer where you can plug in a serial, parallel, or network **cable**. (2) A unique number assigned to a particular Internet **service** on a host machine. For instance, most **MUDs** and **MOOs** require that you

Telnet to a host using a specific port different from the standard Telnet port number. You can usually specify a port number as part of an Internet address, as in *lambda.parc.xerox.com 8888*.

PPP—Abbreviation for *Point-to-Point Protocol*. This is a protocol that lets a computer link to the **Internet** by calling in to a service provider using a modem and a standard telephone line.

properties—Characteristics of an object defining its state, appearance, or value. Often used to mean a program's settings.

property inspector—A viewer that displays the properties of the current selection.

protocol—A set of rules for interaction between software programs on a network. Protocols may include requirements for formatting data, for passing control information back and forth, and for error checking.

public-key encryption—An **encryption** method that requires two unique keys for decrypting the data (one public and one private), making the data secure across public networks. Pretty Good Privacy (PGP) is a well-known public-key encryption system.

query string—The word or phrase you pass to a Web search engine.

QuickTime—A multimedia file format developed by Apple. It is often used for video clips.

radio button—*See* **option button**.

random-access memory (RAM)—Computer memory that temporarily stores information, for instance, software code that you've loaded by launching a program or data that you're processing. Generally, the more of it, the better!

read-only memory (ROM)—Computer memory containing data that cannot be changed by the user and that remains even when the computer is turned off. ROM is used for storing your computer's BIOS, for instance, which is the code that lets you boot up and that performs a variety of low-level functions.

remote—Any system that you can connect to by using only communications devices rather than just local wiring.

remote computer—A computer you link to via telephone lines, satellite, or other communication links.

resolution—The density of an image, expressed in dots per inch.

restore button—The button that replaces the maximize button once a window has been maximized. It lets you return the window to the size it was before maximizing.

reverse lookup—The process of looking up the domain name of an Internet-connected computer when all that's known is the numeric IP address. For instance, you may have a numeric IP address assigned by a **SLIP** or **PPP** access provider, but no associated domain name. When you try to log in to certain security-conscious FTP sites, the host software tries to look up your domain name via DNS reverse lookup and can't find one, so you are not allowed on the system. *See also* **domain-name address**.

RFC—Abbreviation for *request for comments*. An RFC is a proposal or report electronically distributed via the Internet, usually for the purpose of elucidating or helping to define a new Internet technical standard.

robot—*See* **spider**.

RS-232—The standard used by your serial port. RS-232 lines are the individual pins and wires that make up the hardware interface, such as the send data line, the receive data line, and the various hardware handshaking (or hardware flow control) lines.

RTF—*Rich Text Format.* A file format that can be read by many word processing programs across all platforms.

RTS/CTS—*Ready to Send/Clear to Send.* In an RS-232 serial port, the two lines that allow two devices to signal each other when they are ready to send or receive data. This process is known as **hardware handshaking** or hardware flow control. *See also* **RS-232**.

script—A software program that doesn't need to be compiled. It is run by another program "as is," in human-readable form.

scroll bar—The control that lets you move the image or text within a window either horizontally or vertically to view data that is not currently visible.

server—A computer or a program that provides a particular service on a network or on the Internet. Typical services include file access, printing, e-mail, **FTP**, and so on. The computers and software that access servers are called **clients**.

server push—A technique specific to Netscape products whereby a Web server can initiate the transmission of data to the Web **client**. Server push is often used for animation or sound. *See also* **client pull**.

service—A specialized function or utility provided by a **server**.

service provider—An organization, usually commercial, that provides connections to the Internet.

session—A connection between two machines on a network or on the Internet.

shell account—An account with an access provider that lets you access a text-based system for performing routine Internet tasks. You connect to a shell account via Telnet or a dial-up terminal emulation program. Some Internet access providers let you put your own Web pages on their server using a shell account.

shortcut—A desktop icon that can be used as a quick way to launch a program or document. Another word for *hotlink* in a WWW document.

signature—A text file that contains any information that you want to attach regularly to your e-mail messages and network news posts. A signature is usually less than five lines long and contains contact information.

single selection list box—A list box that lets you choose only a single item from a list.

slider—A control that displays a continuous range of values and lets you choose one.

SLIP—Abbreviation for *Serial Line Internet Protocol*. Like **PPP**, this is a protocol that lets a computer link to the Internet by calling in to a service provider using a modem and a standard telephone line.

SMTP—*Simple Mail Transfer Protocol.* The most common protocol for sending e-mail messages over the Internet. *See also* **POP3**.

snail mail—A form of messaging that utilizes carbon-based materials to create and address human-readable data, which is then transmitted over a complex network of streets and air routes by human entities known as "postal employees."

sockets—A software mechanism that allows programs to communicate locally or remotely by setting up endpoints for sending and receiving data. The application programmer does not have to worry about the nuts-and-bolts details of how the data travels from one point to the other, as that is taken care of by the operating system or other resident software. The Windows Sockets API (**Winsock**) uses this concept.

spider—A program that wanders around the Web looking for new content. Links to new sites that it finds may then be added to large directory documents such as Yahoo. Spiders are also known as robots, wanderers, crawlers, and WebCrawlers.

spin box—A control that displays a limited range of values and lets you choose one.

SSL—*Secure Sockets Layer.* A version of the **HTTP** protocol that includes encryption. SSL allows for the secure transfer of sensitive information across the Net, as in financial transactions.

string—Geek-speak for a set of characters. Your name, for instance, is a string.

symbolic link—A name that does not refer to an actual object but points to another name. For instance, on an FTP site, a directory list might include the entry WINDOWS, even though there is no WINDOWS directory at this level. The WINDOWS entry could be a symbolic link to a directory buried much deeper in the file system, such as /pub/micro/pc/GUI/windows. Symbolic links provide convenient shortcuts to actual objects.

synchronous transmission—A method of transmitting data that uses a special timing signal to ensure a set time interval between any two characters. *See also* **asynchronous transmission**.

tag—A special code used in an **HTML** document to indicate how a piece of text or a graphic should be displayed by a Web browser; it may also establish a **hotlink** to another document.

TCP/IP—Abbreviation for *Transmission Control Protocol/Internet Protocol*. TCP/IP is a set of protocols that applications use for communicating across networks or over the Internet. These protocols specify how packets of data should be constructed, addressed, checked for errors, and so on.

Telnet—A program that lets you log in to a remote **host computer** and access its data and services as if you were using a text-based **terminal** attached locally.

terminal—A keyboard and display screen used to access a **host computer**.

terminal emulation—A software program that lets you use a personal computer to communicate with a **host computer**. It transmits special commands and interprets incoming data as if it were a terminal directly connected to the host.

text box—A control that lets you enter and edit text.

title bar—The horizontal bar at the top of a window that includes the window name. The title bar also acts as a handle that can be used to drag the window.

title bar icon—The small icon at the top left corner of the title bar. You can use it to display the pop-up menu. Double-clicking this icon closes the program.

toolbar—A control that provides a defined area for a set of other controls such as icon buttons, drop-down list boxes, and so on.

traffic—Data traveling across a network or across the Internet.

tree control—A control that lets you display a set of hierarchical objects in an expandable outline format.

upload—To send a file to a remote system; the opposite of **download**.

URL—Abbreviation for *Uniform Resource Locator*. A URL is a specially formatted address that a Web browser uses to locate, retrieve, and display a document. The URL includes the Internet address of the data, where it is located on the Web server machine, and what kind of transport protocol is required to retrieve it. URLs are contained in the **hotlinks** within **HTML** documents; they may also be specified by the user of a Web browser "on the fly."

Usenet—A large collection of networked users that communicate using the UNIX-to-UNIX Copy Protocol (UUCP) rather than **TCP/IP**. Usenet is connected to the Internet by gateways, and many Internet users are familiar with its broad range of discussion forums known as newsgroups.

UUCP—*UNIX to UNIX copy.* An older set of network commands for sending and receiving data on dial-up networks.

UUENCODING—A standard for encoding binary data that allows it to be transmitted as 7-bit ASCII information; it is then *UUDECODED* into its original binary form.

WAIS—Abbreviation for *Wide-Area Information Server*. WAIS is a specialized Internet client/server system for researching information in Internet databases.

WAN—*See* **wide area network**.

wanderer—*See* **spider**.

Web—Short for **World Wide Web**.

Web browser—A program for retrieving and viewing **HTML** documents on the **World Wide Web**. Also known as a Web **client**.

WebCrawler—*See* **spider**.

Web document—Any document available on the **World Wide Web**.

Web server—A computer that stores Web documents and allows **Web browsers** to retrieve them over the Internet using the **HTTP** protocol. Also, the software that makes this possible.

wide area network—A group of computers and/or networks connected to one another by means of long-distance communication devices such as telephone lines and satellites, rather than just through local wiring. *See also* **local area network**.

widget—In HTML geek-speak, an object in a Web document that accepts user input. Examples are check boxes, radio buttons, drop-down lists, and so on.

wildcard character—A character used when you specify a file name; it is a variable that stands for any other valid character or characters. The question mark (?) stands for a single character, while the asterisk (*) stands for any string of characters in the file name. For instance, **.txt* means "any file that has the .TXT extension"; *??.txt* means "any file that has a two-letter name and the .TXT extension."

Winsock—Short for *Windows Sockets API*, a software "toolkit" that lets Windows programmers access **TCP/IP** services using a standard interface. Any Internet programs that use this standard, such as e-mail clients, Web browsers, and so on, will work under Windows 95.

World Wide Web (WWW)—An Internet service used for browsing hypermedia documents; the "Internet within the Internet" formed by all the Web servers and **HTML** documents currently online.

XOFF—A special character that's used to control the flow of information between a **DCE** and a **DTE**. When one device receives an XOFF character from the other, it stops transmitting until it receives an **XON**.

XON—A special character used to control the flow of data between a **DCE** and a **DTE**. *See also* **XOFF**.

Index

Internet Resources

Internet Business 500

$29.95, 488 pages, illustrated, part #: 287-9

This authoritative list of the most useful, most valuable online resources for business is also the most current list, linked to a regularly updated *Online Companion* on the Internet. The companion CD-ROM features the latest version of *Netscape Navigator*, plus a hyperlinked version of the entire text of the book.

Walking the World Wide Web, Second Edition

$39.95, 800 pages, illustrated, part #: 298-4

More then 30% new, this book now features 500 listings and an extensive index of servers, expanded and arranged by subject. This groundbreaking bestseller includes a CD-ROM enhanced with Ventana's WebWalker technology; updated online components that make it the richest resource available for Web travelers; and the latest version of Netscape Navigator along with a full hyperlinked version of the text.

HTML Publishing on the Internet for Windows
HTML Publishing on the Internet for Macintosh

$49.95, 512 pages, illustrated
Windows part #: 229-1, Macintosh part #: 228-3

Successful publishing for the Internet requires an understanding of "nonlinear" presentation as well as specialized software. Both are here. Learn how HTML builds the hot links that let readers choose their own paths—and how to use effective design to drive your message for them. The enclosed CD-ROM includes Netscape Navigator, HoTMetaL LITE, graphic viewer, templates conversion software and more!

Bestseller

The Web Server Book

$49.95, 680 pages, illustrated, part #: 234-8

The cornerstone of Internet publishing is a set of UNIX tools, which transform a computer into a "server" that can be accessed by networked "clients." This step-by-step in-depth guide to the tools also features a look at key issues—including content development, services and security. The companion CD-ROM contains Linux™, Netscape Navigator™, ready-to-run server software and more.

Internet Guide for Windows 95

$24.95, 552 pages, illustrated, part #: 260-7

The *Internet Guide for Windows 95* shows how to use Windows 95's built-in communications tools to access and navigate the Net. Whether you're using The Microsoft Network or an independent Internet provider and Microsoft *Plus!*, this easy-to-read guide helps you started quickly and easily. Learn how to e-mail, download files, and navigate the World Wide Web and take a tour of top sites. An *Online Companion* on Ventana Online features hypertext links to top sites listed in the book.

Quicken 5 on the Internet

$24.95, 472 pages, illustrated, part #: 448-0

Get your finances under control with *Quicken 5 on the Internet.* Quicken 5 helps make banker's hours a thing of the past—by incorporating Internet access and linking you directly to institutions that see a future in 24-hour services. *Quicken 5 on the Internet* provides complete guidelines to Quicken to aid your offline mastery and help you take advantage of online opportunities.

Books marked with this logo include a free Internet *Online Companion*™, featuring archives of free utilities plus a software archive and links to other Internet resources.

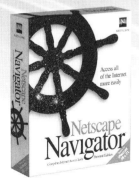

To order any Ventana title, complete this order form and mail or fax it to us, with payment, for quick shipment.

TITLE	PART #	QTY	PRICE	TOTAL

SHIPPING

For all standard orders, please ADD $4.50/first book, $1.35/each additional.
For *Internet Publishing Kit* orders, ADD $6.50/first kit, $2.00/each additional.
For "two-day air," ADD $8.25/first book, $2.25/each additional.
For "two-day air" on the kits, ADD $10.50/first kit, $4.00/each additional.
For orders to Canada, ADD $6.50/book.
For orders sent C.O.D., ADD $4.50 to your shipping rate.
North Carolina residents must ADD 6% sales tax.
International orders require additional shipping charges.

SUBTOTAL = $ _____
SHIPPING = $ _____
TOTAL   = $ _____

Name _____ Daytime telephone _____
Company _____
Address (No PO Box) _____
City_____ State_____ Zip_____
Payment enclosed ____VISA ____MC ____ Acc't # _____ Exp. date_____
Signature _____ Exact name on card _____

Mail to: Ventana • PO Box 13964 • Research Triangle Park, NC 27709-3964 ☎ 800/743-5369 • Fax 919/544-9472

Check your local bookstore or software retailer for these and other bestselling titles, or call toll free:

800/743-5369